IN SOLIDARITY WITH THE EARTH

T&T Clark Explorations in Theology, Gender and Ecology

Series editors
Hilda P. Koster
Arnfríður Guðmundsdóttir

This international book series promotes creative and innovative theological engagements at the intersection of gender and ecology. The series aims to publish books that respond theologically to the multiple changes at different levels in the environmental landscape – such as evolution, climate change, biodiversity, Anthropocene, extinction and de-extinction, technological innovation, food security, animal ethics and other geo-political concerns – and the various ways these changes interact with issues of gender and sexuality. To this end, the books published in this series may intersect with the following fields of study: critical theories of gender, race, class and sexuality; evolutionary and ecological science; new materialism; affect theory; animal studies; and Indigenous cultures and spirituality.

Titles

IN SOLIDARITY WITH THE EARTH

A Multi-Disciplinary Theological Engagement with Gender, Mining and Toxic Contamination

Edited by Hilda P. Koster and Celia Deane-Drummond

t&t clark

LONDON • NEW YORK • OXFORD • NEW DELHI • SYDNEY

T&T CLARK
Bloomsbury Publishing Plc
50 Bedford Square, London, WC1B 3DP, UK
1385 Broadway, New York, NY 10018, USA
29 Earlsfort Terrace, Dublin 2, Ireland

BLOOMSBURY, T&T CLARK and the T&T Clark logo are trademarks
of Bloomsbury Publishing Plc

First published in Great Britain 2024

A catalogue record for this book is available from the British Library.

Library of Congress Control Number: 2023939362

ISBN: HB: 978-0-5677-0608-9
         ePDF: 978-0-5677-0609-6
         eBook: 978-0-5677-0611-9

Series: T&T Clark Explorations in Theology, Gender and Ecology

Typeset by Integra Software Services Pvt. Ltd.

To find out more about our authors and books visit www.bloomsbury.com
and sign up for our newsletters.

CONTENTS

FIGURES AND TABLES

Figures

Table

ACKNOWLEDGEMENTS

As editors we express our sincere gratitude to the authors contributing to this multidisciplinary book for their dedication to our shared project. This book originated in an international symposium and conference organized by the Laudato Si' Research Institute (LSRI) in March and June 2021. Reworking a lecture or conference paper into a book chapter can be challenging under normal circumstances yet due to the Covid pandemic scholars contributing to this project did not have the benefit of an in-person engagement with one another and the audience. We are especially grateful therefore for the diligence with which the authors have integrated the rich discussions of the two originating events into their truly excellent and provocative chapters.

Many people have offered us assistance and encouragement during our work on this book. We are especially grateful to the LSRI staff for their administrative support. Special thanks go to Harriet David for keeping track of loose ends and to Dr Josh Kaiser, whose editorial expertise helped us make technical scientific texts accessible to a broader audience. We are further sincerely grateful to Rosemary Boissonneau, PhD candidate in ecological theology at the University of St. Michael's College in the University of Toronto, whose editorial skills, careful eye, enthusiasm and tireless energy have been indispensable for the completion of the project and made it so much better.

Early on we envisioned that this book would be published with *T&T Clark Explorations in Gender, Theology, and Ecology*, which promotes creative and innovative theological engagements with the multiple ways ecology and environmental concerns intersect with gender and sexuality. We have both been involved with initiating this series and now serve respectively as its co-editor and senior adviser and are therefore especially grateful that the book did indeed find a home here. Our book has been greatly enhanced in content and form by the reviews of Dr Lisa Sideris and Dr Susan Rakoczy, who serve on the board for the book series, as well as two anonymous reviewers. Special thanks also go to Dr Arnfríður Guðmundsdóttir, who, as co-editor for the series, has offered unwavering collegial support and valuable feedback. Heartfelt thanks also to Anna Turton, commissioning editor at T&T Clark, who has enthusiastically embraced this project and whose friendly nudges helped us move the project to its completion. Sinead O'Connor, editorial assistant for theology at Bloomsbury, has further offered invaluable editorial support, especially with the layout of the book and its cover.

As scholars we further owe gratitude to a circle of colleagues who have offered input and inspiration. Special thanks go to the colleagues at our respective professional institutions: LSRI, Campion Hall at the University of Oxford (UK) and the Regis St Michael's Faculty of Theology in the Toronto School of Theology (Toronto, Canada). Their interest in and support for our work truly made all the difference. We are further indebted to the University of St. Michael College for offering funding for valuable research assistance which significantly lightened our editorial work and made the work on this book so much more enjoyable.

Last but never least, we thank our respective circle of friends and both our husbands and daughters for their loving care for us and our work.

We offer our book in solidarity with the courageous struggle of women resisting the destructive impacts of extractive industries on ecosystems and on their communities in today's world. Their struggle and hope for a just and sustainable earth-community energize this book and our collective work.

CONTRIBUTORS

Denise Humphreys Bebbington is Research Associate Professor in the Department of International Development, Community and Environment at Clark University in Massachusetts, Worcester, MA (USA). She is an affiliate faculty member of the Women's and Gender Studies Program and faculty convener of a new earth conversation at Clark. Her research has explored the political ecology of natural gas in Bolivia and the implications of the gas economy for both Indigenous peoples and regional societies; the dynamics of socio-environmental conflict and mobilization linked to natural resource extraction and large-scale infrastructure investments; and the relationship between gender, environment and development, specifically how women gain access to and control over natural resources. Prior to her academic research, she served as Representative to Peru for the Inter-American Foundation (IAF), South American Regional Sub-Director for Catholic Relief Services (CRS) and Latin America Program Coordinator for the Global Greengrants Fund (GGF). She is co-author of *Governing Extractive Industries: Politics, Histories, Ideas* (2018) and *Evaluación y Alcance de la Industria Extractiva y la Infraestructura en Relación con la Deforestación: Amazonía* (2019).

Sharon A. Bong is Associate Professor of Gender Studies at the School of Arts and Social Sciences, Monash University Sunway City, Malaysia. She graduated with a PhD in religious studies (2002) and MA in women and religion (1997), University of Lancaster, UK. She has authored *Becoming Queer and Religious in Malaysia and Singapore* (2020) and *The Tension between Women's Rights and Religions: The Case of Malaysia* (2006) and co-edited *Gender and Sexuality Justice in Asia* (2020), *Trauma, Memory and Transformation in Southeast Asia* (2014) and *Re-imagining Marriage and Family in Asia: Asian Christian Women's Perspectives* (2008). She is former coordinator and consultant to the Ecclesia of Women in Asia and a forum writer for the Catholic Theological Ethics in the World Church.

Lisa Sowle Cahill is the J. Donald Monan, S.J., Professor, Boston College (Massachusetts, USA). Dr Cahill is a past president of the Catholic Theological Society of America (1992–3) and the Society of Christian Ethics (1997–8). She is a fellow of the American Academy of Arts and Sciences. She received her MA and PhD degrees from the University of Chicago Divinity School. Her works include *'Blessed Are the Peacemakers': Pacifism, Just War and Peacebuilding* (2019), *A Theology and Praxis of Gender Equality* (2018), *Global Justice, Christology and Christian Ethics* (2013) and *Theological Bioethics: Justice, Participation, and Change* (2005). *Ethics in Apocalyptic Times: Realistic Hope and Christian Politics* is in progress. She serves on the editorial boards of the *Journal of Religious Ethics*; the *Journal of Catholic Social Thought*; *Theology*; the *Irish Theological Quarterly*; *Asian Horizons* and *Mellita Theologica* (University of Malta).

Sierra Cloud is a graduate of Fort Valley State University (Georgia, USA). She has interned at the University of Pittsburgh in the Particle Based Functional Material Research Experience. Her research interests are in sustainability and water justice.

Celia Deane-Drummond is Director of the *Laudato Si'* Research Institute (LSRI) and Senior Research Fellow in Theology, Campion Hall at the University of Oxford (Great Britain). After beginning her academic career in natural sciences with a focus on plant physiology and agricultural botany, Dr Deane-Drummond retrained in theology, education and environmental ethics. She has a PhD in plant physiology from the University of Reading and a PhD in systematic theology from the University of Manchester. As Director of LSRI, she leads its multidisciplinary research work and develops and fosters its collaborative partnerships and projects with the church and other allied organizations. She is also responsible for LSRI's strategic growth plan and promoting its education and outreach work nationally and internationally. Her main research interests are in theological and ethical engagement with the natural and social sciences on questions related to ecology, genetics, animal studies and anthropology. She was Chair of the European Forum for the Study of Religion and Environment and is currently Vice President of the Science and Religion Forum of Great Britain, a trustee of the International Society for Science and Religion and a visiting Professor in Theology and Science at the Centre for Catholic Studies, Durham University. Her publications include *The Wisdom of the Liminal: Human Nature, Evolution and Other Animals* (2014); *Technofutures, Nature and the Sacred*, ed. with Sigurd Bergmann and Bronislaw Szerszynski (2015); *Ecology in Jürgen Moltmann's Theology*, 2nd edition (2016); *Religion in the Anthropocene*, ed. with Sigurd Bergmann and Markus Vogt (2017); *Theology and Ecology across the Disciplines: On Care for Our Common Home*, ed. with Rebecca Artinian Kaiser (T&T Clark, Bloomsbury, 2018); *The Evolution of Wisdom Volume 1: Theological Ethics through a Multispecies Lens* (2019) and *Shadow Sophia: Evolution of Wisdom Volume 2* (2021).

Josianne Gauthier is a Canadian lawyer with over twenty years of experience in international development and solidarity, focusing on human rights, children's rights, social justice and faith-inspired advocacy work. She joined Coopération Internationale pour le Développement et la Solidarité (CIDSE), an umbrella organization for Catholic development agencies from Europe and North America, as Secretary General in 2017. Before this, she led the Public Engagement, Advocacy and Campaigns teams at Development and Peace – Caritas Canada, the Canadian member of CIDSE, working on an array of international development and policy issues. Her work at CIDSE includes involvement in networks and actions focusing on climate justice, systemic change, and promoting sustainable lifestyles. A mother of three young children, she is also passionate about engaging and forming youth on issues of social justice and integral ecology and communicating about personal commitment and just relationships to broad audiences. In October 2019, she participated in the Synod on the Pan Amazon Region in Rome on behalf of CIDSE.

Marion Grau is Professor of Systematic Theology, Ecumenism and Missiology at the MF Norwegian School of Theology, Religion, and Society (Oslo, Norway). Her teaching interests are in constructive theology and critical intersectional theories. Her current research projects include a constructive theology of energy transitions and climate change. She is the author of *Pilgrimage, Landscape, and Identity: Reconstructing Sacred Geographies in Norway* (2021), *Refiguring Theological Hermeneutics: Hermes, Trickster, Fool* (2014), *Rethinking Mission in the Postcolony: Salvation, Society, and Subversion* (T&T Clark/Continuum, 2011) and *Of Divine Economy: Refinancing Redemption* (T&T Clark/Continuum, 2004).

Linda Hogan is Professor of Ecumenics, Head of School and Director of the Irish School of Ecumenics at the Trinity College Dublin (Ireland). As an ethicist and ecumenist, Dr Hogan has published extensively on religion, gender and human rights. She is the founder of Trinity's College's Ethics Lab, where she helps resolve the ethical challenges encountered by academic and industry partners in the social sciences, life and data sciences and health. Dr Hogan served as vice-provost/chief academic officer and deputy president of Trinity College Dublin. She also serves as Chair of the Board of the Marino Institute of Education and as board member for the Coombe Women & Infants University Hospital, the Irish Council for Bioethics, and Science Gallery. She is an elected member of the International Women's Forum. Among her publications are *From Women's Experience to Feminist Theology* (1998), *Confronting the Truth: Conscience in the Catholic Tradition* (2000), *Keeping Faith with Human Rights*, Moral Traditions Series (2015), Nigel Biggar and Linda Hogan (eds) *Religious Voices in Public Places* (2009), Linda Hogan and Dylan Lee Lehrke (eds) *Religion and the Politics of Peace and Conflict* (2009) and Linda Hogan and A. E Orabator (eds) *Feminist Catholic Theological Ethics: Conversations in the World Church* (2014).

Felicia Jefferson is Associate Professor at the Fort Valley State University (Georgia, USA). Her work, funded by multiple federal grants, has appeared in top science journals, including a recent publication in the *Frontiers in Computer Science*. Her other recent publications include work that used CRISPR-Cas9 technology and an investigation of cognitive decline in patients. Dr Jefferson served as an invited speaker of the 475th meeting of the National Science Board, which advises US Congress and the president, to discuss issues of diversity in academic STEMM (science, technology, engineering, mathematics and medicine). She was also the lead author for a publication by the National Academies of Science, Engineering, and Medicine and presented the study's preliminary results publicly to the National Academies. She is a delegate to National CDEI under ASEE's board of directors and served as the workshop/special session organizing chair for the Brain Informatics' 11th International Conference.

Catherine Keller is George T Cobb Professor of Constructive Theology in the Graduate Division of Religion of Drew University (Madison, New Jersey, USA). Her work on theology covers a spectrum of dimensions: ecofeminist, process, pluralist, political and philosophical. Her books include *From a Broken Web: Separation, Sexism and Self* (1986), *Political Theology of the Earth: Our Planetary Emergency and the Struggle for a New Public* (2018) and *Facing Apocalypse: Climate, Democracy and Other Last Chances* (2021). She is the co-editor of *Postcolonial Theologies (2012), Common Good/s: Ecology, Economy and Political Theology* (2015) and *Entangled Worlds: Religion, Science and the New Materialism* (2017). She holds a PhD in the philosophy of religion and theology from Claremont Graduate School.

H. Kailean Khongsai works in creation care in West London for the environmental ministry A Rocha UK. He is a Church Mission Society, Oxford mission partner. His initial role was in outreach, building bridges among different faith backgrounds and using environmental projects to inspire and teach people to care for the environment. Currently he manages the community side of A Rocha UK through project management, coordinating events and volunteers. He was the pioneer in transforming a three-acre area of derelict land into a beautiful multipurpose green space for people and wildlife in Southall, West London. Originally from Manipur, North-East India, Kailean has an MSc in ecology and an MSc in environmental waste management.

Hilda P. Koster is the Sisters of St. Joseph of Toronto Associate Professor of Ecological Theology and the Director of the Elliott Allen Institute for Theology and Ecology in the Regis St Michael's Faculty of Theology in the University of Toronto (Canada). A native of the Netherlands, she holds a BA and MDiv from the University of Groningen, a ThM from Princeton Theological Seminary and earned her doctorate from the Divinity School of the University of Chicago. Dr Koster's publications on theology, eco-feminism and environmental ethics have appeared in *Theology Today, Modern Theology, The Journal of Religion, The Anglican Theological Review* and *Scriptura*. Among her book-length co-edited/authored publications are *The Gift of Theology: The Contribution of Kathryn Tanner* (2015), *Planetary Solidarity: Global Women's Voices on Christian Doctrine and Climate Justice* (2017) and the *T&T Clark Handbook of Christian Theology and Climate Change* (Bloomsbury, 2019). Dr Koster is the co-editor of the T&T Clark book series *Explorations in Theology, Gender, and Ecology* (Bloomsbury).

Marianna Leite is an international human rights lawyer, researcher, activist and specialist in gender and development, currently affiliated with the University of Coimbra (Portugal). Over the past few years, she has been primarily concerned with gender, business and human rights. This work is very much linked to a robust analysis of structural systems such as (neo)colonialism, patriarchy and neoliberalism. Until December 2020, she was Women's Rights Strategic Adviser at Christian Aid. Prior to that, she was Christian Aid's Global

Lead on Gender and Inequality, working on the development of holistic approaches to gender and intersecting inequalities that ensure equality of outcomes and rights for all.

Kuzipa Nalwamba serves at the World Council of Churches (WCC) as programme director for Unity, Mission and Ecumenical Formation (Geneva, Switzerland). A theologian and educator by training, Dr Nalwamba earned her doctorate at the University of Pretoria (South Africa). Her research was at the intersection of Christian tradition, science and African world views and cosmologies as resources for eco-theology and eco-ethics. Dr Nalwamba was a high school teacher and served in student ministry. She became the first woman general secretary of the Zambia Fellowship of Evangelical Students (ZAFES) and later associate regional secretary and publishing secretary at the Africa region of the International Fellowship of Evangelical Students (IFES). A retired ordained minister of the United Church of Zambia (UCZ), she was congregation minister, school chaplain and lecturer at the UCZ Theological College (Kitwe, Zambia), where she was academic dean. Before joining WCC, she worked at the Council for World Mission (CWM).

Deborah Delgado Pugley is Principal Researcher and Assistant Professor at the Pontificia Universidad Catolica del Peru/Pontifical Catholic University of Peru (Lima, Peru). She has extensive experience in environmental governance and climate policy, particularly regarding Indigenous peoples and tropical forests. Dr Delgado Pugley has conducted interdisciplinary research and extended fieldwork following Indigenous social movements, human and environmental rights, and natural resources management. She has considerable field experience in the Amazon regions of Bolivia and Peru, where she has led research teams on climate change, Indigenous movements, human rights, natural resource management, forestry development and gender.

Oliver Putz is Affiliate Scholar at the Institute for Advanced Sustainability Studies (IASS) in Potsdam (Germany), where he studies the role of religion in a global societal transformation towards more just, equitable and sustainable futures. Before coming to the IASS, he was Assistant Professor of Theology and Science at Santa Clara University in California. Dr Putz holds a PhD in biology from the Freie Universität Berlin (Germany) and a PhD in theology from the Graduate Theological Union, Berkeley. Aside from the role of religion in the Anthropocene, he has conducted research on animal theology, theological anthropology and suffering as a challenge for a contemporary theodicy.

Rheygan Reed is a Neuroscience Bioengineering and Sleep Lab Manager at Fort Valley State University (Georgia, USA) and a graduate student in the Public Health Degree Program at the University of Nevada, Reno (Nevada, USA). She has co-authored multiple research papers on the effects of sleep deprivation on public safety.

Tebaldo Vinciguerra serves the Holy See, initially with the Pontifical Council for Justice and Peace and currently as an official of the Dicastery for Promoting Integral Human Development, created by Pope Francis. He works on environmental issues – chiefly mining, energy, agriculture, water and oceans – in the light of Catholic Social Teaching and participates in many working groups and conferences, including major UN environmental summits and various working groups within the Catholic Church. Previously, he was a researcher on natural disasters at the Center for Strategic Studies of the Italian Ministry of Defense and the coordinator of numerous development projects promoted by the Archdiocese of Lima (Peru). He completed university studies in political science and international studies at the Political Science Institute of Bordeaux (France) and the Faculty of Political Science of Turin (Italy). He co-founded the Italian NGO Puri di Cuore, promoting awareness about and recovery from the dangers caused by pornography. Mr Vinciguerra is married and has three children.

INTRODUCTION

Hilda P. Koster and Celia Deane-Drummond

Today's accelerated forms of extractivism are destroying ecological systems, land-based livelihoods and cultures at an unprecedented scale. Large-scale mining projects, oil and gas development, clear cutting and hydroelectric dams all rearrange landscapes and often use highly toxic chemicals that pollute the soil and the water with grave consequences for ecosystems and people depending on these landscapes for their livelihood and survival. In his address on integral ecology and mining, Pope Francis, following the bishops of Latin America, describes extractivism as

> [t]he action of 'extracting' the greatest amount of materials in the shortest possible time, converting them into raw materials and inputs that industry will use, that will be transferred into products and services that others will market, society will consume and then nature itself will receive in the form of polluting waste – that is the consumerist loop that is being generated at ever greater speed and ever greater risk.[1]

Francis calls special attention to the effects of extractivism on Indigenous and poor, minoritized communities, both in the Global South and North, whose health typically is being sacrificed as collateral damage. Indigenous environmental activist Casey Camp-Horinek (Ponca Nation) hauntingly describes this very connection between fossil fuel development and pollution:

> In my small Ponca tribe, we hold a funeral nearly every week for those who died from fossil fuel-related illnesses. All our families have multiple cases of asthma, cardiovascular disease, and industry-specific cancers. Our wells are so polluted our tribe must now buy water. Our land is so toxic, organic food can't be grown

---

1. *Address of His Holiness Pope Francis to Participants at the Meeting Promoted by the Dicastery for Promoting Integral Human Development on the Mining Industry*, 3 May 2019, pp. 1–4 (3). Available on the Vatican website https://www.vatican.va/content/francesco/en/speeches/2019/may/documents/papa-francesco_20190503_incontro-industria-mineraria.html (accessed 22 November 2022).

within 16 miles. They call it economic progress. We call it environmental genocide.[2]

The harms experienced by communities such as that of Camp-Horinek are not gender neutral. A growing body of research and publications, including documented resistance to mining by grassroots and civil society, has shown that poor minoritized women and girls living in the presence of extractive projects shoulder significant and distinct burdens.[3] Contamination of the land and water by mining and fossil fuel industries puts enormous strain on the daily lives of women and girls, who in the Global South (the majority world!) often are responsible for growing food and collecting clean drinking water—a daily task already made increasingly hard because of climate change-related disasters. And whereas extractive industries encroach on land-based livelihoods that are typically sustained by women, studies focusing on women's participation in mining reflect their limited or non-existent access to jobs, information and benefits.[4] The toxics released by extractive industries further have distinct and serious impacts on women's health: it has been linked to steep increases in ovarian and breast cancers and to miscarriages and premature births.[5] Extractive industries also often lead to spikes in gender-based violence targeted at local women and gender-diverse people. For instance, Canada's National Inquiry into the Missing and Murdered Indigenous Women and Girls[6] crisis identified oil and

2. Casey Camp-Horinek, 'My Tribe Holds a Funeral Every Week for People Killed by Fossil Fuels. This Isn't Progress – It's Environmental Genocide', *Independent*, 4 January 2021, https://www.independent.co.uk/voices/fossil-fuels-trump-land-tribes-b1781438.html (accessed 2 November 2022).

3. Cf. Adriana Eftimie, Katherine Heller and John Strongman, *Mainstreaming Gender into Extractive Industries Projects* (Extractive Industries and Development Series; Washington, DC: The World Bank, 2009). For a detailed study reflecting grassroots activism, see Livia Charles, Safia Cissoko and Osprey Orielle Lake, 'Gendered and Racial Impacts of the Fossil Fuel Industry in North America and Complicit Financial Institutions' (WECAN, 2021), https://www.wecaninternational.org/_files/ugd/d99d2e_918b1e133b2548549b686e4b 6eac4cc3.pdf (accessed 2 November 2022). See also Katy Jenkins, 'Women Anti-mining Activists' Narratives of Everyday Resistance in the Andes: Staying Put and Carrying on in Peru and Ecuador', *Gender, Place & Culture* 24:10 (2017), pp. 1441–59. https://doi.org/10.1 080/0966369X.2017.1387102.

4. For this argument see Denise Humphreys Bebbington's chapter 'Toxic environments' (Chapter 2) in this volume.

5. Joan A. Casey et al., 'Unconventional Natural Gas Development and Birth Outcomes in Pennsylvania, USA', *Epidemiology* 27:2 (2016), pp. 63–72, https://www.ncbi.nlm.nih.gov/ pmc/articles/PMC4738074/ (accessed 2 November 2022).

6. Marian Buller, Michèle Audette, Brian Eyolfson and Qayaq Robinson, *Reclaiming Power and Place: The Final Report of the National Inquiry into Missing and Murdered Indigenous Women and Girls*, 13 June 2019, Volume 1a, Chapter 7, https://www.mmiwg-ffada.ca/wp-content/uploads/2019/06/Final_Report_Vol_1a-1.pdf (accessed 2 November 2022).

gas development on or near Indigenous lands as a major factor in the violence perpetrated against Indigenous women, girls and 2SLGBTQQIA+ people.[7]

In this volume of collected essays, an international consortium of theologians, sociologists and environmental scientists engage with these and other gendered and racial injustices and violent consequences of extractive industries and chemical pollution (often while also referencing climate change-related vulnerabilities) in solidarity with the earth and those living in or near extractive zones. While detailing the ways women and gender-diverse people are negatively affected by extractivist projects, authors also trace their courageous and persistent activism resisting the industry's toxic contamination.[8] As Anna J. Willow details in her insightful book *Understanding ExtrACTIVISM: Culture and Power in Natural Resource Disputes* (2019)[9] worldwide extractivist projects are increasingly met with fierce resistance by those determined to protect their lands, health and livelihoods. Women and gender-diverse people often are on the forefront of these movements and exercise strong leadership. Whereas the latter at times is done by drawing on the leadership roles women traditionally occupy in a particular culture, women and 2SLGBTQQIA+ people have also organized into influential global activist networks, such as the Women, Earth and Climate Activist Network International,[10] and strategically use social media to build multi-scalar alliances, organize conferences and appeal to international authorities like the United Nations.[11]

Attending to gendered vulnerabilities thus requires paying close attention to the gendered effects of extractive projects and toxic pollution without unduly victimizing women and diversely gendered people. There are additional pitfalls that come with a focus on gendered vulnerabilities. We are naming three. First, addressing the ways women and girls are adversely affected by extractive industries might suggest that women and girls are 'innately' more attuned to the natural world.[12] Such essentialist assertions tend to lock women into fixed roles based on traditional divisions of labour and their childbearing capacities. Several authors in

7. The acronym 'SLGBTQQIA' stands for two-spirit, lesbian, gay, bisexual, transgender, queer (or questioning), intersex and asexual. The plus sign represents other sexual identities, such as pansexual or asexual. 'Two-spirit' refers to a person who identifies as having both a masculine and a feminine spirit and is used by some Indigenous people to describe their sexual, gender and/or spiritual identity.

8. See especially the chapters by Marion Grau, Lisa S. Cahill and Sharon A. Bong in this book.

9. Anna J. Willow, *Understanding ExtrACTIVISM: Culture and Power in Natural Resource Disputes* (New York: Routledge, 2019).

10. For insight into the scope of this type of activism see the website of the Women's Earth and Climate Action Network (WECAN) International: https://www.wecaninternational.org/

11. Willow, *Understanding ExtrACTIVISM*, p. 3.

12. For this criticism, see Melissa Leach 'Earth Mother Myths and Other Eco-Feminist Fables: How a Strategic Notion Rose and Fell', *Development and Change* 38:1 (2007), pp. 67–85.

this book detail how in the context of patriarchal, (settler) colonial arrangements essentialist notions are being used to block women's access to jobs and benefits and justify violence against women activists resisting extractive industries.[13] The approach chosen in this book therefore is one of a strategic gender essentialism: the book provisionally accepts the category of 'woman' as a strategy for collective of a focus on gendered vulnerabilities representation in order to pursue political ends.[14]

An additional pitfall is the tendency to treat gendered vulnerabilities in isolation, whereas they typically are aggravated by factors such as sexual orientation, ethnicity, race, religion, illiteracy, age, disability and marital status. Authors contributing to this book therefore utilize an intersectional lens when researching the gendered impacts of extractivism and toxic pollution. Finally, a strategic focus on women should not lose sight of the distinct vulnerabilities of 2SLGBTQQIA+ people living in or near extractive zones who often experience specific forms of gender-based violence and marginalization.[15]

Multidisciplinary approach and integral ecology

The chapters in this book originated in a multidisciplinary, international symposium on 'Women, Mining and Toxic Contamination', which was organized by the Laudato Si' Research Institute (LSRI) at Campion Hall at the University of Oxford (a work of the Jesuits in Great Britain). The symposium brought theologians in conversation with environmental and biological scientists, sociologists and 'practitioners' representing ecclesial organizations focused on eco-justice advocacy. The research symposium subsequently fed into the LSRI launch conference on 'Women Solidarity and Ecology'. The keynote lectures at this conference by Catholic ethicist Linda Hogan and Protestant eco-theologian Catherine Keller frame the multidisciplinary conversations of our book All

13. See for instance the chapters by Denise Humphreys Bebbington, Deborah Delgado and Lisa S. Cahill.

14. For this use of strategic gender essentialism, cf. Raksha Panda et al., 'Strategic Essentialism', *International Encyclopedia of Geography* (Oxford: John Wiley and Sons, Ltd 2016), pp. 1–6. https://doi.org/10.1002/9781118786352.wbieg1170. The concept of 'strategic essentialism' originates with post-colonial feminist thinker Gayatri Chakravorty Spivak and her work on subaltern studies. In Spivak usage, the term 'strategic essentialism' is the idea of an oppressed group intentionally taking on stereotypes about itself to disrupt or subvert the dominance that oppresses or marginalizes it. Cf. Elisabeth Eide, 'Strategic Essentialism and Ethnification: Hand in Glove?', *Nordicom Review* 31:1 (2010), pp. 63–78 (76), https://newdiscourses.com/tftw-strategic-essentialism/ (accessed 22 December 2022).

15. See Taylor Brorby's fine memoir of growing up in the Dakotas (USA), *Boys and Oil: Growing up Gay in a Fractured Land* (New York: Liveright 2022).

chapters, including the keynotes, are extensively reworked versions of the original presentations and reflect the feedback and rich discussions that these original presentations generated.

Our multidisciplinary approach takes its inspiration from Pope Francis' integrated approach to ecology in his encyclical *Laudato Si': On Care for our Common Home* (2015).[16] Francis famously observes that 'we are faced not with two separate crises, one environmental and one social, but rather with one complex crisis which is both social and environmental'. And because of the complex integrated nature of our planetary crises 'strategies for a solution demand an integrated approach to combating poverty, restoring dignity to the excluded, and at the same time protecting nature'.[17] The Pope urges us to reach out beyond our scholarly disciplines when gathering knowledge about and seeking solutions for today's complicated environmental problems. Thus he insists that 'due to the number and variety of factors to be taken into account when determining the environmental impact of a concrete undertaking [such as mining], it is essential to give researchers their due role, to facilitate their interaction, and to ensure broad academic freedom'.[18] Our book is a modest contribution to this endeavour and very much an invitation to others to join in this important work.

Obviously, a book focusing on gendered vulnerabilities sits at times uncomfortably with *Laudato Si'*'s silence on the experiences and contribution of women and other gendered minorities to the movement for ecological justice and ecological theology.[19] Similarly, *Laudato Si'*'s binary, essentializing concept of gender based on heterosexual stereotyping begs to be interrogated within the concrete struggles for a dignified human life amidst the onslaught of extractive industries on vulnerable communities. The theological chapters in this book therefore engage the concept of integral ecology through a critical feminist lens. Yet, as Catherine Keller observes, the challenge before us is twofold: 'we must continue to avow and advance women's rights, needs and aspirations; and at the same time, we must not hold the ecological alliance hostage to the struggle for gender equality'.[20] Authors in this book are engaging this challenge constructively. Also, whereas the focus on human dignity, central to Catholic Social Teaching (CST) and Pope Francis' interpretation of integral ecology, risks reinstating anthropocentrism, scholars contributing to this volume draw

16. Pope Francis, *Laudato Si': On Care for Our Common Home* (Rome: Libreria Editrice Vaticana, 2015), Chapter 4.

17. Pope Francis, *Laudato Si'*, §139.

18. *LS*, §140.

19. For two such feminist critiques of *Laudato Si'*, cf. Ivone Gebara, 'Women's Suffering, Climate Injustice and Pope Francis's Theology: Some Insights from Brazil', and Sharon Bong, 'Not Only for the Sake of Man: Asian Feminist responses to *Laudato Si*'', in Grace Ji-Sun Kim and Hilda P. Koster (eds), *Planetary Solidarity: Global Women's Voices on Christian Doctrine and Climate Justice* (Minneapolis: Fortress Press, 2017), pp. 67–96.

20. Catherine Keller, 'Solidarities of Difficult Difference: Towards a Conviviality of the Earth', Chapter 10 of this volume.

an inclusive understanding of 'integral ecology' into a 'deep solidarity' with the earth. The opposite fear of the risk of biocentrism is less prominent in Pope Francis compared with Pope Benedict XVI, but Roman Catholic anxieties about a watering down of attention to the human by giving more attention to other creatures fail even with respect to human dignity if its conception of the human does not openly welcome and encompass all human beings in their gendered complexity. Drawing again on Keller: 'the intersectionality of gender, sex, race, class is woven of the life of nonhuman bodies. Human justice itself does not materialize in abstraction from our common material life. So integral ecology cannot be dissociated from the ecumenism of feminist struggles. The *ecu* of religious diversity – the *oikumene* – stems etymologically and materially from the same *oikos* that is threatened with oikocide'.[21]

Finally, given the scale and complexity of the topic, a book on extractivism and gender is bound to have its limitations. Ours is no exception. The book's case studies mainly reflect North and South America and, to a far lesser extent, Asia. Obviously extractivism is an enormous concern across the African continent as well. Further studies will need to include case studies from South Africa, Nigeria, and other African countries, with a particular focus on illegal mining sites (*zama zamas*). Other limitations of this book are the relatively limited range of scientific perspectives. Future work will especially need to invite scholars working in ecological and political economics, Indigenous law and international relations to be part of the conversation. And, finally, there is a need for a richer representation of and contribution from minoritized scholars to these important conversations, as well as an engagement with interfaith perspectives.

Structure of the book and overview of chapters

The book is divided into four parts, each consisting of two main chapters and a response by a writer who broadly identifies themselves as being an active 'practitioner'. The first three parts are organized around the gendered effects of contamination by mining and environmental plastics and chemicals. These parts first present a chapter by a social or natural scientist, which then is followed by a chapter written by a theologian. The fourth and final part of the book offers decolonial and post-colonial theological engagements with fracking and the extraction and processing of rare earth minerals. Following the 'See, Judge, Act' method of CST the parts move from an analysis and assessment of multiple situations to a theological interpretation and call for action.

As indicated above, the four main parts of the book are preceded by an opening chapter by Catholic ethicist Linda Hogan and are followed by a chapter by Protestant eco-theologian Catherine Keller. As editors we are further grateful for the epilogue offered by Tebaldo Vinciguerra of the Vatican's Dicastery for

---

21. Catherine Keller, 'Solidarities of Difficult Difference' (emphasis given).

Promoting Integral Human Development, which 2019 meeting on 'Mining for the Common Good' inspired the symposium from which this book arose.

A more detailed description of the different chapters and contributions will serve as a further orientation. In her opening chapter, 'Human rights and the vulnerabilities of gender in the context of climate emergency and extractive industries', Hogan highlights the importance of human rights' discourse for addressing gendered vulnerabilities in the context of climate change and resource extraction. Thus, after offering a comprehensive account of how the vulnerabilities of gender are amplified and re-inscribed as the effects of climate change and of extractive industries become ever more severe, she demonstrates the value of human rights perspectives to address these challenges. Hogan argues that human rights' theory provides a further framework for the Pope's integral approach since it too foregrounds the interconnectedness of the economic, political, environmental and cultural dimensions of the climate crisis and, moreover, does so from the perspectives of vulnerable individuals and communities. At the same time, Hogan's critical focus on the gendered aspects of human rights' discourse challenges Francis' integral ecology to self-critically broaden its scope by attending to the plight of (minoritized) women and gender-diverse persons.

Hogan's chapter is followed by the first main part of the book, which details the gendered effects of large-scale mining, as well as charts the invigorating movement of Indigenous women and two-spirited people resisting extractivism and pipeline construction. In Chapter 2, Denise Humphreys Bebbington, a scholar of international development, draws on three communities directly influenced by mining operations in Bolivia and Peru. She argues that damage to social relations and institutions induced by mining company practices should be understood as a form of socio-environmental contamination; these practices produce significant and highly gendered impacts that require assessment and remediation alongside impacts to the natural environment. Specifically, Bebbington argues that in these male-dominated communities, women often miss out on vital information about health impacts of mining and do not gain equitable access to and control over benefits, whether they are offers of employment, material contributions or financial donations, and projects. Because organizing benefit agreements in a gender-blind way only deepen existing inequalities, solidarity with women in these communities asks that benefit agreements account for the ways mining increases gendered vulnerabilities.

In the following chapter, 'Countering colonial mining: Water protectors, environmental justice and the creation community of saints', ecological theologian and climate activist Marion Grau highlights the essential contribution of Indigenous women and two-spirited activists to the movements confronting extractive industries and protesting climate change. Grau examines several instances of Indigenous activism, with particular focus on Indigenous women's leadership in the #NODAPL Standing Rock anti-pipeline movement and the Fridays for Future movement. At Standing Rock, the focus was on the prophesy Mni Wiconi – water is life. In the camp, water was ritually connected to women, who exclusively were invited to participate in the morning water ritual in the river. The iconography of a young female water protector fighting the Black Snake echoes with Marian imagery and the Magnificat – of young vulnerable women announcing the coming of a different power and a different order. Grau concludes by reflecting on the notion of the community of saints, especially a more cosmically inclusive community as has been envisioned by Elizabeth Johnson, and she ponders expanding it to include not only the brave women leading these movements but also the animals who offer their solidarity as witnesses and inspiration.

Part 1 concludes with a response essay by Marianna Leite, who draws on her experience working on issues of gender, inequality and women's rights at Christian Aid. Although Leite raises concerns about how the guiding question in Bebbington's essay risks essentializing women, she largely commends both authors for not only exposing gendered toxicity but also countering it through the empirical research, theological readings and narratives of resistance that they present.

Part 2, 'Pollutants', focuses on the gendered effects of contamination by environmental plastics and endocrine-disrupting chemicals on environmental health. While not 'technically' concerned with resources extraction these chapters not just detail how minoritized women are exponentially affected by chemical toxins but also trace the grave threat of our world's addiction to oil-based plastics to planetary health. In the first chapter in this part, biological scientist Felicia Jefferson, together with Rhyegen Reed and Sierra Cloud, explores in great detail the impact of exposure to endocrine-disrupting chemicals (EDCs) on Black and Hispanic women and girls. By first providing a short understanding of how the endocrine system works, the authors expose how EDCs are linked to miscarriages and cancers. The chapter, then, examines the gendered and racial practices of corporations using EDCs, which are typically used in female personal care products. In response to the highly alarming results of their research, the authors stress the crucial importance of educating women and the public at large about the adversarial health effects of EDCs. Specifically, they not only stress the need for legislation that regulates the use of EDCs but also hold industries and corporations accountable.

In Chapter 5, 'The ecological *kairos*: Theological reflections on the threat of environmental plastics to organismal and environmental health', German theologian Oliver Putz takes on the threat posed by environmental plastics (EPs). EPs of all kinds pollute virtually all ecological systems, including every ocean basin, freshwater system, terrestrial habitat, the atmosphere and the polar ice caps. Because EPs have a very direct adverse effect on the declining abundance of organisms, they further exacerbate the already devastating impact of other human-caused drivers of extinction, above all land use change and overexploitation. Putz's chapter elaborates on the gendered effects of EPs and biodiversity loss. For reasons of simple biology, women and girls suffer greater adverse health effects from EP toxicity, such as the disruption of endocrine functions. Poverty and gendered social roles exacerbate these risks when, for example, the task of disposing of plastic waste through incineration primarily falls on women and girls, increasing their exposure to toxic fumes from the burning plastics. Whereas the first part of the chapter details the gendered environmental risks of EPs, the second part offers a theological reflection drawing on CST and, in particular, the concept of *kairos*. Here Putz argues that the drastically advanced deterioration of biosphere integrity constitutes what Christians call a *kairos* moment: a time for all possible stakeholders, the world religions included, to address the issue head-on and take immediate action to protect ecosystem health as well as those who are already suffering the consequences of this situation. The aim of Putz's contribution to this volume then is to look at the hazards of plastic pollution-mediated biodiversity loss through the critical lens of CST and address the question of the ecological conversion or *metanoia* that Christians need to experience in light of this intricate socio-ecological dilemma.

Kailean Khongsai responds to the chapters by Jefferson and Putz by drawing on his work with A Rocha (UK), a Christian environmental and community-based conservation organization. Adding a new perspective to the discussion, Khongsai highlights the problems caused by focusing the extensive on exporting of plastic waste from wealthy nations to poorer ones, especially the impacts on women working to recycle plastic waste in many regions of Asia. His chapter concludes with a theological reflection on the need for an ecological conversion: a conversion that is respons-able to the lives of the people most harmed by technocratic neo-capitalism, like those forced to contend with the plastic waste of the rich.

The third part, 'Toxicity', sketches how the toxic contamination of mining is matched by social processes that disempower and often endanger the lives of women resisting extractive industries. In her chapter, 'Toxicity in the times of project-based development: Indigenous women facing oil and gold pollution in the Peruvian Amazon basin', Peruvian sociologist Deborah Delgado Pugley explores Indigenous women's living conditions and activism in areas of the Peruvian Amazon affected by oil pipelines and gold mining. Delgado discusses two case studies. The first study examines how the Indigenous community of Cuninico was affected after spills from a state-owned oil pipeline polluted their water sources and how a women-led collective judicial challenge won for the community comprehensive compensation and remediation from government agencies. The second study investigates how the women of the Amarakeri Communal Reserve challenge the expansion of heavily polluting artisanal gold mining in their lands and how their lives are affected by mercury exposure, threats to their Indigenous traditions and a variety of social ills resulting from the mining. Specifically, Pugley takes aim at the 'project-based logic' that is prevalent in the remediation of toxic environments and that tends to focus on technical elements while not properly monitoring the long-lasting socio-ecological impacts that hinder the rebuilding of resilient environments. Local women rarely gain employment in remediation projects yet typically do suffer harms ranging from sexual violence to difficulty caring for their families due to the continued toxicity of the local ecosystem. The chapter concludes with a call for comprehensive evaluation mechanisms to ensure quality standards and adequate transparent funding of remediation projects as well as a recommendation that extractive industries' toxic effects be studied in a manner that centres the views of women in the affected Indigenous communities.

In Chapter 7, 'Mining and women's activism: Still under the surface of Catholic Social Teaching', Catholic feminist ethicist Lisa Sowle Cahill also draws on social-scientific studies of women's anti-mining activism in Guatemala, Peru and

Ecuador. Her chapter discusses in great detail how women anti-mining activists meet violence, including domestic abuse, physical assault and rape; and how the 'double message' of CST on gender both upholds human rights for all and reinforces the stereotypical 'women's roles' that justify abuse of women who transgress their 'proper' sphere. Cahill explains that 'Catholicism' exists at many levels and in many forms, including individual believers, local communities, Catholic universities, non-profits, NGOs and social justice networks. Some expressions of Catholicism empower women as anti-mining activists, while others enforce gender norms limiting women's agency to the domestic sphere under male authority. Not infrequently, Catholic representatives and institutions participate in patriarchal cultural norms that hinder and often further endanger the lives of women activists. Yet CST and the Catholic Church can be and have been a support to anti-mining activists. For this to be the case, however, the agency of women must receive explicit recognition and more political support. CST must not only formally mandate women's equality but must also 'operationalize' and 'normalize' the voice and agency of women across all its social initiatives and ministries, including support for anti-mining activism. This must include the explicit affirmation of women as political actors and the condemnation of gendered-based violence.

In her response essay, Kuzipa Nalwamba, the World Council of Churches (WCC) Program Director for Unity, brings her native African theological context in constructive conversation with the chapters by Delgado and Cahill. Nalwamba understands the experiences of women in extractive zones as 'epistemologies of lament' that ought to invigorate Christian teaching and action against the toxicity of large-scale mining operations and the neoliberal global capitalism fuelling it.

The case studies in the fourth, and final part of the book demonstrate the need for a decolonial and post-colonial (eco)feminist theological engagement with extractivism. In her chapter, Hilda Koster details the complicated case of fracking for oil on the Berthold Indian reservation in western North Dakota, home of the Mandan-Hidatsa-Arikara (MHA) Nation. Whereas the oil boom has brought much-needed income and even wealth to the MHA nation, it also has led to staggering levels of pollution and turned the Berthold into an epicentre of the Missing and Murdered Indigenous Women, Girls, and Two Spirited People (MMIWG2S) crisis. Detailing this interlocking reality of ecocide and femicide on the Berthold, the chapter draws on the work of Indigenous legal scholars, most notably Sarah Deer (Creek Nation), who demonstrate how the legal complexities by which settler society continues to encroach on tribal sovereignty fuel the 'rape' of Indigenous lands and bodies. The chapter thus insists on the need for an eco-feminist, decolonial engagement with extractivism – an engagement that connects the gender ideology operative in extractive capitalism with the logic of coloniality (the systemic codifications of knowledge and being that continue to render certain people and lands extractable). Aiming to disrupt and subvert such a logic, Koster turns to the work of Potawatomi environmental philosopher Kyle Whyte who situates environmental justice within Indigenous conceptions of social resilience and self-determination that are rooted in *reciprocal* relationships with land and non-human species. The final part of the chapter connects this Indigenous account of environmental justice with Pope Francis' notion of integral ecology and the theological discourse of structural sin. When it comes to an integral ecology that privileges the experience of Indigenous communities in extraction zones, as Pope Francis urges us to do in his Apostolic Exhortation *Querida Amazonia*, there can be no environmental justice without confession of sin and repentance for settler colonial violence.

In Chapter 9, 'Rare earth and rare practice of "integral ecology": A feminist-post-colonial reading of "Save Malaysia, Stop Lynas" protests', post-colonial theologian Sharon Bong examines the current controversy over the license renewal of Lynas, the rare earth processing plant in her native Malaysia. Rare earth ore contains seventeen elements that are indispensable to the manufacture of hi-tech products, such as smart phones, LCD TV screens, computer monitors, wind turbines and electric cars. Whereas the waste generated from processing rare earth elements is highly radioactive and toxic, leading to a spike in birth defects and cancers, under its new license the Lynas plant would produce over 22,000 tonnes of radioactive waste a year while discharging non-radioactive but toxically contaminated liquid into local waterways at a rate of 500 tonnes per hour. In her chapter Bong sketches the consequences of processing rare earth mineral on environmental health. She further proposes a feminist-post-colonial reading of anti-mining activism. Such a reading forefronts the words and actions of those who embrace the land as their 'common home' and presents them as counterpoints to colonization's masculinized meta-narratives. Bong exposes how these meta-narratives maintain the boundaries of purity/pollution through outsourced processing of toxic waste and uphold the concomitant feminization of a post-colonial nation-state as a body that continues to be sullied for profit.

Josianne Gauthier's response draws on her practical experience in human rights and community-based organizing with CIDSE (a family of eighteen Catholic Social Justice organizations across Europe and North America). Gauthier considers how a global solidarity with Indigenous communities' pain and destruction caused by (settler) colonialism's long and enduring intimate and toxic relationship with extractivist economics should be practised. Specifically, she notes that despite international legislation and treaties, countries often fail to support these communities because of other of national economic interests. Highlighting this as 'continued colonialism', Gauthier also names it as a failure to break free from addictions to growth, power and privilege and as a lack of courage to transform or re-imagine economic systems. She invokes Querida Amazonia's notion of 'cultural dream' to suggest we can only care for our Common Home as we care for one another and that we must enter a path of cultural conversion which sees the beauty and value in all cultures and traditions, especially Indigenous cultures that can challenge colonial pasts and patterns.

In her book-end chapter, 'Solidarities of difficult difference: Towards a conviviality of the earth', Catherine Keller picks up on the discussion on solidarity and unpacks *Laudato Si*'s notion of 'common home' or *oikos* through feminist theologies' long labour to dispel any presumption of a commonality won by repressing differences of sex/gender, class, race, religious or species difference. Drawing on process theology, she articulates an alternative posture to *oikos-cide* or the *home-killing* realities brought about through *oikonomia* (economy) – specifically mining. She thus explores two lines of enquiry into gender difference and the common home. In the first, she explores the matter of gender by asking how gender difference matters in relation to all of the differences that materialize as our terrestrial ecology. In the second, she explores how gender difference matters to religious difference in the common home. Keller further examines John Milton's gender-inflected critique and meditation on the open wounds of mining, paralleling his city of pandemonium constructed by the demonic *oikos* of wealth with the current-day fossil fuel industry now steadily bringing human civilization into pandemonium. This hellishly structured disorder of dissociated differences risks not only *Paradise Lost* but planet too. Through this apocalyptic unveiling of capitalist extraction, Keller reveals a *home-keeping* whose commonality is born of a vigorous new global and planetary solidarity of difference. Such a solidarity, she suggests, is constructed by forging challenging alliances, awareness of our intractably entangled interdependence, and creative chaos made possible by liminal spaces of relational vulnerability that allow for hard conversations and increased awareness of our obligations to each other amidst all our difficult differences. Ultimately Keller reminds us that none of our lives are indifferent to each other and that none of our differences should distract from the time-pressed task of earth-healing.

Finally, Tebaldo Vinciguerra's epilogue draws important connections between a structural disrespect for the commons and the neglect of women's lives and experiences in mainstream economics. In this context his essay introduces the *Economia di Francescos* initiative, which aims at developing an ecological economics rooted in Pope Francis' teachings on integral ecology. How might such an ecological economics incorporate women's experiences and ecological wisdom?

Audience and aspiration

It is our hope that our book's focus on gender and extractivism is of interest to both scholars and those working with NGOs, churches and faith-based advocacy groups. Whereas ecological theologians, Christian environmental ethicists and scholars working in theological gender studies are the obvious audience for our book, we believe that both scholars and practitioners will find insights into its chapters that support and strengthen ethical analysis, advocacy and other forms of engagement with the struggles of women and gender-diverse persons against extractive industries. Our book further should be of interest to scholars working on extractivism within the natural and social sciences, especially in human rights and environmental law and scholars in development, environmental and peace studies.

May this book foster earth-healing conversations and practices in deep solidarity with the gendered experiences and subjugated knowledges of vulnerable communities living at the extractive zones of our world.

Chapter 1

HUMAN RIGHTS AND THE VULNERABILITIES OF GENDER IN THE CONTEXT OF CLIMATE EMERGENCY AND EXTRACTIVE INDUSTRIES

Linda Hogan

The alarm bells keep ringing – we are living with a climate emergency. In January 2021 a *Scientific American* article noted that more than 11,000 scientists from 153 countries had endorsed a report confirming that the world is facing a climate emergency and noted that '1,859 jurisdictions (now 1,938) in 33 countries (now 34) have issued climate emergency declarations covering more than 820 (now 826) million people.'[1] While there is some debate about the use of the term 'emergency', there is no doubt about the urgency of the situation. In answer to the question 'why emergency' *Scientific American* says, '[B]ecause words matter.' To preserve a liveable planet, humanity must take action immediately. Failure to slash the amount of carbon dioxide in the atmosphere will make the extraordinary heat, storms, wildfires and ice melt of 2020 routine and could 'render a significant portion of the Earth uninhabitable'.[2] *Laudato Si'* had already rung that alarm and added that 'the human environment and the natural environment deteriorate together', insisting that 'we cannot adequately combat environmental degradation unless we attend to causes related to human and social degradation' which 'affects the most vulnerable people on the planet'.[3] *Laudato Si'* has injected a new sense of purpose and direction into the global response to the climate emergency and has positioned the ethical question as a matter of social justice and of intergenerational solidarity. Moreover, it recognized that the climate challenge is not 'simply one of many, but the broader

1. See https://www.scientificamerican.com/article/the-climate-emergency-2020-in-review/ The current data can be found here: https://climateemergencydeclaration.org/climate-emergency-declarations-cover-15-million-citizens (accessed 14 July 2021).

2. https://www.scientificamerican.com/article/we-are-living-in-a-climate-emergency-and-were-going-to-say-so (accessed 14 July 2021).

3. Pope Francis, *Laudato Si': On Care for Our Common Home* (Rome: Libreria Editrice Vaticana, 2015), p. §48.

backdrop for an understanding of both ecological ethics and social ethics'.[4] Any solution, it argues, must be committed to combatting poverty and inequality, restoring dignity to the excluded and at the same time protecting nature.[5]

This chapter argues that human rights can provide an important framework of response to the climate crisis, one that recognizes the interconnectedness of the economic, political, environmental and cultural dimensions of the climate emergency, particularly the gendered dimensions. The chapter begins by explaining why the language and politics of human rights is vital in the struggle against climate change, and why it provides an important complement and corrective to the integral ecology framework of *Laudato Si'*. It goes on to discuss how climate change threatens human rights, especially the fundamental rights of women and other individuals affected by gender inequality and its intersections. It considers how the vulnerabilities of gender are amplified and re-inscribed by environmental degradation, especially in the extractive industries and their related global trade networks. These industries exemplify the toxic and gendered interplay between the depletion of the earth's resources and the assault on the fundamental rights of individuals and communities. The chapter concludes by highlighting features of a renewed human rights language that can help address some of these challenges and advance a gender-sensitive approach to climate change.

Human rights, gender and integral ecology

Some might question the utility of a category (i.e. human rights) that is integral to modernity and therefore implicated in the economic and political structures that have underwritten the climate emergency. However, I argue that a human rights approach mandates certain ethical and political commitments that are essential if we are to tackle the inequities of climate change, particularly the gendered inequities. Here I am influenced by the climate justice approach promoted by Mary Robinson's *Climate Justice Foundation* which requires commitments on human rights and gender equality as part of the overall agenda to address global warming and stem the tide of climate change[6] and which rejects, as a false dichotomy, trade-offs between human rights and gender equality on the one hand and climate action on the other. Additionally, my approach to human rights is

---

4. Message of the Holy Father Francis to Participants in the 3rd International Conference of Catholic Theological Ethics in a World Church, 'A Critical Time for Bridge-Building: Catholic Theological Ethics Today', in Kristin Heyer, James F. Keenan and Andrea Vicini (eds), *Building Bridges in Sarajevo: The Plenary Papers from CTEWC* (Maryknoll: Orbis Press, 2019), p. xv.

5. Pope Francis, *Laudato Si'* (*LS*), §139.

6. Mary Robinson, *Climate Justice: Hope, Resilience and the Fight for a Sustainable Future* (London: Bloomsbury, 2018) and the *Mary Robinson Climate Justice Foundation* at https://www.mrfcj.org/principles-of-climate-justice/ (accessed 14 July 2021).

embedded in the feminist, decolonial and subaltern reframing of liberal human rights discourse that has sought to divest it of its inherent moral myopia[7] of racism, ethnocentrism and sexism and re-imagine it through a genealogical, multi-religious, intercultural global conversation about what we owe each other.[8] Recent works in Catholic social ethics including William O' Neill's *Reimagining Human Rights, Religion and the Common Good* (2021) and David Hollenbach's *Humanity in Crisis* (2019)[9] continue this tradition of reframing and each positions human rights as a crucial lens through which the demands of Christian witness in the context of a climate emergency can be expressed.

When it comes to the issue of gender, a human rights approach also provides an important corrective to the 'integral ecology' framework of *Laudato Si'*. Much has already been said about the fact that *Laudato Si'* makes no reference to women, even though the majority of the world's poor are women and although there are specifically gendered dimensions to the ecological crisis. Indeed, this gendered 'blindspot' in *Laudato Si'* is itself a reflection of a more deep-seated lacuna in Pope Francis' theological vision, which has been much analysed but which is not the focus of this chapter. A more fundamental concern than the absence of a gendered lens in *Laudato Si'*, however, is how deeply linked the concept of 'integral ecology' is with the 'human ecology' and 'ecology of man' in the theologies of St John Paul II and Pope Benedict XVI each of which posits an essentialist and patriarchal reading of human ecology.[10] Many feminist theologians including Christiana Zenner and Maura Ryan have highlighted how, whether it be in *Centesimus annus, Caritas in veritate*, or in many other documents, Pope Francis' predecessors use the language of human

---

7. This is William O' Neill's term in *Reimagining Human Rights: Religion and the Common Good* (Washington, DC: Georgetown University Press, 2021), p. 11.

8. Linda Hogan, *Keeping Faith with Human Rights* (Washington, DC: Georgetown University Press, 2015), p. 206.

9. David Hollenbach S.J., *Humanity in Crisis: Ethical and Religious Responses to Refugees* (Washington, DC: Georgetown University Press, 2019).

10. 'Human ecology also implies another profound reality: the relationship between human life and the moral law, which is inscribed in our nature and is necessary for the creation of a more dignified environment. Pope Benedict XVI spoke of an "ecology of man", based on the fact that "man too has a nature that he must respect and that he cannot manipulate at will" It is enough to recognize that our body itself establishes us in a direct relationship with the environment and with other living beings. The acceptance of our bodies as God's gift is vital for welcoming and accepting the entire world as a gift from the Father and our common home, whereas thinking that we enjoy absolute power over our own bodies turns, often subtly, into thinking that we enjoy absolute power over creation. Learning to accept our body, to care for it and to respect its fullest meaning, is an essential element of any genuine human ecology. Also, valuing one's own body in its femininity or masculinity is necessary if I am going to be able to recognize myself in an encounter with someone who is different. In this way we can joyfully accept the specific gifts of another man or woman, the work of God the Creator, and find mutual enrichment. It is not a healthy attitude which would seek 'to cancel out sexual difference because it no longer knows how to confront it' (*LS* §55).

ecology to critique contemporary gender theories, including feminist theological accounts of gender.[11] Moreover, for Pope Benedict and also for Pope Francis, there is a strong link between this essentialist reading of gender through the lens of (a particular interpretation of) natural law and the ecological vision that sustains environmentalism. In *Laudato Si'*, Pope Francis continues to insist that 'valuing one's own body in its femininity or masculinity, and thus honouring binary sexual difference (and, presumably, heteronormativity) is crucial in sustaining integral ecologies'.[12]

Thus, while the integral ecology of *Laudato Si'* is indeed a vital resource when tackling climate change, its anchoring in an essentialist view of gender, coupled with its failure to recognize the gendered aspects of the ecological crisis, suggests that it must be supplemented by other frameworks, including from the Christian social ethics tradition, if a gender-sensitive approach to climate change is to be advanced. In this context the language of human rights can be an important resource, particularly when one takes account of its evolution in recent decades in response to feminist, LGBTQI, decolonial and subaltern critiques which have emanated both within and without faith communities. As a moral language that has been shaped in and by different religious and secular traditions, the language of human rights has come to be a 'short-hand' to express the fundamental goods in which people have interests as aspects of their well-being and flourishing.[13] Moreover, this moral language is underwritten and given legal force through a range of international and regional treaties and through national legislation. Thus, human right functions both as a moral language and as a set of overlapping and intersecting legal frameworks – a feature that is particularly significant when seeking to mitigate the impacts of climate change.

The climate emergency and its impact on human rights

In July 2019 UN Special Rapporteur on Extreme Poverty and Human Rights Professor Philip Alston presented a report on *Climate Change and Poverty*[14] to the Human Rights Council during the 41st Session of the General Assembly.

11. As Maura A. Ryan notes this framework reasserts 'the biological basis for the differences between the sexes which [in turn] has implications not only for how we view homosexuality as a social and moral question, but also what we make of traditional gendered roles within the family and, by extension, within society'. See Maura A. Ryan, 'A New Shade of Green? Nature, Freedom, and Sexual Difference' in '*Caritas in veritate*': *Theological Studies* (2010), pp. 335–49 (346).

12. Christiana Zenner, 'The Order of Nature? Integral Ecology and Natural Law', November 4, 2020, https://berkleycenter.georgetown.edu/responses/the-order-of-nature-integral-ecology-and-natural-law (accessed 14 July 2021).

13. I am grateful to Dr Patrick O' Riordan S.J. for this phraseology in his response to my paper delivered at the Women, Solidarity and Ecology Conference, Laudato Si' Research Institute, Oxford, 2 June 2021.

14. Philip Alston, *Climate Change and Poverty* (United Nations: Geneva, 2019), available at https://digitallibrary.un.org/record/3810720 (accessed 14 July 2021).

The report notes that 'climate change threatens truly catastrophic consequences across much of the globe and the human rights of vast numbers of people will be among the casualties. By far the greatest burden will fall on those in poverty', and it goes on to say that 'to date human rights bodies have barely begun to grapple with what climate change portends for human rights'.[15] While many UN bodies have highlighted how climate change negatively impacts the work for sustainable development, equality and poverty alleviation, it was only in 2015 with the signing of the Paris Climate Agreement that an international agreement on climate change put human rights at the centre of its analysis. In doing so it provided a framework for response that foregrounded the interconnectivity between the protection of the environment and the vindication of the rights of vulnerable individuals and communities.

Alston's report describes climate change as a threat that is likely to challenge or undermine the enjoyment of almost every human right in the international bill of rights.[16] Economic and social rights will be significantly impacted. According to the World Bank at 2 degrees centigrade of warming, 100–400 million people will be at risk of hunger, and 1–2 billion more may no longer have access to adequate water. Crop yields would likely be 30 per cent less, even with adaptation measures, and additional deaths in the region of 250,000 annually from malnutrition, malaria and heat stress will likely ensue. By 2050 climate change will likely displace 140 million people in sub-Saharan Africa, South Asia and Latin America. The last fifty years of development, global health and poverty reduction are at risk because 120 million more could be pushed into poverty as livelihoods and assets are more exposed and more vulnerable to natural disasters. People in poverty and those barely above the poverty line are greatly endangered by climate change, with their precarious access to adequate water and sanitation, food, shelter, work, education and health care seriously under threat.[17] Climate change both reflects global inequality and exacerbates it. Inequality between and within nations is growing exponentially year on year and climate change accelerates and amplifies this dynamic. Thus, as the same World Bank report highlights, the poorest half of the world's population – 3.5 billion – is responsible for just 10 per cent of carbon emissions, while the richest 10 per cent is responsible for half.[18] Reinforcing this point, a recent report from the National Academy of Sciences of the United States has found that climate change has already worsened global inequality, with the gap between per capita income in rich and poor countries 25 per cent larger than it would be without climate change.[19]

15. Alston, *Climate Change and Poverty*, no. 1.

16. Alston, *Climate Change and Poverty*, no. 64.

17. World Bank, *Shock Waves: Managing the Impacts of Climate Change on Poverty* (Washington, DC: World Bank, 2016), p. 12, noted in Alston, *Climate Change and Poverty*, no. 36.

18. World Bank, *Shock Waves: Managing the Impacts of Climate Change on Poverty*, p. 12.

19. Noah Diffenbaugh and Marshall Burke, 'Global Warming Has Increased Global Economic Inequality', *Proceedings of the National Academy of Sciences of the United States of America* 116: 20 (May 2019), noted in Alston, *Climate Change and Poverty*, no. 39.

Threats to civil and political rights are also likely amplified because of climate change. The political instability and insecurity caused by climate-induced migration and inequality pose risks of increased xenophobia, racism and nationalism – all of which can undermine the civil and political rights of minorities and immigrants as well as those who have become internally displaced or are refugees. Indeed, one of the reasons the language of climate emergency is so contentious is because state-declared emergencies can often be an occasion to increase government powers and circumscribe civil and political rights. Giorgio Agamben's *State of Exception* highlights how exception or emergency has become a technique of government, and his analysis exposes the political risks associated with the declaration of a state of exception.[20] Nor is the climate emergency immune from authoritarian manipulation or intent, particularly given the political instability that it already occasions. Thus, any adoption of the language of climate emergency must be attentive to the risks it may pose to the protection and promotion of civil and political rights, particularly of those 'outsiders' who are perceived to threaten the security or prosperity of a society.

Mining and its impact on human rights

When we consider the mining and extractive industries specifically similar human rights concerns are evident, both in respect of economic, social and cultural rights and also in terms of civil and political rights. Analyses of the impacts of the mining and extractive industries on economic and social rights disclose a varied picture. High-profile conflicts like those at Standing Rock and in the Democratic Republic of Congo highlight the threats these industries pose to the rights of Indigenous communities and to labour rights.[21] Other analyses suggest that the economic benefits to be derived from the mining and extraction industries can be positive, yet they also present a major risk to sustainable development,[22] not only because of the finite nature of natural resources but also because of the conflicts they generate.[23] The 'natural resource curse' is much analysed, and in many such

20. Giorgio Agamben, *State of Exception* (Chicago: Chicago University Press, 2005), p. 8.

21. See Max Planck Foundation, *Human Rights Risks in Mining*.

22. The concept of sustainable development is now highly contested because it is premised on a model of economic growth and a political economy that is tied to global capitalism. Critics regard this as intrinsically problematic for natural resources and the environment. See John C. Dernbach and Federico Cheever, 'Sustainable Development and Its Discontents', *Journal of Transnational Environmental Law* 4:2 (2015), pp. 247–87. Available online: https://ssrn.com/abstract=2634664 (accessed 15 July 2021). An overview of the debates can be found at https://digitalcommons.du.edu/cgi/viewcontent.cgi?article=1021&context=law_facpub (accessed 15 July 2021).

23. There is extensive literature on this topic. Tony Addison and Alan Roe's *Extractive Industries: The Management of Resources as a Driver of Sustainable Development*

contexts mining and extraction industries have adverse human rights impacts for individuals and communities. Nonetheless, as evidenced by the UNU-WIDER's *Extractives for Development* project, when properly managed by governments the mining and extractive industries can catalyse inclusive, sustainable development and underpin the achievement of fundamental human rights.[24]

In addition to the varied impact that mining has on economic, social and cultural rights, it is clear that the mining industry often has severe and negative impacts on civil and political rights. For example, climate-induced conflicts, whether involving state actors or private corporations, have been a significant and ongoing source of human rights violations against environmental human rights defenders, especially from Indigenous communities. Data is difficult to come by. Nonetheless a number of NGOs and international organization including Amnesty International and Frontline are working to document the scale of this problem. The 2019 a *Global Witness* review of the number of killings of environmental human rights defenders around the world found that between 2002 and 2013 at least 908 people had been killed as a result of protecting their rights to land and the environment, although it acknowledged that figures are likely to be higher.[25] As a result of the advocacy of Frontline and other organizations this issue has finally begun to receive the attention it deserves, and in March 2019 the Human Rights Council adopted a resolution that recognized the critical role of environmental human rights defenders and expressed alarm 'at increasing violations against environmental defenders, including killings, gender-based violence, threats, harassment, intimidation, smear campaigns, criminalisation, judicial harassment, forced eviction and displacement, and recognized that violations are also committed against defenders' families, communities, associates and lawyers'.[26]

(Oxford: Oxford University Press, 2018) gives an excellent analysis of the topic and includes essays from many of the key analysts and actors in this field. The Max Planck Foundation, *Human Rights Risks in Mining a Baseline Study*, 2016, available at https://rue.bmz.de/includes/downloads/BGR_MPFPR__2016__Human_Rights_Risks_in_Mining.pdf (accessed 14 July 2021), provides a comprehensive overview of the key ethical and human rights issues. For some examples of regional analyses see United Nations Development Programme Bangkok Regional Hub and Poverty-Environment Initiative Asia-Pacific of UNDP and UN Environment, *Managing Mining for Sustainable Development,* 2018, http://www.undp.org/content/undp/en/home/librarypage/poverty-reduction/Managing-Mining-for-SD.html (accessed 15 July 2021), and the UN Environment Programme Finance Initiative (UNEP FI) and Global Compact Initiative, *Digging Deeper: Human Rights and the Extractive Sector*, 2018, available at https://www.unpri.org/download?ac=5081 (accessed 15 July 2021).

24. The learnings from this project are captured in Tony Addison and Alan Roe's *Extractive Industries.*

25. https://www.universal-rights.org/urg-policy-reports/environmental-human-rights-defenders-ehrds-risking-today-tomorrow/ (accessed 15 July 2021).

26. https://undocs.org/A/HRC/RES/40/11 (accessed 15 July 2021).

Climate change, human rights and the vulnerabilities of gender

Climate change has a particularly negative impact on the human rights of women and other individuals affected by the inequities and exclusions of gender. The IPCC Fifth Assessment Report notes that this heightened vulnerability to climate change 'is rarely due to a single cause. Rather, it is the product of intersecting social pressures that result in inequalities in socioeconomic status and income, as well as in exposure. Such social processes include, for example, discrimination on the basis of gender, class, ethnicity, age and (dis)ability'.[27] Women constitute the majority of the world's poor and thus are directly impacted by the degradation of natural resources. Additionally, intersecting and multiple sources of marginalization bear on many women's lives. Moreover, traditional cultural values and norms often impede women's capacity to adapt to climate change, thus increasing their vulnerability. Indeed, as has been noted by feminist scholars Nira Yuval-Davis and Valentine Moghadam many decades ago, in times of crisis gender norms often become even more rigid and women frequently bear a heightened responsibility for the transmission of the community's norms and as the guarantors of its cultural identity.[28] This dynamic has become particularly evident as women strive to adapt to climate change and develop new survival mechanisms. Many of the climate-related vulnerabilities that women experience also extend to LGBTQI+ persons who often experience assaults on their fundamental rights because of gender-based violence, discrimination and marginalization and, as highlighted in the ICCP Fifth Report, are therefore particularly affected by climate-induced political and economic instability. Consequently, the work for gender equality is a vital component in building 'the resilience of individuals and communities globally in the context of climate change and disasters'.[29]

The 2019 UN Council for Human Rights Report on gender-responsive climate action[30] examines the impact of climate change on women's lives and enumerates

---

27. 'IPCC, 2014: Climate Change 2014: Synthesis Report. Contribution of Working Groups I, II and III to the Fifth Assessment Report of the Intergovernmental Panel on Climate Change' [Core Writing Team, R. K. Pachauri and L. A. Meyer (eds)]. (IPCC: Geneva, 2015), 1.5., 54, https://www.ipcc.ch/report/ar5/syr/ (accessed 15 July 2021).

28. See Nira Yuval-Davis, *Gender and Nation* (London: Thousand Oaks, New Delhi: Sage Publications, 2004); Valentine Moghadam, *Gender, Nation and Identity: Women and Politics in Muslim Societies* (London: Zed Books, 1994), for detailed discussions of this point.

29. CEDAW no. 12 available at https://tbinternet.ohchr.org/Treaties/CEDAW/Shared%20Documents/1_Global/CEDAW_C_GC_37_8642_E.pf (accessed 15 July 2021).

30. The section below is a summary of the gender-related impacts of climate change as discussed by the UN Report, pp. 4–8. 'Analytical Study on Gender-Responsive Climate Action for the Full and Effective Enjoyment of the Rights of Women Report of the Office of the United Nations High Commissioner for Human Rights, Human Rights Council Forty-First session 24 June–12 July 2019', https://undocs.org/A/HRC/41/26 (accessed 15 July 2021).

the human rights responsibilities of states and other actors, including private corporations and businesses, to implement gender-responsive approaches to climate change. Although primarily focused on women, it also pays some attention to the human rights interests of LGBTQI+ persons. The report delineates the most pervasive and pernicious gender impacts of climate change. The severe impact that climate change has on fundamental economic and social rights – including the rights to an adequate standard of living, food security, housing, medical care and education – has already been noted. However, these impacts are often amplified for women and LGBTQI+ persons. Climate change especially affects women's livelihoods in a number of sectors. For example, 60 per cent of all women at work in South Asia and sub-Saharan Africa are smallholder farmers or engaged in unpaid or poorly paid, time- and labour-intensive agricultural work and therefore adversely affected by climate change. The consequent loss of livelihoods, reduction in incomes and deterioration of working conditions in agriculture and related sectors[31] render women vulnerable to employment and deepening inequalities. Moreover, since gender equality is an important determinant of economic and social security, this also impacts whole communities.[32]

The extractive industries have a comparably negative impact on women's livelihoods, security and rights in many parts of the world[33] and the intersecting dynamics of LGBTQI+, Indigenous, tribal or ethnic identities frequently exacerbate these vulnerabilities. Macdonald cites cases in India and Nigeria where Indigenous women have been 'disproportionately affected by mining and oil and gas projects because they lose access to forest, fields, and fisheries, which they have previously used for food to feed their families'[34] and notes that 'the loss of land-based livelihoods drives more women to sex work in the absence of alternatives'.[35] In addition the traditional patriarchal structures that govern norms associated with land ownership, political participation, decision-making and the representation of the community's interests in negotiations limit women's voices and inhibit their access to finance, technology and resources, including compensation and reparation. They also impede women and LGBTQI+ person's opportunities to mitigate the most severe impacts of the extractive industries on their health and well-being or to adapt and practice climate-smart livelihoods.

31. Global Gender and Climate Alliance, 'Gender and Climate Change: A Closer Look at Existing Evidence' (2016), available at http://wedo.org/wp-content/uploads/2016/11/GGCA-RP-FINAL.pdf. (accessed 15 July 2021).

32. According to Food & Agriculture Organisation (UN) there has been a 55 per cent improvement in food security in developing countries because of women's empowerment. See *Gender Equality and Food Security: Women's Empowerment as a Tool against Hunger* (2013), available at www.fao.org/gender/background/en/ (accessed 15 July 2021).

33. See Catherine Macdonald, 'The Role of Gender in the Extractive Industries', in Tony Addison and Alan Roe (eds), *Extractive Industries: The Management of Resources as a Driver of Sustainable Development* (Oxford: Oxford University Press, 2018), pp. 442–59.

34. Macdonald, 'The Role of Gender in the Extractive Industries', p. 447.

35. Macdonald, 'The Role of Gender in the Extractive Industries', p. 447.

Climate change–induced political and societal instability also impairs health infrastructures and impedes access to health care. It often undermines access to sexual and reproductive rights, which are already under threat in many jurisdictions because of the global mobilization of resistance to reproductive rights. The deepening poverty and related societal instability also make women and LGBTQI+ persons more vulnerable to gender-based violence.[36] Furthermore, climate-induced mobility, including the displacement associated with mining and other extractive industries, elevates the risks of violence for women and LGBTQI+ persons and can contribute to an escalation of human trafficking and forced marriages, all of which undermine gender equality. As a result, the development achievements of the last fifty years pertaining to women's well-being and gender equality[37] risk being reversed.

Women defending their environments also often pay a high price. One such woman was environmental rights defender Fikile Ntshangase whose case opens the 2021 Report of the Special Rapporteur on the situation of human rights defenders.[38]

> She was shot dead in her home in Mtubatuba, South Africa, on the evening of 22 October 2020. Three gunmen fired six shots and she died at the scene. She was 65 years old and had been involved in a dispute over the extension of an opencast mining operation. She was a prominent member of the Mfolozi Community Environmental Justice Organization. Her lawyer told the Special Rapporteur that Mama Fikile had received threats by phone in the middle of the night in June 2019, and she had reported them to the local police. A few months before she was killed, she received more.[39]

Fikile Ntshangase's case exemplifies the situation of environmental human rights defenders across the world, who appear to be particularly vulnerable to attack. The 2021 Report notes that one in two victims of killings recorded in 2019 by OHCHR was working with communities 'around issues of land, environment,

---

36. United Nations, 'Report of the Special Rapporteur on Violence against Women, Its Causes and Consequences', Yakin Ertürk, *Political Economy of Women's Human Rights* at https://undocs.org/A/HRC/11/6 (accessed 15 July 2021).

37. See the most recent report from the United Nations, Department of Economic and Social Affairs, *Progress on the Sustainable Development Goals, the Gender Snapshot 2020* (United Nations: Geneva, 2020), https://www.unwomen.org/-/media/headquarters/attachments/sections/library/publications/2020/progress-on-the-sustainable-development-goals-the-gender-snapshot-2020-en.pdf?la=en&vs=824 (accessed 15 July 2021).

38. United Nations, 'Report of the Special Rapporteur on the Situation of Human Rights Defenders'; Mary Lawlor, *Final Warning: Death Threats and Killings of Human Rights Defenders*, Human Rights Council 46th Session, March 2021, https://undocs.org/en/A/HRC/46/35 (accessed 15 July 2021).

39. Lawlor, *Final Warning*, p. 1.

impacts of business activities, poverty and rights of indigenous peoples, Afrodescendants and other minorities'.[40] In common with all human rights defenders women face risks, including assassination, criminalization, intimidation and assault. However, they also face the added threat of gender-specific violence, including sexual violence, which can have additional adverse social consequences such as stigmatization and discrimination.

Gender-sensitive, human rights–based responses to climate change

Multiple expert reports and decades of development work confirm that the human rights of women and LGBTQI+ persons can only be protected when the impacts of climate change are addressed and that climate change can only be effectively mitigated when the gender-related aspects of its impacts are tackled directly. They are symbiotic and mutually reinforcing. In this final section I highlight a number of the features of human rights language that can help frame a response to the climate crisis and imbue climate action with the urgency and priority it requires. Although there are other features of human rights discourse that are important in the fight against climate change, I will focus on the capacity of this discourse to highlight (i) the essential moral *and* legal nature of our task; (ii) the interdependence and indivisibility of the economic, political, social and cultural dimensions of the challenge and (iii) the imperative to develop the practices of deep democracy.

The human rights obligations of state and non-state actors

The concept of human rights is grounded in the inherent and equal dignity of all human beings, and it sets out the obligating features of this equal dignity. In David Hollenbach's compelling words 'we can say that one human being *is* a kind of *ought* in the face of another'.[41] These obligating features, categorized by Hollenbach into basic needs, core freedoms and essential relationships,[42] ground human rights and impose correlative duties, including the duty to protect and advance human rights wherever they are at risk. Since human rights function both as a moral language and as an international legal framework the question of how and to whom to ascribe the duties of vindicating human rights is important, though contested. As noted by Patrick O' Riordan, 'even in asserting human rights as moral claims, they entail the identification of individuals who have duties to meet those claims'.[43] As legal claims, moreover, the obligations to respect, protect and fulfil human rights claims are clearly specified. Primary responsibility resides with states and, with its option for the poor, the Catholic tradition assigns to states

---

40. Lawlor, *Final Warning*, p. 5.

41. Hollenbach, *Humanity in Crisis*, p. 86.

42. Hollenbach, *Humanity in Crisis*, p. 88.

43. Patrick O' Riordan, response to my paper delivered at the Women, Solidarity and Ecology Conference, Laudato Si' Research Institute, Oxford, 2 June 2021.

a particular duty to address the alarming growth in poverty and global inequality. However, the human rights obligations of businesses are also significant. Yet, notwithstanding the obligations contained in the various legal instruments, this is *the* major failure of contemporary climate action. The Alston report issues a scathing indictment of states' failure to protect human rights in the context of climate change. He is equally damning of corporate actors, not only because of widespread greenwashing practices but also because of the way that neoliberal globalization undermines the economic, social and often civil and political rights of individuals and communities, especially in the Global South. The international character of key human rights standards and treaties, in principle, provides protection for vulnerable communities in the context of the nomadic practices of global industries. However, in practice, enforcement continues to be a challenge.

A focus on human rights thus requires that we have an immediate and honest conversation about the obligations and duties of states and corporate actors, as also about the urgent need for more effective enforcement measures that will hold governments and corporate actors to account for their support of and complicity with international business practices that undermine (women's) human rights and drive climate change.

The interdependence and indivisibility of human rights

While the history of human rights in the twentieth century is in part a story of rival emphases on either civil and political rights or on economic, social and cultural rights, in recent decades the 'doctrine' of the interdependence and indivisibility of human rights has held sway. This comprehensive vision insists that civil, political, economic, social and cultural rights are inherently complementary and equal in importance and that the violation of one damages the achievement of the others.[44] Indeed the Vienna Declaration expanded this to assert the interdependence between human rights, democracy and development, based on the indivisibility of human rights.[45]

A threat that, in Alston's words, 'is likely to challenge or undermine the enjoyment of almost every human right in the international bill of rights'[46] inevitably requires a comprehensive response based on their interdependence and indivisibility. The policies that will be required to ensure respect for economic and social rights (water, land, shelter, livelihood etc.) also require a civic context in which civil and political rights are assured.[47] This is especially important when the

44. Lanse Minkler and Shawna Sweeney, 'On the Invisibility and Interdependence of Basic Rights in Developing Countries', *Human Rights Quarterly* 33 (2011), pp. 351–96.

45. United Nations, 'Vienna Declaration and Programme of Action' (United Nations: Geneva, 1993).

46. Alston, *Climate Change and Poverty*, no. 64.

47. See O' Neill, *Reimagining Human Rights*, pp. 37–44 on the narrative embodiment of rights for a more detailed account of this point.

livelihoods of communities are at risk, whether it be from depletion and extraction of resources, privatization or deregulation. In these contexts, as we see all over the world, governments frequently circumscribe or curtail the basic liberties of citizens and securitize large sections of civic life in order to protect the interests of global capital. Moreover, when we attend to gender, we can see that 'although efforts to shrink and reduce civic space – including freedoms of expression, assembly and association – affect all defenders, they disproportionately impact women human rights defenders who have historically had very limited civic space to begin with, and who also face additional and gender-specific obstacles, risks and violations'.[48]

The commitment to indivisibility also highlights the importance of gender-related rights, including reproductive rights[49] to protect women's freedom and safety as they navigate the threat of climate change. Access to sexual and reproductive services plays a significant role in securing the well-being of women, girls and LGBTQI+ persons and in protecting them from the vulnerabilities associated with gender-based forms of discrimination. The indivisibility of rights also moderates the perceived individualism of human rights discourse.[50] As noted by William O' Neill, when discussing the human rights philosophies of Nyerere and Tutu, 'the rhetorical practice of human rights in our concrete narrative traditions preserves the mutual recognition of agents as worthy of respect, thereby permitting us to speak of moral solidarity'.[51]

Practices of deep democracy and human rights

In the context of civil and political rights, participation rights are especially important since the meaningful and informed participation of individuals and communities of diverse backgrounds is essential for effective climate action. This is not only essential in relation to women and those from minority groups such as LGBTQI+ and Indigenous groups. It is also vital in dealing with the political presentism that systematically excludes the interests and rights of future generations from the conversation about climate change. The deep democracy that is needed to expand the political imagination to include the interests of future generations must also vindicate the participation rights of individuals and communities around the world who today are shut out of the deliberations and

---

48. https://www.ohchr.org/Documents/Issues/Women/WRGS/Supporting_WHRDs_UN_System.pdf (accessed July 2021).

49. Through CEDAW the 'international bill of rights' includes the reproductive rights of women – CEDAW Article 16, 'on a basis of equality of men and women: (e) the same rights to decide freely and responsibly on the number and spacing of their children and to have access to the information, education and means to enable them to exercise these rights'.

50. There is not space to discuss this here. See Linda Hogan, *Keeping Faith*, chapters 1 and 4.

51. O' Neill, *Reimagining Human Rights*, p. 38.

decisions about addressing the climate emergency. Roman Krznaric delineates 'design principles of deep democracy' that structure political and legal processes in a way that will safeguard the interests of disenfranchised youth and future generations.[52] While vital, Krznaric's radically inclusive proposal must take account of those who are currently without voice and influence. The principle of subsidiarity is also important in this regard, particularly as it has been invoked and developed in *Laudato Si'*.[53] Although there is not time to develop this point here, I concur with Lisa Sowle Cahill assessment that *Laudato Si'* not only affirms the multi-polar nature of the contemporary world order, it also reframes and expands the classic understanding of the principle of subsidiarity. In doing so it affirms the importance of a broad-based, civil society–led, inclusive and multi-dimensional approach to climate action. The problem must be tackled top-down *and* bottom-up.

Conclusion

In conclusion, while human rights discourse is limited and flawed, it is nonetheless an important framework through which to pursue the imperatives of climate action. It is, as Hans Jonas says, 'essentially the story of the sacralization of the person',[54] although it is a story which continues to be reshaped by feminist, decolonial and subaltern scholars and activists whose voices disclose new blind spots and reveal new depths of intersectional oppression. The climate emergency has disclosed further blind spots in human rights discourse and has revealed even more deep-seated intersectional injustices. In particular, it suggests that human rights discourse needs to be interrogated in light of its anthropocentrism. Is human rights fatally anthropocentric, or can its remit be expanded to include other animals? In the words of William O' Neill, can a re-imagined human rights discourse animate 'a biocentric or cosmotheandric ethics by which a generalised respect for the concrete other warrants respect for the intrinsic value of nonhuman nature'?[55] Moreover, can the unrealized promise of distributive justice, that was initially bound up with the post-war ideal of human rights, be achieved in the context of climate justice?[56] These and other questions must continue to be

52. Roman Krznaric, *The Good Ancestor: How to Think Long Term in a Short-Term World* (London: Penguin, 2020), pp. 163–93.

53. See Lisa Sowle Cahill, 'Laudato Si': Reframing Catholic Social Ethics', *The Heythrop Journal* (2018), pp. 887–900.

54. Hans Jonas, *The Sacredness of the Person: A New Genealogy of Human Rights* (Washington, DC: Georgetown University Press, 2013).

55. O'Neill quoting Engelbert Mveng, 'Black African Art', in Appiah-Kobi et al. (eds), *African Theology en Route: Papers from the Pan-African Conference of Third World Theologians, Accra, 1977* (Maryknoll: Orbis, 1977), pp. 137–42.

56. Samuel Moyn, *Not Enough Human Rights in an Unequal World* (Cambridge, MA: Belknap Press/Harvard University Press, 2018), p. 11.

grappled with. Yet, notwithstanding the challenges, human rights continue to be an important lens through which the social transformation that is essential for human and planetary flourishing can be pursued. As I have argued elsewhere, human rights function as ethical assertions about the critical importance of certain values for human (and planetary) flourishing, as an emerging consensus generated in intercultural, intersectional and genealogical conversations and as emancipatory politics whose modus operandi is ultimately that of persuasion. Moreover, as 'the grammar of dissent' which is William O Neill's formulation, human rights also become the catalyst for a politics that will necessarily be restorative, 'redeeming what Gutierrez calls "the rights of the poor" or most vulnerable',[57] including rights of redress.

57. O' Neill, *Reimagining Human Rights,* p. 184.

Part 1

MINING

Chapter 2

TOXIC ENVIRONMENTS

Denise Humphreys Bebbington

As the cumulative effects of large-scale natural resource extraction continue to mount across the globe, serious questions have emerged about the wisdom of continuing to extract without regard for the long-term impacts to the environment. In the encyclical letter, *Laudato Si'*, which inspires this collection of chapters, Pope Francis calls us together to address 'the urgent challenge to protect our common home' to reflect on what is happening to our earth.[1] Dean Laplonge gives this call to protect nature a gendered twist and asks us, 'Do women have a better ethics of care towards the environment than men?'[2] If it is the case that they do, he ponders, could this ethics be harnessed to bring reform to an industry such as mining and so reduce its negative impacts? While Laplonge directs his question to the industrial mining sector and the impacts on the bio-physical environment that are generated by extraction, I propose to take up his question as it applies to the increasingly toxic *social* environments that women experience while living in the presence of contaminating extractive activities.

We know from a robust set of studies as well as from casual views of the landscape that modern mining produces significant waste materials.[3] With some minerals, the volume of waste can be very high (for copper and gold, 99 per cent of what is extracted is waste, and even more so for lower grade ores). Mining processes often rely upon highly toxic substances, like cyanide, to extract the minerals from rock and can produce acid mine drainage (the outflow of acidic water from the mine site and from waste materials).[4] We also know that mineral

---

1. Pope Francis, *Laudato Si': On Care for Our Common Home* (Rome: Libreria Editrice Vaticana, 2015), §48.

2. Dean Laplonge, 'The "Un-Womanly" Attitudes of Women in Mining towards the Environment', *The Extractive Industries and Society* 4:2 (2017), pp. 304–9 (304), https://doi.org/10.1016/j.exis.2017.01.011 (accessed 9 January 2021).

3. Gavin Bridge, 'CONTESTED TERRAIN: Mining and the Environment', *Annual Review of Environment and Resources* 29:1 (2004), pp. 205–59.

4. Anthony Bebbington, 'The New Extraction: Rewriting the Political Ecology of the Andes?', *NACLA Report on the Americas* 42:5 (2009), pp. 12–20 (15).

wastes make their way into the air and soil, in addition to waterways, and that such contamination does not stay at the mine site but instead travels and can spread far beyond the initial point of extraction with long-term effects on the environment.[5] With modern mining, enormous quantities of solid wastes are being produced, though mining companies have largely sidestepped discussions of what to do with growing mine wastes and the potential environmental liability that they present to future generations.[6]

We have far less information about the influence of sex and gender on exposure to contaminants, though studies suggest that 'there may be sex and gender differences in exposure to chemicals which can be manifested in sex differences in absorption, distribution, metabolism, storage and excretion.'[7] The effects of pollution on bodies can be significant and vary widely based on exposure and susceptibility levels. As scholars have noted, however, given the enormous sums of investment involved and the potential contributions of royalties and taxes to national coffers, it is no surprise that mining takes over, dominates the landscape and 'assumes superiority over everything else.'[8]

A growing body of ethnographic work by scholars, together with documented resistance to mining by grassroots and civil society activists, reveals the extent of the unequal distribution of benefits and harms experienced by local populations from extractive industry operations in their communities (see also chapters by Koster and Cahill in this volume for a discussion of the impacts on women living in the presence of natural resources extraction in the United States and Latin America).[9] Across a range of mining environments, rural women shoulder significant and distinct burdens in the process of living in the presence of

5. Laplonge, 'The "Un-womanly" Attitudes of Women in Mining towards the Environment', p. 304; Anthony Bebbington and Mark Williams 'Water and Mining Conflicts in Peru', *Mountain Research and Development* 28:3–4 (2008), pp. 190–5 (191, 193).

6. Gavin M. Mudd, 'Australia's Mining Legacies', *ARENA, The Mining Issue* 124 (2013), pp. 19–24.

7. Tye E. Arbuckle, 'Are There Sex and Gender Differences in Acute Exposure to Chemicals in the Same Setting?', *Environmental Research* 101:2 (2006), pp. 195–204 (195), https://doi.org/10.1016/j.envres.2005.08.015 (accessed 4 February 2021).

8. Kuntala Lahiri-Dutt, 'The Megaproject of Mining: A Feminist Critique', in *Engineering Earth* (New York: Springer, 2011), pp. 329–51 (331).

9. Jeffrey Bury, 'Livelihoods in Transition: Transnational Gold Mining Operations and Local Change in Cajamarca, Peru', *The Geographical Journal* 170:1 (2004), pp. 78–91; Gerardo H. Damonte, *The Constitution of Political Actors: Peasant Communities, Mining and Mobilization in Bolivian and Peruvian Andes* (Saarbrucken-Berlin: VDM Verlag, 2008); Anthony Bebbington (ed.), *Social Conflict, Economic Development and the Extractive Industry: Evidence from South America* (London: Routledge, 2011); Kyra Grieco, 'Motherhood, Mining and Modernity in the Peruvian Highlands from Corporate Development to Social Mobilization', in *Negotiating Normativity* (Cham: Springer, 2016), pp. 131–46; Fabiana Li, *Unearthing Conflict* (Durham, NC: Duke University Press, 2015); Tom Perreault, 'Mining,

extractive projects.[10] The impacts of extraction are not gender neutral and can be further aggravated by factors such as ethnicity, illiteracy, age, disability and marital status.[11] Access to jobs and financial opportunities offered by mining projects is not the same for men and women, nor is the distribution of burdens from mining activities that produce contamination.[12]

Studies focusing on women's participation in mining-related negotiation processes involving compensation and benefit-sharing agreements reflect their limited or non-existent presence, leaving women to rely on spouses, male relatives and male community leaders to gain access to information and to benefits.[13] When benefit agreements are organized in a gender-blind way (i.e. through

Meaning and Memory in the Andes', *The Geographical Journal* 184:3 (2018), pp. 229–41; Letizia Silva Ontiveros et al., 'Proyectos de Muerte: Energy Justice Conflicts on Mexico's Unconventional Gas Frontier', *The Extractive Industries and Society* 5:4 (2018), pp. 481–9. See also the Environmental Justice Atlas project, https://ejatlas.org.

10. Ingrid Macdonald and Claire Rowland, 'Tunnel Vision: Women Mining and Communities (Victoria, Australia: Oxfam Community Aid Abroad: 2002); Adriana Eftimie, Katherine Heller, and John Strongman, *Mainstreaming Gender into Extractive Industries Projects* (Extractive Industries and Development Series; Washington, DC: The World Bank, 2009), https://esmap.org/sites/esmap.org/files/Mainstreaming%20Gender%20into%20 Extractive%20Industries%20Projects_Guidance%20Note%20for%20Task%20Team%20 Leaders.pdf (accessed 11 November 2020); Matthew Himley, 'El género y la edad frente a las reconfiguraciones en los medios de subsistencia originados por la minería en el Perú', *Apuntes. Revista de ciencias sociales* 38:68 (2011), pp. 7–35, https://doi.org/10.21678/apuntes.68.618 (accessed 11 September 2020); Ximena S. Warnaars, 'Why Be Poor When We Can Be Rich? Constructing Responsible Mining in El Pangui, Ecuador', *Resources Policy* 37:2 (2012), pp. 223–32. https://doi.org/10.1016/j.resourpol.2011.10.001; Katy Jenkins, 'Women Anti-mining Activists' Narratives of Everyday Resistance in the Andes: Staying Put and Carrying on in Peru and Ecuador', *Gender, Place & Culture* 24:10 (2017), pp. 1441–59. https://doi.org/10.1080/09 66369X.2017.1387102 (accessed 11 January 2021); Leda M. Pérez, Lorena De la Puente and Daniela Ugarte, *Las cuidadoras de los mineros: género y gran minería en Cotabambas* (Lima, Perú: Fondo Editorial Universidad del Pacífico, 2019).

11. Matthew Himley, 'El género y la edad frente a las reconfiguraciones en los medios de subsistencia originadas por la minería en el Perú'.

12. Julia Cuadros, *IMPACTOS DE LA MINERÍA EN LA VIDA DE HOMBRES Y MUJERES EN EL SUR ANDINO: Los Casos Las Bambas y Tintaya* (Lima, Peru: CooperAcción, 2010); James Keenan et al., 'Company–Community Agreements, Gender and Development', *Journal of Business Ethics* 135:4 (2016), pp. 607–15 https://doi.org/10.1007/s10551-014-2376-4 (accessed 9 July 2021).

13. Martha Macintyre, 'Petztorme Women: Responding to Change in Lihir, Papua New Guinea', *Oceania* 74:1–2 (2003), pp. 120–34. https://doi.org/10.1002/j.1834-4461.2003. tb02839.x (accessed 11 November 2021); Gerardo Castillo Guzmán and Laura Soria Torres, *Gender Justice in Consultation Processes for Extractives Industries in Bolivia, Ecuador and Peru* (Lima, Peru: Oxfam, 2011).

male-dominated organizations), women are likely not to gain equitable access to and control over flows of benefits whether they are offers of employment, material contributions or financial donations and projects.[14] Such negotiations can deepen existing inequalities and compound women's sense of exclusion and marginalization.[15] This can lead to ruptures in personal relationships within families, clans and communities, and increasingly toxic social relations.[16] In this chapter, I argue that damage to social relations and social institutions induced by mining company practices should be understood as a form of socio-environmental contamination, producing significant and highly gendered impacts that require assessment and remediation alongside impacts to the natural environment. Following Laplonge's observation, I also want to suggest that women's ethic of care also extends to the protection, where possible, of these social relations.

Extractive projects can produce environmental harms and restrict access to resources (land, water, forests) that women rely on for their productive activities. This can undermine women's livelihoods and their ability to provide for their families, resulting in declining living standards and increased vulnerability. Environmental contamination linked to extractive projects can also significantly increase burdens on women who raise children and provide care to spouses and extended family members. At the same time, increased financial costs linked to health problems, especially chronic illness, result in additional stress and care needs.[17]

Pollution from mining and oil and gas projects also affects farm animals and wildlife which form part of women's economic activities. The toxic impacts observed by women are often dismissed, attributed to women's ignorance or mismanagement, or declared to be falsified claims of contamination. Water contamination from mining is often linked to poor animal health though oftentimes women are told their poor animal husbandry practices are the cause of their animals' sickness, not pollution.

Women who actively resist or speak out about mining may find themselves the target of ostracism and abuse. Those who participate in protests or take on leadership roles may find themselves at odds with family members, neighbours

---

14. Ginger Gibson and Deanna Kemp, 'Corporate Engagement with Indigenous Women in the Minerals Industry: Making Space for Theory', in *Earth Matters: Indigenous Peoples, the Extractive Industries and Corporate Social Responsibility* (Sheffield, UK: Greenleaf, 2008), pp. 104–22.

15. Fabiana Li, *Unearthing Conflict* (Durham, NC: Duke University Press, 2015).

16. Denise Humphreys Bebbington and Anthony Bebbington, 'Extraction, Territory, and Inequalities: Gas in the Bolivian Chaco', *Canadian Journal of Development Studies/ Revue canadienne d'études du développement* 30:1–2 (2010), pp. 259–80.

17. See Auyero and Swistun's chronicle of an urban neighbourhood's struggles to make sense of their experiences with environmental contamination, Javier Auyero and Déborah Alejandra Swistun, *Flammable: Environmental Suffering in an Argentine Shantytown* (Oxford: Oxford University Press, 2009).

and community members, which can complicate important family relationships and networks. In the most extreme cases, they have been subject to violence and killings.[18] The response to women's activism can be found in persistent patriarchal ideas about women's roles and who should and should not be leaders. Across each of these adverse and pernicious responses, the impact is similar, and social relations are ultimately and negatively affected by their activism.

It is also important to acknowledge that not all episodes of environmental harms and threats of harm linked to extractive activities lead to citizen action and protest. Frequently, community inaction is the response to such impacts. Contradictory and confusing statements by authority figures (politicians, doctors, company officials) can contribute to uncertainty and division within the community and inhibit possibilities for collective action.[19] Without clear and robust information, local residents may find it difficult to 'make sense' of environmental contamination.[20]

To develop these ideas around socially toxic mining environments and their emergence from physical contamination, I draw on three experiences involving communities directly influenced by mining operations in Peru and Bolivia. Two of the experiences date back to 2005, when the mining supercycle was well underway, and especially apparent in Peru.[21] I became involved in the two cases from Peru as part of my work with the Global Greengrants Fund. The Bolivian case comes later and is linked to research conducted on natural resource extraction under the Morales/MAS government (2006–19).

La Oroya: Slow violence and toxic relationships

One of my earliest and most heart-wrenching encounters with mining contamination in the Andes was not at a mine site but rather at a mine smelter complex in the high Andes town of La Oroya in central Peru. While I had long travelled through La Oroya en route to other work in the central highlands of Peru, the first time I visited it for an extended period was around the same time it

---

18. Global Witness, an international non-governmental organization based in London, has produced yearly reports documenting human rights abuses against land and environmental defenders since 2012. See the 2020 report, *Last Line of Defence*, for a discussion of who is targeted by the violence at https://www.globalwitness.org/en/campaigns/environmental-activists/last-line-defence/.

19. Javier Auyero and Déborah Alejandra Swistun, 'The Social Production of Toxic Uncertainty', *American Sociological Review* 73:3 (2008), pp. 357–79 (accessed 2 February 2021).

20. Pamela Neumann, 'Toxic Talk and Collective (In)action in a Company Town: The Case of La Oroya, Peru', *Social Problems* 63:3 (2016), p. 433, https://doi.org/10.1093/socpro/spw010 (accessed 3 February 2021).

21. Anthony Bebbington and Jeffrey Bury (eds), *Subterranean Struggles: New Dynamics of Mining, Oil, and Gas in Latin America* (Austin: University of Texas Press, 2013).

appeared on the Blacksmith Institute's list of the Ten Most Polluted Places on Earth.[22] During that visit, I met and worked closely with a local activist Protestant pastor and members of MOSAO (Movimiento para la Salud de La Oroya/Movement for Health of La Oroya), a local social movement organized to advocate for the many families living with the impacts of severe, long-standing contamination from the smelter. On a bad day, the air was thick with toxic smoke pouring from the chimneys as the complex smelted metals that came not just from Peruvian mines, but also from metals shipped in from other regions and countries.[23] Residents of La Oroya reveal very high levels of lead (among other metals) in their blood, some seven times higher than World Health Organization standards.[24] Dr Fernando Serrano, a professor at the St. Louis University School of Public Health's Division of Environmental and Occupational Health in Missouri, USA, who travelled to La Oroya to carry out a study in 2005, was alarmed by the results. In order to reduce children's exposure to the worst of the toxic mix, the US company that ran the smelter, Doe Run Peru,[25] bused the town's youngest residents (under the age of six years) down the mountain, to a special day-care facility in order that they could breathe and play in clean air. What Dr Serrano and his colleagues did not anticipate was the hostile reception that his team of researchers received when they arrived in La Oroya. Called vampires, the team was pelted with eggs and verbally assaulted by local residents, fearful that the team's presence would lead to the closing of the smelter and the loss of jobs.

22. The Blacksmith Institute first listed La Oroya in the top ten in its 2007 report and continued to do so in subsequent years. See http://www.worstpolluted.org/projects_reports/display/61.

23. Marco Aquino, 'In Peru, a Smelter's Future Stirs Fears of Its Toxic Past', https://www.reuters.com/article/us-peru-smelter-idUSKBN14W2L9 (accessed 3 February 2021).

24. A 2005 study revealed the extent of the public health crisis. In addition to confirming high levels of lead in 99 per cent of children from a 1999 study, researchers also identified higher than normal levels of arsenic, cadmium, mercury, antimony, caesium and thallium not only in the local population of La Oroya but also in a village 80 kilometres away (see B. Fraser, 'Peruvian Mining Town Must Balance Health and Economics', *The Lancet* 367:9514 (2006), pp. 889–90).

25. The smelter operated under the trade name Doe Run Peru and was fully owned by the Renco Group, Inc. based in the United States. The complex had moved between private and state ownership, and in 1997, the US-based Doe Run purchased the La Oroya lead smelter and the Cobriza copper mine in Peru from the Peruvian government for $247 million as part of a privatization programme. Doe Run also operated Herculaneum, a lead smelter located in the state of Missouri. In 2001, US government regulators found high levels of lead in local children, and Doe Run initiated a clean-up programme, eventually closing the Herculaneum smelter in 2013. Back in Peru, Doe Run was the target of an intense campaign to clean up its operations, though it was able to revise and postpone environmental remediation plans on several occasions. The Protestant pastor forged ties between MOSAO in La Oroya and families affected by Doe Run's Herculaneum smelter, a strategy that helped put further pressure on Doe Run's operations in Peru.

During our meeting with MOSAO representatives, the severe health challenges faced by families, largely shouldered by mothers, became clear. We also came to experience what was a much more complex and deeply troubling social dynamic in which toxicity invaded every nook and cranny in the town and found its way into everyday social interactions and the individual and collective decision-making of residents. Mothers talked about the experience of giving birth to contaminated children whose bodies grew discoloured and weak. Some of these mothers ultimately buried their children without receiving answers as to what made them sick because they were too afraid to speak out. While few families in La Oroya escaped chronic illness, not all of them would attribute their ill health to the smelter's operations. Indeed, La Oroya is very much a company town where nearly every family has a direct or indirect link to the smelter complex and where many of the town's institutions are supported by the company. At one point, our meeting was interrupted when some unknown individuals came into the hall and sat down. They were asked to leave but declined to do so. The meeting abruptly ended, and later MOSAO representatives explained that the individuals were most likely company 'eyes and ears'. The stakes for La Oroya's residents were high. The all or nothing strategy of the company, in which it would consistently threaten to close its operations if it was not given additional time to put into place an environmental remediation plan, was echoed by workers and others in the town, who, fearful of losing their jobs, silenced those who spoke out through acts of surveillance, harassment and death threats.[26] And as Scurrah observed, many local social mobilizations were in fact in favour of the smelter; these were protests against its potential closure.[27]

La Oroya is an extreme example of a contaminated mining environment with few residents able to escape the long-term effects of living and working in the shadow of everyday pollution. Government efforts to improve public health in the town and to obligate the company to implement an environmental clean-up plan were unsuccessful. After repeated extensions to meet environmental standards, and repeated non-compliance with deadlines, Doe Run Peru declared bankruptcy in 2010, and the smelter reduced its operations as the government and company looked for a solution. However, even with the smelter paralysed, the poisoned social relations of the town continued to mix with the 'fine dust particles that pass easily pass through the mucous membranes, the bloodstream, biological membranes making their way to [residents'] DNA'.[28] Subsequently, the Peruvian

---

26. José De Enchave, Raphael Hoetmer and Mario Palacios Pané (eds), *Mineria y Territorio en el Peru, Dialogos y Movimientos* (Lima, Peru: CooperAcción, Confederación Nacional de Comunidades del Perú Afectadas por la Mineria, Universidad Nacional Mayor de San Marcos, 2009).

27. Martin Scurrah, *Defendiendo Derechos y Promoviendo Cambios* (Lima, Peru: Instituto de Estudios Peruanos, 2008).

28. Mongabay Environmental News, 'Peruvian Town Faces Another 14 Years of Air Pollution from Mine', https://news.mongabay.com/2016/04/peruvian-town-faces-another-14-years-air-pollution-mine/ (accessed 2 February 2021).

government attempted to restart the smelter, but these efforts only further exacerbated divisions and tensions among residents of La Oroya. The toll of living with toxic pollution is especially hard on women who must mobilize their limited financial resources and relationships in order to address the faltering health of their children and their loved ones, while at the same time trying to make sense of their socially and environmentally toxic environments.

Choropampa: The social aftermath of a mercury spill

The next story I want to refer to occurred in Choropampa, in northern Peru. A mercury spill, linked to a contracted truck that was transporting materials from the Yanacocha mine (Minera Yanacocha) in Cajamarca to Lima, set into motion a confrontation that continues to impact local residents. The Yanacocha mine, at the time co-owned by Newmont Mining Company (USA), Buenaventura Mining Company (Peru) and the International Finance Corporation (IFC),[29] the commercial lending arm of the World Bank, was the largest, most profitable gold mine in 2000 when the accident occurred.[30] As the truck flipped, it spilled about 150 kilograms of mercury along a dirt highway and into an adjacent drainage canal in the market town of Choropampa.[31] Local villagers as well as visitors from the city of Cajamarca gathered up the shiny liquid believing it was valuable and then hid the material in their homes even after mine representatives warned them that the mercury was toxic (presuming this was a ruse by the company to get the metal back). Only about one-third of the spilt mercury was recovered. Some thousand local residents are thought to have been affected by the spill and suffered a range of health impacts.

Initially, the company was slow to respond to the accident and first placed blame for the spilt mercury on the trucking firm. Only later did the company move into full public relations crisis mode. Mine managers implied that weak villager compliance in returning the mercury to them was a cause of their ill health. Mine representatives and medical officials portrayed health complaints as self-inflicted, morally questionable and lacking validity. Women residents, now wary of local health officials at a clinic funded by the mine, were told that the symptoms of toxic reaction that they and their children had experienced were fabrications. Indeed, a 2001 report by Peru's Defensoría del Pueblo (Human Rights Ombudsman) was

29. Over subsequent years, the International Finance Corporation (IFC) and then later the Buenaventura Mining Company gave up their shares.

30. Jeffrey Bury, 'Livelihoods in Transition: Transnational Gold Mining Operations and Local Change in Cajamarca, Peru', *The Geographical Journal* 170:1 (2004), pp. 78–91.

31. A subsequent review of the accident by the IFC, a partner in the Yanacocha mine at the time of the accident, found that the canisters holding the mercury were not properly secured. The IFC sold its interests in the Yanacocha mine in 2017 to Japan's Sumitomo Metal Mining Company, Ltd.

highly critical of government and company actions in responding to the crisis. The report pointed to signed contracts between the company and affected villagers that constrained those receiving compensation and health services from speaking about the accident. The contracts contained clauses that protected Minera Yanacocha and the transport company, Ransa Comercial, S. A., from assuming responsibility for the spill and from any further legal action by residents. In exchange, Yanacocha agreed to provide residents with health insurance to address health problems linked to the spill. Most of the residents agreed to the contract. Unable to read and write, most residents signed with their thumbprints.[32]

The insertion of company confidentiality clauses into the negotiated agreements with communities is an understudied but ubiquitous practice in which companies offer money or material compensation in exchange for silence and acquiescence.[33] These company endeavours to contain information often circumvent community consensus-based decision-making practices by preventing community leaders and authorities from fully divulging the content of agreements or establishing monitoring processes to ensure compliance with agreements. Such practices may eliminate the immediate problem for companies, but ultimately, they erode the possibility of open and transparent discussions within communities, undermining the mechanisms that build and sustain trust and cooperation among local residents. In Choropampa, not only did the toxic spill poison bodies, the mercury spill helped contaminate relations between those living in Cajamarca and the mine.

A documentary produced about the Chorompampa spill[34] captures the highly divisive conflict pitting the town's residents against mine company managers and doctors and then against each other as they struggle over whether to take offers of employment and compensation (and be silenced), or to continue to fight the company and government. There are no good choices. In one of the film's most emotional scenes, the camera reveals that it is the town's women who angrily confront the police and demand that Choropampa's young mayor stand up to company officials and seek justice. Their desperation and sense of helplessness are palpable at the same time as their courage is in full view.

Nearly twenty years after the spill, the residents of Choropampa continue to live with the consequences of the mining accident, attributing their ill health to mercury exposure and to a lack of access to adequate health care. The economy of the town has suffered as well – local farmers have encountered reductions in

32. Defensoria del Pueblo, 'INFORME DEFENSORIAL N° 62 : EL CASO DEL DERRAME DE MERCURIO QUE AFECTÓ A LAS LOCALIDADES DE SAN SEBASTIÁN DE CHOROPAMPA, MAGDALENA Y SAN JUAN, EN LA PROVINCIA DE CAJAMARCA' (Lima, Peru: Defensoría del Pueblo, 2001), https://www.defensoria.gob.pe/wp-content/uploads/2018/05/informe_62.pdf (accessed 4 January 2021).

33. Bebbington and Bebbington, 'Extraction, Territory, and Inequalities: Gas in the Bolivian Chaco'.

34. *Choropampa: The Price of Gold*, DVCAM, directed by Ernesto Cabellos and Stephanie Boyd (Lima, Peru: Guarango, 2002).

demand for what are perceived by some to be contaminated crops. Unable to make a living, many families moved away. Cajamarca lawyer and socio-environmental activist Mirtha Vásquez, who served as one of Peru's three vice presidents during Peru's interim government of 2020–21, and subsequently as prime minister from late 2021 to early 2022, is a strong advocate for national guidelines to treat people affected by heavy metal contamination. Vásquez notes that families impacted by contamination may not fully understand the long-term challenges that they are facing when they sign agreements with companies. 'Over time people [in Choropampa] began to realise the damage … was not as simple as they were told, it was permanent damage.'[35]

Challapata, Oruro: Keeping mining contamination away

The third and final story comes from highland Bolivia, where a proposed mining project ran headlong into a persistent and effective grassroots coalition resisting the establishment of mining. Oruro is a region that suffers from high levels of environmental contamination linked to mineral extraction, and this legacy is well documented as are the increasingly tense conflicts over water.[36]

Under the populist government of Evo Morales and his party, the Movement towards Socialism (2006–19), natural resource extraction became the foundation for national development and investment in social programming. Authorities in Oruro promoted the slogan: 'Oruro was, is and will be a mining territory'.[37] However support for natural resource extraction is not universal in Bolivia and the rapid, often uncontrolled expansion of mining has unleashed disagreements 'between the state, the private sector and social movements over the territorial, environmental and human implications of [mining's] expansion'.[38]

The municipality of Challapata, about 120 kilometres from the City of Oruro in Bolivia's high plains, benefited early on from the construction of

35. Noah Moeys, 'The Village Still Suffering from Peru Mercury Spill Fallout – after 20 Years', *The Guardian*, 2 April 2020, https://www.theguardian.com/global-development/2020/apr/02/the-village-still-suffering-from-peru-mercury-spill-fallout-after-20-years (accessed 3 February 2021).

36. Tom Perreault, 'Climate Change and Climate Politics: Parsing the Causes and Effects of the Drying of Lake Poopó, Boliva', *Journal of Latin American Geography* 19:3 (2020), pp. 26–46; Riley Mulhern et al., 'Contesting the Social License to Operate: Competing Visions and Community Exclusion on the Bolivian Altiplano', *The Extractive Industries and Society* 9 (2022), https://doi.org/10.1016/j.exis.2020.08.014 (accessed 2 June 2022).

37. Emilio R. Madrid Lara et al., 'Coro Coro and Challapata: Defending Collective Rights and Mother Earth against Development Mining Fetishism', *Environmental Justice* 5:2 (2012), pp. 65–9 (66). https://doi.org/10.1089/env.2011.0027 (accessed 10 January 2021).

38. Anthony Bebbington, 'The New Extraction: Rewriting the Political Ecology of the Andes?' pp. 13–14.

the Tacagua Dam and irrigation system, an ambitious development project implemented in the early 1960s. The project created a highly productive farming/livestock/dairying region. Women play important roles in managing animals and in dairying activities. The success of the region's livestock producers led to a government-installed dairy processing plant which President Evo Morales himself inaugurated in 2011.

The history of this proposed mine extends back some three decades. In 1993, a consortium of Bolivian and Canadian mining interests began prospecting in the area of Achachucani Hill, adjacent to the Tacagua Dam. Important mineral deposits were found, among them gold. However, before the company could establish a project, villagers in the region executed a direct action, a *bloqueo* or roadblock, on the main highway between Oruro and Potosí. The company quickly withdrew its personnel and stopped further work. In 2007, with world gold prices approaching record highs, a new Canadian company, Castillian Resources, restarted the project. The community responded with another *bloqueo* and pressured departmental authorities to evict the company. Anticipating resistance from some sectors, the company deployed financial resources in an aggressive strategy to win the hearts and minds of local villagers using local media to convince residents of the benefits of mining. Local activists counter that the company is actively seeking to foster confusion and division within communities with this strategy.[39]

Women play leading roles in keeping Challapata mining free. They see the company's media campaigns as disrespectful, a provocation and a campaign of harassment. They fear that the company will be successful at dividing community members, especially through offering employment opportunities to young people. Here women are responsible for administering water resources, serving as water judges and on irrigation committees, and the potential loss of water resources and livelihoods energizes their collective struggle. They are keenly aware of the challenges they face. In response, they have created their own social media campaign 'The Women Are Water' with links to other groups and campaigns around Latin America.[40] In this sense, the example of Challapata has a slightly more positive edge insofar as women have been able to push back against some of the pollution of the social environment and have been able to protect and win back collective spaces in the community.

Conclusion

The experiences described above reflect very different sets of challenges for living in mining environments. In the two cases from Peru, highly toxic physical

39. Madrid Lara et al., 'Coro Coro and Challapata: Defending Collective Rights and Mother Earth against Development Mining Fetishism', p. 67.

40. Cf., 'We, Women Are Water 2020' at https://gaggaalliance.org/tag/mujeres-de-challapata/

environments, the product of long-term pollution and mining accidents, have produced toxic social environments. In both environments, women struggle to make sense of the contamination. In the third case from Bolivia, social toxicity has been fostered even without environmental contamination, as the mining company uses a range of techniques designed to weaken social ties or at least the ties that bind together resistance, as part of a suite of 'tactics of dispossession'.[41]

What the different cases share is the production of more complicated, fractured, fractious and indeed toxic social environments that have emerged as a result of the presence of mining or the prospect of mining. While the accumulated contamination of these social environments damages, in one way or another, everyone who lives in them, women have borne the effects of these increasingly difficult social relationships in ways affected by their own, gendered positionalities. It is not my purpose here to suggest that they have been impacted 'more' than other identity-based groups in these communities but merely to note that they have been impacted in ways that are painful and significant and that are mediated by their identities as women. Nor do we necessarily have to have a view on whether women have a stronger ethic of environmental and social care than do men to see the value in Laplonge's provocation. His question is helpful to bear in mind always in discussions of ways to repair both the social and environmental harms done by mining. Elements of such repair are, perhaps, visible in parts of the Challapata case.

Rather than looking to women to utilize 'their caring ethic' to defend and save the environment from the harms caused by mining operations, governments and companies need to take seriously not only the accumulating material toxicity in mining environments but also the toxic social impacts of mining.[42] They must also recognize and respond to the implications of deteriorating social environments for the long-term quality of life in, and sustainability of, rural communities. Ultimately, it is the companies and governments' responsibility to reverse this deterioration. However, as they imagine strategies of restoration, they will have much to learn from the specific ways in which rural women have experienced the suffering caused by the ways in which these social environments have been damaged, as well as from ways in which women have responded collectively to these impacts.

For *Laudato Si'* and efforts to convert its theological messages into practice and policy, the implication of these cases is that it remains vital not to lose sight of the

41. Thomas Frederiksen and Matthew Himley, 'Tactics of Dispossession: Access, Power, and Subjectivity at the Extractive Frontier', *Transactions of the Institute of British Geographers* 45:1 (2020), pp. 50–64 (52).

42. Laplonge, 'The "Un-womanly" Attitudes of Women in Mining towards the Environment', p. 304.

gendered dimensions of human and industrial despoliation of the earth. Equally important is to recognize the ways in which the cry of the poor and processes of ecological conversion are themselves also gendered. Perhaps more than anything, these cases insist on centring gender in our readings of environmental change, our readings of the encyclical and our reflections on which actors will chart the pathways towards a restored common home.

Chapter 3

COUNTERING COLONIAL MINING

WATER PROTECTORS, ENVIRONMENTAL JUSTICE AND THE CREATION COMMUNITY OF SAINTS

Marion Grau

Transitioning from colonial mining practices requires a different way of imagining, engaging and using energy, different practices for its use and supply. The struggle for the energy transition we are in is fiendishly complex, and simple answers defy the situations. How can recent examples of climate action help tell a story about the just energy transitions we need while refusing to sacrifice Indigenous lands and resources to mine resources for green technologies?

Alliances among Indigenous activists, environmental and religious organizations have become more common during the last years of climate action. During the COP26 in Glasgow, religious leaders from around the globe urged to strengthen partnerships between religious and Indigenous leaders to help save the planet.[1] This chapter gathers threads of such partnerships and the ways they might be framed in a constructive theological framework for decolonial climate justice.

Drawing on the resistance against the Dakota Access pipeline in 2016 and the ongoing resistance to green colonialism in Arctic Indigenous lands (Sápmi), the chapter seeks to gather practices and narratives to imagine and live in and through these energy transitions. At Standing Rock, water protectors offered compelling narratives and images to reframe the struggle against toxic extractivism through the motto 'Water is life – *Mni Wiconi*'. Sámi and environmental activists worked together to block a proposed copper mine in Repparfjorden in Northern Norway. Colonial heritage and trauma flow together in both cases. Pressure to extract copper for the energy transition or to build on traditional reindeer grazing grounds to construct wind farms is a form of green imperialism that triggers intergenerational colonial trauma. For many Indigenous people, the struggle against colonial extractions is also a spiritual struggle. Religious communities who see the struggle for climate justice as a theological crisis and a call to action can

---

1. See https://religionnews.com/2021/11/04/cop26-event-urges-partnership-between-religious-indigenous-leaders-to-save-planet/ (accessed 27 April 2022).

form alliances that resist such colonial projects and work for a more just transition by developing principles of energy justice.

Contesting colonial petro-cultures involves a critique of toxic masculinity, various forms of extractivism, and developing a theology of energy justice transitioning towards building a global community. In need of stories that imagine different ways of living on a warming planet, we might imagine a cloud of witnesses that struggle for the planet as a kind of *communio sanctorum* giving glimpses of community, of 'companions in hope'.[2]

Contesting colonial petro-cultures: Rethinking energy and protecting Indigenous lands

Moving towards justice in energy transition from fossil fuels necessitates taking into account existing energy inequities. Some energy systems are burdened with aging fossil infrastructure and lagging upgrades to less polluting and more efficient technology. Transitioning to renewables without addressing energy justice will tend to heighten existing inequalities. Thus, many critical energy scholars worry that a renewable transition, without being led by democratic and just processes, could just as easily work to entrench existing power relations, while at the same time failing to produce truly sustainable communities.[3]

Meanwhile, purveyors of petroleum dependence continue to proliferate metanarratives of the necessity of 'being anointed with the oil of power', which is claimed to provide stable and reliable energy. The study of petro-cultures has contributed to the realization of the degree to which oil has made us into what is often called modern people, shaping our existence while narrating us into networks of colonial power and commerce far afield.[4] Some of these powers are connected to petro-masculinity, a toxic mix of racism, misogyny and climate denial.[5] How do the claims of petro-culture to save humanity hold us enthralled in oil as an 'opium for the masses' (Marx) and the 'energy of slaves',[6] and how can we wean ourselves from its paralyzing and destructive powers? If petroleum is a kind of unholy sacrament, an extreme unction towards death, how can these addicted societies die to oil? What does religion beyond petroleum look like? What stories of energy justice and critiques of energy domination schemes need we articulate?

2. Elizabeth A. Johnson, *Friends of God and Prophets: A Feminist Theological Reading of the Communion of Saints* (Ottawa: Novalis, 1998), p. 202.

3. Cara Daggett, 'Energy and Domination: Contesting the Fossil Myth of Fuel Expansion', *Environmental Politics* 30:4 (2021), pp. 644–62.

4. Sheena Wilson, Adam Carlson and Imre Szeman (eds), *Petrocultures: Oil, Politics, Culture* (Montreal: McGill-Queen's University Press, 2017), p. 3.

5. Cara Daggett, 'Petro-Masculinity: Fossil Fuels and Authoritarian Desires', *Millennium: Journal of International Studies* 47:1 (2018), pp. 25–44 (25).

6. Cf., Andrew Nikiforuk, *The Energy of Slaves: Oil and the New Servitude* (Vancouver: Greystone Books /D&M Publishers, Inc., 2012).

Even as the outright denial of climate change is beginning to dissipate, manipulative communication strategies such as greenwashing, deflection, division, delay and other assorted forms of misdirection aim to blunt efforts to push for energy transitions.[7] The constructive work of theology in this time and place concerns the rethinking of narratives infused with passionate attachment to petro-culture and the discerning of how to tell theopoetic transition stories that help nudge us into increasingly post-petroleum energy relations. This work includes a reimagining of gifts and gift-giving as Eu-Charis (the good gift) in ways that indeed are freely given but oblige to responsible reciprocity if the gift is to be honoured and life to be valued.

Decolonizing energy transitions: Between poisonous domination and sacred gift

Humans have used energy in various ways throughout history, and their usage continues to be in flux.[8] A scientific introduction to energy studies suggests that the energy regimes of Greenland Inuit and medieval Viking settlers were profoundly mismatched, one having adjusted to the possibilities and challenges of the land and seascape, thus enabling survival, the other having failed to adjust and, eventually, ending in extinction.[9] Cara Daggett suggests that we need new narratives for the energy transition, and that the blossoming of *alternative energy stories*, countering patterns of domination by fuel, and featuring political innovations that more equitably and sustainably organize energy, will be as important as new energy tools, and perhaps more so.[10]

Similarly, in *Bataille's Peak*, Allan Stoekl proposes that 'postsustainability' demands a radical reconceptualization of energy, no longer as a resource but (again) as vitality – *en ergon* – as processes that are constantly in flux and evolving. Stoekl argues that energy is intimately tied to a desire to manage the Self.[11] Framed theologically, energy narratives represent human efforts to manage God and the world, often at the cost of other humans, animals and landscapes that are set apart for energy extraction. Energy desires and energy economics are connected to how we *might* imagine the world, how deity manifests and is experienced. Were one to construct a theology of energy, better descriptions of what energy might be and a recognition that energy is fundamentally resistant to control are necessary.[12]

7. For a fuller account of such strategies, see Michael Mann, *The New Climate War: The Fight to Take Back Our Planet* (New York: Public Affairs, 2021).

8. As for example described by historian of energy, Vaclav Smil.

9. Thomas Schlabbach and Viktor Wesselak, *Energie: Den Erneuerbaren Gehört die Zukunft* (Berlin: Springer, 2020), p. 15.

10. Daggett, 'Energy and Domination', p. 647.

11. Allan Stoekl, *Bataille's Peak: Energy, Religion, and Postsustainability* (Minneapolis: University of Minnesota Press, 2007), p. 125.

12. Randy Schroeder, 'Getting into Accidents: Stoekl, Virilio, Postsustainability', in *Petrocultures: Oil, Politics, Culture*, 358, citing Stoekl, *Bataille's Peak*, pp. iv–x.

Post-fossil ideas of energy in a theological mode necessitate energy stories that inspire different ways to relate to creation and its inhabitants. The protest at Standing Rock provided hints towards a different way of engaging energies and their spiritual/material manifestations while highlighting the challenges that counter such attempt.

Wrestling the Black Snake: Pushing back at colonial energy extraction

Indigenous peoples have been affected by colonial mining for centuries and have experienced great cultural and spiritual devastation. In recent years, there has been a renaissance of tribal cultures and defence of the land, ironically represented by the fight against a pipeline through tribal lands in North Dakota, a dedicated oil state. In 2016, I had the opportunity to spend some days at the Standing Rock (ND) protests against the North Dakota Access Pipeline at Standing Rock (ND) – days that offered a glimpse that another world is possible,[13] one in which a different way of relating to the land, to the Sacred and to each other was palpable as a something that was entering a more conscious state of concrescence. Some have called it a 'movement of movements', exemplary of 'environmental struggles writ large'.[14] I travelled to the camp after a local Dakota member of the clergy had invited religious leaders to come to Standing Rock to help support the movement by coming to the site of struggle and participating in a ceremony of repentance for the churches' participation in the colonial process. In particular, clergy representatives for the denominations renounced the Doctrine of Discovery, a theological doctrine that had lent support to the depropriation of Native peoples in the Americas. Representatives from most mainline denominations were present and read the common declaration. Weeks later, thousands of US veterans travelled to the camp for a show of solidarity as well as an expression of apology for the fraught relationship of the US military as part of the colonization process.[15] These encounters also triggered a need for tribal members to come to engage transgenerational colonial trauma that resurfaced during these events, despite the difficulties of encounter with non-native visitors to the camp that had to be socialized into a culture of respect for the hosts and reciprocity of giving.

Though tenuous and temporary, a sense of community emerged during powerful days of being present and paying attention. In particular, Standing Rock offered a meeting site for tribal peoples, settler descendants, environmental activists and religious leaders. The encounters offered inspiration and learning about how eco-justice resistance movements might be developing in the future.

What made the #NODAPL (No Dakota Access Pipeline) environmental action a milestone in the fight against fossil fuels was that it was started and

---

13. Julie Sze, *Environmental Justice in a Moment of Danger* (Berkeley: University of California Press, 2020), p. 29.

14. Sze, *Environmental Justice in a Moment of Danger*, p. 25.

15. Sze, *Environmental Justice in a Moment of Danger*, p. 45.

remained centred on Indigenous peoples, and among them especially women and youth. Violence, especially against Indigenous women, has been particularly prominent in extractive contexts, and several activists made specific links between environmental abuse and domestic violence.[16] Though Indigenous peoples represent only 5 per cent of the global population, the lands they call home contain 80 per cent of the world's biodiversity, and very often lands that are subject to mining, the establishment of dams, fracking and all kinds of extractive activities that damage people and the land.[17] The tribal hosts resisted efforts to centre away from Indigenous peoples as hosts and guardians of the land and educated visitors who did not understand this or were interested in romanticizing the gathering. The messaging also was consistently that Standing Rock was a ceremony, rather than a protest, camp or music festival. Alcohol and drugs were prohibited, and violators were asked to leave the camp. Instead, people were invited to be in prayer – whatever that meant to them – and to listen, gather around the sacred fire and contemplate their own story in relationship to the protection of water. The unapologetic spiritual focus was another important factor that made this gathering different from other more secular or loosely pluralistically framed environmental movements and made particular demands on the internal attitudes of visitors.

This may also have been the reason why religious representatives in particular were invited. Clergy, bishops and seminary students showed up in large numbers, joined by Jews, Quakers, Muslims, Buddhists and pagans, representing a unique gathering of religious tribes in themselves. The ceremony offered access to a glimpse of a different spiritual polity, and a 'transformative politics for non-Native allies'.[18] This was done while ensuring that Indigenous sovereignty remained at the core. Thus, #NODAPL provided a vision of a different power dynamics and decentred white supremacy by centring Indigenous leadership, such as the Indigenous Environmental Network (IEN).[19]

The welcome and the solidarity of the camp, the willingness to share food, sleeping areas, clothes, and the spiritual impulses of the camp hinted at a 'comradeship [...] made in the struggle'[20] which gave hints at a remaking of a common identity that might be able to transcend the legacies of racism, dispossession and imperialism. One of the transformative possibilities the ceremony offered was a chance to imagine new identities, even as the transgenerational trauma of colonization, dispossession and violence emerged and was triggered by the heavy-handed presence of militarized police and the hostility of many settler-descendant neighbours.

The protest was led primarily by youth and women, witnessing to the increasing impact of young Indigenous activists at the forefront of climate justice

---

16. Sze, *Environmental Justice in a Moment of Danger*, p. 41.
17. Sze, *Environmental Justice in a Moment of Danger*, p. 28.
18. Sze, *Environmental Justice in a Moment of Danger*, p. 30.
19. Sze, *Environmental Justice in a Moment of Danger*, p. 32.
20. Sze, *Environmental Justice in a Moment of Danger*, p. 44.

activism.[21] Activists highlighted the relationship between gender-based violence and environmental violence, arguing that 'abuse of the Earth and of women are connected'.[22] Standing Rock provided 'for a brief moment in time, a collective vision of what the future could be'.[23] It has come to stand as an 'iconic battle for environmental justice'[24] and provided many with a sense of a large community coming together across differences to change the way land, water and energy are used and distributed – away from the oppressive, colonial logic of extraction and enrichment of the few. The communal rituals at Standing Rock took on a new and heightened meaning in those days, whether it was being initiated into the camp, gathering near the Sacred Fire, sharing and receiving food, swapping clothes, praying, smudging sage, talking and connecting, rituals of repentance or common prayer.

Water protectors encouraged those participating in the ceremony to take the movement for environmental justice home with us and to continue imagining its next steps: working locally to educate and engage more people, divesting from petroleum dependency and imagining alternatives, continuing to building a 'movement of movements' in new and yet unimagined ways.[25] Though the ceremony of the camp was not to last, the experience inspired many to a renewed engagement to help usher in the end of petrocapitalism and its destructive extractivist legacies. After the #NODAPL camps were disbanded, activists went back to their home communities, rebuilding Indigenous communities, pushing for divestment from fossil industries, studying, gathering, creating rituals that help articulate grounding earth spiritualities or rethinking life on a vulnerable planet.

The narrative elements of the story of resistance included the water protectors who would stand in ceremony, proclaiming 'water is life' pitted in a struggle against the Black Snake – symbolizing the fossil fuel energy economy and in particular the infrastructure of delivery of pipelines and the danger they represent to life-giving rivers.

Defeating the Black Snake is described as both a spiritual and economic quest. Dismantling the toxic streams of oil and its spills includes many practices: blocking the building of infrastructure, going to court against further developments or making fossil fuels unprofitable through divestment campaigns. The latter seems to finally show some success, at least at the stock market. Still too many fossil fuel projects persist accompanied by hell-bent forms of climate action delay and heavy behind-the-scene manipulations. One glaring tactic of delay of needed energy

---

21. Sze, *Environmental Justice in a Moment of Danger*, p. 27.

22. Sze, *Environmental Justice in a Moment of Danger*, p. 41.

23. Nick Estes and Jaskiran Dhillon (eds), *Standing with Standing Rock: Voices from the #NODAPL Movement* (Minneapolis: University of Minnesota Press, 2019), p. 5.

24. Sze, *Environmental Justice in a Moment of Danger*, p. 28.

25. Sze, *Environmental Justice in a Moment of Danger*, p. 50.

transitions is represented by the staggering number of fossil fuel representatives present at the COP26 negotiations in Glasgow.[26]

Unsurprisingly, Rachel Maddow, following the track of corruption and anti-democratic manoeuvring of white supremacist billionaires on either side of Cold War lines, found major ties between oil and gas investments and oligarchs and billionaires with autocratic political leanings. We continue to witness an ongoing unveiling of the entanglement of authoritarianism and petroleum, racism and misogyny.[27] Attempts to repress or raise doubts about the reliability of climate scientists and protestors often go along with toxic petro-masculinity – a gendering of fuel engines as masculine and other energy forms as weak or insignificant – a caricature of gender essentialism that is often directed at climate activists, frequently represented by young women, many of them Indigenous and from the Global South. This violence towards women and land is especially visible in petroleum extraction. The 'man camps' that arise as petro-infrastructure is built have long been connected to the rape, abduction and vanishing of Indigenous women. In North Dakota, for example, the incidence of violence and abuse against women rose sharply during the time of the Bakken oil boom, and close to 100 per cent of this violence was committed by non-Indigenous men, bringing new meaning to the term 'toxic masculinity'.[28]

The #NODAPL Standing Rock pipeline protest made visible a shift in the spiritual economies of tribal communities. A trans-tribal alliance fought back against the delivery system of petro-culture, the 'Black Snake' of petroleum and the attached infrastructure that delivers it via Indigenous lands, pipelines.[29] Standing Rock provided a convergence point for Indigenous groups who had become increasingly organized and activist on land and water issues. Further afield, Indigenous peoples throughout Canada have protested several of the points

---

26. https://gizmodo.com/glasgow-climate-negotiation-leaves-room-for-fossil-fuel-1848 053158 (accessed 29 April 2022).

27. Rachel Maddow, *Blowout: Corrupted Democracy, Rogue State Russia, and the Richest, Most Destructive Industry on Earth* (New York: Crown, 2019); See also Darren Dochuk, *Anointed with Oil: How Christianity and Crude Made Modern America* (New York: Basic Books, 2019).

28. Michelle Cook, 'Striking at the Heart of Capital: International Financial Institutions and Indigenous Peoples' Human Rights', in *Standing with Standing Rock: Voices from the #NODAPL Movement* (Minneapolis: University of Minnesota Press, 2019), pp. 103–57 (112–13). For an ecofeminist/decolonial reading of the violence against Indigenous women and two-spirit people in the context of fracking in the Bakken see Hilda Koster's chapter in this volume.

29. https://religiondispatches.org/decolonizing-thanksgiving-at-standing-rock-a-black-friday-report/ (accessed 27 February 2022). See also Hilda P. Koster, 'Trafficked Lands: Sexual Violence, Oil, and Structural Evil in the Dakotas', in Grace Ji-Sun Kim and Hilda P. Koster (eds), *Planetary Solidarity: Global Women's Voices on Christian Doctrine and Climate Justice* (Minneapolis: Fortress, 2017), pp. 155–78.

at which fracked natural gas from north-eastern British Columbia is intended to connect to the Western Canadian coast via the Coastal GasLink Pipeline.[30] This case illustrates how extractive petro-culture dissects and destroys the integrity of land and water, just as Indigenous life in reciprocity with land and water has been disrupted through extractive colonial policies. Land rights issues reach back into the time of British coloniality. Like the water protectors at Standing Rock, the western Canadian tribal group of the Wet'suwet'en resists the building of pipelines on their lands[31] and livelihoods, while others demonstrate against the development of Line 3 in Minnesota.[32]

Sheila Watt-Cloutier, an Inuit climate activist, connects the 'dispiritedness' of Indigenous communities, the 'self-destruction and suicide rates', and violence against Indigenous women to this devastation of the human-nature bond.[33] The jobs and profits of 'extraction industries have a history of failure in creating a sustainable economic boost in the territories they occupy'.[34] Watt-Cloutier argues that 'many of these industries, unless they reinvent themselves entirely, have the potential to cause further disconnect and severance' for Inuit. She asks: 'What will mining, oil and gas, and, in fact, all extractive industries do to our already-vulnerable collective hunter spirit?'[35] She asks how 'our hunters, men, women, and youth, those who have known the wisdom of the land, feel at the end of a workday spent digging up and destroying the very land they have held sacred' as jobs bring short-term profits but long-term destruction.

I propose that the 'reparations ecologies' we might imagine be framed as a theopolitics that remembers 'the violence and inequality of modernity'. As such they seek emancipatory modes and further restorative justice, highlighting 'intersectional, feminist, and global coalition politics'.[36] Further, it is crucial to 'remain hopeful in the face of catastrophic histories, including the end of a way of life',[37] and in the face of the 'aggressive indifference'[38] of interests invested in colonial white supremacy and the depraved indifference of climate action delay. Even so, argues Sze, it may be possible that 'those most vulnerable [...] are arguably also the

30. Canadian church leaders have released a letter voicing support of Indigenous resistance against this pipeline project: https://www.anglicanjournal.com/church-leaders-sign-statement-of-support-for-wetsuweten/ (accessed 27 February 2022).

31. https://bc.ctvnews.ca/tensions-building-in-wet-suwet-en-territory-as-b-c-pipeline-conflict-continues-1.5672253 (accessed 27 February 2022).

32. https://www.theguardian.com/environment/2021/aug/10/protesters-line-3-minnesota-oil-gas-pipeline (accessed 27 February 2022).

33. Sheila Watt-Cloutier, *The Right to Be Cold: One Woman's Story of Protecting Her Culture, the Artic and the Whole Planet* (Toronto: Penguin, 2015), p. 293.

34. Watt-Cloutier, *Right to Be Cold*, p. 291.

35. Watt-Cloutier, *Right to Be Cold*, p. 293.

36. Sze, *Environmental Justice in a Moment of Danger*, pp. 78, 80–1.

37. Sze, *Environmental Justice in a Moment of Danger*, p. 81.

38. Sze, *Environmental Justice in a Moment of Danger*, p. 88.

most prepared for the postcarbon, postcapitalist future, in part because they have survived in the face of socially and politically sanctioned death'.[39]

Protecting the waters: Political spirituality at Standing Rock

Ceremony focuses attention so that attention becomes intention. If you stand together and profess a thing before your community, it holds you accountable.[40]

Mni Wiconi! 'Water is life'. The call of the Water Protectors at Standing Rock suggests that water is a gift to be managed responsibly. Instead, 'water has been tricked'; it has been polluted, bottled, fracked, 'corrupted, and instead of a bearer of life, it must now deliver poison'.[41] Water comes with strings of responsibility attached and disregards results in its poisoning.

Some have seen parallels between the young women at Standing Rock who led the fight against the Black Snake and Mary the Virgin who is often depicted crushing the head of a snake. Whatever imaginary folk may be braiding (Leduc's term, also invoked in the title of Wall Kimmerer),[42] if some part of us is to survive and enter into surely very different covenantal relationships, we have to relearn how to live in a changed world in cross-cultural covenants of reciprocity. Iconic images of a young female water protector fighting the Black Snake invoke Marian imagery and the Magnificat, of young women announcing the coming of a different power and a different order. At Standing Rock women performed the water ritual each morning, highlighting the responsibility of women in this spiritual economy of thanksgiving.[43] When Mary is highlighted as the one who crushes the (Black) snake, a very different picture emerges, one that resists the patriarchal and gender-complementary readings of her and other women by Roman Catholic officials. Such images pull her out of the shadow of the patriarchal frame that pertains throughout the papal encyclopaedia *Laudato Si'*, and which ignores the fact that women are generally most affected by climate change while marginalizing women's and especially Roman Catholic ecofeminists' contributions to ecological theologies.[44] While *Laudato Si'* offers some recognition of the climate crisis, there are other aspects of patriarchal theology and authoritarian structure that

---

39. Sze, *Environmental Justice in a Moment of Danger*, p. 92.

40. Robin Wall Kimmerer, *Braiding Sweetgrass: Indigenous Wisdom, Scientific Knowledge, and the Teachings of Plants* (Minneapolis: Milkweed Editions, 2013), p. 249.

41. Kimmerer, *Braiding Sweetgrass*, p. 315.

42. Timothy B. Leduc, *A Canadian Climate of Mind: Passages from Fur to Energy and Beyond* (Montreal: McGill-Queen's University, 2016).

43. Kimmerer, *Braiding Sweetgrass*, p. 94.

44. Celia Deane-Drummond, 'Foreword', in *Planetary Solidarity*, pp. xxi–xxv (p. xxvii); see also Ivone Gebara, 'Women's Suffering, Climate Injustice, God, and Pope Francis' Theology: Some Insights from Brazil', in *Planetary Solidarity*, pp. 67–79 for a critique of the unsatisfactory treatment of gender and women in the encyclical.

remain firmly in place, and where there is no willingness to show mercy or take responsibility for past abuses by the Roman Catholic Church.[45] If it is then that we seek to launch a faithful response, that always also means a critical account of our own traditions and institutions.

Mary's association with blue and the heavens and stars, as well as the crusher of the serpent brings up interesting possibilities of imagining for Mary as the patroness of water protectors and those seeking transitions away from the Black Snake of petro-culture. In the image of the Pietà, she holds the body of her child, like all those embracing children who have become victims of destructive state violence.

Repparfjorden: Green colonialism and Sámi land rights

Arctic peoples and species experience amplified effects of climate change around the world. The Arctic is increasingly becoming a site of profound change, profound loss and death. We know that traditional life cycles, migration patterns and wisdoms are already being profoundly affected by climate change. Indigenous peoples of the Arctic, their livelihoods densely interwoven with the elements and species of Arctic regions, have been suffering a combination of trans-generational cultural and ecological genocide.

Indigenous energy regimes were developed to remain within the resource limits of the place and its inhabitants, seeking to live in a balance that ensures future generations' thriving. While these tender balances of thriving were always subject to fluctuations, they are now severely disrupted by the modern extractive technologies during colonial Arctic expansion. Since Indigenous modes of living generally reflect what secular Westerners consider to be spiritual or religious modes of perception, one of the most debilitating effects of colonization has been the disregard, supersession and secularization of Indigenous peoples' ancestral landscapes, histories and cosmologies.[46] Colonial differentiations between nature and culture replaced the land as a relative with progressively and exponentially extractive cultures. It begs the question whether in some instances 'culture' was all too congruent with extractivism.

Land is central to many Indigenous peoples, and some suggest it should be a doctrinal topic in Native American theology.[47] In many Indigenous cultures,

45. See the various incidents of unwillingness to apologize for the graves of children found on the grounds of former residential schools, or the lack of clear leadership on responding to victims of sexual abuse perpetrated by priests (REFS).

46. Sámi speak about belonging to the land, rather than the land to them, in a mode similar to that of many Indigenous peoples.

47. Clara Sue Kidwell, Homer Noley, George E. Tinker and Jace Weaver, *A Native American Theology* (Maryknoll: Orbis Books, 2001).

cosmogonies frame creation as 'relative, not as a resource'.[48] Such narratives 'carefully encouraged Indigenous societies in the Americas to have a reciprocal, intentional, environmentally sustainable relationship with the natural world', aiming to forestall infringement of these limits.[49] Circumpolar Arctic Indigenous peoples have their own locally specific sacred geographies, sites and maps.

Our sense of place is determined by the context, and for many Indigenous cultures this means that narratives of identity and place are 'geo-mythological'.[50] Creation myths represent various narrating and understanding the energies of a particular life world.

For many people, recovering or maintaining a sense of happiness in a sacred geography/landscape helps counter the despiritualization of geography and the loss of a sense of place. To counter the shrinkage and diminishment of place in the throes of petro-culture and the dynamics of efficient, fast travel, of the contraction of space, modes of pilgrimage both enable and stand in critical difference to these forms of collapsed and exploited place. Mourning the loss of place and relations to it is also being negotiated through rituals and liturgies.

The colonial destruction of Sámi lifeways and landscapes affects people's sense of place. Historically, the cultural imperialism and forced assimilation into Norwegianness were a part of the religious politics of the Reformation and its connection to more zealous and doctrinaire versions of faith.[51] Another major impact was the colonial division of Sámi into 'true' reindeer holding, nomadic Sámi, and those who were not and were slated to be assimilated. This division was over time also internalized by the Sámi and continues to divide.[52] Furthermore, ideas of cultural hierarchy contributed to the fact that some Swedish clergy assisted racial biologists in removing human remains from Sámi graves.[53] These experiences remain present as intergenerational cultural trauma, which affects relations and is part in a mix with Arctic amplification. 'Sometimes, environmental racism and attacks on land rights and Native lands reflect the attacks on the few by the majority.'[54]

48. Daniel Morley Johnson, 'Reflections on Historical and Contemporary Indigenist Approaches to Environmental Ethics in a Comparative Context', *Wicazo Sa Review* 22:2 (Fall 2007), pp. 33–55.

49. Johnson, 'Reflections on Historical and Contemporary Indigenist Approaches to Environmental Ethics in a Comparative Context', p. 38. This did at times include warning children that the oversize ancestor of a small animal they might mistreat would come back to take revenge on them for torture or killing without need.

50. Jace Weaver, 'Revelation and Epistemology – We Know the Land, the Land Knows Us: Places of Revelation, Place as Revelation', in Steven Charleston and Elaine Robinson (eds), *Coming Full Circle: Constructing Native Christian Theology* (Minneapolis: Fortress, 2015), pp. 27–53 (29).

51. Daniel Lindmark and Olle Sundström (eds), *The Sami and the Church of Sweden: Results from a White Paper Project* (Möklinta: Gidlunds Forlag, 2018), p. 209.

52. Lindmark and Sundström, 'The Overall Results of the White Paper Project', p. 211.

53. Lindmark and Sundström, 'The Overall Results of the White Paper Project', p. 211.

54. Sze, *Environmental Justice in a Moment of Danger*, p. 20.

Similar processes of disruption and devastation occurred in other circumpolar Indigenous contexts. Often, churches were an ambivalent influence in colonial contexts, at times preserving, at other times helping to break down Indigenous practices by promoting settlement and residential schooling, as well as educational practices as cultural imperialism.

State and church worked to assimilate the Sámi. Church officials often functioned as the handmaidens to colonial education and knowledge production. Sámi were slowly stripped of access to land for subsistence living which put them under significant economic pressure. Their technologies were seen as primitive and their spirituality condemned as heathen. One of the tools of colonial repression was the modern practice of scientific travel and mapping. Thus, images produced by early modern Scandinavian scientist-travellers 'portray how the negotiation for power over the landscape also includes a visual production of the landscape, a production that is representative of and significant for intruders and settlers as well as for the imagination of the local population'.[55] This dynamic extended to the way landscape was depicted in art and image in historic Scandinavian science literature which often worked 'as a colonizing tool to expand the Christian empire to the Nordic north. Churches and sacred places had an obvious significance in the construction of the landscape as national terrain'.[56]

During the protests at Standing Rock, intergenerational trauma manifested in the challenges; the past grief impacted the current action. Environmental destruction and cultural repression are often tied together, then and now. Recently, for example, the Fosen wind turbine park in Trondelag was recognized as infringing on the rights of Sámi to 'practice their unique culture' by the Supreme Court of Norway.[57] Cultural oppression has often gone along with a polemic against Indigenous ritual. Similarly, a repression of spirituality exists in the modern climate movement. Truth and reconciliation commissions must often come to terms with the intergenerational trauma of the past without closing their eyes towards the effects such colonization continues to have on Arctic Indigenous peoples today.

In the summer of 2021, Indigenous and environmental activists blocked construction equipment at the proposed site of the Nussir copper mine and put out a call to join them in camp and support them. Activists were able to delay the onset of construction throughout the summer. In order to show quick, unbureaucratic support that centred a Sámi perspective of respect for the relations of life in the fjord, three theologians wrote a call to action gathering signatures from key figures in Sápmi. During the blockade against the proposed copper mine

---

55. Sigurd Bergmann, *Religion, Space, and the Environment* (New Brunswick: Transaction, 2014), p. 223.

56. Bergmann, *Religion, Space, and the Environment*, p. 224.

57. https://www.domstol.no/enkelt-domstol/hoyesterett/avgjorelser/2021/hoyesterett-sivil/hr-2021-1975-s/ (accessed 27 February 2022).

in the Repparfjorden in Northern Norway, Sámi activists interpreted a walrus's presence in the Repparfjorden at the time of the blockade of the construction as an animal teacher, indicating an ancestral presence. Animals speak through their actions, and we humans better listen and respect their needs for an intact place. An appeal seeking to support Sámi Christians in their resistance against the ocean dumping site for the toxic waste projected to emerge from the proposed Nussir copper mine cited a passage in the Book of Job that suggests that animals are teachers of humans: 'But ask the animals, and they will teach you; the birds of the air, and they will tell you; ask the plants of the earth, and they will teach you; and the fish of the sea will declare to you' (Job 12.7-8). This wisdom is echoed by the Sámi poet Áillohaš. Both teach that birds and animals can interact and communicate with us.

> We should therefore be particularly attentive when [animals] act in unusual ways. In Sámi traditions, we find many stories about Máttut – the female ancestors of living beings. Every animal has a Máddu, an Ancestral Mother. Salmon, halibut, seagulls sailing over the fjord – all have their ancestors. Máttut are very large, but they only show themselves to us when we torture their children or take more than our fair share of the Earth´s resources. According to Sámi tradition, we are forbidden to hunt or fish in such a manner that we risk the anger of the ancestral mothers, the Máttut.[58]

Soon after the theologians' call to action was published online, the firm that had guaranteed the financing of the mine pulled out due to environmental reasons, stopping plans to begin construction.

Instances of green colonialism are becoming more frequent as energy transitions are becoming more urgent. Government agencies may approve these kinds of projects, at times whether or not they make any financial or environmental sense. The common political practice of delaying the transition away from fossil fuels to other energy forms increases the pressure that is put on Indigenous and other territories attractive to mining. Energy transition often requires precious metals or land use in areas that are at a distance from urban centres. Often such extractive projects are hidden behind a facade of greenwashing and may continue colonial patterns of depropriation. Often Indigenous lands are targeted for extraction when the majority population in urban centres resist a project close to their sphere of interest.[59] Extractive economies are based on a degenerative process rather than a regenerative, sustainable dynamic – and thus a far cry from relations of mutual obligation and gift-giving.

---

58. https://www.opprop.net/ellos_vuotna (accessed 29 April 2022).
59. This was the case at Standing Rock, where the pipeline initially was to run near Bismarck, ND, and was rerouted onto the reservation after protests of the settler community.

Gift-giving and responsibility

A great longing is upon us, to live again in a world made of gifts. I can scent it coming, like the fragrance of ripening strawberries rising on the breeze.[60]

In some strands of Christian tradition, divine grace is described as undeserved, unforceable and without appropriate response. There are good reasons to assert this, as it counteracts certain problematic tendencies in human relationality to the Divine, especially the tendency to bargain, compel and attempt to force by various means divine support for one's own purposes.[61]

John Milbank reserves redemption and forgiveness as a divine 'true gift'. God remains only a giver and is never a recipient in a gift exchange. Thus, the God-given gift is a 'transcendental category'[62] in a way that structures theological discourse about creation, grace, incarnation, atonement, the church and spirit, all of which have been described as a 'gift'. This gifting and the related *methexis* as a 'sharing of being and knowledge in the Divine'[63] flow only in one direction: from God to humans, and from there to other humans, but never towards 'him'.

Such 'sovereign' lack of the need for reciprocity is echoed in representations of British colonial logic.[64] There are echoes between theological and imperial language: the image of the sun, who gives light but does not receive anything back, God, the ungiven giver and the sovereign who 'gives and does not expect'. The theological image of grace as a gift all too closely parallels imperial propaganda. This image of God builds upon a long but increasingly problematic tradition of casting God as a propertied male owner and humanity as an impoverished, lacking, feminized recipient. We are in our nothingness before 'him',[65] and yet the metaphor is unstable, and nothingness is gendered, a kind of 'feminine lack' in giving.[66] This phrasing repeats classic tropes of divine economy such as the commerce of the *conubium* and perpetuates a problematic gendering of the human-divine relationship where the propertied divine bridegroom seeks to marry a feminized, unworthy whore-bride,

60. Kimmerer, *Braiding Sweetgrass*, p. 32.

61. See also Terra Rowe's book *Toward a Better Worldliness: Ecology, Economy and the Protestant Tradition* (Minneapolis: Fortress, 2017).

62. John Milbank, *Being Reconciled: Ontology and Pardon* (London: Routledge, 2003), p. ix.

63. Milbank, *Being Reconciled*, p. ix.

64. David Murray, *Indian Giving: Economics of Power in Indian-White Exchanges* (Amherst: University of Massachusetts Press, 2000), p. 55.

65. Note Milbank's insistent use of the male pronoun for God. Milbank, *Being Reconciled*, p. 46 et passim.

66. I have explored the issue of the feminization of giving in strands of traditional interpretations of women in the gospels and their excessive giving (which has also been read as foreshadowing Jesus' abundant giving of his life) in more detail in Grau, *Of Divine Economy: Refinancing Redemption* (London: T&T Clark 2004), pp. 99–107.

giving 'her' a new body.[67] Such unidirectional power needs not to ask for permission and cannot only not be responded to but also is not responsible to the masses of feudal serfs, peasants, workers and disinherited. And it matches all too closely the power claimed by the authoritarian billionaire class and their promotion of toxic petro-masculinity as the very snake oil to cure our every ill. I ask therefore: In a context of creeping environmental destruction and tragically unavoidable severe climate chaos, is it tenable to claim that divine grace does not need a responsible human agent? Does a sense of creation as 'gift' in this context not compel a rethinking of what responsible human relationships to the land might look like?

Nanabozho, the culture hero of Anishinaabe culture, represents the personification of the life force and its dual capacities. His twin brother generated as much imbalance as the brother was dedicated to engendering balance, and whose arrogance of power pushed unlimited growth and threw humility to the wind.[68] That duality of human nature is well represented in the oral stories and narratives of many cultures – the way we undo ourselves and our communities, then and now. Further, the Anishinaabe monster Windigo represents that within us that cares more for our own survival than anything else, with a heart made of ice and a ravenous hunger that increases the more it devours, ending in uncontrolled consumption.[69]

The blessing/curse scenarios of the Deuteronomic tradition seem to illustrate a similar dynamic: Respect the good relations, or you will be disrespected, and the land will reject you. Ironically, it is this emphasis on reciprocity that Christians have often read as oppressive, as the jealousy of the Old Testament God, a favourite supersessionist reading strategy.

Recent studies have now also more closely explored the ideas of gift in biblical texts. Barclay reminds us that Mauss suggests that the idea of a given without concern for reciprocity is a modern invention, particularly that of Reformation theologians.[70] More specifically, he argues that in Graeco-Roman and Jewish practices, a gift can be *unconditioned* (free of prior conditions regarding the recipient) without also being *unconditional* (free of expectations that the recipient will offer some 'return').[71]

Indeed, 'benefits were generally intended to foster mutuality, by creating or maintaining social bonds', where the expectation of reciprocity 'created cyclical patterns of gift-and-return' and thus, what seems in modern terms to be paradox – 'that a "free" gift could also be obliging – is entirely comprehensible in ancient terms'.[72] The fact that a benefit is undeserved and cannot be earned does not mean it does not oblige. Further, it is important to note that in all this, Paul 'stands *among* fellow Jews in this discussion of divine grace, not apart from them in a unique or

67. John Milbank, 'The Midwinter Sacrifice', in Graham Ward (ed.), *The Blackwell Companion to Postmodern Theology* (Oxford: Blackwell, 2001), pp. 107–30 (128).

68. Kimmerer, *Braiding Sweetgrass*, pp. 205, 212.

69. Kimmerer, *Braiding Sweetgrass*, pp. 304–5.

70. John M. G. Barclay, *Paul and the Gift* (Grand Rapids: Eerdmans, 2015), p. 37.

71. Barclay, *Paul and the Gift*, p. 312.

72. Barclay, *Paul and the Gift*, p. 312.

antithetical position'.[73] This is to counteract the supersessionist readings of Pauline grace as radically innovative or different from all Jewish traditions.

But what if what is also visible here is an echo on 'cultures of gratitude', on an economy of Thanksgiving that is also present in the biblical imaginary and that in the Reformation has been superseded by an economy of (cheap) grace? Has this grace, especially in its iterations as Protestant Work Ethic, lured us away from these relations of gratitude and reciprocity, or can rereadings of grace as the undeserved divine gift that invites reciprocity be heard anew? Cultures of gratitude necessitate lives of respect and reciprocity rather than mere lip service.

That wisdom of life can be threaded from biblical narrative as from Indigenous creation stories. The breakdown of relationships of respect and mutuality marks many creation stories. Skywoman Falling is dependent for her survival on muskrat who offers their life as sacrifice to bring up the mud from which the cultures that Skywoman seeds can develop. Timothy Leduc's cross-cultural theological reflection on the lands and spiritual geography of Ontario and Eastern Canada shows Skywoman's figure as related to Notre Dame/Our Lady, the Stella Maris, the star over the waters, each an ancestral woman whose presence and wisdom have helped frame the spiritual worlds she represents.[74] Leduc suggests a braided recovery of the spiritual ancestors of all Canadians, bringing together Indigenous and settler ancestors and their braided descendants and narratives in order to imagine a 'climate of mind' that can locate ancestral and present sacrality in land and urban environment. Wall Kimmerer envisions similarly a 'polyculture of complementary knowledges'[75] that is necessary to defeat monocultures of science and production.

Communion of saints: Critical decolonial hagiographies

In order to honour the witnesses to environmental destruction of ecosystems and therefore also local communities, we can lift up these persons as exemplars of the community of saints that provide models of engagement and can be inspiring for others. That is, through sharing, and raising awareness of their struggles more broadly, we can critically reconstruct the notion of the community of saints, without romanticizing their stories. Some historic female Catholic saints appear to have been victims of sexual or gender-based violence and were lifted up as having escaped that violence in some way. The percentage of female saints appears not to have risen above 30 per cent before the 1500s, and female saints were always in the minority.[76] Yet, indeed, in the early Church, 'all Christians were saints', and

---

73. Barclay, *Paul and the Gift*, p. 314.

74. Leduc, *A Canadian Climate of Mind*, p. 156.

75. Kimmerer, *Braiding Sweetgrass*, p. 139.

76. Robert Bartlett, *Why Can the Dead Do Such Great Things? Saints and Worshippers from the Martyrs to the Reformation* (Princeton: Princeton University Press, 2013), pp. 146–7.

the word applied to every member of the Christian community, not to an elite', and did not refer to 'heroic or perfect' persons but simply the faithful.[77] Some of the saints are associated with animals, or landscapes – St Francis the most famous of them but also Paul the Hermit, St Cuthbert, St Blaise and others.[78] And despite the medieval focus on churches and relics, it remains clear that many saints were associated with wells and springs and thus retained a sense of the sacred in and through landscapes and elements.[79]

A number of women might be called environmental martyrs, risking violence not for some kind of glory, but rather in the sense of being witnesses who speak out for environmental justice.[80] Such martyrs and saints would not be modelled on patron saints which repeat hierarchical power structures but rather imagine an egalitarian community of the saints. Water protectors could be seen, then, as persons marking water as sacred and defending its ability to continue to give life in a way that combines elements of pre-Christian Indigenous senses of sacred place and the association of witnesses (martyrs) or holy persons with a well. I have no interest in a super-sessionist readings of water protectors as persons of Christian faith but merely note the sense of the sacred in the landscape and the way in which person and element can intersect in marking sacredness.

Influencers abound on social media, dealing in a variety of ritualized forms of self-promotion as well as activism. Beyond the 'liturgies' of self-sanctification, social media has also provided many with role models that can show us the possibilities of human and transspecies solidarity. What new role models and saints might we imagine for our time of climate and energy transition? If saints can be said to present us with an image of an internal or external struggle to bring forth that possibility of saintliness that resides in each and every one of us, the common human struggles, how might we imagine aspects of such critical reconstruction?

The Catholic feminist theologian Elizabeth Johnson distinguishes two models of sainthood, one framed according to a biblical model of community, and the Roman model of patronage that was the main target of Reformation criticism.[81] Mark Dukes' Dancing Saints from Saint Gregory of Nyssa in San Francisco and Nadia Bolz-Weber, who speaks of All Saints as a 'feast of splendid nobodies',[82] release saints from the twin dangers of romanticization and dismissal. Each of these was intended to help crack open the issue of saints and sainthood in ways that invited listeners and viewers into the effort to do this work publicly. Nadia Bolz-Weber hints at an egalitarian and ethically complex approach

---

77. Bartlett, *Why Can the Dead*, p. 15.
78. Bartlett, *Why Can the Dead*, pp. 390–1.
79. Bartlett, *Why Can the Dead*, p. 621.
80. Celia Deane-Drummond, 'Foreword', in *Planetary Solidarity*, p. xxvi.
81. Johnson, *Friends of God and Prophets*, p. 92.
82. Johnson, *Friends of God and Prophets*, p. 8.

of communion of saints.[83] In true Lutheran fashion, humans are an un/holy mixture of all saints and all sinners, *simul iustus et peccator*. The shadow that haunts all our attempts to be ethical actors requires acknowledgement, rather than repression.[84]

Elizabeth Johnson's reconstruction of the community of saints further proposes that a reconstruction of sainthood should resist the marginalization of female saints, the patriarchal depiction of female saints and the hierarchical nature of the patron saint.[85] She emphasizes that the community of saints includes the entire people of God, not just an elite group of the dead that functions as patrons to be petitioned for favours and healing.[86] The early Christian martyrs refused to offer gestures of civic piety to the Roman Empire's cult,[87] but under the auspices of Roman imperial religion, saints were integrated in the Roman patron-client system, which replicates a hierarchical system of negotiation through favours. For Johnson this changes the understanding of sainthood into something fundamentally unequal, and it is exactly this quality of the cult of saints that the Reformers attacked.[88] Instead, she sees saints as companions of hope, in the paradigm of friendship with God and each other, and inspiring examples to maintain moral responsibility and resist amnesia.[89] Johnson also expands the notion of the communion of the saints to the entire cosmos,[90] beyond the anthropocentrism of most accounts. Johnson argues that consigning the dead to utter extinction undermines the basis for an ecological ethics that includes the primordial *communio sanctorum*, all of creation.[91]

Johnson's sense of *communio sanctorum* might open up to lifting up animal saints. A Finnish environmental campaign to 'Save the Norps' uses a seal 'icon' logo for their campaign to protect the endangered Saima ringed seals. The logo, sold on T-shirts, posters and bags, shows a seal floating vertically in the water, looking at the observer, featuring a halo.[92] This marking of the seal as saintly pushes the boundaries of human-centred hagiography.

83. The church Bolz-Weber founded is called House of All Sinners and Saints (http://houseforall.org/). Based on her experiences, she wrote a book entitled *Accidental Saints* where she develops a Lutheran theology of sainthood, of *simul iustus et peccator*, justified and sinner at the same time. Nadia Bolz-Weber, *Accidental Saints: Finding God in All the Wrong People* (New York: Convergent Books, 2015).

84. Personal conversation with Einar Vegge (20 July 2017).

85. Johnson, *Friends of God and Prophets*, pp. 27–9.

86. Johnson, *Friends of God and Prophets*, p. 87.

87. Johnson, *Friends of God and Prophets*, p. 71.

88. Johnson, *Friends of God and Prophets*, pp. 92, 108.

89. Johnson, *Friends of God and Prophets*, p. 167.

90. Johnson, *Friends of God and Prophets*, p. 2.

91. Johnson, *Friends of God and Prophets*, pp. 240, 242.

92. https://www.luontokauppa.fi/tuote/save-the-norps-college (accessed 28 February 2022).

In some Christian hagiography, animals functioned as visualization of the demonic spirits that taunted St Anthony in the desert and other saints.[93] On the other hand, saints like St Cuthbert and St Francis were known for their ability to befriend and interact with animals.[94] St Cuthbert was on a missionary journey with a poor boy, an eagle and a large fish caught by the eagle. The boy was getting hungry and anxious for food. Then they saw an eagle hunting for fish. Cuthbert was compassionate with the boy's hunger and said: 'God is able to provide for us today through the ministry of this eagle.' When the eagle had caught a fish, the boy approached the eagle. The eagle dropped the fish and flew away, and the boy took the fish and ran back to Cuthbert. But Cuthbert said to him: 'Why have you not given our fisherman his share?' The boy understood, cut the fish in half and returned half of it to the riverbank where the eagle found it and returned to eat it. This story shows a saint who understands the competition of humans and animals for food but emphasizes the need for both to be able to eat and have enough (Vita Sancta Cuthberti, Book ii.). Putting the halo on a contemporary endangered seal species indicates that the seal needs protection, rather than adoration. A halo is thus a symbol of multiple meanings, indicating something or someone to be remembered, uplifted, respected and marked as holy in some way. Such gestures of respect can also be verbal.

In the text of a call to action for the protection of the Repparfjorden, a walrus appears as a source of ecotheological wisdom, a fellow inhabitant of the fjord who has things to teach us. Sámi observers had noticed the walrus demonstratively taking up place in the fjord near the proposed mining site. In Sámi traditions, stories are told that if an animal is tortured or abused, the giant female ancestor of a particular species will come and hold responsible for those that torture or treat disrespectfully their descendants.[95] The walrus, like Bileam's donkey, spoke eloquently through its presence, and the German funder of the mine eventually pulled the funding for the mine and the Repparfjorden remains intact, for now.

More than ever before, we need not only more democracy, but also a 'democracy of all species', as US Indigenous botanist Robin Wall Kimmerer invokes.[96] Our use and addiction to certain forms of energy are at the heart of the problem. In order to be able to embody aspects of such a democracy of all species, we need to reconstruct our theologies, rituals and liturgies to reflect a relationality of respect and one of *energy humility* for the walruses, fjords and plains of this planet.

93. Bartlett, *Why Can the Dead*, pp. 77, 387–8.

94. Bartlett, *Why Can the Dead*, p. 391.

95. Lovisa Mienna Sjoberg, 'Válmmas Máilbmi – en Färdig Värld', *Klimat Och Miljø* (2021) *Dagboken Med Krkoalmanacka 2021–2022* (Varberg: Argument förlag, 2021).

96. Kimmerer, *Braiding Sweetgrass*, p. 58.

A PRACTITIONER'S RESPONSE TO DENISE
HUMPHREYS BEBBINGTON AND MARION GRAU

Marianna Leite

Through my previous role at Christian Aid, I was invited to act as respondent during the mining session of the *Laudato Si'* Research Institute's symposium entitled Women, Mining, and Toxic Contamination that took place on 3 March 2021 and, subsequently, the symposium's book on mining, gender and toxic-contaminations. I was particularly tasked with reviewing Denise Humphreys Bebbington's chapter 'Toxic environments' and Marion Grau's chapter 'Countering colonial mining: Water protectors, environmental justice and the creation community of saints'. Therefore, this response focuses on the main threads I identified in both chapters and their overlaps. It concludes with brief suggestions on the possible way forward.

Reaction to Humphreys Bebbington's chapter 'Toxic environments'

The chapter utilizes two guiding questions present in Dean Laplonge's 2017 article which inquires whether 'women have a better ethics of care towards the environment than men', and if so, 'could this ethics be harnessed to bring reform to an industry such as mining and so reduce its negative impacts?'

Bebbington applies these guiding questions to 'the increasingly toxic social environments that women experience living in the presence of contaminating extractive activities'. She points out that we have 'far less information about the influence of sex and gender on exposure to contaminants and affirms that some studies (such as Arbuckle's 2006 piece) suggest that 'there may be sex and gender differences in exposure to chemicals which can be manifested in sex differences in absorption, distribution, metabolism, storage and excretion'.

Bebbington draws on three powerful case studies in La Oroya and Choropampa, in Peru and Challapata, in Bolivia. She argues that damage to social relations and social institutions induced by the practice of mining corporations should be understood as a form of 'socio-environmental contamination' producing significant and highly gendered impacts that require assessment and remediation alongside impacts to the natural environment. Following on from Laplonge's observation, she suggests that women's ethic of care also extends to the protection, of these social relations.

The author brings to light an issue that is of crucial importance: the differentiated impacts of extractive industries. Her chapter examines how gender dynamics as well as other social factors such as ethnicity, illiteracy, age, disability and marital status may further compound existing inequalities and women's sense of exclusion and marginalization. Although Bebbington does not suggest that women have been impacted 'more' than other identity-based groups in these communities, she affirms that '[r]ather than looking to women to bring "their caring ethic" to defend and to save the environment from the harms caused by mining operations, governments and companies need to take seriously not only the accumulating material toxicity in mining environments but also the toxic social impacts of mining'.

This is a timely piece that addresses emerging issues such as, for example, the ones connected to the mining disaster of Brumadinho that took place in Brazil in 2019. While working to assist the victims of the disasters, Christian Aid and the Movement of those Affected by Dams (MAB) were able to confirm that the women who were affected by the Brumadinho disaster face challenges that are specific to their gender. These include lack of acknowledgement by the community, patriarchal stereotypes that might prevent women from taking up leadership roles, hostility, harassment and repression, domestic violence or threats of violence as a consequence of their activism, the unpaid care burden related to young children or other family members, sexual assault and intimidation in public places, non-recognition from interlocutors in negotiations, including companies and public authorities, as well as slander and defamation.[1] The Brumadinho findings are similar to the ones observed in La Oroya, Choropampa and Challapata. This unfortunately seems to indicate that gender disparities are common in other similar contexts.

I therefore agree with Bebbington when it comes to framing the damage to social relations and social institutions as a form of socio-environmental contamination. Notwithstanding, I wonder if the argument would have been strengthened if it departed from a different guiding question. Bebbington mentions, for instance, that persistent patriarchal ideas about women's roles and leadership negatively affect women environmental defenders. I have an inkling that it might have been beneficial if she could have taken a step further by also acknowledging that essentialized narratives about women may also reinforce existing patriarchal dynamics. For example, I question if the article would have been strengthened

---

1. Christian Aid, 'Engendering Business and Human Rights: Applying a Gender Lens to the UN Guiding Principles on Business and Human Rights and Binding Treaty Negotiations', 2019, https://www.christianaid.org.uk/sites/default/files/2019-05/Engendering%20Business%20and%20Human%20Rights_1.pdf. (accessed 1 May 2022).

by a more in-depth approach to gender and, therefore, a guiding question that would take into account the socially constructed roles without necessarily reinforcing them.

In 'Mothers at the Service of the New Poverty Agenda', Maxine Molyneux states that in recent years female poverty, as distinct from the gender dimensions of poverty, has acquired considerably more policy attention. As a result of that, policy analysis and packages have had a tendency of approaching gender in a restrictive and, at times, unhelpful way.[2] For example, the Progresa/Oportunidades Mexican poverty reduction programme unintendedly overburdened women with responsibilities and reinforced socially constructed roles.[3] Oportunidades aimed to improve human development by focusing on children's education. The programme departed from an assumption that is similar to Laplonge's guiding questions, which is that women are better at managing resources and are more likely to make family-oriented decisions and spending. This perception that women are supposedly more 'ethical' led to the creation of conditional cash transfers centred around the responsibility of mothers. This would, in principle, be fine if it were not for the fact that those mothers are already overburdened by the unequal division on labour.

Humpreys Bebbington did acknowledge this tension in her conclusion. Why then am I bringing this example to the forefront? Well, I believe that when we are proposing solutions to the dire effects mining has on women's lives, we must also make sure to try to challenge structural issues responsible for these symptoms. Bebbington does this really well to an extent but I would say only from a partial point of view. She advances the concept of *social toxicity* to argue, through the analysis of the three cases studies, that women living in mining environments have to endure the effects of toxic social environments fostered even without environmental contamination. This is a powerful concept that surely should be explored further as it enables us to understand the voracious and often invisible effects of neoliberalism on communities' social fabric.

For example, Bebbington points out how community members may be pressured to stand against one another to secure their jobs and prevent any forms of accountability. Similarly, she underscores the role of international financial institutions (such as the International Financial Corporation's role in the Yanacocha Mine) as well as the complete lack of transparency and clear information sharing in settlement agreements. This is surely a testament of the ubiquitous presence of corporations in these settings. To help complement Bebbington's claims, I would therefore argue that women's higher vulnerability to irresponsible mining and toxic contamination is not only due to negative corporate practices but also connected

2. Maxine Molyneux, 'Mothers at the Service of the New Poverty Agenda: Progresa/ Oportunidades, Mexico's Conditional Transfer Programme', *Social Policy & Administration* 40:4 (2006), pp. 425–49 (432).
3. Molyneux, 'Mothers at the Service of the New Poverty Agenda: Progresa/ Oportunidades, Mexico's Conditional Transfer Programme', p. 432.

to deeply embedded patriarchal concepts and narratives that constrain all of us, women and men, in all our diversity, within corporations or society at large, to toxic masculine and feminine roles. Understanding how neoliberalism reinforces patriarchy in mining contexts would enable us to have a more comprehensive understanding of and solutions to the issue of toxicity, be it environmental, social or both.

Reaction to Marion Grau's chapter on 'Countering colonial mining'

Grau's chapter looks at water protectors' contributions to climate justice discussions and how they imagine different ways of creating and distributing energy systems. The theologian asks, 'How can recent examples of climate action help tell a story about the just energy transitions we need while refusing to sacrifice Indigenous lands and resources to mine resources for green technologies?' This, she claims, is important as it connects to energy desires and energy economics (i.e. how one might imagine the world and how one might be connected to the divine).

Grau further postulates that various energy economies 'have influenced human ideas of the sacred, of divine power' and that these relationships have changed throughout history. If we want to change energy relations towards less oppression and more energy justice, we have to imagine different ways of creating and distributing energy systems. Indigenous women's perspectives have been central in linking the sacred with energy and should therefore remain central in any energy-related solution.

The author rightly argues that to merely push for a green transition is not enough. In fact, she states that the push for renewable energy can entrench power imbalances just as much as fossil fuels if they are not led by democratic and just processes. This means that the transition from oil and gas 'must also take into account existing energy inequities'.

Grau equates petroleum to a kind of unholy sacrament, an extreme unction towards death. As an alternative to this spiritual death, she offers an example, or gifts (good gifts) as she puts it, from the 2016 Standing Rock pipeline protest. This case study embodies the reciprocity needed for the good gift to be honoured and life to be valued. It stands in direct opposition to the 'ecocidal colonial violence' caused by the undying thirst for fossil fuels. It also exists as a testimony of the violence created by the unbalanced relationship with creation and the erosion of social fabric between us and our brothers and sisters. Similar to Bebbington', Grau, highlights the often invisible damage to social relations and social institutions induced by irresponsible mining practices. For instance, the toxic masculinity of non-Indigenous men is noted as responsible for 100 per cent of the cases of abuse against Indigenous women in North Dakota. Just as Indigenous women are raped so is our mother earth. In a way, this could be understood as a form of 'socio-environmental contamination' put forth by Bebbington.

Furthermore, Grau's analysis of the 'sovereign' lack of gift in colonial narratives is remarkable. She argues that divine gift giving is typically construed as flowing in an unidirectional and linear way which fails to acknowledge the possibility of a reciprocity between humans and the divine. In this spectrum, God is seen 'as a propertied male owner and humanity as an impoverished, lacking, feminized recipient'.

This realization brings us to a conclusion that is similar to that of Bebbington's article – the fact that we can no longer be silent as we are called to uphold human dignity for all creation. As Christians, or rather as people of faith, we are called to share in God's mission of justice, peace and respect for all Creation and to seek for all humanity the abundant life which God intends. Within scripture, through tradition, and from the many ways in which the spirit illumines our hearts today, we discern God's gift of dignity for each person and their inherent right to acceptance and participation with the community. In 'Song of the Prophets',[4] Christian Aid states that sometimes, in our denial or despair, we do not listen well to the *real* prophets or catch their imaginative vision. Instead, Grau proposes the creation of a 'Communion of Saints' – 'to honour the witnesses to environmental destruction of ecosystems' and 'provide models of engagement and can be inspiring for others'. For instance, the Indigenous women described by Grau fight the 'oil snake' and all the sins it represents. Just like the Holy Mary, they are the true prophets as they call people to behave differently and to do what is right. 'They help us all face up to the future we are walking towards and that we are creating for future generations.'[5]

This profound analysis leaves us thirsty for action. For example, Grau recommends framing mainstream counter-colonial narratives of just energy transitions in terms of gifts and gift-giving that are freely given but 'oblige to responsible reciprocity if the gift is to be honoured and life to be valued'. This can be a transformative way to overcome the trauma of colonial extractions and create decolonial hagiographies.

Grau's notion of 'good gifts' might inspire others, in particular faith actors, to refrain from being silent in the face of the environmental injustices. Of course, it is impossible to predict what the future might entail but, at least, we are equipped with new narratives, new theologies and new realities that are being slowly conceived.

I assume more research on counter-colonial narratives that dismantle petromasculinity is needed just as much as we thirst for examples of resistance to social toxicity. The scholarship might equally feel the need to tackle the idea of feminine values (not necessarily through women and girls) as a tool to counteract

4. Christian Aid, 'Song of the Prophets: A Global Theology of Climate Change', 2020, https://www.christianaid.org.uk/sites/default/files/2020-05/song-of-the-prophets-theology-climate-change-report-May2020.pdf. (accessed 1 May 2022).

5. Christian Aid, 'Song of the Prophets', p. 6.

toxic petromasculinity and the pervasive exploitative masculinity driving mining and extraction. That is, how values normally understood as feminine – but not necessarily inherent or exclusive to women and girls – might help us strike a balance in counter-narratives and political strategies. How might values such as caring for the earth, peaceful living, love for one another and unity drastically change theologies and practices of toxicity, extraction and exploitation?

Conclusion

The two pieces discussed above end with a ray of hope. They present suggestions and examples for the way forward, either through empirical research, theological readings or activisms. Humpreys Bebbington's example of successful women-led resistance in Challapata demonstrates that counter-narratives cannot only wield positive results; they can, in fact, be fundamental in harnessing these transformative outcomes. Grau's reconstruction of theologies towards relationality of respect and reciprocity is essential to disrupting petromasculinity as the *modus operandi* of toxic extractive systems.

Further understanding how neoliberalism reinforces patriarchy in extractive contexts and how narratives and theologies enable toxicity and exploitation would enable us to have a more comprehensive set of alternatives and solutions to the issue of toxicity, be it environmental, social or both. I believe it is really relevant to continue to document and lift successful stories of women-led resistance, in all their diversity, to foster and support different means of existing and of producing counter-narratives. In a sense, both essays push for balance – balance in how we connect to feminine and masculine values, in Indigenous and non-Indigenous knowledge and praxis, in how we relate to each other and with the environment as God-given gifts. This is core to enabling our communion with nature and one another. We are all custodians of the environment, and we have a fundamental and inexorable responsibility to imagine new ways of coexisting with nature and ensuring those imaginaries become reality.

Part 2

POLLUTANTS

Chapter 4

UNDERSTANDING THE IMPACT OF ENVIRONMENTAL CONTAMINANTS ON WOMEN FROM INDUSTRIAL POLLUTANTS

Felicia Jefferson with Rheygan Reed and Sierra Cloud

This chapter demonstrates how endocrine-disrupting chemicals (EDCs) negatively impact human health, particularly the health of women. The chapter begins with a short description of how the endocrine system works before exploring the impact of everyday pollutants on women's endocrine physiology. The working hypothesis in this research is that industrial pollution contributes to miscarriages, shorter life and cancers in women – especially women of colour, who are disproportionately affected through higher rates of exposure to EDCs. The chapter argues that educating women about their endocrine system, the environment and the chemicals used by industrial companies can positively impact women's health and will contribute to wider public discussion of the adverse health effects of EDCs.

Overview of the endocrine system

The endocrine system consists of several organs that release hormones responsible for controlling nearly all the biological processes in the human body. The thyroid gland, for instance, releases thyroid hormones which control vital bodily functions including breathing, heart rate, body temperature, menstrual cycles and the nervous system. During infancy and childhood, thyroid hormones are essential for proper brain development.[1] Likewise, the parathyroid glands, located next to the thyroid gland in the neck, regulate calcium levels that contribute not only to a healthy nervous system but to healthy muscles and bones. The adrenal cortex, the outer part of the adrenal gland located above the kidneys, regulates

---

1. Maria Segni, 'Disorders of the Thyroid Gland in Infancy, Childhood and Adolescence', in K. R. Feingold, B. Anawalt, A. Boyce et al. (eds), *Endotext [Internet]. South Dartmouth (MA): MDText.com*, Inc.; 2000–12, 21 March 2012, https://www.ncbi.nlm.nih.gov/pubmed/25905261 (accessed 6 July 2022).

body metabolism by releasing cortisol, the stress hormone and aldosterone, which controls blood pressure. The pancreas assists the digestive system and controls blood sugar by releasing insulin into the bloodstream. The pineal gland, whose function was last to be discovered, releases both melatonin to regulate the circadian rhythm cycle and reproductive hormones along with the ovaries and testes. In short, these – and other – glands of the endocrine system collectively regulate metabolism, growth and development, sexual function, reproduction and mood.[2]

Because the endocrine system does not utilize ducts to store hormones, the continual, healthy functioning of the system is of paramount importance to every organ in the body. If the endocrine system becomes compromised in its ability to regulate hormone levels or to maintain a proper feedback loop, disease can occur. While diabetes is the most common disease associated with the endocrine system, other diseases, including hypothyroidism, thyroid cancer and hyperglycaemia, can also arise.

The impact of environmental pollution on women's endocrine physiology

The 1996 publication, *Our Stolen Future*, by Theo Colborn, Dianne Dumanoski and John Peterson Myers, was the first book to publicize the concept of endocrine disruption.[3] The book proposed that chemical pollution is threatening the intelligence, fertility and survival of the human race.[4] Indeed, many chemical compounds found in the environment can interfere with the body's endocrine system and contribute to adverse health outcomes. These EDCs can also be found in products such as pesticides, metals, additives or contaminants in food, personal care products and cosmetics.[5] EDCs have been associated with chronic illnesses in women, especially endometriosis, polycystic ovary syndrome, breast cancer, heart disease and even obesity. This link between EDCs and adverse health conditions means that educating women about their endocrine system, the environment and what companies are doing with their products can positively impact women's health.

---

2. H. S. Chahal and W. M. Drake, 'The Endocrine System and Ageing', *The Journal of Pathology* 211:2 (2007), pp. 173–80. https://doi.org/10.1002/path.2110.

3. Theo Colborn, Dianne Dumanoski and John P. Myers, *Our Stolen Future: Are We Threatening Our Fertility, Intelligence, and Survival? A Scientific Detective Story* (New York: Plume Publishing, 1996).

4. Richelle D. Björvang and Pauliina Damdimopoulou, 'Persistent Environmental Endocrine-Disrupting Chemicals in Ovarian Follicular Fluid and *in Vitro* Fertilization Treatment Outcome in Women', *Upsala Journal of Medical Sciences* 125:2 (2020), pp. 85–94. https://doi.org/10.1080/03009734.2020.1727073.

5. Antonia M. Calafat, Xiaoyun Ye, Lee-Yang Wong, Amber M. Bishop, Larry L. Needham, 'Urinary Concentrations of Four Parabens in the U.S. Population: NHANES 2005–2006', Environmental *Health Perspectives* 118:5 (2010), pp. 679–85. https://doi.org/10.1289/ehp.0901560.

Examples of problematic EDCs

One example of an EDC linked to adverse health is bisphenol A (2,2-bis (4-hydroxyphenyl) pro173 pane). This chemical, better known as BPA, is a human-made, non-steroidal, carbon-based compound belonging to the diphenylmethane derivatives and bisphenols, with two hydroxyphenyl groups. Most notably, BPA is a monomer for polycarbonate plastics, epoxy resins and thermal receipts. BPA can be easily released from the polymer product in which it is present and can migrate into the environment where it then can enter the body through ingestion, inhalation and adsorption.[6] The use of cosmetics is one means of exposure, but the primary source of exposure occurs by consuming food and drink contaminated with BPA from polycarbonate bottles and cans coated with epoxy resins.[7] Moreover, high temperatures liberate BPA at higher concentrations. As temperatures rise, the ester bond linking BPA molecules in polycarbonate and resins undergoes hydrolysis, resulting in the release of free BPA into food, beverages and the environment.[8] Breast milk, dental sealants, air, dust and water are all sources of exposure to BPA.

When it enters the body, BPA has the ability to bind to oestrogen receptors and mimic oestrogenic activities.[9] BPA is classified as an environmental oestrogen, yet it is also considered an EDC because research has shown the detrimental effects it plays on the neurological development of foetal tissues, reproductive health of both men and women, and wildlife. Field studies indicate that there are increases

6. Karolina Mikołajewska, Joanna Stragierowicz and Jolanta Gromadzińska, 'Bisphenol A – Application, Sources of Exposure and Potential Risks in Infants, Children and Pregnant Women', *International Journal of Occupational Medicine and Environmental Health* 28:2 (2015), pp. 209–41. https://doi.org/10.13075/ijomeh.1896.00343.

7. K. Mikołajewska et al., 'Bisphenol A – Application, Sources of Exposure and Potential Risks in Infants, Children, and Pregnant Women'; A study conducted on the amount of BPA detected in food storage cans that were covered in epoxy resin found that the average content of BPA in meat products was 110 μg BPA/kg of meat (17380 μg/kg). This study shows that the average amount of meat per meal is 18.7μg per meal, which is a very low unit compared to the standard μg amount. Cf. Hoa H. Le, Emily M. Carlson, Jason P. Chua and Scott M. Belcher, 'Bisphenol A Is Released from Polycarbonate Drinking Bottles and Mimics the Neurotoxic Actions of Estrogen in Developing Cerebellar Neurons', *Toxicology Letters* 176:2 (2008), pp. 149–56. https://doi.org/10.1016/j.toxlet.2007.11.001.

8. K. Sakurai and C. Mori, 'Fetal Exposure to Endocrine Disruptors', *Nihon Rinsho: Japanese Journal of Clinical Medicine* 58:12 (2000), pp. 2508–13.

9. Wade V. Welshons, Susan C. Nagel, S. and Frederick S. von Saal, 'Large Effects from Small Exposures. III. Endocrine Mechanisms Mediating Effects of Bisphenol A at Levels of Human Exposure', *Endocrinology*, 147 (6 Suppl) (2006), pp. S56–S69. https://doi.org/10.1210/en.2005-1159.

in reproductive abnormalities in mammals, reptiles, birds and several fish species following exposure to oestrogenic EDCs.[10]

Another example of an EDC is diethylstilboestrol (DES), which is chemically akin to BPA. DES was utilized as a medicinal product between 1940 and 1971, often prescribed to pregnant women to prevent miscarriage, premature labour and other related pregnancy issues.[11] In the 1950s, however, utilization of DES declined due to studies showing no correlation with the prevention of pregnancy mishaps.[12] While DES may be more potent than BPA and has been eradicated due to the increase in cancers and foetal morbidity associated with its use, both chemicals are synthetic oestrogens with similar functions in the body. Thus, questions about whether BPA in small amounts caused adverse health effects in women and/or in foetuses arose at least five years ago and remain relevant today.

One final class of chemical compounds of concern to women's health are parabens, which are present in 80 per cent of personal care products.[13] Although parabens are used as safety mechanisms for consumers, Consumer Ingredient Review denotes specific concentration limits that cause adverse effects in women.[14] Exposure to parabens occurs through dermal contact/ absorption from various personal care and cosmetic products, inhalation and ingestion from food and beverage processing.[15] Over the past years, parabens have been found in an array of body care products such as topical creams, deodorants and lotions.

10. Ethan D. Clotfelter, Alison M. Bell and Kate R. Levering, 'The Role of Animal Behaviour in the Study of Endocrine-Disrupting Chemicals', *Animal Behaviour* 68:4 (2004), pp. 665–76. https://doi.org/10.1016/j.anbehav.2004.05.004.

11. Nancy Langston, *Toxic Bodies* (New Haven: Yale University Press, 2010).

12. Edward C. Dodds, L. Goldberg, Wilfred Lawson and Robert Robinson, 'Estrogenic Activity of Certain Synthetic Compounds', *Nature* 141 (2010), pp. 247–8. https://doi.org/10.1038/141247b0.

13. Dorota Błędzka, Jolanta Gromadzińska and Wojcieh Wąsowicz, 'Parabens: From Environmental Studies to Human Health', *Environment International* 67 (June 2014), pp. 27–42. https://doi.org/10.1016/j.envint.2014.02.007.

14. Xiaoyun Ye, Amber M. Bishop, John A. Reidy, Larry L. Needham, Antonia M. Calafat, 'Parabens as Urinary Biomarkers of Exposure in Humans', *Environmental Health Perspectives* 114:12 (2006), pp. 1843–6. http://www.jstor.org/stable/4119595 (accessed 6 July 2022).

15. Antonia M. Calafat, Xia. Ye, L. Y. Wong, A. M. Bishop and L. L. Needham, 'Urinary Concentrations of Four Parabens in the U.S. Population: NHANES 2005–2006', *Environmental Health Perspectives* 118:5 (2010), pp. 679–85. https://doi.org/10.1289/ehp.0901560.

EDCs in wastewater

Several studies have documented the problem of human exposure to harmful EDCs through contaminated drinking water.[16] EDCs enter source water, finished drinking water and distribution (tap) water via municipal wastewater discharge. Pharmaceuticals flushed from households also enter into water systems due to failed removal during water treatment.[17] Before water discharge, water is treated through a multistage wastewater treatment plant, constructed to eliminate wastewater via a three-fold system. Preliminary treatment includes removal of solid material. Wastewater is then screened to eliminate large, inorganic components including paper and plastics. Further screening is completed to ensure the removal of fine grits and silt particles. Primary treatment then involves transferring wastewater to sedimentation tanks to remove solid particles of organic materials (flocculation). Once completed, primary sediment can settle and separate, through gravity, from wastewater. Despite the grand amount of solid material removed in this stage, high levels of efflux remain in the amount of dissolved oxygen needed to decompose organic material and dislodge solids and nutrients.

Though municipalities enforce regulations to prevent contamination of water from waste discharge, there are many examples of EDCs and other unregulated organic concentrations of contaminated water present in the water supply. In a study conducted by Benotti and colleagues, eleven of the most frequently found compounds were pharmaceuticals such as atenolol, atrazine, carbamazepine estrone, gemfibrozil, meprobamate, naproxen, phenytoin, sulfamethoxazole, TCEP and trimethoprim at a mean concentration of 10 ng/L, with the exception of sulfamethoxazole, found in source water at 12 ng/L, TCEP (120 ng/L), and atrazine, found in source finished and distribution water systems at concentration levels of 32, 49 and 49 ng/L.[18] Although these concentrations may only show a single pharmaceutical at sub-µg/L levels, researchers speculate that the long-term risk to humans from any is negligible. Atrazine is a commonly used herbicide in agriculture in the United States to prevent weeds in crops such as maize and sugarcane. It is also used on turfs, such as sports arenas and golf courses, and residential lawns. However, in 2004 it was banned in the European Union due to persistent levels of groundwater contamination. In 2007, the US Environmental Protection Agency (EPA) classified Batrazine as an endocrine disruptor due to

16. 'Endocrine Disruption', Endocrinology Web Review, *Nature Reviews*, 4 September 2017, https://www.nature.com/collections/bgbvkwbrvk/#:~:text=Endocrine%2Ddisrupting%20 chemicals%20(EDCs),health%20but%20to%20global%20health (accessed 6 July 2022).

17. Mark J. Benotti, Rebecca A. Trenholm, Brett J. Vanderford, Jane C. Holady, Benjamin D. Stanford and Shane A. Snyder, 'Pharmaceuticals and Endocrine Disrupting Compounds in U.S. Drinking Water', *Environmental Science & Technology* 43:3 (2009), pp. 597–603. https://doi.org/10.1021/es801845a.

18. Benotti et al., 'Pharmaceuticals and Endocrine Disrupting Compounds in U.S. Drinking Water'.

delays in puberty in animal research. Concern about the prevalence of EDCs in the environment is evident from medical professionals, environmental scientists, drinking water municipalities, government agencies and the public.

Effects of EDCs on foetal development

One concerning characteristic of EDCs is the ability of such chemicals to interrupt the process of foetal development during pregnancy.[19] Both phthalates[20] and bisphenols, found within the food supply, are sources of exposure to EDCs.[21] Pacyga states that due to their short half-lives (less than twenty-four hours), exposure to phthalates and bisphenols is best characterized by analysis of urine (as opposed to blood).[22] She and her colleagues found that the use of plastic containers in pregnancy was associated with higher urinary phthalate metabolites, whereas canned food consumption was associated with higher urinary BPA concentrations.[23]

Not only can exposure to phthalates and bisphenols result in unhealthy pregnancies and births but also in behavioural problems and health issues for the child after birth. Exposure of the foetus to BPA has been linked to increased anxiety in children, symptoms of depression and weakened behavioural control by the time children reached three years old. In the study conducted by Zlatnik, the weakened behavioural control was more pronounced in girls than boys. BPA also causes adverse effects within the reproductive system. The phenyl groups of BPAs mimic oestrogen and attach themselves to the oestrogen receptor. Zlatnik states that BPA can interfere with normal foetal neurodevelopment.[24] In 2011, a study was conducted of 240 children by Braun and colleagues. This study identified a correlation between foetal exposure to BPA and adverse behaviours, using maternal urine sampling and the behavioural outcomes of their children born up to the age of three.[25]

19. Benotti et al., 'Pharmaceuticals and Endocrine Disrupting Compounds in U.S. Drinking Water', p. 599.

20. Benotti et al., 'Pharmaceuticals and Endocrine Disrupting Compounds in U.S. Drinking Water', p. 600.

21. Marya G. Zlatnik, 'Endocrine-Disrupting Chemicals and Reproductive Health', *Journal of Midwifery & Women's Health* 61:4 (2016), pp. 442–55, https://doi.org/10.111/jmwh.12500.

22. Diana C. Pacyga, Sheela Sathyanarayana and Rita S. Strakovsky, 'Dietary Predictors of Phthalate and Bisphenol Exposures in Pregnant Women', *Advances in Nutrition (Bethesda, Md.)* 10:5 (2019), pp. 803–15, https://doi.org/10.1093/advances/nmz029.

23. Pacyga et al., 'Dietary Predictors of Phthalate and Bisphenol Exposures in Pregnant Women', p. 809.

24. Marya G. Zlatnik, 'Endocrine-Disrupting Chemicals and Reproductive Health', *Journal of Midwifery & Women's Health* 61:4 (2016), pp. 442–55, https://doi.org/10.1111/jmwh.12500.

25. Zlatnik, 'Endocrine-Disrupting Chemicals and Reproductive Health', p. 444.

Studies also show that a chemical like DES creates toxins that can be passed from one generation to the next. Zlatnik highlights such generational effects when she states that daughters of mothers who took DES during pregnancy have a subsequent high risk of several adverse reproductive outcomes, including rare vaginal cancers and cervical incompetence.[26] Moreover, a correlation between foetal exposure to DES and depression/anxiety was first established in 1983 and later confirmed by the Nurses' Health Study, which includes a longitudinal cohort study of women, and other studies in 1994 and 2022.[27]

Both DES exposure and psychiatric illness are similar in their health impacts. DES exposure in women results in multiple health outcomes, which leads to risk of depression. Titus and colleagues performed models consisting of women who were either exposed to DES or not, along with close monitoring of the fourteen medical states commonly associated with exposure to DES. The fourteen DES-linked medical conditions were present in those who were exposed to DES: clear cell adenocarcinoma of the vagina/cervix, infertility, early pregnancy loss, second trimester pregnancy loss, preeclampsia, ectopic pregnancy, preterm delivery, stillbirth, neonatal death, cervical intraepithelial neoplasm 2+, breast cancer at age 40 or above, early menopause, coronary artery disease, and myocardial infarction.[28] Titus and colleagues also discuss how the risk of depression increased in women who were exposed to DES while in gestation. A report based on data from the Nurses' Health Study showed that, history of depression at study baseline was higher in women who were exposed prenatally.[29]

In light of the evidence that EDCs lead to adverse health outcomes, it is also important to note that studies of both pregnant women and women in biomonitoring cohorts have shown that women want – and believe they deserve – more information on their likely personal exposures to environmental chemicals.[30] Questionnaires used in Zlatnik's studies reveal several things: women are sometimes unaware of hazards of environmental toxins; women worry about potential toxins but don't trust the resources they find in the public sphere; healthcare providers should be adequately informed about EDCs before advising their patients.[31]

26. Zlatnik, 'Endocrine-Disrupting Chemicals and Reproductive Health', p. 453.

27. Linda J. Titus et al., 'Prenatal Diethylstilbestrol Exposure and Risk of Depression in Women and Men', *Epidemiology* (Cambridge, Mass.) 30:5 (2019), pp. 679–86. https://doi-org/10.1097/EDE.000000000000.1048.

28. Titus et al., 'Prenatal Diethylstilbestrol Exposure and Risk of Depression in Women and Men', p. 685.

29. Titus et al., 'Prenatal Diethylstilbestrol Exposure and Risk of Depression in Women and Men', p. 685.

30. Zlatnik, 'Endocrine-Disrupting Chemicals and Reproductive Health'.

31. Zlatnik, 'Endocrine-Disrupting Chemicals and Reproductive Health', p. 447.

Exposure to EDCs in light of racial, ethnic and socio-economic disparity

In recent years, two groups – the American College of Obstetricians and Gynaecologists (ACOG) and the International Federation of Gynaecology and Obstetrics (FIGO) – have argued that 'the evidence that links exposure to toxic environmental agents and adverse reproductive and developmental health outcomes is sufficiently robust' and that timely action is necessary to identify and reduce exposure while addressing the consequences.[32] More specifically, both groups recognized that while exposure to harmful chemicals is everywhere, people with lower income are disproportionately affected. Hence, actions taken to prevent harm from EDC exposure in women are not only a question of gender equality but also a matter of equality in society at large.[33]

One 2018 study reviewed the evidence linking unequal exposures to EDCs with racial, ethnic and socio-economic diabetes disparities in the United States. The study found that the dramatic rise in US diabetes rates correlates closely with synthetic chemical production and that epidemiological, animal and cellular data demonstrates that EDCs can interfere with insulin secretion and action as well as with other pathways that regulate glucose homeostasis.[34] Moreover, the study found that exposure to several toxicants has been prospectively linked to diabetes risk; these toxicants include PCBs,[35] organochlorine (OC) pesticides, various chemical constituents of air pollution, BPA and phthalates – all of which are more likely to affect African Americans, Latinos and low-income individuals because of higher exposure.[36]

In a study conducted twenty-five years ago, women with high PCB levels exhibited increased instances of diabetes (incidence density ratio 2.3 [95 per cent CI 1.25–4.34]).[37] A previous study was conducted on the relationship between

32. R. D. Björvang and P. Damdimopoulou, 'Persistent Environmental Endocrine-Disrupting Chemicals in Ovarian Follicular Fluid and *in Vitro* Fertilization Treatment Outcome in Women', *Upsala Journal of Medical Sciences* 125:2 (2020), pp. 85–94.

33. Björvang and Damdimopoulou, 'Persistent Environmental Endocrine-Disrupting Chemicals in Ovarian Follicular Fluid and *in Vitro* Fertilization Treatment Outcome in Women', p. 88.

34. Daniel Ruiz, Marisol Becerra, Jyotsna S. Jagai, K. Kerry Ard and Robert M. Sargis, 'Disparities in Environmental Exposures to Endocrine-Disrupting Chemicals and Diabetes Risk in Vulnerable Populations', *Diabetes Care* 41:1 (2018), pp. 193–205. https://doi.org/10.2337/dc16-2765.

35. Max Weintraub and Linda S. Birnbaum, 'Catfish Consumption as a Contributor to Elevated PCB Levels in a Non-Hispanic Black Subpopulation', *Environmental Research* 107:3 (2008), pp. 412–17. https://doi.org/10.1016/j.envres.2008.03.001.

36. Weintraub and Birnbaum, 'Catfish Consumption as a Contributor to Elevated PCB Levels in a Non-Hispanic Black Subpopulation', pp. 414–15.

37. Weintraub and Birnbaum, 'Catfish Consumption as a Contributor to Elevated PCB Levels in a Non-Hispanic Black Subpopulation', p. 412.

phthalates and insulin resistance. The study found that Mexican Americans ($P = 0.001$) and non-Hispanic Black adolescents ($P = 0.002$) had significant increments in HOMA-IR (HOMA-insulin resistance) with a higher level of high MWPs or bis(2-ethylhexyl) phthalate that were not observed in non-Hispanic whites ($P \geq 0.74$).

In addition, traffic-related air pollution compromises chemicals including nitric oxide (NO_x), ozone and particulate matter (PM). Nationwide studies have shown that African Americans and Latinas are exposed to significantly more $PM_{2.5}$ and that ethnic and racial disparities in exposure to traffic-related air pollution exceed those between income groups. It is also true that racial differences in NO_2 exposure are greater in large metropolitan centres compared with small to medium areas, a reflection of racial and ethnic segregation around traffic corridors in major US cities. African Americans and people with lower incomes also have higher BPA levels than the population at large. The precise reason behind these high levels of BPA is unclear, but it may have to do with minimal access to fresh food and more dependence on processed foods. Disparities in BPA exposure may contribute to metabolic disease burden because increasing evidence associates BPA with diabetes. This means that African Americans, Latinos and the socio-economically disadvantaged are more susceptible to exposure to diabetogenic pollutants, which are an important contributor to diabetes. Thus, an improvement in environmental health could help reduce the risk of diabetes and address some of the racial and socio-economic disparities already mentioned.

The impact of EDCs on women of colour

Black women have higher levels of exposure to phthalates and parabens than white women. According to Helm, Black women in the United States have higher rates of obesity, diabetes and preterm birth than white women – all conditions potentially impacted by EDCs.[38] Previous research discovered that EDCs found in hair products – heavily used in the African American community because of the association between hair and personal identity – are important factors which contribute to hormone-mediated diseases. For example, use of hair oil and hair relaxers is associated with earlier menarche, higher incidence of fibroids and increased risk of breast cancer.[39] When Black women purchase more products containing EDCs, including fragrances, feminine hygiene material and deodorizing products, they are more at risk to exposure when compared to white women.

38. Jessica S. Helm, Marcia Nishioka, Julia G. Brody, Ruthann A. Rudel and Robin E. Dodson, 'Measurement of Endocrine Disrupting and Asthma-Associated Chemicals in Hair Products Used by Black Women', *Environmental Research* 165 (2018), pp. 448–58. https://doi.org/10.1016/j.envres.2018.03.030.

39. Helm et al., 'Measurement of Endocrine Disrupting and Asthma-Associated Chemicals in Hair Products Used by Black Women', pp. 449–50.

The use of fragrances, in particular, was positively associated with urinary metabolite levels of diethyl phthalate (DEP) in a study of pregnant African American and Dominican women in New York City. Moreover, data from the National Health and Nutrition Examination Survey (NHANES) showed that reported use of vaginal douches, which are heavily marketed to Black women as aesthetic products, was associated with higher urinary metabolite levels of DEP in Black compared with white women. Hair products are also a source of exposure and health disparities. Black women and children often use hormone-containing hair and skin products almost every day – much more often than white women and children – and some professional hair-straightening products contain and release substantial amounts of formaldehyde.

Previous and current research studies tie the chemicals in these hair products to breast cancer, which is the second leading cause of death in women in the United States. Black women are comparatively more affected by breast cancer relative to white women, and it is possible that hair products play a role in this disparity. Tetch notes that hair and personal care products have been gaining increasing attention in breast cancer research.[40] A study by Stiel and colleagues looked at environmental oestrogen, EDCs and placenta-derived ingredients found in hair products used primarily by African American women. The authors concluded that there is evidence that the use of hair products is a risk to early breast cancer in Black women. In addition, Myers and colleagues assessed ethanol extracts of eight personal products frequently used by African Americans for estrogenic and anti-estrogenic activity in a human breast cancer cell line cultured in the laboratory.[41] These authors detected estrogenic activity in oil, hair lotion, extra-dry skin lotion, toner, tea-tree hair conditioner and cocoa butter skin cream. Thus, these hair and skin-care products contained similar ingredients that may act as if they are oestrogen functioning.

In another study, Helm and colleagues examined eighteen hair-care products including hot oil treatments, anti-frizz/polish products, leave-in conditioner, root stimulator, hair lotion and relaxer.[42] The researchers targeted sixty-six chemicals for analysis based on evidence of their association with endocrine disruption or asthma, their expected presence in consumer products and analytical capacity. Two chemicals, 4-t-nonylphenol and octyphenol diethoxy late, had a level of detection (LOD) at or below 1 μg/g while most of the other chemicals had levels less than 2.5 μg/g. However, higher levels were found in decamethylcyclopentasiloxane (D5) (17.2 μg/g), octamethylcyclotetrasiloxane (D4) (5.2 μg/g) and benzo-phenone-3 (BP-3) (4.8 μg/g). Furthermore, the products analysed contained more cyclosiloxanes fragrance chemicals, DEP and parabens than chemicals from other chemical classes.

40. Dede Teteh et al., 'The Black Identity, Hair Product Use, and Breast Cancer Scale', *PloS one* 14:12 (2019), pp. 1–15. https://doi-org/10.1371/journal.pone.0225305.

41. Teteh et al., 'The Black Identity, Hair Product Use, and Breast Cancer Scale', p. 2.

42. Helm et al., 'Measurement of Endocrine Disrupting and Asthma-Associated Chemicals in Hair Products Used by Black Women', p. 449.

The study also found that nonylphenols were present in 30 per cent of products and antimicrobials, BPA, ethanolamine's, glycol ethers and high MWPs were present in fewer than 20 per cent of products. In addition, 78 per cent of the products included parabens that acted as preservatives. The study found the low MWP DEP, commonly used as a solvent in fragrances and fragranced products, present in 78 per cent of hair products and at higher concentrations (median: 47 µg/g; maximum: 2,450 µg/g) than other phthalates and most other targeted chemicals. At least one of the three cyclosiloxanes was found in 67 per cent of the products in the same study.

Linalool, limonene and HHGB (or Galaxolide) were most found in 40 per cent of products. Seventy-two per cent of the products had at least one UV filter, which is used as an activator ingredient in products like sunscreen. Glycol ethers were not found in many of the products; however, three of the eight ethers were found in hair root stimulators and relaxers. Further, 39 per cent of the alkylphenols were detected in seven of the eighteen products with concentrations above 10 µg/g. Helm concludes that, given the exposure and endocrine-mediated health disparities experienced by Black women, new research and regulatory activities should consider the effects of ethnic differences in product use on exposures and health.[43]

This chapter has already highlighted the adverse effect of exposure to EDCs during the prenatal period. Indeed, studies show that higher exposure to EDCs during the prenatal period, including EDCs commonly found in personal care products, has been linked to a number of adverse child health outcomes including low birthweight and preterm birth. Interestingly, non-Hispanic Black women, as well as women from certain Asian subgroups, are two times more likely to have a low-birth weight infant, suggesting the need to determine whether differences in phthalate exposure could contribute to racial and ethnic disparities in birthweight.[44]

A study conducted by the Puerto Rico Test site for Exploring Contamination Threats (PROJECT) evaluated 1,090 Puerto Rican women. This study states that in an average pregnancy, during each interquartile range, increased monobutyl phthalate (MBP) concentrations were associated with a 42 per cent increase in the odds of a preterm birth (odds ratio = 1.42 95 per cent CI 1.07, 1.88). Other adverse health outcomes linked to higher exposure to EDCs also exist, such as neurobehavioral, asthma and allergic disease outcome.[45] Chan and colleagues

43. Helm et al., 'Measurement of Endocrine Disrupting and Asthma-Associated Chemicals in Hair Products Used by Black Women', p. 456.

44. Marissa Chan, Carol Mita, Andrea Bellavia, Machaiah Parker and Tamarra James-Todd, 'Racial/Ethnic Disparities in Pregnancy and Prenatal Exposure to Endocrine-Disrupting Chemicals Commonly Used in Personal Care Products', *Current Environmental Health Reports* 8:2 (2021), pp. 98–112. https://doi.org/10.1007/s40572-021-00317-5#citeas.

45. Chan et al., 'Racial/Ethnic Disparities in Pregnancy and Prenatal Exposure to Endocrine-Disrupting Chemicals Commonly Used in Personal Care Products', p. 99.

conducted a study to understand the current state of the literature on racial/ethnic differences in chemical exposures occurring during pregnancy and the prenatal period that are linked to potentially modifiable risk factors.

The study focused on eight chemicals or classes of chemicals previously identified as chemicals of concern found in PCPs (phthalates, parabens, benzophenone-3, triclosan, cyclic volatile methyl siloxanes, formaldehyde-releasing preservative, 1, 4-dioxene and diethanolamine) and their impact on women of different racial and ethnic backgrounds in the contiguous United States and Puerto Rico. One insight from the study concerned phthalate acid esters, a class of industrial and multiuse chemicals that can be found in a variety of consumer products. These phthalates are found everywhere in the environment: not only in consumer products (including personal care products) but in food, indoor air, indoor dust and the air inside vehicles. Moreover, due to their short half-life (from five hours to less than twenty-four hours), concentrations are representative of recent exposure compared to chronic or cumulative exposure.

Chan's work focused on studies reporting information on low MWPs, such as DEP, di-iso-butyl phthalate (DiBP) and di-*n*-butyl phthalate (DBP), which are used in solvents, medications and personal care products.[46] In addition, a study conducted by Chan's colleague, James Todd, evaluated urinary phthalate metabolite concentrations in a diverse cohort and found higher concentrations of MBP, MiBP, MBzP and MEP among non-Hispanic Black women, Hispanic women and women who selected 'other' as their race/ethnicity as compared to non-Hispanic white women. Specifically, non-Hispanic Black women had a baseline specific gravity-adjusted geometric mean (GM) MEP of 286.0 μg/L compared to 98.7 g/L for non-Hispanic white women.[47] Intriguingly, the metabolite monoethyl phthalate rate decreased for Hispanic women throughout pregnancy. However, the MEP rate increased in late pregnancy for non-Hispanic Black women. Chan and colleagues found that these findings reflected higher exposure to personal care product phthalates, such as DBP and DEP, during pregnancy, which may illustrate differences in modifiable product use by race/ethnicity.[48]

Racial and ethnic disparity in pregnancy outcomes remains one of the most challenging public health problems. Consistently, infant mortality and low birthweight rates have been at least twice as high for Black women compared to white women.[49] The developing foetus and neonates are especially susceptible

---

46. Chan et al., 'Racial/Ethnic Disparities in Pregnancy and Prenatal Exposure to Endocrine-Disrupting Chemicals Commonly Used in Personal Care Products', p. 101.

47. Chan et al., 'Racial/Ethnic Disparities in Pregnancy and Prenatal Exposure to Endocrine-Disrupting Chemicals Commonly Used in Personal Care Products', p. 101.

48. Chan et al., 'Racial/Ethnic Disparities in Pregnancy and Prenatal Exposure to Endocrine-Disrupting Chemicals Commonly Used in Personal Care Products', p. 102.

49. Nalini Ranjit, Kristine Siefert and Vasantha Padmanabhan, 'Bisphenol-A and Disparities in Birth Outcomes: A Review and Directions for Future Research', *Journal of Perinatology: Official Journal of the California Perinatal Association* 30:1 (2010), pp. 2–9. https://doi.org/10.1038/jp.2009.90.

to EDC exposure resulting in adaptions and organizational changes that appear to predispose them to later dysfunctions.[50] Most effects of developmental exposure to EDCs appear to be irreversible; indeed, some of these effects may even be transgenerational; i.e. they lead to epigenetic alteration in the germ line and thus have biological impacts on all subsequent generations.[51]

As this chapter has already shown, BPA, used as an industrial plasticizer, contains estrogenic properties. Dental fillings, plastic food and water containers, baby bottles, food wrap, and the lining of beverage and food cans present multiple routes for BPA to enter the body. There are studies that have researched the BPA in the blood of pregnant women and newborns. Ranjit and colleagues discovered that BPA is found in concentrations of 1–18 ng/mL in the maternal serum, 1–10 ng/mL in amniotic fluid and cord serum taken at birth, and up to 100 ng/g in the placenta.[52] Breast milk is an additional route of transfer of maternal BPA to offspring: one study reported BPA in more than 60 per cent of human breast milk samples tested levels up to 6.3 ng/mL.

There is also evidence that shows that BPA attaches to the oestrogen receptor, which then activates oestrogen receptor-mediated gene expression that occurs when BPA acts as if it was oestradiol. Studies have shown that prenatal exposure to BPA, in vivo, is associated with changes in hypothalamic pituitary gonadal axis function, mammary development and cognitive function as well as specific behavioural changes in the offspring.[53] Ranjit and colleagues found that because BPA mimics oestrogen in its actions, continued exposure to BPA during gestation is likely to have an impact on the developmental trajectory of the foetus.[54] Recent reports state that while exposure to BPA can cause foetal death and reduced birthweight and growth during infancy, these effects occur only at high levels of exposure, and therefore, risks are negligible.

As noted, BPA has been shown to account for most estrogenic activity that leaches from landfills into the surrounding ecosystem, i.e. into communities in which African Americans are more likely than whites to reside. Studies show that the fast-food restaurants and grocery stores in African American communities are less likely to contain healthy food options, no matter the income. Thus, as Ranjit states, African Americans are more likely to be at higher risk of exposure to EDCs.[55]

50. Ranjit et al., 'Bisphenol-A and Disparities in Birth Outcomes: A Review and Directions for Future Research', p. 2.

52. Ranjit et al., 'Bisphenol-A and Disparities in Birth Outcomes: A Review and Directions for Future Research', p. 3.

51. Ranjit et al., 'Bisphenol-A and Disparities in Birth Outcomes: A Review and Directions for Future Research', p. 2.

53. Ranjit et al., 'Bisphenol-A and Disparities in Birth Outcomes: A Review and Directions for Future Research', pp. 3–4.

54. Ranjit et al., 'Bisphenol-A and Disparities in Birth Outcomes: A Review and Directions for Future Research', p. 4.

55. Ranjit et al., 'Bisphenol-A and Disparities in Birth Outcomes: A Review and Directions for Future Research', p. 7.

Another cause of perinatal morbidity and mortality, followed only by prematurity, is intrauterine growth restriction (IUGR). Infants that have low birthweight and IUGR have high perinatal morbidity and mortality rates. The risk of neonatal death for infants weighing 2,000–2,499 grams at birth is four times higher than for infants weighing 2,500–2,999 grams and ten times higher than for infants weighing 3,000–3,499 grams.[56] Ranjit and colleagues found that, for surviving neonates, the risks of IUGR and low birthweight extend into the post-neonatal period and include a greater risk of mortality and an increased risk for a host of adverse health and developmental outcomes, including lower mean intelligence quotient scores and a higher instance of cognitive impairment. Diseases like cardiovascular disease, hypertension, type 2 diabetes and obesity are risk diseases resulting from IUGR. Ranjit states that a growing body of evidence suggests that the effects of IUGR/low birthweight are intergenerational due to shared environmental factors, genetic factors or both.[57]

A study by the Washington State intergenerational Study of Birth Outcomes found that low maternal birthweight conferred a two-fold increase in the risk of low birthweight offspring and a 30 per cent greater risk of preterm delivery among African Americans, Hispanics and whites.[58] Ranjit and colleagues found that if BPA exposure is shown to be a contributor to disparities in birth outcomes, this implies the need to intervene in those macro-level systems – governmental and regulatory, business, industry and community – that shape African American women's disproportionate exposure or enhanced susceptibility to BPA.[59]

EDCs and infertility

Over the past years there has been a decline in fertility among both men and women.[60] Factors such as late childbearing and low sperm count have attributed to the decline, but accumulating evidence suggests that the cause of infertility is EDCs. BPA has been found in follicular fluid of women with infertility issues[61] as

56. Ranjit et al., 'Bisphenol-A and Disparities in Birth Outcomes: A Review and Directions for Future Research', p. 8.

57. Ranjit et al., 'Bisphenol-A and Disparities in Birth Outcomes: A Review and Directions for Future Research', p. 8.

58. Ranjit et al., 'Bisphenol-A and Disparities in Birth Outcomes: A Review and Directions for Future Research', p. 8.

59. David Crews and John A McLachlan. 'Epigenetics, Evolution, Endocrine Disruption, Health, and Disease', *Endocrinology* 147 (6 Suppl) (2006), pp. S4–S10. https://doi.org/10.1210/en.2005-1122.

60. David S. Guzick and Shanna Swan, 'The Decline of Infertility: Apparent or Real?', *Fertility and Sterility* 86:3 (2006), pp. 524–6. https://doi.org/10.1016.j.fernstert.2006.05.027.

61. Ronit Machtinger, Catherine M. Combelles, Stacey A. Missmer, Katharine F. Correia, Paige Williams, Russ Hauser and Catherine Racowsky, 'Bisphenol-A and Human Oocyte Maturation in Vitro', *Human Reproduction* 28:10 (2013), pp. 2735–45. https://doi.org/10.1093/humrep/det312.

well as the umbilical cords of Japanese babies along with other EDCs.[62] This is of exigent concern because animal studies have shown that exposure of oocytes to BPA has led to meiotic arrest.[63] Maturation of oocytes occurs from the splitting of the meiotic spindle and the cytoplasm, allowing for maturation in preparation for fertilization.[64] When this process is reprimanded, oocytes cannot continue to maturation. Therefore, exposure to chemicals like BPA may be detrimental.

Clinical studies have shown an inverse relationship between urine/serum concentrations of BPA, the number of oocytes retrieved and peak oestradiol (E2) levels in women undergoing in-vitro fertilization (IVF).[65] BPA has been shown to compete with E2 for binding with the oestrogen receptor alpha, one of the two oestrogen receptor subtypes.[66] Interestingly, BPA has two unsaturated phenol rings while oestradiol is an aromatized C18 steroid with a hydroxyl group at 3-beta concentrations and not BPA at all. Data found that as the BPA concentrations increased, the viability of the oocytes decreased and often lead to degradation. Lenie and colleagues found that oocytes exposed to 30 mM BPA during follicular development slightly reduced granulosa cell proliferation and lower-than-normal oestrogen production. According to the EPA and the US Food and Drug Administration (FDA), 50 μg/kg/ day is the safe daily consumption of BPA in humans. Additionally, 18 per cent of the oocytes were able to resume normal progression through meiosis after stimulation of oocyte maturation.[67]

Similarly, in a 2003 report of an in-vivo study, concern was raised by meiotic abnormalities occurring in untreated female mice who were exposed to polycarbonate cages and bottles impaired by alkaline detergents.[68] Numerous

62. K. Sakurai and C. Mori, 'Fetal Exposure to Endocrine Disruptors', *Nihon Rinsho. Japanese Journal of Clinical Medicine* 58:12 (2000), pp. 2508–13.

63. Machtinger et al., 'Bisphenol-A and Human Oocyte Maturation in Vitro.'

64. Victor Y. Fujimoto, Dongsul Kim, Frederick S. vom Saal, Julie D. Lamb, Julia A. Taylor and Michael. S. Bloom, 'Serum Unconjugated Bisphenol A Concentrations in Women May Adversely Influence Oocyte Quality during in Vitro Fertilization', *Fertility and Sterility* 95 (2011), pp. 1816–19. https://doi.org/10.1016/fertnstert.2010.11.008.

65. E. Mok-Lin et al., 'Urinary Bisphenol A Concentrations and Ovarian Response among Women Undergoing IVF', *International Journal of Andrology* 33:2 (2010), pp. 385–93. https://doi.org/10.1111/j.1365-2605.2009.01014.x.

66. Iain A. Lang et al., 'Association of Urinary Bisphenol A Concentration with Medical Disorders and Laboratory Abnormalities in Adults', *JAMA* 300:11 (2008), pp. 1303–10. https://doi.org/10.1001/jama.300.11.1303.

67. Sandy Lenie, Rita Cortvrindt, Ursula Eichenlaub-Ritter and Johan Smitz, 'Continuous Exposure to Bisphenol A during in Vitro Follicular Development Induces Meiotic Abnormalities', *Mutation Research/Genetic Toxicology and Environmental Mutagenesis* 651:1 (2008), pp. 71–81. https://doi.org/10.1016/j.mrgentox.2007.10.017.

68. F. Pacchierotti, R. Ranaldi, U. Eichenlaub-Ritter, S. Attia and I. D. Adler, 'Evaluation of Aneugenic Effects of Bisphenol A in Somatic and Germ Cells of the Mouse', *Mutation Research/Genetic Toxicology and Environmental Mutagenesis* 651:1 (2008), pp. 64–70. https://doi.org/10.1016/j.mrgentox.2007.10.009.

studies suggest that low BPA concentrations do affect the division of oocytes due to the degradation of the mitotic spindle.[69] BPA does this by negatively interacting with the mitotic spindle.[70] Also, BPA micronuclei were predominantly positive when characterized for kinetochores. This proved that it induced chromosome loss in anaphase.[71] Collectively, the in-vivo and in-vitro studies provided significant evidence that BPA disrupts meiosis, negatively affecting oocyte division and causing infertility issues. As mentioned in a 2003 article by Crews and colleagues, when studying EDCs, or endocrine active substances, exposure must be considered within the context of an individual's endocrine background. Vertebrate model systems provide direct evidence for the effects of EDCs on genetic background and on future generations (offspring). Human interactions are more difficult to decipher as these are not laboratory-contained experiments.

Previous studies of the correlation between BPA and endometriosis generated inconsistent results that were limited by the participant sampling framework, insufficient sample size and/or use of serum with transient concentrations instead of urine to measure specific BPA concentrations. Therefore, a study by Upson and colleagues utilized data from the Women's Risk of Endometriosis Study to obtain participants and data to assess a relationship between high BPA urine concentrations and endometriosis.[72] Concerning ovarian endometriosis, there was no strong evidence that BPA has negative effects. On the contrary, there were statistically positive correlations with total BPA concentrations in urine and non-ovarian endometriosis. This suggests that BPA may affect the normal dynamic structural changes of hormonally responsive endometrial tissue during menstruation, promoting the establishment of refluxed endometrial tissues in non-ovarian endometriosis.

While there is limited research on this topic, there is significant evidence showing an association between BPA concentrations in urine and miscarriage. An important determinant of reduced fertility is failed implantation, which is thought

---

69. Pacchierotti et al., 'Evaluation of Aneugenic Effects of Bisphenol A in Somatic and Germ Cells of the Mouse', p. 2.

70. Erika Pfeiffer, Brigitte Rosenberg, Susanne Deuschel and Manfred Metzler, 'Interference with Microtubules and Induction of Micronuclei in Vitro by Various Bisphenols', *Mutation Research/Genetic Toxicology and Environmental Mutagenesis* 390:1 (1997), pp. 21–31. https://doi.org/10.1016/S0165-1218(96)00161-9.

71. Leanne Lehmann and Manfred Metzler, 'Bisphenol A and Its Methylated Congeners Inhibit Growth and Interfere with Microtubules in Human Fibroblasts in Vitro', *Chemico-Biological Interactions* 147:3 (2004), pp. 273–85. https://doi.org/10.1016/j.cbi.2004.01.005.

72. Kristen Upson, Sheela Sathyanarayana, Anneclaire J. De Roos, Holger M. Koch, Delia Scholes and Victoria L. Holt, 'A Population-Based Case–Control Study of Urinary Bisphenol A Concentrations and Risk of Endometriosis', *Human Reproduction* 29:11 (2014), pp. 2457–64. https://doi.org/10.1093/humrep/deu227.

to account for 50–75 per cent of pregnancy failures.[73] Implantation is orchestrated by a series of hormones sent from endocrine glands; therefore, chemicals such as BPA, which can strongly influence and disrupt endocrine signalling, can disrupt the process of implantation. Takai and colleagues highlighted an increased failure of intrauterine implantation in mice after exposure to relatively low levels of BPA.[74] In pups, after a single round of BPA administration, a decrease in litter size and in the number of implantation sites was evident.[75] Also, the same effects occurred in mice after either ingestion of BPA or after subcutaneous single dosage rounds of BPA were administered.[76] However, it was unknown whether the decreased implantation sites were due to the adverse effects of BPA on the uterus and/or embryos.

To test, mice were fertilized, and their uterus was flushed to release embryos and/or blastocysts. Some mice were unable to obtain fertilization from the levels of BPA, releasing unfertilized eggs. In turn, it was suggested that 100 mg/kg/day had inimical effects on embryonic status and development. Only 67 per cent of the mice successfully hatched their eggs. Berger and colleagues recently demonstrated that 100 mg/kg/day caused a reduced percentage of implantation sites in mice.[77] BPA not only affected preimplantation but also the post implantation of the mice. Circumstantial evidence can be observed by the reduction of litter size. The study suggests that BPA negatively affects embryo transport, development and uterine receptivity, consequently, increasing the risk of miscarriages. In addition, urinary levels can be measured to assess how much BPA is within the body. A recent study found that 93 per cent of women tested had adequate levels of BPA in their urine. As stated previously, there could be an association between urine levels and

75. Sarah M. Zala and Dustin J. Penn, 'Abnormal Behaviours Induced by Chemical Pollution: A Review of the Evidence and New Challenges', *Animal Behaviour* 68:4 (2004), pp. 649–64. https://doi.org/10.1016/j.anbehav.2004.01.005.

74. Yahushi Takai et al., 'Preimplantation Exposure to Bisphenol A Advances Postnatal Development', *Reproductive Toxicology* 15:1 (2000), pp. 71–4. https://doi.org/10.1016/S0890-6238(00)00119-2.

73. Nick S. Macklon, Joep P. M. Geraedts and Bart C. J. M. Fauser, 'Conception to Ongoing Pregnancy: The "Black Box" of Early Pregnancy Loss', *Human Reproduction Update* 8:4 (2002), pp. 333–43. https://doi.org/10.1093/humupd/8.4.333.

76. Shuo Xiao, Honglu Diao, Mary A. Smith, Xiao Song and Xiaoqin Ye, 'Preimplantation Exposure to Bisphenol A (BPA) Affects Embryo Transport, Preimplantation Embryo Development, and Uterine Receptivity in Mice', *Reproductive Toxicology* 32:4 (2011), pp. 434–41. https://doi.org/10.1016/j.reprotox.2011.08.010.

77. Robert G. Berger, Trina. Hancock and Denys DeCatanzaro, 'Influence of Oral and Subcutaneous Bisphenol-A on Intrauterine Implantation of Fertilized Ova in Inseminated Female Mice', *Reproductive Toxicology* 23:2 (2007), pp. 138–44. https://doi.org/10.1016/j.reprotox.2006.09.005.

implantation failure in humans. Women that underwent IVF also gave urine test samples to see if there was a correlation between infertility and increased levels of BPA. There was a positive correlation between the two entities.

Conclusion

The foregoing chapter has detailed the consequences of EDCs and their effects on women's health and has led to several conclusions.

First, there is a need for more research on the prevention of toxic levels of chemical modifiers that lead to adverse health consequences in both humans and animals. As the chapter has shown, a chemical such as BPA, both a xenoestrogen and EDC, is hazardous to both women's reproductive health and health in general. The analogous, more potent xenoestrogen, DES, has previously been overturned by the FDA and removed from the market due to its adverse effects on pregnancy and increase risks of cancer. Because women in general, and women of colour, in particular, are undoubtedly the largest group of consumers of cosmetics and various types of creams and personal products, they are disproportionally affected by EDCs. There is a great need for more research on the prevention of toxic levels of these chemical modifiers and a need for levels of antimicrobial mechanisms to be monitored closely so as not to dampen their potential benefits by their adverse effects.

Secondly, though specific levels in the concentration of BPA can be considered safe, in larger concentrations there are still very harsh consequences to the health of the environment.[78] Although some levels of BPA or other EDCs may be considered safe, what has yet to be determined is the level of contamination variance across individuals. There is no clear way in which to assess an individual's daily contact with BPA, either naturally or synthetically. Though sparse concentrations of BPA exposure may not lead to hindrances in women's health, its impact in higher concentrations, as detailed in current research, raises enough concern to question the adequacy of current environmental protection laws. Parabens, for instance, have shown significant associations with breast cancer and endometriosis. Though they may not directly be the cause of these ailments, they do, however, raise serious concerns about the increased risk of poor health outcomes in women.

Lastly, at the intersection of the negative effects of urban heat islands and growing interest in green infrastructure design in urban areas there exists a potential longer term solution for mitigation that warrants exploration. Vertical greenery systems theoretically offer the most practical and abundant space per

---

78. Jane Muncke, 'Endocrine Disrupting Chemicals and Other Substances of Concern in Food Contact Materials: An Updated Review of Exposure, Effect and Risk Assessment', *The Journal of Steroid Biochemistry and Molecular Biology* 127:1 (2011), pp. 118–27. https://doi.org/10.1016/j.jsbmb.2010.10.004.

square foot in an urban environment for increasing vegetation cover. They also offer a combination of benefits from both the vegetation itself and pavement cooling mitigation techniques. Additionally, they offer solutions for key associated consequences of urban heat islands, namely reduced energy consumption, reduced air pollution and greenhouse gas emissions, and a positive impact on human health. Although there are limitations to large-scale implementation, vertical greenery systems have proven useful in urban heat island mitigation.

Chapter 5

THE ECOLOGICAL *KAIROS*

THEOLOGICAL REFLECTIONS ON THE THREAT OF ENVIRONMENTAL PLASTICS TO ORGANISMAL AND ENVIRONMENTAL HEALTH

Oliver Putz

Humanity finds itself at an existential crossroads, and our decisions on what to do next will decide the future of all life on earth. This is not so much an alarmist exaggeration as it is a sober assessment of the current state of affairs. For the past two centuries, our destructive impact on the planet has been so extensive that before too long an irreversible overall destabilization could be imminent.[1] In some cases, such 'points of no return' (tipping points) may already have been reached.[2] Take, for example, the anthropogenic loss of biodiversity, the extent of which has biologists worried we might be facing a sixth mass extinction event.[3] If this turns

1. Will Steffen et al., 'Planetary Boundaries: Guiding Human Development on a Changing Planet', *Science* 347:6223 (2015), pp. 1259855-1-10.

2. In a recent paper, Chris Boulton and colleagues conclude that three quarters of the Amazon rainforest has lost its resilience since the early 2000s, 'risking dieback with profound implications for biodiversity, carbon storage and climate change at a global scale'. Chris A. Boulton, Timothy M. Lenton and Niklas Boers, 'Pronounced Loss of Amazon Rainforest Resilience since the Early 2000s', *Nature Climate Change* (2022), https://doi.org/10.1038/s41558-022-01287-8. It seems that at least in the Amazon rainforest, tipping points may already have been reached. While it is not clear what ramifications we have to expect, it is certain that they will have a global impact on the Earth Systems and many of its spheres (i.e. biosphere, atmosphere, hydrosphere).

3. By biodiversity, or biological diversity, I mean the variety of life in all its many manifestations. Biologists usually distinguish three groups of diversity (ecological, organismal and genetic), within which elements are organized in nested hierarchies, with each element subsuming all the elements grouped beneath it. The three groups are linked, so that some elements are shared by different groups. See Kevin J. Gaston, 'Biodiversity', in Navjot S. Sodhi and Paul R. Ehrlich (eds), *Conservation Biology for All* (Oxford: Oxford

out to be so, the biosphere's complex web of life that has evolved over eons will collapse without sufficient time to gradually reorganize itself; the entire system will shift rapidly and irrevocably to a new equilibrium.[4] Whether such a catastrophic alteration of the biosphere would spell doom for humanity is unclear, but that it will come at great suffering for all is an incontrovertible fact. Our actions today will determine the trajectory of the Earth System in the near and far future. We must choose now what we want this future to be.

To the ancient Greeks, such a critical point in time demanding decisive action was known as *kairos*.[5] Unlike *chronos*, the quantitative measure of sequential time, *kairos* has a qualitative character, for it is in such moments that we must weigh options based on values and world views, decide on an action in line with said views, and act accordingly. Paul Tillich appropriates this understanding of *kairos*, which he describes as a moment 'pregnant with a new understanding of the meaning of history and life'.[6] Of course, the central *kairos* moment for Christians is the Incarnation marking the transition of history into the Kingdom of God, but, as Tillich points out, history abounds with second order *kairoi* in which the prophetic Spirit arises in the Church and demands a re-evaluation of the current situation.[7] In these, as there were, 'secondary' boundary situations between the

University Press, 2010), p. 27. For sixth mass extinction, see Anthony D. Barnosky et al., 'Has the Earth's Sixth Mass Extinction Already Arrived?', *Nature* 471 (2011), pp. 51–7; Anthony D. Barnosky et al., 'Introducing the Scientific Consensus on Maintaining Humanity's Life Support Systems in the 21st Century: Information for Policy Makers', *The Anthropocene Review* 1:1 (2014), pp. 78–109; Gerardo Ceballos et al., 'Accelerated Modern Human-induced Species Losses: Entering the Sixth Mass Extinction', *Science Advances* 1:5 (2015), p. e1400253.

4. 'Rapidly', here, must be understood in geological terms, where millennia are but a blink of an eye. So-called pulse disturbances, such as the large asteroid impact responsible for the extinction of the dinosaurs 66 million years ago, act instantaneously both on the ecological (within one or a few generations) and the evolutionary (changes becoming manifest within populations) level, whereas push disturbances unfold over several millions of years followed by a rather brief period of peak impact driving the system into a new constellation. Nan Crystal Arens and Ian D. West, 'Press-Pulse: A General Theory of Mass Extinction?' *Paleobiology* 34:4 (2008), p. 464. For evolutionary biologists and geologists, even the latter scenario is ultimately 'rapid' compared to the more slow-paced evolutionary change in biological diversity playing out over tens or hundreds of millions of years.

5. John E. Smith, 'Time, Times, and the "Right Time"; "Chronos" and "Kairos"', *The Monist* 53:1 Philosophy of History (1969), pp. 1–13.

6. Paul Tillich, *Systematic Theology, Volume 3* (Chicago: The University of Chicago Press, 1963), p. 369.

7. Paul Tillich, 'Kairos (1922)', in Christian Danz, Werner Schüßler and Erdman Sturm (eds), *Ausgewählte Texte* (De Gruyter Texte) (German Edition) (Berlin: Walter de Gruyter, 2008), p. 51.

'not yet' and the 'already' of the Kingdom,[8] the existential decisions at hand must be negotiated in light of the central *kairos* as their criterion. In other words, how to respond to the emerging trials of a specific time (*kairos*) and place (*topos*) must be determined relative to the perceived meaning of the absolute universal transformation that was the Incarnation. These moments of challenge, then, are to Christians always also opportunities to actualize the Kingdom more fully. That in doing so Christians also negotiate the meaning and possibility of their theistic faith is self-evident.

In this chapter, I want to argue that we live in the 'ecological *kairos*' that demands of us an existential decision on how to respond to the current ecological crisis, and in which monotheistic religions must negotiate the meaning of existence as well as the validity and implications of their faith. I will illustrate the nature of this boundary situation by taking a closer look at the systemic interplay of the disastrous effects of anthropogenic plastic pollution for both environmental and human health. In particular, I will focus on the impact environmental plastics have on the loss of biodiversity and the threat this poses to women's health and well-being. Fully aware of the complexity of the challenge, I nevertheless want to discuss a possible first step towards a solution, namely a radical ecological conversion that involves the fundamental reorientation of our existential concern onto creation.

The Plastic Age

Since their introduction in the early days of the twentieth century, plastics have become one of the most ubiquitously utilized human-made materials to date, surpassed only by steel and cement.[9] What makes these synthetic and semi-synthetic organic polymers so desirable for industrial and general consumer use are their specific properties, above all their malleability and durability. When heated, plastics can be formed into a variety of shapes, assuming practically any degree of rigidity warranted when cooled down. It is due to these favourable qualities that plastic production has exponentially increased, currently running at an annual global output that is somewhere around 400 million metric tons (MMT), a mass

---

8. Paul Tillich, *Systematic Theology, Volume 2* (Chicago: The University of Chicago Press, 1957), p. 164.

9. The first synthetic plastic, *Bakelite*, was introduced already in 1907, but it was in the 1950s that plastic production began to soar (a time known as the 'Great Acceleration'). Roland Geyer, Jenna R. Jambeck and Kara Lavender Law, 'Production, Use, and Fate of All Plastics Ever Made', *Science Advances* 3 (2017), p. e1700782; World Steel Association (1978–2021), Steel Statistical Yearbooks, www.worldsteel.org/steel-by-topic/statistics/steel-statistical-yearbook (accessed 19 January 2022); U.S. Geological Survey (1996–2021), Cement Statistics and Information, https://www.usgs.gov/centers/national-minerals-information-center/cement-statistics-and-information (accessed 19 January 2022).

equivalent to over three quarter that of the world population.[10] With a revenue of 468 billion US dollars in 2018 in China alone, plastics are of tremendous growing economic interest.[11] Market predictions see a continuous rise of production and revenue for the coming years.[12] There cannot be any doubt that this truly is the Plastic Age.

Environmental plastics as persistent pollutants

Just as production is soaring to new heights, plastic trash is increasing at an exponential rate with much of it ending up in the natural environment where it poses a severe risk to biosphere integrity and human health.[13] Part of what makes plastic debris so hazardous is its extreme longevity. Composed of organic monomers that are usually derived from non-biodegradable fossil hydrocarbons, plastic remains in the environment for an indefinite time after it has been discarded. While chemical and biological degradation are possible in principle, lack of technological know-how, high costs and low efficiency prevent either from being part of our current disposal strategies. As a result, the large majority of commercially used plastics are basically non-degradable and are either dumped in landfills or burnt in incinerators.[14] Plastic debris that escapes into the environment is often transported

10. Roland Geyer estimates the annual global plastic production in 2017 at 438 MMT (348 MMT polymer resins, 62 MMT polymer fibres, 27 MMT additives), which equates to 77.2 per cent of the mass of the world population in 2017 (7.6 billion). Roland Geyer, 'Production, Use, and Fate of Synthetic Polymers', in Trevor M. Letcher (ed.), *Plastic Waste and Recycling* (Cambridge, MA: Academic Press, 2020), pp. 13–32 (16). For calculation of relative plastic mass see Hannah Ritchie and Max Moser, 'Plastic Pollution', https://ourworldindata.org/plastic-pollution (accessed 15 January 2022). The mass of all plastic ever produced outweighs the current total mass of all terrestrial and marine animals combined. Emily Elhacham et al., 'Global Human-Made Mass Exceeds All Living Biomass', *Nature* 588 (2020), pp. 442–4 (443).

11. Accounting for 32 per cent of the global production in 2020, China remains the largest plastic producer worldwide. Statista: https://www.statista.com/statistics/282732/global-production-of-plastics-since-1950/ (accessed 15 January 2022).

12. Mini B. Tekman et al., *Impacts of Plastic Pollution in the Oceans on Marine Species, Biodiversity and Ecosystems* (Berlin: WWF Germany, 2022). If the historical trend of the past seventy years was to continue, global annual primary production would reach 1,100 MMT in 2050.

13. Linn Persson et al., 'Outside the Safe Operating Space of the Planetary Boundary for Novel Entities', *Environmental Science & Technology* 56:3 (2022), pp. 1510–21.

14. Of the 380 MMT of EP litter generated in 2017, 210 MMT were discarded and 100 MMT incinerated (Geyer, *Plastic Waste and Recycling*, 2020). See also Trevor Zink and Roland Geyer, 'Material Recycling and the Myth of Landfill Diversion', *Journal of Industrial Ecology* 23:3 (2019), pp. 541–8, Trevor Zink and Roland Geyer, 'Material Recycling and the Myth of Landfill Diversion', *Journal of Industrial Ecology* 23:3 (2019), pp. 541–8. https://doi.org/10.1111/jec.12808.

over large distances to even the most remote areas. Whether in the air, as fallout in the Polar regions, on the tops of the highest alpine ranges or in the deepest reaches of the oceans, plastic debris can be found in every part of all Earth System spheres.[15] Here, it accumulates and breaks down into ever smaller pieces under the influence of UV light and mechanical forces. Its enormous volume, ubiquitous environmental dispersion and longevity have made plastic debris a distinctive stratal component that is now considered one of the key geological markers for the Anthropocene.[16]

In comparison to incineration or landfill disposal, recycling offers a far more environmentally favourable waste management strategy, but unfortunately, turning recovered litter into secondary material is not without its challenges. Above all, it constitutes a sound strategy only when the production of primary (virgin) material is being reduced or, better even, terminated altogether. Given that the very opposite is the case, and that primary production is even increasing, recycling remains an ultimately ineffective attempt at reducing the environmental impact of plastics. Another serious drawback of recycling is that most plastics in use are composites of different polymers that cannot be separated easily. Chemical depolymerization, which is technically possible, is currently very limited. And even though new technologies to break down polymers are being developed, at this point plastic recycling mostly involves mechanical recycling of thermoplastics, where old material is heated (thermal softening or plastication) and subsequently extruded into newly desired shapes.[17] Since most of the resulting secondary material is of lesser technical and economic value and not suitable for its originally intended use, virgin polymer is added during the recycling process.[18] Even if such 'downcycling' could be turned into 'upcycling' and produce secondary material of higher quality, all plastic polymers can undergo only a limited number of recycling

---

15. Fauziah Shahul Hamid et al., 'Worldwide Distribution and Abundance of Microplastic: How Dire Is the Situation?', *Waste Management & Research* 36:10 (2018), pp. 873–97.

16. Jan Zalasiewicz et al., 'The Geological Cycle of Plastics and Their Use as a Stratigraphic Indicator of the Anthropocene', *Anthropocene* 13 (2016), pp. 4–17.

17. Zoe O. G. Schyns and Michael P. Shaver, 'Mechanical Recycling of Packaging Plastics: A Review', *Macromolecular Rapid Communications* 42 (2021), https://doi.org/10.1002/marc.202000415.

18. Schyns and Shaver, 'Mechanical Recycling of Packaging Plastics: A Review'; Geyer, 'Production, Use, and Fate of Synthetic Polymers', pp. 23–4. Chemical or microbial depolymerization of EP mixtures is a possible technological approach around this problem, but it is, at least currently, too expensive or not developed sufficiently for general use. See for example V. Tournier et al., 'An Engineered PET Depolymerase to Break Down and Recycle Plastic Bottles', *Nature* 580 (2020), pp. 216–20; Wolfgang Zimmermann, 'Biocatalytic Recycling of Polyethylene Terephthalate Plastic', *Philosophical Transactions of the Royal Society A* 378 (2020), http://dx.doi.org/10.1098/rsta.2019.0273.

rounds and will eventually have to be disposed permanently.[19] Altogether, then, it is not surprising that overall only 9 per cent of all plastic ever produced has been recycled.[20] In fact, only 2 per cent of all plastic packaging material, which comprises the greatest fraction of all newly produced plastics, is currently effectively recycled every year.[21] While none of this is reason enough to abandon recycling altogether, it nevertheless underscores the importance of a well-thought-out exit strategy regarding the global plastic economy. As of now, plastics will remain a permanent hazardous environmental pollutant for millennia to come.

The impact of environmental plastics on biodiversity

Concern about plastic pollution usually focuses on the debris build-up in the natural environment, but this emphasis underplays the complexity of the threat these materials present to ecological and human health even when still in use. Already during the production of plastics, an assortment of hazardous air pollutants (HAPs), such as carcinogenic benzene and toluene, can be released unless adequate safety measures are in place.[22] Once in use, functional plastics leach chemical additives that can, among other things, disrupt the endocrine

---

19. Reiner Pilz coined the terms 'downcycling' and 'upcycling' in 1994 in an interview with Thornton Kay for SalvoNEWS, *SalvoNEWS* 99 (1994) p. 14, https://www.salvoweb.com/files/sn99sm24y94tk181119.pdf (accessed 10 March 2022). Pilz was referring to other building materials (e.g. wood), but the terms caught on and are now used widely, including for plastic 'recycling'.

20. Zink and Geyer, 'Material Recycling and the Myth of Landfill Diversion'; Schyns and Shaver, 'Mechanical Recycling of Packaging Plastics: A Review'; Geyer et al., 'Production Plastics Ever Made'. Today, around 14 per cent of the global plastic waste is recycled.

21. Ellen MacArthur Foundation, 'The New Plastics Economy: Rethinking the Future of Plastics and Catalysing Action', https://emf.thirdlight.com/link/cap0qk3wwwk0-13727v/@/#id=1 (accessed 16 February 2022). According to the study, in 2013, 4 per cent of plastic trash that entered the recycling process was lost, while 8 per cent was downcycled in cascaded recycling; 14 per cent was incinerated, 32 per cent leaked outside collection systems and 40 per cent ended up in landfill.

22. Unfortunately, production plants quite frequently emit a wide range of chemicals that will negatively impact human health. Apart from the HAPs, these include nitrogen oxide, carbon monoxide, filterable particulate matter, large particulate matter, fine particulate matter, sulphur oxides, volatile organic compounds (VOCs), ammonia and carbon dioxide equivalents. See David Azoulay et al., *Plastic & Health: The Hidden Costs of a Plastic Planet*, Report Center for International Environmental Law, https://www.ciel.org/wp-content/uploads/2019/02/Plastic-and-Health-The-Hidden-Costs-of-a-Plastic-Planet-February-2019.pdf (accessed 10 February 2022).

system of humans, animals and even plants, thereby causing cancer, birth defects and other developmental abnormalities.[23] Even professional plastic disposal still runs the very likely risk of releasing toxic chlorinated aromatic compounds as well as greenhouse gases during incineration, one of the most common ways of discarding the material permanently.[24] Given the breadth of adverse actions plastics exert in their various forms and at all stages of their life cycle, it is best to frame plastic pollution in terms of *environmental plastics* (EPs), an umbrella category under which all synthetic or semi-synthetic organic polymers either in use or discarded can be subsumed. When it comes to EPs as a driver of extinction it is important to recognize that *all* plastic in use, no matter whether new or recycled, needs to be considered just as much as plastic in production or plastic litter.

Plastic pollution may not be the primary driver of the present biodiversity crisis, but that is no reason to underestimate its perilous potentials. Researchers estimate that at present approximately 100 species are vanishing each year for every million species, a loss that exceeds the extinction rate in the absence of human actions by 1,000 times.[25] According to the *Living Planet Report* published by the WWF in 2020, the loss of vertebrate wildlife between 1970 and 2016 averages roughly 70 per cent, and it is safe to assume that the situation is even worse for invertebrates and plants.[26] The International Union for Conservation of Nature (IUCN) Red List of Threatened Species estimates that up to 1 million species of plants and animals are

---

23. Linda G. Kahn, Claire Philippat, Shoji F. Nakayama, Rémy Slama and Leonardo Trasande, 'Endocrine-Disrupting Chemicals: Implications for Human Health', *Lancet Diabetes & Endocrinology* 8:8 (2020), pp. 703–18; Christopher W. Tubbs and Claire E. McDonough, 'Reproductive Impacts of Endocrine-Disrupting Chemicals on Wildlife Species: Implications for Conservation of Endangered Species', *Annual Review of Animal Biosciences* 6 (2018), pp. 287–304; Jennifer E. Fox, Marta Starcevic, Philip E. Jones, Matthew E. Burow and John A. McLachlan, 'Phytoestrogen Signaling and Symbiotic Gene Activation are Disrupted by Endocrine-Disrupting Chemicals', *Environmental Health Perspectives* 112:6 (2004), pp. 672–77.

24. Alan Blankenship et al., 'Toxic Combustion By-Products from the Incineration of Chlorinated Hydrocarbons and Plastics', *Chemosphere* 28:1 (1994), pp. 183–96; Thomas Astrup, Jacob Møller and Thilde Fruergaard, 'Incineration and Co-combustion of Waste: Accounting of Greenhouse Gases and Global Warming Contributions', *Waste Management & Research* 27:8 (2009), pp. 789–99.

25. Stuart L. Pimm et al., 'The Biodiversity of Species and Their Rates of Extinction, Distribution, and Protection', *Science* 344:6187 (2014), 1246752. https://www.science.org/doi/10.1126/science.1246752.

26. The exact number is 68 per cent of vertebrate wildlife populations that were lost in the given timeframe. World Wildlife Fund for Nature, 'Living Planet Report 2020. Bending the Curve of Biodiversity Loss', https://livingplanet.panda.org/en-us/ (accessed 18 December 2021). The conclusion that numbers for invertebrate and plants may be similar or worse is based on the fact that these organismic groups are even more susceptible to the main drivers of extinction, including, as it were, plastic pollution.

currently facing extinction.[27] These staggering numbers rival those of the most dramatic extinction events in earth history, which is why biologist consider them the clear marks of a beginning sixth mass extinction.[28] How much of it is caused by EP pollution is anyone's guess; pollution in general is only the third-biggest cause of extinction after land-use change and overexploitation.[29] However, evidence of EPs affecting natural populations detrimentally either on a physical, physiological, ecological or epidemiological level is mounting.

The physical impacts EPs have on wildlife populations may be the most widely known side effect of environmental plastic pollution. Everyone is familiar with images of large piles of EP trash or with the huge oceanic plastic patches, often many million square kilometres in size.[30] Flooding in low-lying areas due to EP-debris clogging natural and human-made drainage systems is by now a rather common phenomenon, perhaps too common to be generally recognized as the danger it is.[31] Floods drown significant numbers of individual plants and animals of often already vulnerable populations. They also aid the reproduction of pathogens and of disease vectors, thus putting wildlife populations and humans

27. Intergovernmental Science-Policy Platform on Biodiversity and Ecosystem Services, 'Global Assessment Report on Biodiversity and Ecosystem Services' (2019), https://ipbes. net/global-assessment (accessed 2 January 2022). For 2021, the IUCN Red List evaluated a total of 142,577 species, of which 40,084 were listed as threatened (i.e. critically endangered, endangered or vulnerable), but since less than 5 per cent of all described species have been evaluated, the actual number is expected to be much higher. See IUCN Red List, 'Summary Statistics', https://www.iucnredlist.org/resources/summary-statistics (accessed 12 March 2022). Cf., Robert H. Cowie, Philippe Bouchet and Benoit Fontaine, 'The Sixth Mass Extinction: Fact, Fiction or Speculation?' *Biological Reviews* 97 (2022), pp. 640–63.

28. Barnosky et al., 'Earth's Sixth Mass Extinction?', p. 51; Gerado Ceballos, Paul R. Ehrlich and Peter H. Raven, 'Vertebrates on the Brink as Indicators of Biological Annihilation and the Sixth Mass Extinction', *Proceedings of the National Academy of Sciences USA* 117:24 (2020), pp. 13596–602.

29. World Wildlife Fund for Nature, 'Living Planet' (2021).

30. Floral C. Mihai, 'Rural Plastic Emissions into the Largest Mountain Lake of the Eastern Carpathians', *Royal Society Open Science* 5 (2018), 72396. https://dx.doi.org/10.1098/rsos.172396; Laurent Lebreton et al., 'Evidence that the Great Pacific Garbage Patch Is Rapidly Accumulating Plastic', *Scientific Reports* 8 (2018), 4666. https://doi.org/10.1038/s41598-018-22939-w; Matts B. O. Huserbråten, Tore Hattermann, Cecilie Broms and Jon Albretsen, 'Trans-polar Drift-pathways of Riverine European Microplastic', *Scientific Reports* 12 (2022), 3016. https://doi.org/10.1038/s41598-022-07080-z.

31. In fact, EP debris has been found to cause blockages of drainage systems much faster than organic matter due to the great flexibility of the material that assures tighter obstructions. Dorien Honingh et al., 'Urban River Water Level Increase through Plastic Waste Accumulation at a Rack Structure', *Frontiers in Earth Sciences* 8 (2020), 28. https://doi.org/10.3389/feart.2020.00028.

at even greater risk.[32] Plastic trash transported by flash floods, rivers or wind often becomes a problem to animals far removed from the original dumpsite. For instance, plants and sessile animals frequently get smothered by large plastic sheets, such as bags or tarpaulins, easily carried by water or air currents for literally thousands of miles. Deprived of oxygen, sunlight or nutrients, these organisms die instantly.[33] Equally hazardous to population health is the entanglement of aquatic and terrestrial animals with lost fishing gear, string, packing, hay bale twine or other filamentous plastic materials.[34] If not drowned or asphyxiated immediately, thusly incapacitated creatures either starve over time or become afflicted with severe and long-lasting health issues that ultimately shorten their life and prevent them from reproducing. It may seem as if physical implications of EP pollution are too localized to actually become a major threat to biosphere integrity but given the enormous amount of EP trash in the natural environment, they have become a serious driver of extinction, particularly in already vulnerable populations.

This is also true for the physiological threats of EP, of which there are many. Take for example the release of toxic materials from ingested plastic objects mistaken for food by different animals. While the consumption of macroplastics (debris larger than 5 millimetres) can cause fatal physical obstructions of the digestive tract, ingested microplastic (debris smaller than 5 millimetres) or nanoplastic (debris of 1–1,000 nanometres) leaches a slew of chemical additives that cause physical harm, ranging from genotoxicity (e.g. chromosome breakage in leukocytes, oxidative damage to DNA) to reproductive and developmental effects (e.g. spontaneous aborts, infertility, developmental abnormalities) to cancer.[35] Particularly in case of aquatic animals, plasticizer leachates can

---

32. Legesse Adane and Driba Muleta, 'Survey on the Usage of Plastic Bags, Their Disposal and Adverse Impacts on Environment: A Case Study in Jimma City, Southwestern Ethiopia', *Journal of Toxicology and Environmental Health Sciences* 3:8 (2011), pp. 234–48.

33. Murray R. Gregory, 'Environmental Implications of Plastic Debris in Marine Settings – Entanglement, Ingestion, Smothering, Hangers-on, Hitch-Hiking and Alien Invasions', *Philosophical Transactions of the Royal Society B* 364 (2009), pp. 2013–25. https://doi/10.1098/rstb.2008.0265.

34. Susanne Kühn, Elisa L. Bravo Rebolledo and Jan A. van Franeker, 'Deleterious Effects of Litter on Marine Life', in Melanie Bergmann, Lars Gutow and Michael Klages (eds), *Marine Anthropogenic Litter* (Cham: Springer Open, 2015), pp. 75–116 (77); Andrea K. Townsend and Christopher M. Barker, 'Plastic and the Nest Entanglement of Urban and Agricultural Crows', *PLoS ONE* 9:1 (2014), e88006. https://doi.org/10.1371/journal.pone.0088006.

35. Tekman et al., *Impacts of Plastic Pollution*, https://wwfint.awsassets.panda.org/downloads/wwf_impacts_of_plastic_pollution_on_biodiversity.pdf (accessed 15 January 2022); Shyam Sundar and Jaya Chakravarty, 'Antimony Toxicity', *International Journal of Environmental Research and Public Health* 7 (2010), pp. 4267–77; Kellie Boyle and Banu Örmeci, 'Microplastics and Nanoplastics in the Freshwater and Terrestrial Environment: A Review', *Water* 12 (2020), 2633. https://doi.org/10.3390/w12092633.

also be taken up via the gills or skin and still cause the same set of adverse physiological effects.[36] Whether by ingestion or absorption, many leachates are known endocrine disruptors that interfere with normal hormonal functions by mimicking natural hormones or blocking their access to specific cellular receptors, thereby causing disease.[37] Since many of these toxins can pass the blood-brain barrier, they can alter behaviours, further heightening the danger of EP pollutants to biodiversity.[38]

Naturally, the adverse effects of EPs on biosphere integrity become quite complex when taking on an ecological perspective. One rather disturbing example of this may be the ingestion of EP debris just discussed. As it turns out, mistaking plastic debris for natural prey can be the result of long-evolved adaptive behavioural programmes going awry under new anthropogenically altered ecological conditions. Organisms base their behavioural and life history decisions on environmental cues, but when such visual or chemical cues are emitted by debris rather than prey, the triggered stereotypical and genetically constrained behaviour can prove entirely maladapted and deadly. Turtles mistake clear plastic bags for jellyfish; fish follow the smell of microplastic covered by the same bacteria that give natural food items their specific odour.[39] What once assured proximate survival and ultimate biological success now is the source of demise. These 'evolutionary traps' may very well cause irreparable losses for populations and

---

36. Mi Jang et al., 'Relative Importance of Aqueous Leachate versus Particle Ingestion as Uptake Routes for Microplastic Additives (hexabromocyclododecane) to Mussels', *Environmental Pollution* 270 (2021), https://doi.org/10.1016/j.envpol.2020.116272.

37. The commonly used definition of an endocrine disrupting chemical is 'an exogenous agent that interferes with the synthesis, secretion, transport, binding, action, or elimination of natural hormones in the body that are responsible for the maintenance of homeostasis, reproduction, development, and/or behavior'. Thomas M. Crisp et al., 'Environmental Endocrine Disruption: An Effects Assessment and Analysis', *Environmental Health Perspective* 106 (1 Suppl) (1998), p. 12. For uptake of endocrine disruptors from functional EPs, see Emma L. Teuten et al., 'Transport and Release of Chemicals from Plastics to the Environment and to Wildlife', *Philosophical Transactions Royal Society B* 364 (2009), pp. 2027–45; Giuseppe Latini, Alberto Verrotti and Claudio De Felice, 'DI-2-Ethylhexyl Phthalate and Endocrine Disruption: A Review', *Current Drug Targets – Immune, Endocrine & Metabolic Disorders* 4:1 (2004), pp. 37–40; Amy L. Lusher, N. A. Welden, P. Sobral and M. Cole, 'Sampling, Isolating and Identifying Microplastics Ingested by Fish and Invertebrates', *Analytical Methods* 9:9 (2017), pp. 1346–60.

38. Boyle and Örmeci, 'Microplastics and Nanoplastics', 2633.

39. Tekman et al., *Impacts of Plastic Pollution*; Matthew S. Savoca, Chris W. Tyson, Michael McGill and Christina J. Slager, 'Odours from Marine Plastic Debris Induce Food Search Behaviours in a Forage Fish', *Proceedings of the Royal Society B* 284 (2017), 20171000, https://doi.org/10.1098/rspb.2017.1000.

even entire species,[40] as does bioaccumulation of plastic additives in apex predators feeding on organisms lower in the food chain.[41] Relatively low levels of toxins in prey organisms can reach dangerous extents when consumed in great amounts, thus magnifying the adverse effects of such additives as phthalates, bisphenols or other plasticizers consumed by predators at the top of the food chain.

A frequently underestimated ecological impact of EP pollution is the spread of invasive species, a potential driver of extinction.[42] Diverse communities of organisms, including toxic microorganisms, fast-growing seaweeds and invertebrates with extremely broad phenotypic plasticity, can be transported by currents or winds across entire oceans to areas where they, then, cause great damage by outcompeting local and endemic species. Unfortunately, plastic flotsam appears more efficient than natural oceanic rafts (e.g. wood) in dispersing alien macrofauna.[43]

However, plastic flotsam or airborne debris are vectors not only for exotic species but also for bacterial pathogens, rendering EP pollutants an epidemiological risk. Polymers in the oceans might be colonized by potential pathogens, such as *Escherichia coli* or *Aeromonas salmonicida*, which survive the passage and cause disease in northern star coral (*Astrangia poculata*) or different fish species.[44]

40. For the term 'evolutionary traps', see Martin A. Schlaepfer, Michael C. Runge and Paul W. Sherman, 'Ecological and Evolutionary Traps', *Trend in Ecology & Evolution* 17:10 (2002), pp. 474–80. The extent of the impact evolutionary traps may have on biodiversity loss is a function of (i) the availability of plastics in the environment, (ii) an individual's acceptance threshold and (iii) the overlap of cues given by natural foods and plastics. See Robson G. Santos, Gabriel E. Machovsky-Capuska and Ryan Andrades, 'Plastic Ingestion as an Evolutionary Trap: Toward a Holistic Understanding', *Science* 373 (2021), pp. 56–60.

41. Juan J. Alava, 'Modeling the Bioaccumulation and Biomagnification Potential of Microplastics in a Cetacean Foodweb of the Northeastern Pacific: A Prospective Tool to Assess the Risk Exposure to Plastic Particles', *Frontiers in Marine Sciences* 7 (2020), 566101. https://doi.org//10.3389/fmars.2020.566101.

42. Jose Carlos García-Gómez, Marta Garrigós and Javier Garrigós, 'Plastic as a Vector of Dispersion for Marine Species with Invasive Potential: A Review', *Frontiers in Ecology and Evolution* 9 (2021), https://doi.org/10.3389/fevo.2021.629756; Monteserrat Vilà and Philip E. Hulme (eds), *Impact of Biological Invasions on Ecosystem Services* (Cham: Springer Nature, 2017).

43. García-Gómez, Garrigós and Garrigós, 'Plastic as a Vector of Dispersion for Marine Species with Invasive Potential: A Review'.

44. Charlotte J. Beloe, Mark A. Browne and Emma L. Johnston, 'Plastic Debris as a Vector for Bacterial Disease: An Interdisciplinary Systematic Review', *Environmental Science & Technology* 56:5 (2022), pp. 2950–8; Manca Kovac Viršek, Marija N. Lovšin, Špela Koren, Andrej Kržan and Monika Peterlin, 'Microplastics as a Vector for the Transport of the Bacterial Fish Pathogen Species *Aeromonas salmonicida*', *Marine Pollution Bulletin* 125:1–2 (2017), pp. 301–9.

The quick growth of aquaculture as a source of seafood has only increased the problem.[45]

What makes EP pollution such a serious threat to biodiversity, then, is (i) its enormous extent, (ii) the multiplicity of its effects, including physical, physiological, ecological and epidemiological threats, as well as (iii) its interplay with other drivers of extinction, especially with regard to already vulnerable or endangered populations. Our plastic-dependent lifestyles have added greatly to the dramatically accelerating anthropogenic biodiversity loss that is perhaps the most pressing ecological crisis we face today.

Direct and indirect effects of EP driven biodiversity loss on women's well-being

The effects of biodiversity loss are felt by all, no matter where in the world, but the extent of the impact depends on a variety of key factors, chief among them economic status and gender.[46] More than half of the world's poor live in rural areas where they depend disproportionally on natural resources (i.e. ecosystem services) for food, water, medicine and fuel.[47] For them, losing biological diversity and, with it, the productivity of the ecosystem bear far more significant ramifications than for the wealthy. The implications are even bigger for women and girls who make up the great majority of the poor worldwide (approximately 70 per cent).[48] Moreover, due to their specifically assigned roles within their societies, girls and

45. Jake Bowley, Craig Baker-Austin, Adam Porter, Rachel Hartnell and Ceri Lewis, 'Oceanic Hitchhikers – Assessing Pathogen Risks from Marine Microplastic', *Trends in Microbiology* 29:2 (2020), https://doi.org/10.1016/j.tim.2020.06.0111; Dandi Hou et al., 'Assessing the Risks of Potential Bacterial Pathogens Attaching to Different Microplastics during the Summer–Autumn Period in a Mariculture Cage', *Microorganisms* 9 (2021), 1909. https://doi.org/10.3390/microorganisms9091909.

46. Jamie D. Bechtel, *Gender, Poverty and the Conservation of Biodiversity: A Review of Issues and Opportunities* (Chicago: MacArthur Foundation Conservation White Paper Series, 2010), p. 2, https://www.macfound.org/media/files/csd_gender_white_paper.pdf. *This is a white paper, and as such stands for itself.*

47. Bechtel, *Gender, Poverty and the Conservation of Biodiversity: A Review of Issues and Opportunities*, p. 4.

48. Bechtel, *Gender, Poverty and the Conservation of Biodiversity: A Review of Issues and Opportunities*, p. 5. The exact fraction of women among the world's poor is disputed, though. In a recent study, Doss and colleagues conclude that a 'larger proportion of female-headed households than male-headed households have incomes (or consumption expenditures) below the poverty line'. Cheryl Doss, Ruth Meinzen-Dick, Agnes Quisumbing and Sophie Theis, 'Women in Agriculture: Four Myths', *Global Food Security* 16 (2018), pp. 69–74, https://doi.org/10.1016/j.gfs.2017.10.001. However, since the figure is still frequently used also in governmental outlets, I will use it here, though with caution.

women in poor rural areas use natural goods quite differently from boys and men, which further exacerbates the problem. That in these societies women usually are not granted the same legal, social or political standing only makes matters worse.[49] Under many regimes, women are not entitled to land ownership, even though they are the ones responsible for working the land and assuring its productivity.[50] It is an indisputable fact that today the catastrophic anthropogenic loss of biological diversity is a particularly serious threat for girls and women, especially in disadvantaged communities.

While the challenges are manifold, including such fundamental problems as food and health security, perhaps the central problem that the loss of natural resources presents to girls and women is that it limits their access to education and other forms of empowerment. Gender-specific roles can differ between cultures. Yet, in most communities of the developing world, women are still responsible for resource management, including collecting firewood and water, as well as 60–80 per cent of the food production (agriculture, fishing, forestry) and animal husbandry.[51] All these tasks are becoming more difficult as the declining biodiversity is causing ecosystem health to worsen and, in turn, ecosystem services to diminish.[52] As resources are dwindling, women and young girls must travel

49. Bechtel, *Gender, Poverty and the Conservation of Biodiversity: A Review of Issues and Opportunities*, p. 7.

50. Rekha Mehra, *Women, Land, and Sustainable Development* (Washington: International Center for Research on Women Working Paper No. 1, 1995), p. 6. Exact numbers of what proportion of land globally is owned by women are not yet unavailable, but estimates range from as little as 2 per cent (Women's Environment & Development Organization, 'Biodiversity', https://wedo.org/what-we-do/our-focus-areas/biodiversity/, accessed 22 March 2022) to as high as 20 per cent (United Nations Human Rights Special Procedures, https://www.ohchr.org/sites/default/files/Documents/Issues/Women/WG/Womenslandright.pdf, accessed 22 March 2022). Either way, the gender disparity is quite extensive.

51. USAID, 'Fact Sheet: Food Security and Gender', https://www.oecd.org/dac/gender-development/46460857.pdf (accessed 12 March 2022). This figure, like the 70 per cent fraction of women among the poor, is also contested by Doss and colleagues. Doss et al., 'Women in Agriculture', p. 70.

52. Dilys Roe, Nathalie Seddon and Joanna Elliott, *Biodiversity Loss Is a Development Issue: A Rapid Review of Evidence*, Issue Paper (London: International Institute for Environment and Development, 2019), http://pubs.iied.org/17636IIED, accessed 12 March 2022; P. V. Satheesh, 'Issues Concerning Gender and Biodiversity', unpublished manuscript, https://www.iied.org/sites/default/files/pdfs/migrate/17636IIED.pdf (accessed 21 December 2021). For the correlation of biodiversity and ecosystem health and productivity, see Anthony D. Barnosky et al., 'Introducing the Scientific Consensus on Maintaining Humanity's Life Support Systems in the 21st Century: Information for Policy Makers', *The Anthropocene Review* 1:1 (2014), pp. 78–109 as well as David Tilman, Forest Isbell and Jane M. Cowles, 'Biodiversity and Ecosystem Functioning', *Annual Review of Ecology, Evolution, and Systematics* 45 (2014), pp. 471–93. https://doi.org/10.1146/1nnurey-ecolsys-120213-091917.

farther for clean water and firewood, spend more time on finding fodder for the animals, work the fields longer to assure a sufficient yield or fish for extended periods at more distant sites. For young girls, this usually means that they cannot attend school regularly.[53] Without a substantial education, they are bound to remain trapped in a poor economic situation that only gets worse as the ecological conditions keep deteriorating. Adult women must work even harder to support their families and communities and, on top of it, are more exposed to violence and sexual harassment.[54] What is more, their specific roles have made women well-versed resource managers with a keen understanding of systemic interconnections of biological diversity on various levels. This vital technical and traditional know-how has made women the foremost custodians of biodiversity. Syphoning away extra time from this critical function into such mundane activities as extended water or wood collecting due to resource depletion translates directly into missed opportunities for restoring biological diversity where it counts.[55] It is no exaggeration to think of the widening social and gender gap as one of the most pressing social corollaries of the synergism of anthropogenic EP pollution and biodiversity loss. As Kariuki Muigua observes, 'gender is now considered to be a key consideration for equitable and effective biodiversity conservation practice since ethically, ensuring gender-equitable participation is a cornerstone for respecting, protecting, and promoting human rights and for not disadvantaging anyone in the process of conserving biodiversity'.[56]

Apart from these social implications of EP pollution and anthropogenic extinction, there are medical ones that also affect women and girls more severely than men and boys. Partially, this is due to simple biology, particularly sex-specific physiological differences in the endocrine control of organ systems. But in part, the problem has the same social origin discussed above, namely a gender division that benefits males and disadvantages females. As mentioned before, a prominent consequence of declining biosphere integrity is the lack of crop quality. The great sensitivity of ecosystem health to decreasing grassland plant diversity has long been established.[57] The same relationship is observable in the oceans, where

53. Women's Environment & Development Organization, 'Biodiversity'. See also Dinesh Kumar Maurya, 'Education and Biodiversity: An Overview', *Iconic Research and Engineering Journals* 4:6 (2020), pp. 13–6. https://www.irejournals.com/formatedpaper/1702542.pdf (accessed 21 March 2022).

54. Women's Environment & Development Organization, 'Biodiversity'.

55. R. Mishra, 'Conservation of Agro-biodiversity by Women', in M. Kumar and S. K. Verma (eds), *Environmental Ethics and Law* (New Delhi: VL Media Solutions, 2020), pp. 44–50.

56. Kariuki Muigua, 'Gender Perspectives in Biodiversity Conservation', *Journal of Conflict Management & Sustainable Development* 7:4 (2021), p. 81.

57. Tilman et al., 'Biodiversity and Ecosystem Functioning', p. 473. Interestingly, studies that involve diversity restoration demonstrate quite convincingly that this process is reversible by reintroducing lost species. For instance, Tilman and colleagues were

In Solidarity with the Earth

commercial overexploitation of marine vertebrates and invertebrates has lowered ocean productivity on a regional scale.[58] With the loss of system productivity, food production declines so that there is not enough premium quality food to go around. What is available goes to a selected few, which in many poor agrarian societies are the men and male children.[59] Women and girls are expected to be content with leftovers, even though they produce, cook and serve the food. As P. V. Satheesh points out, self-denial among women is a valued cultural trait.[60] The health implications especially for young girls, but also for adult women involved in daily strenuous agricultural labour, are obvious. Malnutrition constitutes a rather dangerous condition that when occurring in childhood can lead to growth-related permanent health problems (e.g. stunting, wasting, chronic energy deficiency).[61] Of course, the food shortages that are linked to anthropogenic biodiversity loss also affect men, but culturally maintained gender differences heighten the health risk for women and girls dramatically.

In case of EP toxicity, greater adverse health implications for women are primarily rooted in physiological differences between men and women, although

able to reach the same productivity (biomass) as would the addition of 54 kilograms of fertilizer per hectare per year by merely changing the number of grass species on the plot from four to sixteen. David Tilman, Peter B. Reich and Forest Isbell, 'Biodiversity Impacts Ecosystem Productivity as Much as Resources, Disturbance, or Herbivory', *Proceedings of the National Academy of Sciences USA* 109:26 (2012), pp. 10394–7. https://doi.org/10.1073/pnas.1208240109.

58. Thomas Luypaert, James G. Hagan, Morgan L. McCarthy and Meenaskhi Poti, 'Status of Marine Biodiversity in the Anthropocene', in Simon Jungblut, Viola Liebich and Maya Bode-Dalby (eds), *YOUMARES 9 – The Oceans: Our Research, Our Future* (Cham: Springer Open, 2020), pp. 57–82 (60).

59. Suniti Neogy, 'Gender Inequality, Mothers' Health, and Unequal Distribution of Food: Experience from a CARE Project in India', *Gender and Development* 18:3 (2010), pp. 479–89; Subarna Ghosh, Liton C. Sen, Sujan K. Mali, Md. Muzahidul Islam and Jhantu Bakchi, 'The Role of Rural Women in Household Food Security and Nutrition Management in Bangladesh', *Asian Journal of Women's Studies* 27:3 (2021), pp. 441–59 (445).

60. Satheesh, 'Issues Concerning Gender and Biodiversity', p. 4.

61. Gautam K. Kshatriya and Subhendu K. Acharya, 'Gender Disparities in the Prevalence of Undernutrition and the Higher Risk among the Young Women of Indian Tribes', *Public Library of Science ONE* 11:7 (2016), e0158308. https://doi.org/10.1371/journal.pone.0158308. In an explanation of the observed undernutrition, the authors observe: 'It would be worth mentioning here that male members of the studied tribes were observed to have easy access to nutritional and diet facilities as compared to the female members because males receive early and extensive social freedom to access income generating activities. Young women, on the other hand in the tribal societies are mostly confined to the domestic and household work by keeping away from most of the income generating activities which broadly limit their buying capacity and independent access to food by broadly affecting their nutrition', pp. 18 and 22.

exposure risks are further heightened by underlying social rules. In many rural communities of the developing world, women bear the responsibility for waste management, including disposing of plastic trash by incineration.[62] Without the necessary safety precautions in place, these women are exposed to the toxic fumes that contain dioxins, furans and persistent organic compounds (POPs), all linked to severe health issues, including cancer.[63] But even without these cultural gender biases, women are at a significantly greater risk of suffering the toxic effects of compounds leaching from EPs, and the reason is simply biology. This is the case with those plasticizers and other additives that have been shown to disrupt normal endocrine functions. Particularly prepubescent and pubescent girls have suffered the varied consequences of endocrine disruption, such as an early onset of puberty that might be associated with a variety of reproductive problems and an increased risk for developing breast and other hormonally driven cancers during the lifetime.[64] Other known problems of endocrine disruption in girls and women include birth defects, reduced fertility, impaired immune functions, endometriosis, polycystic ovary syndrome, heart disease, neurological problems, behavioural changes and obesity.[65] Environmental plastics in baby bottles, water bottles, personal care

62. Patrick A. Bowan, Lee F. Anzagira and Che A. Anzagira, 'Solid Waste Disposal in Ghana: A Study of the Wa Municipality', *Journal of Environment and Earth Science* 4:4 (2014), pp. 10–16; Joshua O. Babayemi and K. T. Dauda, 'Evaluation of Solid Waste Generation, Categories and Disposal Options in Developing Countries: A Case Study of Nigeria', *Journal of Applied Sciences and Environmental Management* 13:3 (2009), pp. 83–8. https://doi.org/10.4314/jasem.v13i3.55370.

63. Helen Lynn, Sabine Rech and Margriet Samwel-Mantingh, *Plastic, Gender and the Environment: Findings of a Literature Study on the Lifecycle of Plastics and Its Impacts on Women and Men, from Production to Litter* (Utrecht, Annemasse Cedex, Munich: Women Engage for a Common Future, 2017), pp. 41–2.

64. Rosa Lauretta, Andrea Sansone, Massimiliano Sansone, Francesco Romanelli and Marialuisa Appetecchia, 'Endocrine Disrupting Chemicals: Effects on Endocrine Glands', *Frontiers in Endocrinology* 10 (2019), 178. https://doi.org/10.3389/fendo.2019.00178; L. Lucaccioni, V. Trevisani, L. Marrozzini, N. Bertoncelli, B. Predieri, L. Lugli, A. Berardi and L. Iughetti, 'Endocrine-Disrupting Chemicals and Their Effects during Female Puberty: A Review of Current Evidence', *International Journal of Molecular Sciences* 21 (2020), 2078. https://doi.org/10.3390/ijms21062078.

65. Lucaccioni et al., 'Endocrine-Disrupting Chemicals' (2020); World Health Organization and United Nations Environment Programme, 'State of the Science of Endocrine Disrupting Chemicals – 2012', WHO, https://www.who.int/ceh/publications/endocrine/en/ (accessed 2 February 2021); Jabou Jagne, Dominque White and Felicia Jefferson, 'Endocrine-Disrupting Chemicals: Adverse Effects of Bisphenol A and Parabens to Women's Health', *Water Air Soil Pollution* 227:6 (2016), 182. https://doi.org/10.1007/s11270-016-2785-3; Linda G. Kahn, Claire Philippat, Shoji F. Nakayama, Rémy Slama and Leonardo Trasande, 'Endocrine-Disrupting Chemicals: Implications for Human Health',

products, tin can linings or wrapping film all have been identified as sources of endocrine-disrupting substances (e.g. bisphenol A, nonylphenol, and phthalates), which accumulate in the adipose tissue and over time exert their disruptive actions on the endocrine system.[66] In their chapter in this volume, Felicia Jefferson and Sierra Cloud are addressing the issue of plastic-mediate endocrine disruption in great detail, which is why I will refrain from discussing it here any further. Let it suffice to say that when it comes to endocrine disruption, women certainly are at a greater risk than men.

Radical ecological conversion in light of the suffering of creation: Human and non-human, female and male

What, then, is theology to make of this complex relationship of environmental plastic pollution, anthropogenic biodiversity loss, and the disproportionate suffering of young girls and women? Perhaps, and here I am trying neither to be obvious nor simplistic, it is important to first acknowledge both the extent and the complexity of what is the socio-ecological crisis. Seemingly unrelated consequences of human actions appear upon closer analysis to be intricately and causally linked in a complicated and self-enforcing feedback system. Today's ecological *kairos* is not a climate change problem. It is not the fallout of a commencing anthropogenic sixth mass extinction or the product of the deadly eutrophication of rivers and oceans due to our overuse of industrialized fertilizers. Neither overpopulation nor

Lancet 8 (2020), pp. 703–18. https://doi.org/10.1016/S2213-8587(20)30129-7. In many countries, bisphenol A has been banned from food-packaging plastic products, including baby bottles, but the very common and as of yet unregulated substitutes, bisphenol S and F are as hormonally active as bisphenol A with very similar endocrine-disrupting effects. Joanna R. Rochester and Ashley L. Bolden, 'Bisphenol S and F: A Systematic Review and Comparison of the Hormonal Activity of Bisphenol a Substitutes', *Environmental Health Perspectives* 123 (2015), pp. 643–50. https://doi.org/10.1289/eph.1408989.

66. Maricel V. Maffini, Beverly S. Rubin, Carlos Sonnenschein and Ana Soto, 'Endocrine Disruptors and Reproductive Health: The Case of Bisphenol-A', *Molecular and Cellular Endocrinology* 254–5 (2006), pp. 179–86; Jane Muncke, 'Exposure to Endocrine Disrupting Compounds via the Food Chain: Is Packaging a Relevant Source?', *Science of the Total Environment* 407 (2009), pp. 4549–59; Jane Muncke, 'Endocrine Disrupting Chemicals and Other Substances of Concern in Food Contact Materials: An Updated Review of Exposure, Effect and Risk Assessment', *Journal of Steroid Biochemistry & Molecular Biology* 127 (2011), pp. 118–27; Daniel Salazar-Beltrán, Laura Hinojosa-Reyes, Edgar Ruiz-Ruiz, Aracely Hernández-Ramírez and Jorge Luis Guzmán-Mar, 'Phthalates in Beverages and Plastic Bottles: Sample Preparation and Determination', *Food Analytical Methods* 11:1 (2018), pp. 48–61; Herald J. Geyer et al., 'Bioaccumulation and Occurrence of Endocrine-Disrupting Chemicals (EDCs), Persistent Organic Pollutants (POPs), and Other Organic Compounds in Fish and Other Organisms Including Humans', in B. Beek (ed.), *Bioaccumulation: New Aspects and Developments* (Heidelberg: Springer Verlag, 2000), pp. 30–59.

the excessive overconsumption of resources by the wealthy few is what defines the crisis at our hand. The inequitable distribution of wealth has resulted in massive poverty worldwide, but that too is not the mainspring of all calamities. It is all these things – and more – each exerting its specific influence in synergy with the other, thus intensifying the overall disaster and speeding up its progression so that increasingly little time is left to prevent the Earth System from reaching dangerous tipping points. What is more, our everyday actions matter, for they contribute and boost each of these individual factors driving the socio-ecological crisis. Using plastic products, often not even a matter of choice anymore, but a forced inevitability, drives the loss of biological diversity as well as the galloping poverty in underdeveloped countries and, especially, the poverty of women. Our actions have consequences, but unlike in previous centuries and millennia, in today's globalized world, the consequences are extremely far-reaching. Connecting biodiversity loss to plastic pollution and women's well-being everywhere makes this quite clear.

I believe that it also elucidates the extent of the problem we face and which, despite increased news coverage and the activism of students everywhere, has still not been fully realized by the majority of those responsible for the situation. The current ecological crisis is the most dangerous threat to human survival in the history of our species. Even the two world wars of the twentieth century did not match its catastrophic potential, which says a lot. We are not merely losing a few more species we could have saved; we are jeopardizing the integrity of the entire biosphere thereby risking the very survival of the planet. Drowning in heaps of plastic trash is no longer just the fate of festering megacities in developing countries alone; it is the reality of the entire planet. All this is unfolding increasingly fast so that our window of opportunity is shrinking literally with every moment we fail to act. We will not be able to reverse the process; extinct biodiversity is lost for ever and not even the most ingenious technology will be able to remove all plastic debris from the environment. At best, we can hope to curb the development and slowly restore at least some of the ecological parameters that have defined the Holocene, thereby dampening future suffering, human and non-human, female or male.[67]

Realizing the immensity of the issue can be so overwhelming that one ends up paralyzed before the challenge, incapable of deciding what to change first, and ultimately changing little or nothing. That we live in a world where living unsustainably is made much easier than living sustainably does not make the situation any better. Still, we may take solace in the fact that even the smallest step taken can make a difference. A cliché, no doubt, but if the socio-ecological interconnections I have been talking about here show us anything, it is that

---

67. The Holocene was the relatively benign geological epoch that followed the last ice ages and had made it possible for humanity to flourish. Whether we have left it already and transitioned into the Anthropocene, a new geological era characterized by the immense and severe impact of human activity, is somewhat disputed, but the consensus on the matter is growing.

individual acts do actually matter. And just as individual deeds can have adverse ramifications reaching around the world, so can other personal efforts help alleviate the problem.

Be that as it may, accepting the interconnectedness of which I speak here is of course the necessary condition for the possibility of transitioning into an integral world view, to which Pope Francis' encyclical *Laudato Si'* calls 'every person living on this planet'.[68] Insisting on a fractured view of reality means to remain stuck in the *technocratic paradigm*, which for the Pope is the root cause of the trouble in which we find ourselves. This, I would argue, is precisely why it is helpful to think of the current crisis as an ecological *kairos*. As mentioned above, what for the Christian defines secondary *kairoi* is that they mark the boundary between the 'already' and 'not yet' of the Kingdom of God. They can be moments in which the Church is to recognize and embrace a heretofore ignored positive development – for the young Tillich, this was the European Christian socialist movement of the 1920s. However, they can also be moments of deep crisis, which must be seen for what they are – threats to the coming of the Kingdom that require the prophetic spirit to be roused in the Church. The socio-ecological crisis of our days is such a critical moment in time when the meaning of our existence, of our relationship to God, and the possibility of our faith are at stake. When Pope Francis calls for a paradigm change from technocracy towards integrality, he does speak prophetically, fully recognizing the *kairos* character of our times.

Where the technocratic paradigm sees humanity as autonomous, powerful, free to make use of all that it can explain and dominate, the integral view proposed by the Pope as the antidote to the crisis focuses on interconnectedness. Here, human beings, just like all other creatures, are seen as part of a greater whole, which itself is an intricate network of interactive, contingent parts. Science can hint at this ontological association, but it cannot capture it exhaustively. It can find echoes of interconnectedness in the balanced flows of energy and materials between the different spheres of the Earth System or in the cosmological account of an evolving universe that originated in an infinitesimally small point containing all the energy and space-time, the initial singularity Georges Lemaître called so astutely the 'cosmic egg'.[69] However, for Pope Francis, this connection goes much deeper and far beyond scientific models. This universe is creation. All that we know, ourselves included, shares that one origin, the divine act that brought forth

68. Pope Francis, *Laudato Si': On Care for Our Common Home* (Rome: Libreria Editrice Vaticana, 2015).

69. Lemaître first described the origin of the universe as 'a Cosmic Egg exploding at the moment of creation' in 1933 at a conference at the Mount Wilson observatory in California, which was attended also by Albert Einstein, who according to the local newspapers applauded Lemaître's presentation, stating that it had been 'the most beautiful and satisfactory explanation of creation to which I [Einstein] have ever listened'. See G. Haitel, *Origins and Grand Finale: How the Bible and Science Relate to the Origin of Everything, Abuses of Political Authority, and End Time Predictions* (Bloomington: iUniverse, 2014), p. 9. (It has

creation out of nothing (*creatio ex nihilo*) and has maintained it in being (*creatio continua*). It is here that the ultimate root for integrality lies. Human beings belong to this creation, to the web of life on earth, as fellow creatures to all other creatures and, like them, divinely endowed with intrinsic value that cannot be quantified. From this and from the fact that we wield exceptional powers that enable us to damage our common home irreversibly, it follows that we have an exceptional responsibility. This is what sets the theological notion of creation apart from scientific ideas like Big Bang cosmology or biological evolution; it subsumes these scientific insights and adds to them a normative quality that is drawn from an integral perspective on ultimate reality. Our destructive treatment of creation opposes this integrality and, with it, the Christian idea of our contingent relationship to God as well as to all other creatures. Instead of relating to other life in creaturely fellowship, we have made them steppingstones, means to our desired ends, and thereby suspended the possibility of realizing the divine kingdom. In this sense, then, we are committing an 'ecological' sin by holding on to our selfish technocratic views. It is this insistence on our perceived personal rights, which are merely the fallout of an overextended luxurious lifestyle, that puts the coming of the Kingdom at risks and demands us to change radically. It demands an ecological conversion, that is, a conversion that embraces our shared ontological nature as fellow creatures.

John Paul II coined the term 'ecological conversion' and in doing so hinted at the kind of change the ecological *kairos* demands of us.[70] In *Laudato Si'*, Pope Francis adopts the notion as the key step in the transition from the technocratic paradigm as the root cause of the problem into an integral framework as its only feasible remedy. One must appreciate the scope of such an undertaking. While it involves a change in behaviour, ecological conversion is more than just a collective behaviour change. It requires a change in heart and soul, an essential *volte-face* that reaches to the very roots of our individual selves and of our social, political and cultural institutions. What is needed, then, is a *radical* conversion that constitutes a *fundamental reorientation of our existential concern away from selfish egocentrism towards a caring relationship with all of creation, and thus, with God.*

been said that Einstein was in fact referring to Lemaître's idea that cosmic rays had been generated in the primordial fireworks of the early universe. The theory turned out wrong but anticipated the prediction of the entire universe being suffused by a cosmic background radiation composed of ancient photons released by the Big Bang put forth by Ralph Alpher, George Gamow and Hans Bethe. See Ralph A. Alpher, Hans Bethe and George Gamow, 'The Origin of Chemical Elements', *Physical Review* 73:7 (1948), pp. 803–4). In his scientific publications, Lemaître referred to the beginnings of the universe a little less poetically as the 'primeval atom'. See George Lemaître, 'L'hypothèse de l'atome primitif', *Revue des Questions scientifiques* 1948, pp. 321–39.

70. John Paul II, 'General Audience, Wednesday 17 January 2001', *Vatican Website*, https://www.vatican.va/content/john-paul-ii/en/audiences/2001/documents/hf_jp-ii_aud_20010117.html.

When he introduced the notion of ecological conversion in a general audience at the turn of the century, John Paul II was talking merely about a gradually growing phenomenon in parts of the global society that he deemed worthy of emulating. And yet, he apparently identified in it a changed perspective that was of another quality than mere activism for the environment. Using the term 'conversion', he acknowledged a certain spiritual dimension that theology knows as *metanoia*, a transformative change of heart in and through spiritual reorientation back towards God.[71] For him, there was more than just 'physical' ecology at risk. Our reckless actions threaten 'a "human" ecology which makes the existence of creatures more dignified, by protecting the fundamental good of life in all its manifestations and by preparing for future generations an environment more in conformity with the Creator's plan'.[72] In a sense, then, ecological conversion is less the passage into something new, as would be the conversion to another faith, than repentance and the return to our true, God-intended being.[73]

And yet John Paul II did not further flesh out what this ecological *metanoia* would have to look like. Nor, for that matter, did Pope Francis, who mentions this most central demand almost as briefly as his predecessor.[74] Neither leaves any doubt that the deeply spiritual transformation radical ecological conversion demands cannot be divorced from its religious dimension, but when it comes to making concrete suggestions on how to proceed, *Laudato Si'* remains rather pragmatic and lays out the blueprint for a global transdisciplinary conversation on the matter.[75] However, such a dialogue is only possible when its participants have already become aware of the necessity for change, which suggests that at least to some degree, they have undergone a change of heart. The ultimate problem, though, is *how* one may achieve this, which is why chapter six of the encyclical focuses on what lies at the very heart of Christian life – human development towards integrality.[76]

'Many things have to change course', Francis writes, 'but *it is we human beings above all who need to change*'.[77] Only when we assume a habit of deep concern for each other and the world around us can we hope to avert the looming catastrophe. As far as Pope Francis is concerned, that would require at the very least raising awareness of 'our common origin, our mutual belonging, and of a future to be

71. R. Schnackenburg, 'Metanoia', in Josef Höfer and Karl Rahner (eds), *Lexikon für Theologie und Kirche*, Volume 7 (Freiburg i.B.: Verlag Herder, 1962), pp. 356–9; Karl Rahner, 'Conversion', in Karl Rahner (ed.), *Encyclopedia of Theology: The Concise Sacramentum Mundi* (New York: Crossroad, 1975), pp. 291–5.

72. John Paul II, 'General Audience, 17 January 2001', p. 4.

73. Etymologically, conversion originates from the Latin *convertere*, viz. turn back. Thus, the German translation of ecological conversion as *ökologische Umkehr*, i.e. ecological turning back, is indeed quite adequate. In its Spanish original, *Laudato Si'* refers to *conversión ecológica*. Pope Francis, *Laudato Si'*, §216.

74. Pope Francis, *Laudato Si'*, §216–21.

75. Pope Francis, *Laudato Si'*, §163–201.

76. Not surprisingly, the chapter is headlined 'Ecological Education and Spirituality'.

77. Pope Francis, *Laudato Si'*, §202, my emphasis.

shared with everyone'.[78] In other words, we face a cultural as well as a spiritual challenge, and the needed 'renewal' requires the education of the whole person – an 'ecological catechesis', as it were.[79] The world is in trouble largely because we have lost our spiritual anchor, and so it is by means of ecological and spiritual education that we can once again understand ourselves more adequately, leave the technocratic paradigm behind and move forward into the holistic framework of integral ecology.[80] A massive undertaking, no less.

Massive indeed, but not really a matter of choice. To Christians, undergoing this total existential reorientation is tantamount to a life of virtue.[81] It is a common and universal duty, not the least because protecting the Earth System is an act of respecting a common good.[82] Moreover, it is a necessary aspect of creaturely fellowship and, as such, part of what God intended for us to do. In the end, however, ecological conversion is merely one aspect of the constant reconciliation with God, neighbour, and creation to which Christians are already called.[83] And since humans are social beings, radical ecological conversion has both a personal and a communal dimension.

So far, so good, but what of women and girls? Are we to say that men and boys are in more need of ecological *metanoia* than they are? I believe, that would be an oversimplification of the actual problem, for which, at least in the wealthy industrial world, women and men share responsibility equally. What makes it important for Christians to reflect on the position of women and young girls is that in doing so we opt for the poor, just as *Laudato Si'* reminds us to do. Curiously, though, women as the primary bearer of the burden of the ecological crisis are virtually absent from *Laudato Si'*, which at best suggests that the Church itself has a long way to go, at worst revealing a continuous blind spot on the part of the hierarchy. Either way, what this oversight of women's suffering as a central social

---

78. Pope Francis, *Laudato Si'*, §202, my emphasis.

79. For more on the concept of ecological conversion, see Timothy Howles, John Reader and Martin John Hodson, '"Creating an Ecological Citizenship": Philosophical and Theological Perspectives on the Role of Contemporary Environmental Education', *Heythrop Journal* 59:6 (2018), pp. 997–1008.

80. 'The External Deserts in the World Are Growing, Because the Internal Deserts Have Become So Vast', Pope Francis, *Laudato Si'*, §217.

81. Pope Francis, *Laudato Si'*, §217. See also Celia Deane-Drummond, 'Biodiversity and Ecological Responsibility: Wonder, Value and Paying Attention to All Creatures', *Antonanium* XCVI (2021), pp. 87–113.

82. Pontifical Council for Justice and Peace, *Compendium of the Social Doctrine of the Church*, Part II, Chapter 10, iv (London: Bloomsbury, 2004), p. 235.

83. The Pope refers to his namesake Saint Francis of Assisi when he concludes that 'a healthy relationship with creation is one dimension of overall personal conversion, which entails the recognition of our errors, sins, faults and failures, and leads to heartfelt repentance and desire to change'. Pope Francis, *Laudato Si'*, §218. In a sense, then, the position of the encyclical is not new but places a heretofore less-stressed emphasis on reconciliation with *all of creation* and not only with our neighbour and God.

implication of the ecological crisis indubitably reveals is that the Church as an institution is in deep need of an ecological *metanoia*. The cry of the poor is first and foremost – at least to about 70 per cent – the cry of women and girls, and it is time the Church heeds it.

If the ecological *kairos* demands of us an existential choice, an ecological *metanoia* or radical ecological conversion, it requires the community of the faithful to negotiate in an open and participatory fashion the meaning of human existence, confer our species' position in the world, and finally the possibility of our faith in light of the 'signs of the time'. Herein lies the power of the *kairos* moment, namely that it goes much beyond any attractive incentives motivating behaviour changes and deeper than any intellectual considerations of scientific data informing our choices. Opting for sustainable development, for protecting the diversity of life, for the poor, women and girls in particular, and for changing one's use of plastic is to the Christian not simply a discussion of environmentally and socially sound actions; it is the deliberate and existential negotiation of the meaning and possibility of the Christian faith. The socio-ecological crisis constitutes an opportune moment to act so that the 'kingdom of God manifests itself in a particular breakthrough' of the prophetic Spirit.[84] Thus is the ecological *kairos*.

In Conclusion

The overall aim of this chapter was threefold. First, it set out to argue that the anthropogenic socio-ecological crisis of our time constitutes a *kairos* moment that necessitates radical ecological conversion. Second, it sought to link three pressing challenges of today's socio-ecological crisis – anthropogenic biodiversity loss, EP pollution and its severe consequences for human and ecological health, and the special vulnerability of women and young girls in this crisis – to underscore the complexity of the situation, thereby strengthening the claim that humanity has indeed arrived at an existential crossroads where, from a Christian perspective, a decisive choice is inevitable. Third, it meant to lay out theologically, at least to a certain degree, what such an ecological *metanoia* would entail. Could this argument have been made looking at either biodiversity loss or EP pollution alone or, for that matter, any other aspect of the ecological crisis with its social ramifications? Absolutely. However, what I hope makes identifying the relationship between plastic use, the loss of life and women's suffering helpful is that it drives home how we do live in an interconnected world and that our actions, may they be as simple as using plastic products, have far reaching implications. In the end, we can no longer claim ignorance or justify our indecisiveness with simple economic concerns. As Christians, we must face the challenge our species has created, and which is by far the most dangerous crisis this planet has ever seen, asking ourselves honestly to what we believe ourselves called and what it means to be a creature in full fellowship with the rest of creation and God.

84. Paul Tillich, *Systematic Theology, Vol. 3* (Chicago: The University of Chicago Press, 1963), p. 370.

A PRACTITIONER'S RESPONSE TO
FELICIA JEFFERSON AND OLIVER PUTZ

H. Kailean Khongsai

The chapters by Oliver Putz and Felicia Jefferson examined the impact of environmental plastic wastes. Plastic is becoming a serious transboundary threat to the natural environment and human health, with researchers predicting an increase in plastic waste unless adequate steps are taken to turn our consumptive habits around. Putz is arguing that we live in the 'ecological *kairos*' that demands of us an existential decision on how to respond to the ecological crisis. In this chapter, I will respond to Putz' chapter with occasional reference to Jefferson's contribution. My response is based on my professional experience with waste management in Southeast Asia and its effects on informal workers, especially women and girls.

Increase and impact of plastic waste production

It is evident that plastics bring many societal benefits. Plastics are inexpensive, lightweight, strong, durable, corrosion-resistant materials, with high thermal and electrical insulation properties. The diversity of polymers and the versatility of their properties are used to make a vast array of products that bring medical and technological advances, energy savings and numerous other societal benefits. Plastics further have a range of unique properties. They can be used at a very wide range of temperatures, are chemical- and light-resistant, and are very strong and tough but can be easily worked as a hot melt. It is this range of properties together with their low cost that has driven the current annual worldwide demand for plastics to reach 245 million tonnes.

With the exponential increase of plastics, plastic waste production is soaring to new heights as well and much of it is ending up in the natural environment where it poses a severe risk to biosphere integrity and human health. Concerns about usage and disposal are diverse, however, and include accumulation of waste in landfills and in natural habitats, creating physical problems for wildlife from ingestion or entanglement in plastic. Other negative effects of plastic waste are due to chemicals leached into the environment.[1]

Putz's chapter is particularly informative in detailing the technical and technological challenges that come with recycling plastic waste. Whereas chemical and biological degradation are possible in principle, the lack in technological know-how, high costs and low efficiency prevent either from being part of our current disposal strategies. Chemical depolymerization, which is technically possible, is currently very limited too. And while new technologies to break down polymers are being developed, at this point plastic recycling mostly involves mechanical recycling of thermoplastics, where old material is heated (thermal softening or plastication) and subsequently extruded into newly desired shapes.

Despite the technological difficulties, Putz does prefer recycling over landfill and incineration as a more environmentally sound form of plastic waste management. Recycling does remain expensive and rather inefficient, however. The presence of additives and impurities also complicates the recycling procedure and decreases both the yield and quality of the recovered product. It is not clear to me therefore that a landfill or incineration facility, if properly managed, is always the less-preferable solutions.

The impact of plastic waste on women's health:
A perspective from South Asia

Both Putz and Jefferson detail the devastating effects that endocrine-disrupting chemicals (EDCs) has on human health, particularly the health of minoritized women of color.[2] The issues mentioned are transnational: they manifest themselves especially in poor communities in both the minority and majority world. Drawing from my experience as a person from Southeast Asia (India), I am acutely aware that most developing/underdeveloped countries struggle with population growth, growing waste, limited infrastructure and a heavy reliance on the informal sector for collection of waste. In Asia, informal workers contribute to over 95 per cent of some types of plastic recovered for recycling, with women making up the majority of the informal workforce in certain regions.[3]

1. L. N. Vandenberg, R. Hauser, M. Marvus, N. Olea and W. V. Welshons, 'Human Exposure to Bisphenol A (BPA)', *Reprod. Toxicol* 24:2 (August–September 2007), pp. 139–77. https://www.sciencedirect.com/science/article/abs/pii/S0890623807002377 (accessed 2 September 2022).

2. Oxfam International: 'Why the Majority of the World's Poor Are Women' (2022). https://www.oxfam.org/en/what-we-do/issues/gender-justice-and-womens-rights (accessed 12 September 2022).

3. Statesman News Service, 'Forgotten Women's Uplift', *The Statesman*, 18 May 2022, https://www.thestatesman.com/opinion/forgotten-womens-uplift-1503073199.html (accessed 12 September 2022).

In patriarchal societies such as India and other Asian countries, women traditionally take on the role of homemakers but with the rising costs of living, they have little choice but to seek for extra income for their household. As a result, a disproportionate percentage of women are found working as informal waste workers – often collecting materials from general dumping sites, bins and roadsides with little or no safety equipment at all. Sadly, this practice is now deeply rooted in the traditional social-economic system. Therefore, it is recognized that while exposure to harmful chemicals is everywhere, poorer section of the community with lower income are disproportionately affected an observation brought home also by Jefferson's study.

Addressing the issue will not be simple. Both Putz and Jefferson do emphasize the importance of educating women. It is an undeniable fact that education empowers women by making them aware of their own rights and safety. More broadly speaking, education and training also allow women to transition from informal work to formal employment. Yet while education is key, some Asian scholars argue that without men helping to alleviate women's plight, education will not provide a lasting solution for the marginalization of poor women in South Asia.[4] These scholars in particular stress the need of changing the division of labour at the grassroots level, which implies that men should get involved in daily survival tasks – tasks that often involve picking materials from open dumping site for reusing or recycling and selling, in addition to gathering food, fuel and water. Most of all, however, there is a need for further study with regard to building effective awareness concerning social rights and justice (access to education, legal recourse against crime, access to health care etc.) and a better way for women to exercise such rights.

The impact of plastic wastes exports

Whereas Putz and Jefferson both provide much detail on the gendered effects of plastic and chemical waste, they do not delve into the export of plastic waste and its impact on the world's poor. Unfortunately, one quarter of the world's population does not have access to a proper waste collection system, and many middle- and low-income countries have poor waste management policy and infrastructure. Yet despite this reality, many wealthy countries send their waste overseas because it is cheap and helps meet their own recycling targets and reduces domestic landfill. According to Tearfund Charity, it is the poorer countries that are shouldering much of the burden of the global waste habit. Between 400,000 and

---

4. Cf., Alphonsus D'Souza, Lalrindiki Ralte and Yangkahao Vashum (eds), *The Quest for The Quest for Harmony: Christian and Tribal Perspectives* (Assam, India: North-East Social Research Centre, 2013).

1 million people die each year in developing countries because of diseases caused by mismanaged waste.[5]

According to World Economic Forum report in Agbogbloshie, Ghana, many of the people working on the electronic waste (e-waste) dumping sites suffer nausea, headaches and injuries, while others have died of cancer at young age.[6] This is because plastics found in e-waste are rarely recycled due to their complex composition and hazardous additives. Instead, they are being dumped and often burnt. Exporting plastic waste might be a legitimate and lucrative 'green-washing' industry for Western countries, but it has life-threatening effects on people who are poor and whose governments are weak.

International environmental law often lacks an awareness that humans depend on natural ecosystems. It further does not provide a clear and compelling direction or encouragement for countries and/or states to work collectively towards a common goal. Yet without common, practical and acceptable global environmental legislation, i.e. legislation that can be applied within a domestic jurisdiction of a state, social, economic and environment degradation and its impact on women and girls cannot be addressed.

Theological reflection and conclusion

In his chapter, Oliver Putz presses upon his readers that our current ecological crises are a matter of grave social concern as our treatment of nature has far-reaching ramifications for the most vulnerable people around the world. He reads our current crisis as an ecological *kairos*. He explains that without adopting an integral vision and practice that draws together the social and the ecological, our current ecological crisis cannot be resolved. On the societal level, an integral vision would mean a shift from a technocratic, neo-capitalist economic model to an integral common good approach. Putz thus agrees with Pope Francis' account of integral ecology in *Laudato Si'* that what is needed is a fundamental reorientation of our existential concern away from selfish egocentrism towards a caring relationship with *all* of creation. This reorientation is nothing less than a 'conversion' (*metanoia*) since the transformative change of heart it requires very much involves a spiritual reorientation back towards God. Yet while this reorientation is what is most needed when it comes to the wealthy minority world, one wonders what it is those who are suffering the consequences of the technocratic neo-capitalist economy may hope for? Should not their struggles and

5. Tearfund, 'The Burning Issue of the Plastic Crisis', 24 April 2020, https://www.tearfund.org/stories/2020/04/the-burning-issue-of-the-plastic-crisis (accessed 12 September 2022).

6. World Economic Forum, Report, 16 May 2019), https://www.weforum.org/agenda/2019/05/this-is-what-the-world-s-waste-does-to-people-in-poorer-countries/ (accessed 12 September 2022).

pain, but also their resilience, courage and longings be central to this conversion that is so urgently required of the wealthy?

Today we do indeed stand at the edge of a world facing ecological disaster. Some of this is simply brought on by poor stewardship and bad management. However, some of this may also be our reaping of what we have sown in terms of moral disobedience, most notably in the form of greed. The failure to keep to God's ways has an inevitably negative effect on the land as well as on our relationship with one another and God.[7] Putz concludes that humanity has arrived at an existential crossroads where from a Christian perspective a decisive choice is inevitable. At this juncture, I would like to draw upon Pope Francis's encouraging word: 'Yet all is not lost. Human beings, while capable of the worst, are also capable of rising above themselves, choosing again what is good, and making a new start, despite their mental and social conditioning.'[8] Although we live in very complex and challenging times, we can reverse the brokenness of this world.

7. David Bookless, *Planet Wise: Dare to Care for God's World* (Nottingham: Inter-Varsity Press, 2008), p. 57.

8. Pope Francis, *Laudato Si': On Care for Our Common Home* (Rome: Libreria Editrice Vaticana, 2015), §205.

Part 3

TOXICOLOGY

Chapter 6

TOXICITY IN THE TIMES OF PROJECT-BASED DEVELOPMENT

INDIGENOUS WOMEN FACING OIL AND GOLD POLLUTION IN THE PERUVIAN AMAZON

Deborah Delgado Pugley

The Amazon is going through overwhelming socio-ecological transformations due to demographic shifts, nurtured colonization and the cumulative effect of several industrial activities on its ecosystems.[1] Although deforestation does not have an industrial scale in the Peruvian Amazon basin, cycles of migration, urbanization and the expansion of small-scale agriculture and artisanal mining are pervasive drivers of land-use change.[2] Stories about complex, unintended and rather negative consequences of these developments on their well-being are conveyed by all Amazonian Indigenous peoples.[3] Nowadays, the global society is aware that the Amazon basin is the biggest standing tropical forest in the world and yet is an extremely fragilized biome, intertwined with arid and toxic environments that are replacing important forests and clean water sources.

1. Roel Brienen, Oliver Phillips, Ted Feldpausch et al., 'Long-Term Decline of the Amazon Carbon Sink', *Nature* 519 (2015), pp. 344–8. https://doi.org/10.1038/nature14283; Carlos Nobre et al., 'Land-Use and Climate Change Risks in the Amazon and the Need of a Novel Sustainable Development Paradigm', *Proceedings of the National Academy of Sciences* 113:39 (2016), pp. 10759–68. https://doi.org/10.1073/pnas.1605516113.

2. Vanessa Romo, *Perú: deforestación por minería de oro en Madre de Dios es la más alta en los últimos 32 años* (Lima: Mongabay, 2018); Deborah Delgado, 'A Toxic Development: Pollution and Change in an Amazonian Oil Frontier', in Sabrina Joseph (ed.), *Commodity Frontiers and Global Capitalist Expansion* (London: Palgrave Macmillan, 2019), pp. 255–77; Nilton Rojas Briceño et al., 'Deforestación en la Amazonía peruana: Índices de cambios de cobertura y uso del suelo basado en SIG', *Boletín de la Asociación de Geógrafos Españoles* 81:2538 (2019), pp. 1–34.

3. Antoine Acker, *Volkswagen in the Amazon: The Tragedy of Global Development in Modern Brazil* (Cambridge: Cambridge University Press, 2017); Davi Kopenawa, *The Falling Sky* (Massachusetts: Harvard University Press, 2013); Laura Rival, *Trekking through History: The Huaorani of Amazonian Ecuador* (New York: Columbia University Press, 2002).

Large oil companies have historically made critical decisions on the developing of extraction sites in coordination with Amazonian national states without taking into consideration the opinion of local communities.[4] More recently, gold mining has made a rather massive, decentralized push in the Amazon, taking the shape of numerous small ventures. Local gold entrepreneurs exploiting scattered sites in the rivers and forests do not try to influence the national state laws for private investment or environmental standards. They focused on exerting their influence over subnational levels of governance, disrupting national authority.[5] Thus, both oil and gold industries are now taking very different paths as oil prices fluctuate immensely and the price of gold keeps rising.

The way in which gold and oil have intervened in the Amazonian landscapes exerts a strong influence on people's daily lives. Evidence shows that the toxic effects of extraction disproportionately impact the well-being of women and children.[6] Considering this overarching process, this chapter engages with experiences of women from two Amazonian Indigenous peoples: the Kukama women of the village of Cuninico, who after a series of oil spills affecting their water sources, strive for fair reparation, and the Harambut women of the Amarakaeri Communal Reserve, who coexist and challenge the expansion of artisanal gold mining in their lands. This chapter examines the state's provisions that allow these situations to occur nationwide and the margins open for Indigenous women's agency that must make life viable in their lands and allow them to gain control over their collective destinies.

4. Martí Orta-Martínez and Matt Finer, 'Oil Frontiers and Indigenous Resistance in the Peruvian Amazon', *Ecological Economics* 70:2 (2010), pp. 207–18. https://doi.org/10.1016/j.ecolecon.2010.04.022; George Stetson, 'Oil Politics and Indigenous Resistance in the Peruvian Amazon: The Rhetoric of Modernity against the Reality of Coloniality', *The Journal of Environment & Development* 21:1 (2012), pp. 76–97. https://doi.org/10.1177/1070496511433425; John Andrew McNeish, 'Resource Extraction and Conflict in Latin America', *Colombia Internacional* 93 (2018), pp. 3–16. https://doi.org/10.7440/colombiaint93.2018.01.

5. Viviana Hidalgo and Eduardo Dargent, 'State Responses to the Gold Rush in the Andes (2004–2018): The Politics of State Action (and Inaction)', *Studies in Comparative International Development* 55:4 (2020), pp. 516–37. https://doi.org/10.1007/s12116-020-09314-5; Marjo de Theije and Marieke Heemskerk, 'Moving Frontiers in the Amazon: Brazilian Small-Scale Gold Miners in Suriname', *Revista Europea de Estudios Latinoamericanos y del Caribe* (2009), pp. 5–25. http://www.jstor.org/stable/25676373.

6. Elizabeth Vallejo Rivera, *Implicancias de la minería informal sobre la salud de mujeres y niños en Madre de Dios* (Lima: Sociedad Peruana de Derecho Ambiental-SPDA, 2014); David Gonzalez, Aubrey Arain and Luis Fernandez, 'Mercury Exposure, Risk Factors, and Perceptions among Women of Childbearing Age in an Artisanal Gold Mining Region of the Peruvian Amazon', *Environmental Research* 179 (2019), 108786. https://doi.org/10.1016/j.envres.2019.108786.

This chapter chooses to explore these two salient cases because they help us approach how toxicity becomes prevalent in a forested environment and how Indigenous women act to make life possible in adverse conditions. In the first case, it is remarkable how after a significant oil spill caused by a failure of a state-owned pipeline, the Kukama women of Cuninico took the leadership of collectively formulating and presenting a judicial case against several agencies of the Peruvian state that could have avoided the disaster.[7] After a long legal battle in January 2021, a decision by the Peruvian Supreme Court supported their right to comprehensive compensation and remediation. In the south of the Peruvian Amazon basin, the Amarakaeri Communal Reserve resists a gold rush that has surrounded its collective land with mining extraction sites. Women are taking a stand against medium-scale artisanal gold mining, as the mining activities and waste have direct negative effects on their health and security. The indirect effects on soil and water quality, water scarcity and raising temperatures are gaining salience. The women are partnering with conservation initiatives at hand, including Payments for Ecosystem Services schemes aimed at avoiding deforestation, in order to preserve their lands in an area devastated by alluvial gold mining.

Methodological approach

Keeping a strong ethical stand, based on mujerista theology,[8] this chapter uses mixed methods to give an empirical account of the experiences that women have shared with me along many visits to the field. Mujerista theology is a conceptual framework used in thinking and understanding women struggles for liberation from distinct experiences of subjugation. By utilizing archives, oral history, ethnography and participant observation, mujerista theology has constituted a gate for interdisciplinary approaches that explore how Latina women navigate their ethnic gendered positions in church and other settings. Migration, ethnicity, class, gender and faith intersect for women in this study and elsewhere.[9] Mujerista theology argues that true sharing of power leads to mutuality. Using mutuality as a starting point for building knowledge demands us to give serious consideration to what 'the other' is saying: not only to try to understand it and respect it but also to be willing to accept what is said as valid and good for all.[10] It is in this spirit that

7. The more than 99,000 gallons of oil spilled affected the communities of the Kukama people located in Cuninico, San Francisco, Nueva Esperanza and Santa Rosa, near the contaminated area.

8. Ada Maria Isasi-Díaz, *Mujerista Theology: A Theology for the Twenty-First Century* (Maryland: Orbis Books, 1996).

9. Sujey Vega. 'Mujerista Theology', in Taylor Petrey and Amy Hoyt (eds), *The Routledge Handbook on Mormonism and Gender* (New York: Routledge, 2020), pp. 598–607.

10. Isasi-Díaz, *Mujerista Theology*.

dialogues with women were undertaken and are being presented in this chapter. Discourses, interviews and collaborations seek to share experiences, perspectives and knowledge that is good for us all.

The experiences of Indigenous women in the Amazon basin are of course diverse among them according to their different historical process, ethnical origins and subjective experiences. This diversity should be acknowledged, and any method for social analysis should recognize the importance of every singular experience, according to its respect and recognizing its intrinsic value. The reflections of this chapter try to build on this approach. A significant part of the exchanges that inspired this chapter occurred during the lockdown due to the Covid-19 pandemic. I used a combination of virtual and face-to-face qualitative techniques. Interviews were conducted during 2020 and 2021 with Amarakaeri women leaders and commoners. Fieldwork was conducted in 2017 in Cuninico and sustained contact with women leaders, lawyers and specialists followed until 2021. Our dialogues regarding this issues and other matters took place frequently.

The challenges of oil and mining for governance

As Tania M. Li points out, to govern, in the sense elaborated by Michel Foucault, is to direct conduct, optimize processes and devise interventions to secure the 'welfare of the population, the improvement of its condition, the increase of its wealth, longevity, health, etc'.[11] In a post-colonial context, governing to enhance the welfare of populations merges with the endeavour glossed with the label 'development',[12] alongside the pursuit for profit that can sometimes be framed as the making of sustainable economies.

Increasing the welfare of communities by using extractive industries' wealth for the benefit of national economies is recognized as a big challenge that Amazonian states face. In fact, the political challenges posed by oil, gas and mining industries to public administrations lay both on the fact that big investors move into countries and regions with small economies and on the

---

11. Michel Foucault, 'Governmentality', in Graham Burchell, Colin Gordon and Peter Miller (eds), *The Foucault Effect: Studies in Governmentality* (Chicago: University of Chicago Press, 1991), pp. 87–105.

12. Tania M. Li, 'Governing Rural Indonesia: Convergence on the Project System', *Critical Policy Studies* 10:1 (2016), pp. 79–94. https://doi.org/10.1080/19460171.2015.1098 553; David Ludden, 'India's Development Regime', in Nicholas Dirks (ed.), *Colonialism and Culture* (Ann Arbor: University of Michigan Press, 1992), pp. 247–87; Donald Moore, 'The Crucible of Cultural Politics: Reworking "Development" in Zimbabwe's Eastern Highlands', *American Ethnologist* 26:3 (1999), pp. 654–89. http://www.jstor.org/stable/647442; Tania Li, *The Will to Improve: Governmentality, Development, and the Practice of Politics* (Durham, NC: Duke University Press, 2007).

particulars of oil, gas and mining investments.[13] Typically, such investments entail strains for governance regarding space-planning and public regulation. First, their 'enclave' character, which can limit the width of their impact, generates an intense local footprint. Second, high rents coming from these investments on resource extraction allow for the concentration of rent. As rent concentrates, power concentrates as well in certain agencies of the state, spreading poor governance and corruption. Sometimes this compromises states' capacity to deliver quality public goods and services[14] and limits as well its ability to deliver predictability to investors over time.[15] Predictability is inherently hard to achieve as market volatility around prices can make the benefits unpredictable in the long run, and the inherent exhaustibility of the resources makes any benefit timeline-finite. Fiscal regimes for oil, gas and mining tend to be complex, and corporate taxpayers tend to be few. This makes tax payments opaque for the public and disproportionately large relative to the rest of the tax base.

Significant social and environmental impacts, particularly on local communities, and an asymmetry in dealings between expert companies and often-inexpert governments have a long-lasting impact for societies' well-being.[16] The intergenerational character of the oil and mining legacy of this investment is usually underestimated, although institutionalism analyses the blueprint of these industries and its impact.[17]

In the case of Peru, institutional reforms and regulations on environmental standards have been introduced alongside liberal reforms. This was done to mitigate the effects of opening the extractive sector to global investment. Social unrest characterized the period of expansion of industrial extraction of minerals and oil, and the regulations reacted and tried to anticipate further unrest, as we can see in the next table.

The growing set of national environmental provisions shows a performative effect on how toxicity is handled in the territory. The practice of monitoring environmental problems and tracking them has increased over time, but current provisions are far from assembling an institutional framework that guarantees a better governance. Evidence of suitable functioning of monitoring and reporting,

13. World Bank, *Riqueza y sostenibilidad: Dimensiones sociales y ambientales de la minería en el Perú* (Lima: Banco Mundial, 2015).

14. International Monetary Fund, *Managing Natural Resource Wealth (MNRW-TTF)* (United Kingdom: IMF, 2010).

15. World Bank, *Riqueza y Sostenibilidad*.

16. Eduardo Zegarra Méndez, José Carlos Orihuela and Maritza Paredes, *Minería y economía de los hogares en la sierra peruana: impactos y espacios de conflicto* (Lima: GRADE, 2007).

17. Eduardo Dargent, José Carlos Orihuela, Maritza Paredes and María Eugenia Ulfe, *Resource Booms and Institutional Pathways* (Cham: Springer International Publishing, 2017).

Table 6.1 Timeline of laws and regulations that rule the mining environment in Peru.

Year	Regulatory milestone	Legal framework
1991	The Law for the Promotion of Investments in the Mining Sector and the Legal Framework for the Growth of Private Investment were adopted	DL 708 y DL 757
1997	The Environmental Management Structural Framework (MEGA) was created, and the foundations of a National Environmental Management System were laid	Conam Board of Directors Decree 001-97
1998	The Regulation for Environmental Quality Standards and Maximum Permissible Limits was approved	DS 044-98
2001	The Law of the National System of Environmental Impact Assessment (SEIA) was admitted, whose regulation would appear 7 years later	Law 27446
2004	The law that regulates mining environmental liabilities was accepted	Law 28271
2005	The General Law of the Environment was admitted, which repeals and replaces the Code of Environment and Natural Resources	Law 28611
2005	'Osinergmin' was created, which assumes the main role in mining inspection	Law 26734
2008	Summit point on the construction of the Peruvian environmental institutionalism. The Environmental Assessment and Enforcement Agency (OEFA) was established. The Ministry of Environment absorbed the Council on the Environment. Inspection functions were transferred to OEFA. INRENA disappeared; the water functions went to the National Authority of Water ANA (Law 29338)	Law Decree 1013. Law that creates the MINAM
2009	Regulation of the National System for Environmental Impact Assessment – SEIA	Supreme Decree 019-2009-Minam
2010	OEFA assumed competences of mining environmental control	Board of Directors Resolution 003-2010-OEFA/CD
2014	'Environmental package' law was created that establishes tax measures, simplification of procedures and permissions for the promotion and dynamization of investment in the country. Cut the ORFA's tax and collection functions, reduced the deadlines for submitting EIAs and removed the authority of the Minam to continue creating protected areas	Law 30230
2015	On 28 December 2015, Senace assumed the functions of evaluating the EIA-d, modifications and ITS, as well as the process of citizen participation of the Energy and Mines Sector	N° 328-2015-Minam

Source: José Carlos Orihuela and Alba Granados, 'Institucionalidad ambiental minera: entre el discurso legal y las prácticas de gobierno', in *¿Una oportunidad perdida? Boom extractivo y cambios constitucionales en el Perú* (Gerardo Damonte, Barbara Göbel, Maritza Paredes, Bettina Schorr and Gerardo Castillo (eds); Lima: Fondo Editorial PUCP, 2021), pp. 225–51.

as well as some administrative sanctions, do appear in the literature.[18] Nevertheless, the respect of human rights and the promotion of integral security for local communities are seriously compromised.

A core limit of current environmental policy and regulation that we can observe on the ground is that they do not go beyond what I will call here the 'project-logic'. This term refers to a logic of power that imposes a limited time frame for action and a refrained responsibility on the environmental consequences of industrial interventions. Thus, even if public institutions are responsible for monitoring extraction sites as well as sanctioning bad practices, these do not guarantee responsible behaviour from either national or private enterprises. We will show in the next two sections how the 'project-logic' works on the ground.

Cuninico: Building a voice for justice out of environmental grief

The northern Amazon has been a site of oil exploration since the 1920s, but exploitation became significant only during the revolutionary military government (1968–75), which started with the exploration of Trompeteros (Loreto, Corrientes basin) by the public company Petroperú in 1971. The enthusiasm awakened by this oil discovery increased when the Occidental Petroleum Company (Oxy) found other deposits in the area. Later it was clear that these deposits were worthwhile but not of great volume. The Peruvian Amazon oil production peaked in 1979 at about 129,000 barrels per day, and there has been a steady decline in oil extraction ever since, but the presence of the oil industry never stopped.

Building an oil pipeline in the Amazon was one of the most ambitious infrastructure projects ever introduced in the Peruvian part of this immense basin. The construction of the oil pipeline had an enormous impact. It demanded cutting through the forest, using significant workforce, and introducing new and sometime toxic materials. All this movement disturbed the forest and redistributed local population, introducing new, stronger migration trends to the area.

Living in polluted lands

In 2014, a significant spill of 2,358 barrels of crude happened at kilometre 42 of section I of the pipeline that unites the extraction sites of the Peruvian Amazon to the coast. This was very close to the village of Cuninico, recognized as a native

---

18. Pedro Herrera and Oscar Millones, '¿Cuál es el costo de la contaminación ambiental minera sobre los recursos hídricos en el Perú?,' *Cuaderno de Trabajo* 321 (Lima: Pontificia Universidad Católica del Perú, 2011), pp. 44–9.

community of the Kukama people, and it affected its water stream. State-owned Petroperú, operator of the Norperuano Pipeline (ONP), hired the men of the community to clean it up. In this way, ONP acted arbitrarily, 'remediating' spills on a limited basis instead of restoring the landscape and ecosystem.

Between 2012 and 2020, the state oil company Petroperú signed contracts for more than 482,370,000 soles (about $141,873,000) with five companies to remedy spills of crude oil caused by technical defects to the Norperuano Pipeline.[19] It is worth noting that these interventions did not implement monitoring and assessment mechanisms.

After years gone past, we know well that insufficient remediation in polluted sites has many consequences. In the case of the Cuninico, during our fieldwork, 100 per cent of people surveyed indicated that the oil spill continued to affect their health five years after the event. The most common symptoms for both children and adults were nausea, headaches, stomach pain and allergic reactions (hives). Medications received at the health centre (an hour away by boat) were only useful to relieve pain and allergies momentarily.[20] No treatment for the toxic exposure was made available either during the remediation operations or after them, and the community was consistently surrounded by heavy metals in water and soil for years.

The toxicity of the environment directly affects women's work managing the resources necessary for care-giving tasks. Before the spill, Cuninico had abundant game and was well known for its fishery. Women produced good-quality crops as well, including citrus fruits, mandioca and banana. Before the oil spill, it was common to drink and cook with stream water in Cuninico.

Food security was seriously disrupted by the lack of proper remediation of the spill. During the cleaning campaign after the spill, food distribution was deficient, and local inflation of food prices took place. Food prices never recovered. Water remains contaminated to this day, so the residents mainly rely on rainwater. In fact, 95 per cent prefer to use rainwater for drinking, and 87.5 per cent do not use the water from the stream as it is particularly polluted. When there is no rain, they are forced to collect river water both for drinking and cooking. After six years since the oil spill, the main concerns of women are still the lack of water and their inability to find enough adequate food for their families. On top of this, women spend a good part of their day going to the health centre to check their children's health.

Additionally, there is the burden of a post-disaster pollution economy that progressively took more importance. Their families' men engage in 'cleaning'

19. Guiovani Hinojosa and Luis Enrique Pérez, *El Estado no verifica la calidad de millonarias labores de remediación de derrames de petróleo en la Amazonía* (Lima: Convoca, 2021).

20. Deborah Delgado, 'A Toxic Development: Pollution and Change in an Amazonian Oil Frontier', in Sabrina Joseph (ed.), *Commodity Frontiers and Global Capitalist Expansion* (London: Palgrave Macmillan, 2019), pp. 255–77.

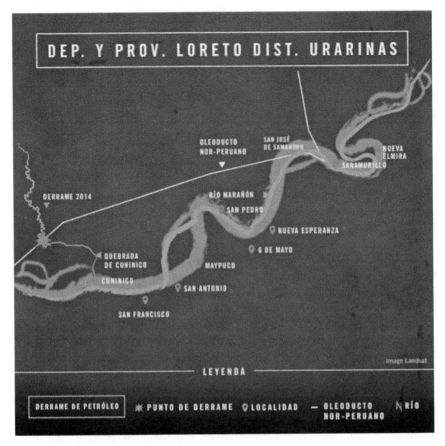

Figure 6.1 Map of the 2014 Cuninico oil spill in relation with the communities of the Urarina District. Loreto, Peru.

Source: Amnesty International, 2017.

activities promoted by the oil company. These operations that are overseen by third-party enterprises are sometimes managed by Indigenous men. The injection of money for remediation has created a labour market that has, yet again, negative effects on the communities. Indigenous men from different ethnicities travel to nearby communities affected by oil pollution, seeking work and flooding the communities with demand for food and shelter. They work long hours exposed to pollutants, and once the work is done and some money is kept, they go back to their communities. This economic activity around pollution is having direct impacts on their health. Increased levels of mercury in urine were detected on men involved in oil spill remediation and for women who relied on surface water for household needs.[21]

Overall, the replacement of the local economy by a monetized system for labour and commodity trade ends up affecting women, who very often support their family economy through their work in agroforestry and fisheries. Their engagement in the pollution economy is limited, and their households depend on an increase of women labour.

Efforts towards getting her voice heard

Facing this difficult set of circumstances, women have undertaken collective action, mobilizing their alliances with the Catholic church, human right lawyers NGOs and the national roundtable on poverty eradication. As most women stayed in the community while men worked in nearby polluted sites, they were active agents in forming a case against the state with the support of their families. For months the women gathered testimonies on how the spill was mishandled by Petroperú and how it affected their lives.

Men supported women's leadership in protesting the oil enterprise and agreed that both women and men would represent the community during their depositions in the Human Rights Interamerican Court. The collective effort led by the women of Cuninico thus gained public relevance as it achieved a judicial denunciation of state institutions, urging these institutions to take measures to avoid disaster and respond to emergencies once they were reported. Juan Carlos Ruiz Molleda, a lawyer and adviser to the Cuninico, Nueva Esperanza, Nueva Santa Rosa and San Francisco communities impacted by the 2014 spill, has worked directly with these women. After a long legal battle, in September 2019, the Loreto regional government approved the first health plan to address the fallout of the disaster. Over the course of three years, the government planned to implement nearly $700,000 in health measures for the four communities.

When the 2020 decision of the Supreme Court of Peru reached the community, there was a celebration of women's efforts but not joy. As Talita Paraná puts it:

We have won a battle, yes, against some monsters. But we cannot be happy because along this path we have lost lives, like my husband's, who died with cancer and with blood problems. Everything that has happened to us is sad because several of us are sick and we will continue to die. Because life is priceless, our life has no spare, nobody can replace it. That's why I say that all

---

21. Jena Webb, 'Mercury Concentrations in Urine of Amerindian Populations Near Oil Fields in the Peruvian and Ecuadorian Amazon', *Environmental Research* 151 (2016), pp. 344–50. https://doi.org/10.1016/j.envres.2016.07.040.

this does not bring joy, but it does generate enormous pride because we see that there is justice, because we verify that we know how to defend ourselves, that we are worthy and that we have rights, even though we are in a lost corner of the country.[22]

Environmental suffering, losing family members and one's health are not things that can be truly remediated. However, the pursuit of justice does restore a sense of human worth and dignity; this is a gift of the women to the their community and their ancestral territory.

The Amarakaeri case: Mercury and insecurity

Mercury is among the ten most dangerous chemicals for public health and is a priority concern for the 128 signatory countries of the Minamata Convention. Mercury emissions to the atmosphere increased 20 per cent between 2010 and 2015, with South America, sub-Saharan Africa and Southeast Asia as the main contributors. Approximately 80 per cent of mercury emissions in South America are from the Amazon, and the exposures of the Amazonian populations are from two to six times the reference doses.[23] Mercury exposure related to artisanal and small-scale gold mining (ASGM) has raised environmental and public health concerns globally. Exposure to mercury, a potent neurotoxin that bio-accumulates in fish, is especially of concern to women of childbearing age (WCBA) and to children in high fish-consuming populations.[24]

22. Judgement of the Supreme Court, https://tc.gob.pe/jurisprudencia/2020/03799-2018-AC.pdf. Noviembre 24, 2020. Original quote: "'Hemos ganado una batalla, sí, contra unos monstruos. Pero no podemos estar alegres porque en este camino hemos perdido vidas como la de mi esposo, muerto con cáncer y también con afectaciones en la sangre. Todo lo que nos ha ocurrido es una tristeza, porque varios estamos enfermos y vamos a seguir muriendo. Porque la vida no tiene precio, nuestra vida no tiene repuesto, nadie la cambia," lamenta, "por eso digo que todo esto no me genera alegría, pero sí un enorme orgullo porque vemos que sí hay justicia, porque comprobamos que sabemos defendernos, que sí valemos y que tenemos derechos, aunque estemos en un rincón perdido del país." https://www.idl.org.pe/caso-cuninico-construyendo-la-historia-del-peru/ (accessed 20 May 2022).

23. Maria Elena Crespo-Lopez et al., 'Mercury: What Can We Learn from the Amazon?', *Environment International* 146 (2021), 106223. https://doi.org/10.1016/j.envint.2020.106223.

24. Beth Feingold, Axel Berky, Heileen Hsu-Kim, Elvis Jurado and William Pan, 'Population-Based Dietary Exposure to Mercury through Fish Consumption in the Southern Peruvian Amazon', *Environmental Research* 183 (2020), 108720. https://doi.org/10.1016/j.envres.2019.108720.

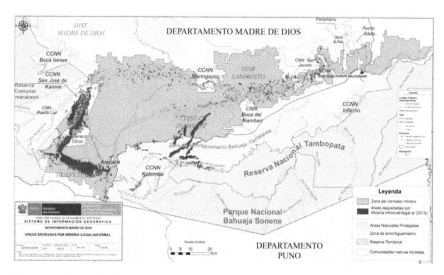

Figure 6.2 Map of affected areas by illegal/informal mining in Madre de Dios.
Source: Ministry of the Environment of Peru, 2015.

Most of the alluvial gold mining in the Peruvian Amazon is concentrated in the region of Madre de Dios. It is an activity that has reached record heights from 2007 to the present, although its presence in the region is precolonial. As early as 1981, the national census highlighted the growth of some mining conglomerates such as Laberinto, Huepetuhe, Mazuko or Caychive, caused by 'the continuous arrival of immigrants of mainly Andean origin.'[25] Once these extraction sites were consolidated, the construction of the interoceanic highway and high gold prices motivated the escalation of mining operations, facilitated by the influx of a stationary workforce. It is estimated that in the first decade of the twenty-first century, gold mining activities released 400 tons of mercury into the environment in Madre de Dios.[26]

Amarakaeri Communal Reserve has a rich history of self-organization and leadership in conservation. Its members have strengthened their institutions to become accountable and efficient as conservation actors. They have developed a model for reducing deforestation and forest degradation that is coherent both with national policies and their cultural heritage. Since the gold rush is so significant in Madre de Dios, commoners have been very involved in mining operations; they have both resisted and worked for this industry.

25. Elena Borasino and Luis Escobedo, 'Conflictos por uso de la tierra en Madre de Dios: análisis institucional y espacial en el marco de la carretera Interoceánica', *SEPIA: Perú: el problema agrario en debate* (Lima, 2010), pp. 573–605.

26. Fernando Osores, Jaimes Rojas and Carlos Manrique, 'Minería informal e ilegal y contaminación con mercurio en Madre de Dios: Un problema de salud pública', *Acta Médica Peruana* 29:1 (2012), pp. 38–42.

Viewed from the ground, two types of alluvial gold mining can be distinguished: artisanal (or small-scale mining) and medium-scale mining. From the point of view of Harambut communities, these differ in several aspects such as their use of technology or machinery, the length of time and the intensity of their activities, the social relationships they establish with the community members, the alliances they support with subnational governments, and the level or degree of their capacity to destroy or to degrade the ecosystem.[27]

The areas with medium-scale mining that use heavy machinery have gone through drastic social changes. Indigenous communities are losing their ways of relating to the environment and their customary knowledge about traditional livelihoods provided by their immediate surroundings. Local water cycles are not working the way they used to, and dry seasons are more severe and extended. This affects agriculture and fisheries. Threats against the culture and ancestral knowledge emerge, and there is a loss of traditional socio-economic activities.

Interviewees indicate that threats are felt especially when Indigenous women move outside their territory for daily activities or when they leave their lands permanently to establish themselves in neighbouring villages and mining towns. Women report facing sexual aggressions while shopping at mining centres or going through them to reach the region's capital. As one young woman from Puerto Luz points out:

> Women have to go shopping in mining towns. Women in general, and the youngest, are subject to all kinds of sexual aggression. Those [mines] with activities within the community are worse because their workers are present within the community. The miners carry diseases, drinking problems, and bring violence.
>
> (Community member of Puerto Luz)

They are harassed by miner workers and sometimes menaced with violence if their communities have recently resisted their presence. The relationships are tense and become openly contentious if women and men from the communal reserve resist miners in any way. Women tend to stay silent, move quickly and avoid contact with miners as they go through their camps and villages. More dramatically, as they move out of their communities, the risk of being trapped in human-trafficking networks is real. Many of the sex-trafficking victims come from farming communities of the Andean highlands, but local Indigenous women are also potential victims.

On the other hand, Harambut women also play a very important role in defending the territory, participating in the evictions of illegal goldminers, alongside communal watchers, and leaders. Women with their families have participated in brigades in charge of defending the integrity of their territories. Although patrolling the forest is traditionally a masculinized undertaking, they

---

27. Woman leader of Shipetiari, interview by author, Madre de Dios, June 2020.

help in several tasks maintaining the camps, cooking and monitoring the reserve. Taking part in these necessary actions to dissuade the expansion of gold mining is very risky. Women are scared about what might happen to their children by way of retaliation. In this regard, Jaime comments: 'In Puerto Luz, women have been key in evicting strangers from the community. Women are very exposed. Women themselves are going to help to evict the miners, so they also play an important role. [After acting] the risks are latent, and no one is safe, neither men nor the women.'[28]

In this hostile context, self-care is an element that should be explored in depth as women face many threats to their security. Self-care is both a necessary act of physical and psychological protection and a political strategy to sustain and promote the work of defenders.[29] Indeed, according to Bernal the lack of self-care is as much itself a form of violence, as it is the consequence of violence. It was found that stress or work overload due to defence work manifests itself in discomforts and diseases, such as muscular ailments, gastrointestinal disorders, among others, that affect the immune system and make defenders more vulnerable to diseases. Women talk about the stress they experience thinking about their children and their partners exposed to this kind of violence.

The fight for keeping an extremely threatened territory is exhausting. Actors working on conservation alongside the Amarakaeri reserve do recognize it. Park rangers call on society as a whole to pay attention to what is happening in these 'remote' areas and no longer tolerate death threats, acts of violence, aggression and mistreatment against men and women who protect Indigenous land and parks. Alleviating the stress on these families could improve enormously their quality of life.

Do harms caused by projects call for project-based responses?

In many countries of the Global South, development, extraction and infrastructure projects of different types are more significant in shaping daily lives of rural people than national policy. The toxicity produced by these projects, as

---

28. Jaime, interview by Damaris Herrera, assistant of the author, Madre de Dios, June, 2021.

29. Jane Barry and Vahida Nainar, *Insiste, Persiste, Resiste, Existe: Women Human Rights Defenders' Security Strategies, Front Line International Foundation for the Protection of Human Rights Defenders* (Colorado: Kvinna Foundation, 2008); Karen Bennett, Danna Ingleton, Alice Nah and James Savage, 'Critical Perspectives on the Security and Protection of Human Rights Defenders', *The International Journal of Human Rights* 19:7 (2015), pp. 883–95. https://doi.org/10.1080/13642987.2015.1075301.

both cases show, has long-lasting effects that outlast any project-based remediation initiative. In fact, a project-based approach to manage industrial toxic consequences is not suited for the objective of remediating toxic environments from the very start. Projects are temporary work efforts that try to keep a clear beginning and end in time. Following a project-logic, remediation measures selectively recognize certain system failures and assume acting upon toxic environments under a minor time and space scope. The limited scope of the intervention allows projects to proliferate without building back resilience in broadly affected environments in the case of mining and oil-related toxicity. There is now evidence that remediation and toxicity control have been broadly ineffective and are rarely assessed in the Peruvian Amazonian context.

To understand the proliferation of this institutional behaviour, the notion of 'technical project' as a restricted form of government, proposed by Li, is enlightening. Projects serve as vehicles for channelling funds to favoured members of the elite, giving them power to organize labour and to discipline villagers who are told to wait patiently for state largesse to come their way.

We can observe that, faced with the challenge of responding to toxic environments, states and investors tend to use a project logic. Projects are a flexible element in state budgets that make funds flow. Money for remediation, or for gold mining control, can flow into localized activities for a brief time, giving the impression of action combatting a toxic environment. In the meantime, concessionary enterprises can cease to exist once the project ceases to be profitable.

Purposely framing the scope and impact of infrastructure for extraction to its construction phase can give the impression of control. Describing technically the abandonment of a drilling site, identifying concession sites for alluvial small-scale gold mining (ASGM), establishing client-provider relations with local majors and policemen are all short-term project-based endeavours, each one in their own way. They leave out of the analysis several of the development consequences and ethical considerations by using a technical language or serving themselves of technicalities and vacuums in the legal framework. They both engage in short-term assemblages of actors that disrupt ecosystems and introduce modifications, framing them as 'unintended' and tending to leave them out of the planning. The introduction of pipelines or equipment for ASGMs as 'technical projects' (designed with a particular aim and limited liability) seize to be just that to become material elements embedded in the lives of people and landscapes. Petroperú's projects as well as inspection and law enforcement over alluvial gold mining fail to properly monitor this long-lasting socio-ecological interaction.

In both cases analysed in this chapter, Indigenous women have coped with several oppressive circumstances that can be reflected in the way they spend their time, their perspectives on the future of polluted lands, as well as in having limited experiences of time and place. Work overload, anguish and uncertainty about ways of meeting their immediate needs burden their daily experience. The risks taken by their family members to work or to defend their land, as well as their own efforts to confront miners and care for their children, are now part of their strategies of risk management and collective care.

In one case, as the infrastructure was state-owned, after a hard battle for compensation, a long-lasting pursuit of justice has now finally reached its goal. The work of assessing the impact of the toxic environment on the lives of community members and the local ecology will establish a precedent for all the affected areas at the national level.

Women's assessment of the consequences of toxic environments for the community's daily life confirms that project-based remediation should not stand alone. A sound management of chemicals is urgent at this point in time. In 2015, the state created, at the insistence of the native communities of that region, the Contingency Fund for Environmental Remediation, capital destined to the rehabilitation of areas affected by hydrocarbons. Such resources are administered by the National Environment Fund (FONAM), a private non-profit entity specialized in raising resources for projects in favour of nature. Later, it transferred this responsibility to PROFONANPE, another private non-profit entity similar in nature to its predecessor. So far, the state has injected 183,000,000 soles ($50,800,000) into the fund for the execution of the remediation. And another transfer of 88,000,000 soles ($24,444,000) was expected for the first quarter of 2021. Thus, it would have ensured 271,000,000 soles to clean Loreto (more than $75,277,000), but, according to authorities in charge, this only represents 40 per cent of what is needed. A similar action plan has been designed for Madre de Dios and mercury remediation. There is a considerable budget at stake for future remediation efforts in the Peruvian Amazon basin, and yet there is still no evaluation of the interventions' quality, and tenders continue to work in small areas without an ecosystem vision. Its effectiveness can hardly be verified. Without a coherent approach that regards toxic environments as socio-ecologically connected landscapes, these efforts are hardly going to restore any resilience.

Conclusion

The expansion of toxic environments is an Amazonian tragedy that illustrates a regional misdirection exceeding the Peruvian territory. Amazonian countries have taken for granted the ecological and social resilience of this biome and underinvested in its people. All Amazonian states are overlooking the steps needed to promote the well-being of Indigenous peoples, women and children. This chapter shows that by working under a 'project logic', states and industries have detached the promotion of national economic development from the the daily lives of people. In doing so, the consequences of otherwise profitable mining and oil operations for local collectives were not taken into consideration, even when public environmental provisions are adopted. As a result, those legal environmental provisions that we can observe for the Peruvian case fail to protect the well-being of people in the Amazon.

It is important to stress that ethical reflections on the Amazonian development project are, consequently, extremely limited, and a sustained dialogue with Indigenous peoples was and still is circumvented. Ethical reflections that engage with Indigenous women's experiences and perspectives remain a critical step for development, which is unavoidably based on sharing certain values on what counts as 'good' social change.

This chapter tried to show that the 'project-logic', prevalent in how we frame industrial intervention, remediation efforts, and its deficient results, does not enable society to have an adequate space for ethical reflection. Considering this, a new turn should be taken. This chapter maintains that in order to be imactful the effects of extractive materiality and its resulting toxicity should be analysed beyond the declared aims of a technical project. Pollution due to extractive activity has a legacy that should not be approached following a project-based logic.

Reflecting upon the 'project logic' will entail avoiding its tendency to cancel or overlook several elements needed to restore ecosystems and address long-term societal harms societies. Toxic environments need encompassing approaches that largely exceed project-based reparation. To start a productive dialogue, women's visions are particularly relevant as they have a different take on time and engagement as they do not consider their relationship to their communities as a short-term responsibility.

Women's visions of long-term commitment are being reflected in their daily choices: their practices of care, their collective action for food security and their legal actions regarding environmental defence and conservation. Enterprises and state might consider that the management of chemicals is urgently needed, and the involvement of local communities to deal with this introduced materiality could help fragilized landscapes. For now, the use of law has offered some hope for justice among certain communities. However, even if justice is achieved in courts, pressure for an ethical and accountable action on toxicity is necessary.

Chapter 7

MINING AND WOMEN'S ACTIVISM

STILL UNDER THE SURFACE OF CATHOLIC SOCIAL TEACHING

Lisa Sowle Cahill

The focus of this chapter is the Roman Catholic response to women's activism against mining in Latin America, particularly in the Amazon. The Amazon basin is home to more than a third of the world's primary forests and a major source of oxygen for the entire earth. The 2015 encyclical of Pope Francis, *Laudato Si'*,[1] targeted environmental degradation as a special concern of Catholic Social Teaching (CST). The subsequent 2019 Synod on the Amazon prioritized that region and made it clear that the peoples of the Amazon are the key sources of wisdom and action for its more environmentally just future.

In 2014, the nine Catholic bishops of the Amazon, together with the Conference of Latin American bishops, the Confederation of Latin American religious orders, Caritas Latin America, and the Brazilian Bishops' Conference, formed a network of activism and support for environmental justice in the Amazon and for its peoples, wildlife and habitats. This alliance, the Panamazonian Ecclesial Network (REPAM)[2], now inclusive of hundreds of Catholic organizations and initiatives, was instrumental in convening the Synod on the Amazon and has the mission of carrying through on its agenda. Despite the fact that women representatives to the Synod were excluded from voting on proposals, the leadership of REPAM affirmed the voice and role of women, along with their 'courageous dedication for life until the last consequences'.[3] Mining damage disproportionately affects women, and women's participation in mining protest is strong. Indeed, women's leadership

---

1. Pope Francis, *Laudato Si': On Care for Our Common Home* (Rome: Libreria Editrice Vaticana, 2015).

2. REPAM (Red Eclesial Panamazónica, https://redamazonica.org/) was officially formed in 2014. Its purpose is to advocate for the rights of the Indigenous peoples and for environmental justice for the Amazonian basin and its inhabitants.

3. Mateo González Alonso, 'REPAM Praises the "Courageous" Commitment of the Women of the Synod, beyond Their Exclusion from the Vote', *Vida Nueva*, 29 October 2019, https://www.vidanuevadigital.com/2019/10/29/la-repam-alaba-el-compromiso-valiente-de-las-mujeres-del-sinodo-mas-alla-de-su-exclusion-en-la-votacion/ (accessed 25 June 2021).

is encouraged by some local ministries within the purview of REPAM, and that support has risen to new prominence with the accession of Cardinal Pedro Ricardo Barreto to the REPAM presidency in 2020. Yet explicit solidarity with women's political activism, in gender-equal terms, has yet to feature conspicuously at the highest levels of 'official' CST. Scholars maintain that the significance of women's participation in the anti-mining movement has thus far not been adequately recognized in social science research,[4] a lacuna I would argue also exists in CST analyses of mining and its impacts. Women in the Amazon, in Latin America more generally, and indeed worldwide, face constraining binary gender norms that limit their ability to exercise public and political roles, norms that are reinforced by religious teaching even within faith traditions that claim to promote respect for women. Full-scale support for women's political power collides with standards of 'feminine' domesticity that Catholicism still conveys and that undoubtedly are strong in the Amazon.

In Latin America, Roman Catholicism is the dominant religious institution and wields significant influence despite declining levels of adherence. Women activists both accept and reject religiously validated norms defining women's roles in domestic and maternal terms. Women own but renegotiate feminine identities as mothers and caregivers to support political participation in the name of families, communities and future generations, as well as of the earth itself.[5]

In the Amazon and elsewhere on the continent, Catholic agencies and representatives have been active supporters of Indigenous peoples' rights to land, to traditional ways of life, and to protection from the disastrous environmental incursions of, for example, resource extraction, logging, industrial farming, cattle raising and pollution.[6] More often than not, the leaders of Indigenous resistance

---

4. Katy Jenkins, 'Women Anti-mining Activists' Narratives of Everyday Resistance in the Andes: Staying Put and Carrying On in Peru and Ecuador', *Gender, Place and Culture: A Journal of Feminist Geography* 24 (2017), pp. 1441–59 (1444–5). https://doi.org/10.108 0/0966369X.2017.1387102; Kalowatie Deonandan and Rebecca Tatham, 'The Unexplored Dimensions of Resistance to Extractivism in Latin America: The Role of Women and NGOs', in Kalowatie Deonandan and Michael L. Dougherty (eds), *Mining in Latin America: Critical Approaches to the New Extractivism* (London and New York: Routledge, 2016), pp. 273–83 (274).

5. On this point, I would like to thank Rev. Dr Kuzipa Nalwamba, who responded to my chapter draft during the Online Symposium – Women, Mining, and Toxic Contamination, Laudato Si' Research Institute Campion Hall, University of Oxford, March 2021. Dr Nalwamba noted that the identities of Indigenous women are neither static nor insulated from the various forces at play in their environments. This made it possible for me to appreciate that 'feminine' identities and role performances are not necessarily 'essentialist' and may in fact work against patriarchal control at the practical level.

6. See Vatican News staff writer, 'Amazonia: Mining Continues to Pose Threat to Indigenous Land', *Vatican News*, 24 June 2021, https://www.vaticannews.va/en/world/ news/2021-06/brazil-amazon-region-mining-deforestation.html (accessed 25 June 2021);

movements are women, who face violent retaliation, driven by a combination of profit motive, power struggle and gender bias. Despite the Catholic Church's opposition to dangerous means and levels of resource extraction, women's anti-mining agency has not been publicized in Catholic initiatives to regulate mining, although the picture is changing. In fact, the Church as institutional teacher and social leader has failed to challenge directly enough the prevalent cultural norms that legitimate gender bias and violence against women activists. The thesis of this chapter is that official CST should name and proclaim the rightful and indispensable character of women's role in anti-mining protests, thus normalizing women's environmental and political leadership for Church, society and the broad environmental justice movement for which *Laudato Si'* calls.

Mining, toxicity and women

Since the 1990s many countries in Latin America have turned to the extractive industries as a source of development that can attract foreign capital, creating a lightly regulated business environment that international mining corporations are eager to join. The growth of industrial mining (legal and illegal) has depleted easily accessible supplies of high-grade ore, creating scarcity and competition, while drastically increasing deforestation, land and water toxicity, and displacement of Indigenous peoples. Mining has become a source of financing for corrupt government officials and for illegally armed combatants vying to control the resource trade. Since its inception, the mining industry in Latin America has been met by protest and resistance movements from within local communities. Women are important agents both of resistance and of counter-resistance when their families benefit financially from the mining industry.[7]

One of the most important negative effects of mining for women is toxicity that is caused, for example, by improper disposal of waste materials (especially mercury) that are used to separate precious metals from ore. While artisanal mining is a traditional income-producing activity in some areas of the Amazon, intensified mining, industrial mining, large-scale mining and illegal mining have increased the presence of deadly toxins. Mercury waste from gold mining, for example in the Madre de Dios River in Peru,[8] is deposited in rivers and leeches into

Eduardo Campos Lima, 'Brazilian Church Commission Examines Mining's Impact on Local Communities', *National Catholic Reporter*, 25 February 2020, https://www.ncronline. org/news/earthbeat/brazilian-church-commission-examines-minings-impact-local-communities (accessed 25 June 2021).

7. See Denise Humphreys Bebbington, 'Toxic Environments', and Deborah Delgado Pugley, 'Toxicity in the Times of Project-Based Development: Indigenous Women Facing Oil and Gold Pollution in the Peruvian Amazon Basin', in this volume.

8. Rebekah Kates Lemke, 'The Pull of Peru's Gold Rush', *Catholic Relief Services*, 30 December 2016, https://www.crs.org/stories/peru-illegal-gold-mining-climate-change (accessed 12 February 2020).

the ground around mining sites. Mercury severely affects the nervous, digestive and immune systems, as well as lungs, kidneys, skin and eyes. Poisoning through food and water sources, and through the inhalation of mercury vapours, has long-term consequences for all those working or residing near the mines.

Children are exposed to special dangers by toxicity. Environmental toxins can be transmitted in utero and through breastfeeding and can cause genetic damage that will have a multigenerational effect. According to the World Health Organization,

> foetuses are most susceptible to developmental effects due to mercury. Methylmercury exposure in the womb can result from a mother's consumption of fish and shellfish. It can adversely affect a baby's growing brain and nervous system. The primary health effect of methylmercury is impaired neurological development. Therefore, cognitive thinking, memory, attention, language, and fine motor and visual spatial skills may be affected in children who were exposed to methylmercury as foetuses.[9]

This in turn disproportionately affects their mothers and other caregivers, who are typically women and girls.

In Tegucigalpa, Honduras, to take another case, the 2009 closing of the San Martin mine (headquartered in Canada) has left a long legacy of harm. The construction of the mining site cut into mountains and exposed sulphur banks which were left open, exposing residents to skin diseases and cancer. Despite some efforts of the Canadian parent company, Goldcorp, to clean up and reforest the site, the results have been insufficient. Sources of toxicity remain, including leakage of cyanide into rivers.[10] A Honduran journalist tells of an eighteen-year-old mother and her eighteen-month-old daughter who are both sick and losing their hair.

> Their health problems began at birth. Both were born ill, they were born with the brand of mining companies within their bodies, a brand that came to the valley at the beginning of 2000 and installed itself in the waters of the rivers and water sources that the valley communities have always used. They used the waters from these rivers well before Goldcorp Inc. arrived. They used the water during the eight years of mining exploitation at Goldcorp's San Martin Mine, and they continue to use it during the seven years following the mine's closure.[11]

9. World Health Organization, 'Fact Sheet: Mercury and Health'. Available online: https://www.who.int/news-room/fact-sheets/detail/mercury-and-health (accessed 12 February 2020).

10. The Global Sisters Report is a project of the US publication *National Catholic Reporter*. Cf., https://www.globalsistersreport.org/

11. Martin Calix, 'The Valley of Despair', April 2019, cited at The Violence of Development: A companion website to the Pluto Press book by Martin Mowforth, https://theviolenceofdevelopment.com/the-valley-of-despair/.

Women are burdened in multiple ways when water and ground become contaminated. Women are responsible for domestic well-being, daily sustenance, and home-based agriculture and livestock. Women need to use scarce resources, both time and money, to access alternative water and food supplies. And while gender bias often excludes women from the economic benefits of working for the extractive industries, there are still millions of women worldwide who engage in small-scale mining, bringing increased personal exposure risk.[12] Systemic gender inequality pervades the ways governments and businesses engage with local communities in consultation and decision-making about the initiation of potentially harmful mining projects and about corporate accountability for accidents that cause pollution, as well as for waste materials that are improperly disposed of and left behind in large quantities when a mine's resources are exhausted and the mining site is closed. Moreover, mining attracts human traffickers and sets the scene for rape and other forms of gender-based violence.

Within communities affected by mining, women are among the most important yet least powerful stakeholders. The Brazilian theologian Ivone Gebara captures women's reality with these words: 'There is no doubt that the social division of labor, of power, and therefore of the great social and political decisions are shaped by gender inequality ... The short and long term effect of these decisions is a burden on women's lives.' Above all, we must remember 'the women from black, indigenous, and minority groups, whose presence is often forgotten because they are considered "lesser than" white women'.[13] In a Vatican press conference on the Synod in 2019, the head of the Episcopal Conference of Bolivia, Bishop Ricardo Centellas, lamented that gender inequality likewise infects Catholic attitudes and practice: 'women have a very strong presence in the Church, but their participation in decision-making is almost invisible'.[14]

Despite multiple intersecting disadvantages, however, it would be wrong to conclude that women do not exercise agency successfully against land and water exploitation, taking on problems like toxic effects on their own health and that of families and communities, community control over mining and toxicity, and mobilization for change. Pope Francis aptly recognizes women's courage in his first encyclical *Evangelium gaudium*: 'Doubly poor are those women who endure situations of exclusion, mistreatment and violence, since they are frequently less able to defend their rights. Even so, we constantly witness among them impressive examples of daily

12. For development of these points, see Oxfam International, *Position Paper on Gender Justice and the Extractive Industries*, March 2017, www.oxfam.org.

13. Ivone Gebara, 'Women, Climate, God, and Pope Francis', in Grace Ji-Sun Kim and Hilda P. Koster (eds), *Planetary Solidarity: Global Women's Voices on Christian Doctrine and Climate Justice* (Minneapolis: Fortress, 2017), pp. 67–79 (71).

14. *Vatican News*, 'Amazon Synod Briefing: Role of Women, Inculturation, Synodality', 23 October 2019. Available online: https://www.vaticannews.va/en/vatican-city/news/2019-10/amazon-synod-briefing-role-of-women-inculturation-synodality.html (accessed 9 February 2020).

heroism in defending and protecting their vulnerable families."[15] Across the globe, women are pivotal actors in resistance to large-scale extractive development.

Mining in a culture of gender inequality

In Latin America, women in the professions, politics and activism tend to identify more positively with women's traditional family roles than do similarly engaged women in the North. Latin American women' activists typically promote their authority on the basis of their maternal identities, and to regard difference-minimizing feminisms as foreign, capitalist or neocolonial in origin. Indigenous women in particular are likely to see gender roles as complementary and to claim that women have distinct gifts, such as a closer link to nature, and to the spirits and deities that inhabit forests, rivers and mountains. Women are unique bearers of ancestral traditions and spirituality.[16]

'Maternalism' is a term created by social scientists to denote political advocacy for women's full access to economic and political roles, for the value of women's maternal virtues, and for the accommodation of the demands of mothering (especially of infants and young children) by the workplace. The concept originated primarily among middle-class, white, US and European women, who wanted to expand their own social agency, while decreasing inequalities between middle-class and 'working class' women and children. Positively, maternalist politics can challenge the boundaries between masculine and feminine, public and private, and state and civil society. On the downside, however, by emphasizing caretaking attributes like other-directedness, nurturance, emotional support, morality and the priority of children, maternalism can reinforce gender stereotypes, conflating all women with motherhood and ascribing familial responsibilities more to women than to men. This discourages men from assuming an equal share or throwing their support behind the cultural and institutional changes necessary to make domestic equality sustainable.[17] In the case of Latin American women politicians, 'maternal ideals historically created a "supermadre" or "militant mother" frame that uniquely legitimated' women's candidacies, while nevertheless positioning their caretaking roles as structural barriers to their political careers.[18]

---

15. Pope Francis, *Evangelii Gaudium* (Rome: Editrice Libreria Vaticana, 2013).

16. Jasmine Gideon and Alejandra Ramm, 'Motherhood, Social Policies, and Women's Activism in Latin America: An Overview', in Jasmine Gideon and Alejandra Ramm (eds), *Motherhood, Social Policies, and Women's Activism in Latin America* (Cham, Switzerland: Palgrave Macmillan, 2020), pp. 1–11 (3).

17. Gideon and Ramm, 'Motherhood, Social Policies', p. 2. See also Catalina de la Cruz, 'The Persistent Maternalism in Labor Programs', in *Motherhood, Social Policies*, pp. 245–66.

18. Susan Franceschet, Jennifer M. Piscopo, and Gwynn Thomas, '*Supermadres*, Maternal Legacies, and Women's Political Participation in Contemporary Latin America', *Journal of Latin American Studies* 48 (2016), pp. 1–32 (30). https://doi.org/10.1017/S0022216X15000814.

Moreover, women can mobilize maternal identities, values and prerogatives across the political spectrum, from the political inclusion of the poor and excluded, to the promotion of class privilege, racism, fascism or even genocide.[19] Maternalist political rhetoric is no less polyvalent for women mining activists. Nevertheless, women's environmental actions, initiatives and movements on the whole empower women, even if for different ends, and even when women define their identities around motherhood and domesticity.

Two studies from Chile display a gender-subversive role of maternal rhetoric, both for women who seek access to mining's profits and for those who seek to rein in the damaging behaviour of extractive companies. In the case of two mines operated by the state-run Codelco Company, women have been integrated into large-scale copper mining, traditionally a man's job. Factors favouring change have included cultural shifts towards equality, fostered by President Michelle Bachelet's first administration (2006–10); and an anticipated shortage of skilled labour, along with a shift from physical strength to technological expertise as a qualification for employment. As of 2015, women still constituted less than 10 per cent of all workers; only about 1 per cent of employed women were executives on one end, and of blue-collar workers, on the other; while 88 per cent of women were administrators, and 10 per cent supervisors and professionals.[20]

On one level, women's inclusion in the labour force has had little impact on women's traditional maternal role, since working women still carry principal responsibility for home and family. In fact, women use maternal qualities (reasonableness, cooperation, commitment to the job) to defend their place in the mining hierarchy, including labour union participation; 'while this limits their full integration into the work force, it also allows them to criticize the way in which men work and participate in activities', for example, by criticizing union corruption.[21] Although women seek to be recognized as women-workers or '*compañeras*', the mother is still 'the predominant image of women' in the labour unions, which have a '*machista*' culture'.[22] Both men and women workers hypothesize a conflict between mining work and maternal responsibilities, with men warning women that misfortune could befall children during their absence and some women criticizing others who get pregnant while employed. In fact, women hold up benefits to ease the conflict (e.g. day care, leaving work earlier) as targets for union activity. Maternalist discourse may make it harder for women to integrate fully into the workforce, but it gives women, as mothers, an entry point to jobs and a way to maintain social approval despite transgressing occupational expectations.

19. Jadwiga E. Pieper Mooney, '"Taking the Nature out of Mother": From Politics of Exclusion to Feminisms of Difference and Recognition of Rights', in *Motherhood, Social Policies*, pp. 39–67.

20. Nicolás Angelcos, 'Women Miners, Labor Integration, and Unionization', in *Motherhood, Social Policies*, pp. 219–43 (223–4).

21. Nicolás Angelcos, 'Women Miners, Labor Integration', p. 220.

22. Nicolás Angelcos, 'Women Miners, Labor Integration', pp. 235, 232.

The second case concerns the city of Arica in the north of Chile, on the border with Peru, which, after a period of mid-century economic prosperity, was in effect turned into an unregulated toxic waste dump by the Chilean Promel Company. Promel had contracted with a large Swedish mining corporation to process tons of sludge but instead left it in an industrial lot. In the 1980s, the government built a series of public housing projects on affected land, without informing residents of danger. In the 1990s, a university investigation and neighbourhood mobilization led to a clean-up, but the wide range of contamination was inadequately managed.

Then the '14 Female Leaders' group (*las 14 dirigentes*) took shape for action. The largely working-class members were apolitical until confronted with a threat to their families. They engaged in collective action including protests, roadblocks, hunger strikes and calls for meetings with authorities, while forming strategic alliances with politicians. They withstood disparaging responses as medical professionals and others blamed them for not taking adequate care of their children and with the alienation of husbands, partners and families, who saw the women as neglecting their domestic duties. The persistence of the fourteen female leaders finally won public notice on the national news following a television programme featuring testimony of dozens of women, mostly mothers. Their efforts gained new legislation requiring a broad response to all future environmental conflicts in Chile, including betterment of neighbourhoods, relocation of residents, and health, education, and environmental services. Women's voices were heard, and their agency was effective. The mothers of Arica did not overturn existing gender categories.[23] They did destabilize the hierarchies those categories usually represent by surmounting their boundaries.

A case from Guatemala is the El Tambor mine, owned by a US company. The mine received its operating license in 2014, despite an incomplete environmental impact statement, no construction permit and a mining moratorium. The La Puya resistance movement has blockaded the entrance to the mine since 2010, protesting both the release of arsenic into local water supplies and the disproportionate consumption of water by the mine operation itself. The government shut down the mine in 2016 as a result of community persistence, legal measures and international publicity.[24] The company then used international trade agreements

23. Evelyn Arriagada, "*Las madres del plomo*": Women's Environmental Suffering in Northern Chile', *Motherhood, Social Policies*, pp. 145–65.

24. Institute for Policy Studies, Common Dreams, 'Mining the Depths of Corruption: New Report Exposes Omissions and Misrepresentations in Nevada-Based Mining Company's Claims in $400 Million Suit against Guatemalan Government', *The Progressive Newswire*, 24 August 2020, https://www.commondreams.org/newswire/2020/08/24/mining-depths-corruption-new-report-exposes-omissions-and-misrepresentations (accessed 29 June 2021); Ellen Moore, 'International Organizations Speak out on Multimillion-Dollar Claim against Guatemala over Failed Mine at La Puya', *Earthworks*, 21 January 2019. Available online: https://www.earthworks.org/blog/international-organizations-speak-out-on-multimillion-dollar-claim-against-guatemala-over-failed-mine-at-la-puya/ (accessed 29 June 2021).

to seek arbitration asking the Guatemalan government asking the Guatemalan government for a $400 million compensation for lost expected income. Women take their turn in twenty-four-hour shifts at the blockade, women position their bodies in the road to block machinery, and women along with male counterparts seek out judicial remedies. At the El Tambor site, women 'are still expected to perform their traditional gender roles'. Women 'cook, serve the meals to the men, clean the site and take care of the children, all this in addition to their daily household chores'.[25] Nevertheless, despite the double burden that maternal and domestic identities place on women, the functional meaning of traditional roles is being reconfigured from within by the crucial part women play in protest leadership.

Rural Andean women in the very different historical, cultural and political contexts of Ecuador and Peru carry on similar types of 'everyday resistance' to large-scale mining developments, affected by yet also affecting gender expectations and disparities.[26] Miranda from Ecuador is concerned about mining's impact on water quality and quantity because 'the men go out to work, they don't stay at home. The woman has to see to the cooking, washing, bathing the children, everything'. Women's connections with water are reinforced by their connection to the earth, expressed through the motif of Pachamama or Mother Earth. Luisa from Peru, where women are primary agriculturalists, explains that 'many women get involved in this struggle for the good of their children, the good of their land'.[27] Women in the Andes perceive themselves to have a 'natural affinity with the land, as women and mothers'.[28] They mobilize out of an appreciation of place, territory and rural livelihoods that have been passed on for generations.[29] As mothers, women see themselves as having more concern than men for future generations, children and grandchildren.[30] Ana María, Violeta and Angélica, all involved in the Guatemalan El Estor mine conflict, express that women are more concerned about the future than the men, both about what tomorrow holds for their children and communities and also about whether traditions will be passed on.[31]

Not only the imagery of environmental responsibility is gendered for these Andean women, so are their practical strategies: female solidarity, consciousness building and networking with related initiatives. At the Fenix mine in El Estor, located next to the country's largest lake, the Indigenous Q'eqchi have been

25. Deonandan and Tatham, 'Unexplored Dimensions of Resistance', p. 277.

26. See Katy Jenkins, 'Unearthing Women's Anti-Mining Activism in the Andes: Pachamama and the "Mad Old Women"', *Antipode* 47:2 (2015), pp. 442–60. https://doi.org/10.1111/anti.12126; Jenkins, 'Staying Put and Carrying On'.

27. Jenkins, 'Unearthing Women's Anti-mining Activism in the Andes', p. 449.

28. Jenkins, 'Unearthing Women's Anti-mining Activism in the Andes', p. 450.

29. Jenkins, 'Staying Put and Carrying On', p. 1453.

30. Jenkins, 'Unearthing Women's Anti-mining Activism in the Andes', p. 451.

31. Kalowatie Deonandan, Rebecca Tatham and Brennan Field, 'Indigenous Women's Anti-mining Activism: A Gendered Analysis of the El Estor Struggle in Guatemala', *Gender and Development* 25 (2017), pp. 405–19 (409). https://doi.org/10.1080/13552074.2017.1379779.

displaced through calculated government violence, including rape and massacres, in order to make way for mining development. Effluent from the mine's refinery pollutes Lake Izabal, leading to compromised water supply, illnesses and birth deformities.[32] Women's commitment to sisterhood and collective action gives them a connection to the long-standing land rights struggles in which their mothers and grandmothers may have participated or which they remember from childhood.[33]

Women's resistance takes place largely at the community level, rather than on the political stage of court cases and legislative battles. At the same time, 'everyday spaces' are 'politicized' and 'intertwined with local, national, and global scales and processes'.[34] Despite upheaval and conflict, women maintain continuity both of everyday resistance and everyday life by incorporating disruptions while "'staying put'" and "'carrying on'".[35] Unbowed by opposition and obstacles, women recruit other women to the cause by building on the common experiences of women to create unity: land, water, community and the futures of their children.[36] In 'bridge leadership', women within the anti-mining movement liaise with other movements to build solidarity, movement strength and broader social cohesion.[37]

Women's mining resistance is sure to encounter pushback, and not infrequently it is violent. The masculine cultural ideal of *machismo* (and its religiously validated counterpart for women, *marianismo*)[38] helps explain not only why violence against women and girls is so pervasive but also why it is protected by a culture of impunity. According to a 2017 United Nations report, Latin America has the world's highest rate of gender-based sexual violence.[39] Outspoken women who lead mining protests, or even engage in protests that take time from household duties, or undermine the control of male family members, can easily experience domestic abuse. They are further subject to reprisals by agents of the mine, by the government and by adversarial community members.

Meanwhile, because foreign investment in mining is advantageous for national and regional governments, protest has become increasingly criminalized and acts of actual and threatened violence are commonplace.[40] The instigator of the

32. Deonandam et al., 'Indigenous Women's Anti-mining Activism', p. 408.

33. Deonandam et al., Indigenous Women's Anti-mining Activism', pp. 412–13.

34. Deonandam et al., 'Indigenous Women's Anti-mining Activism', pp. 413–14.

35. Jenkins, 'Staying Put and Carrying On', p. 1447.

36. Deonandam et al., 'Indigenous Women's Anti-mining Activism', pp, 413–14.

37. Deonandam et al., 'Indigenous Women's Anti-mining Activism', p. 415.

38. See Peter M. Beattie, 'Beyond Machismos: Recent Examinations of Masculinities in Latin America', *Men and Masculinities* 4 (2002), pp. 303–8. https://doi.org/10.1177/109718 4X02004003005.

39. United Nations Human Development Report, 2017. Available online: https://www. undp.org/content/dam/rblac/docs/Research%20and%20Publications/Empoderamiento%20 de%20la%20Mujer/UNDP-RBLAC-ReportVCMEnglish.pdf (accessed 29 June 2021).

40. Jenkins, 'Staying Put and Carrying On', pp. 1448, 1451.

Guatemalan El Tambor blockade, Yolanda Oquelí, has been targeted with attempted assassination. Honduras, home of the murdered environmental defender Berta Caceres, is the scene of a continuing series of killings of activists.

In the case of the Andean women, dramatic confrontations with mine representatives are a relatively infrequent part of a long process. Mining companies wear down or win over resisters by providing employment opportunities and free 'gifts' of household supplies and other bribes. Yet acts of 'everyday' resistance within the community (such as not associating with neighbours who support the mine) have persisted; along with it, community fragmentation has grown. Women's friendships and alliances have been disrupted as women whose husbands or family members work in the mines line up against those who protest its dangers. Opposition of women against other women assumes gendered terms, such as calling adversaries 'mad old women' and 'Pachamamas', meaning unintelligent, unsophisticated and uneducated. Gender norms function as vehicles of social control, producing isolation and high social costs for women who persist in action against the mines. But women's female or maternal self-definition, as connection to the land and solidarity with other women, can yield practices that renegotiate from the ground up the social power open to women.

To gain strength and leverage despite local opposition and intimidation, activist women expand their political reach. They join forces with regional networks, for example the Frente de Mujeres Defensoras de la Pachamama (Front of Women Defenders of Pachamama) in Ecuador, and the international women's organization ULAM (Union Latinoamerica de Mujeres – Union of Latin American Women). Creating or joining a recognized organizational structure gives women more collective power and more authority to negotiate with the state. More broadly, all local resistance initiatives need connections and networked political power to produce the kind of legal and judicial changes that result in enforced and sustainable regulation of mining companies and, for that matter, internal commitment to more socially responsible business practices on the part of the mining companies themselves.[41]

Studies of women's mining protests yield three important points. First, women's activism is carried out within the gendered spaces and constraints that are part of the social milieux of the specific women. In Latin America as in most cultures, socially prescribed gender expectations assign women to domestic roles, especially motherhood, and see public political and economic roles for women as outside the norm and even as offensive to traditional values and ways of life. Even when women

41. In May 2019, Vatican representatives, including Cardinal Peter Turkson (Dicastery for Integral Human Development), mining industry leaders committed to more socially responsible business models (under the auspices of the Development Partner Institute), and representatives of Catholic NGOs and social justice organizations convened at the Vatican for a symposium called 'Mining and the Common Good' and were addressed by Pope Francis, https://www.vaticannews.va/en/pope/news/2019-05/pope-francis-mining-indigenous-rights-development-common-home.html.

are participating equally with men in resistance actions, they are responsible for all the same household and family responsibilities ordinarily required of women.

Second, women share in the fundamental world view and gender conceptions of their culture and so express their protest in 'maternalist' ways that are coherent with that world view. Indigenous women and women who identify as *campesinas* (peasants) themselves use traditional conceptions of womanhood to motivate and justify their activism. However, these conceptions of what is womanly are put into practice in ways that, in effect and practically, reconfigure women's social place.

Third, because women's mining activism consequently transgresses role expectations at the behavioural and political levels, it threatens the status quo of male-oriented social power. This provokes hostility, retaliation and even violence.[42] In other words, women's mining resistance presents 'a microcosm of the larger society'.[43]

As a result of the activist women's involvement and empowerment, attitudes and expectations have begun to change in the outlooks of both women and men. 'In challenging the exploitation wrought by extractive development, women are simultaneously confronting the gender inequities and power disequilibrium within their own societies and also within their households.'[44] The social world is changing. In 2019, FENAMAD, an organization of thirty-seven Indigenous communities in the Madre de Dios region of the Peruvian Amazon, hosted a women's forum in the regional capital of Puerto Maldonado. Women gathered to share experiences and unite in their fight against the extractive industries, deforestation and domestic violence. As one participant attested, 'I have a husband from the community, and he is at home with the kids, cooking dinner … As mothers, we are trying to teach gender equality and show every day that women are fishing, women are farming, women are leading.'[45]

Theological interpretations and insights

Latin American feminist theology

Feminist theology is a reflection on women's experience in light of the gospel. It includes a diagnosis of selfish interests, cruelty and violence, in their personal and structural versions, as sinful. More fundamentally, it is inspired by women's

42. Mary Durran, 'Bolivia: The Impact of a Mine on a Community's Women', 1 November 2012, Caritas Canada, https://www.devp.org/en/blog/bolivia-impact-mine-communitys-women (accessed 6 March 2020).

43. Deonandan and Tatham, 'The Unexplored Dimensions of Resistance to Extractivism in Latin America', p. 277.

44. Deonandan and Tatham, 'The Unexplored Dimensions of Resistance to Extractivism in Latin America', p. 276.

45. Andrew J. Wright, 'Indigenous Women in the Peruvian Amazon Are Leading the Fight for Rights', *Sojourner*, 18 September 2019, https://sojo.net/articles/indigenous-women-peruvian-amazon-are-leading-fight-rights (accessed 13 March 2020).

trust in the redeeming presence of God in Jesus Christ and in confidence that interpersonal and social healing will bring victories for justice. Yet suffering and sin still blight the world, despite the gospel proclamation that Christ is risen and creation made new. One important source of hope is the solidaristic action of Christian communities (with other people of good will), who work courageously and with determination, who stand together and take risks, so that relations and structures might become more compassionate, humane and just. Women's mining activism is a source of such hope.

Latin American and Latina-US women's theologies speak to the transformation of women's suffering by the shared *praxis* of hopeful resistance. They put the practical, particular and local before the universal and doctrinal. According to the Cuban American theologian Ada María Isasi-Díaz, women engage continually in *la lucha* (the struggle) against the adversities of life in *lo cotidiano* (the everyday). *Lo cotidiano* refers to everyday reality, but it also refers to critical awareness of reality, and to taking responsibility for transforming reality, even if only by managing to survive.[46] Indigenous and *campesina* women who lead their communities in mining protests are bravely and successfully carrying on *la lucha*. Women gather strength from the very fact that 'formerly subjugated people' have become 'subjects of our own histories' and 'central characters in our own narratives'. This happens when women in Guatemala, Chile, the Andes and the Amazon jump the fences of gender categories and turn motherhood into a politically subversive *praxis*. When subjugated knowledge interrupts received narratives, the result can be an epistemological 'shock' that opens up and reorders what is considered authoritative.[47]

> *Lo cotidiano* embraces our struggles and our fiestas, our birthing, living and dying; *lo cotidiano* extends to our loving and, tragically, to our hating. *Lo cotidiano* is nurtured by our religious beliefs, the political, our utopias, and those eschatological glimpses we perceive when we are able to take a few steps toward justice. ... Let us not forget *lo cotidiano* as an intrinsic element of woman-centered liberation theologies.[48]

Isasi-Díaz interprets Jesus Christ (*Jesucristo*) as the one who accompanies his disciples in *lo cotidiano*, sharing the suffering, sustaining the struggle, and leading all towards an experience of God's 'Kin-dom' (kingdom or reign of God, in biblical terms), a *familia* of God 'united by bonds of friendship, of love and care, of community'.[49] For Isasi-Díaz, the *praxis* from which Latin American and Latina (US Hispanic) women's theology springs is inclusive and liberatory. The

---

46. Ada María Isasi-Díaz, *La Lucha Continues: Mujerista Theology* (Maryknoll: Orbis, 2004), pp. 100–1.

47. Isasi-Diaz, *La Lucha Continues*, p. 93.

48. Isasi-Diaz, *La Lucha Continues*, p. 104.

49. Isasi-Diaz, *La Lucha Continues*, p. 248.

'Kin-dom' of Jesus Christ (kingdom or reign of God) is a community of friendship and care. Yet the historical *lucha* against oppression still requires conflict with historical marginalization and suffering, including the subordination and silencing of women.

The Mexican-American feminist theologian María Pilar Aquino reinforces this point. Feminist theology (inclusive of men allies) strengthens 'resistance and transformative practices'[50] and celebrates victories of social renewal. It explicitly addresses the desires and hopes 'of oppressed women' for 'a new reality of full citizenship, fiesta and well-being'.[51] From their experience, women recognize God as mother. They recognize the Holy Spirit counselling, consoling and encouraging in a maternal mode. Women are experiencing God as a God of life, as on their side, as calling them to be active participants in processes of liberation and to resist patriarchy everywhere, in society and church.[52]

Gender in recent Catholic Social Teaching

Considering that as recently as 1930, Pope Pius XI, in *Casti connubii*, was proclaiming that women should be obedient to their husbands and that women's equality even in the family and childrearing would be 'a crime',[53] the explicit endorsement of basic gender equality in family and society by official Catholic teaching since the Second Vatican Council (1965) is a remarkable advance. A good representative is the view of Pope John Paul II that 'it is important to underline the equal dignity and responsibility of women with men' and that 'there is no doubt that the equal dignity and responsibility of men and women fully justifies women's access to public functions'.[54] Even more remarkably, this same pope praises 'the great process of women's liberation', lamenting that women 'have often been relegated to the margins of society and even reduced to servitude' and offering an apology: 'And if objective blame, especially in particular historical contexts, has belonged to not just a few members of the Church, for this I am truly sorry.'[55]

In his 2020 encyclical *Fratelli tutti*, Pope Francis calls for 'social friendship' as the basis of social and environmental justice and specifies repeatedly that men and women are included on equal terms. Yet he grants that, although women and men 'possess the same dignity and identical rights', 'we say one thing with words,

---

50. María Pilar Aquino, 'Latin American Feminist Theology', *Journal of Feminist Studies in Religion* 14 (1998), pp. 89–107 (93).

51. Aquino, 'Latin American Feminist Theology', p. 93.

52. María Pilar Aquino, *Our Cry for Life: Feminist Theology from Latin America* (Maryknoll: Orbis, 1993), pp. 131–6.

53. Pius XI, *Casti connubii* (Rome: Editrice Libreria Vaticana, 1930), §74–5.

54. John Paul II, *Familiaris consortio* (Rome: Editrice Libreria Vaticana, 1981), §22–3.

55. John Paul II, *Letter to Women* (Rome: Editrice Libreria Vaticana, 1995), §3.

while 'our decisions and reality tell another story'.[56] To this point, while 66 per cent of local Catholic communities in the Amazon region are women, only 33 per cent of those in decision-making positions are women.[57] A very likely explanation for this discrepancy lies in the reality that the Church's internal structures and socio-political advocacy do not in fact advance equal dignity and rights for women and men. In fact, along with endorsements of theoretical equality, Catholic teaching documents prescribe a model of gender complementarity that tacitly prioritizes women's maternal, familial and domestic roles and curtails their public participation if that is thought to compromise domesticity. According to John Paul II, all women have a 'maternal' personality, and a service-oriented 'feminine genius' for which the model is Mary, wife, mother, handmaid and servant of the Lord. 'Putting herself at God's service, she also put herself at the service of others: a *service of love*.'[58] This ambiguous framework opens the door to selective readings and poses an acute problem of ecclesial complicity in injustice, in countries or regions that are predominantly Catholic, and in which cultural norms prescribe subordination of women similarly to *Casti connubii*.

Pope Francis, Laudato Si' *and the Amazon Synod*

Laudato Si' develops CST in highly significant ways, one of the most important of which is its turn to local and regional governments, civic organizations and civil society to produce results in the face of powerful interests that obstruct change. In calling the Amazon Synod, Pope Francis recognized that CST must emanate and develop from the grassroots and periphery, as well as from ecclesial leadership. Women constitute the majority of the Catholic grassroots and certainly of the periphery. Yet neither *Laudato Si'* nor the Apostolic Exhortation *Querida Amazonia* (2020) highlights the vital work of women as agents of political transformation or recognizes women's potentially huge contribution to the popular mobilization in favour of the planetary justice for which *Laudato Si'* calls.

Positively, *Laudato Si'* uses imagery of the earth as mother and sister to evoke compassionate action from humans, but trades nevertheless on stereotypes of women's family-defined identities, and as awaiting rescue, unable to assert their own rights. These characterizations fail to recognize and critique gender inequalities in the tradition of CST historically or the subordination of women within the family in virtually every society past and present. They reinforce the same gender stereotypes that make it difficult for real women to be advocates for

---

56. Pope Francis, *Fratelli Tutti* (Rome: Editrice Libreria Vaticana, 2020), §23.

57. Andrew J. Wright, 'Women Forge New Path for Catholic Church in Amazon', *Sojourners*, 4 November 2019, https://sojo.net/articles/women-forge-new-path-catholic-church-amazon (accessed 13 March 2020). The data is from the *Pan-Amazonian Atlas* produced by the Pan-Amazonian Ecclesial Network (REPAM).

58. John Paul II, 'Letter to Women', 10.

justice in the very communities most impacted by environmental destruction.[59] Interestingly, however, although *Laudato Si'* presents the Virgin Mary in agency-reducing terms (as a wounded mother who grieves), her spouse Joseph is a good antidote to 'toxic masculinity'; he tenderly cares for wife and child, showing that men who serve (not command) are most truly strong.[60]

Women and women's action, particularly that of Indigenous women, were certainly in view at the 2019 Synod on the Amazon. A delegate to the Amazon Synod, Sr Roselei Bertoldo, affirmed women's own view of themselves as ecclesial agents. 'We are church, and we do church.' Women claim to be and want to be protagonists in the church, with recognized roles, wisdom and authority.[61] The final document of the Amazon Synod and the 2020 Apostolic Exhortation *Querida Amazonia* make progress by identifying women as deserving special attention. Positively, *Querida Amazonia* praises women's roles but, disappointingly, cautions that such roles must 'reflect their womanhood'.[62] Such language can sound patronizing, and not only can be but is used to license violence against women who do not conform to 'womanly' norms. While few Catholic spokespersons or agencies would approve the inequality of women outright, the fact is that relatively few make the defence of women's equality a practical priority or make every effort to ensure that the equal roles of men and women are realized in their own ministries.

Women's activism and Church support

Encouragingly, some local churches and ministries do politically empower women, although these women and their advocacy still have low visibility in the Church's public profile. The Catholic Church in Peru has been a strong supporter of Indigenous communities, training community leaders and drawing on national and international Catholic and political networks to push back against transnational corporations.

In the Loreto region of Peru, two Augustinian priests, Manolo Berjón and Miguel Ángel Cadenas, have fended off incursions from multiple oil spills, most notably in Cuininico, as well as a waterway that would connect Peru to Brazil by

59. The many who have developed similar points include Nichole Flores, Emily Reimer-Barry, Anne Clifford, Ivone Gebara, Tina Beattie and Austin Ivereigh.

60. Pope Francis, *Laudato Si'*, §241–2. On Joseph, see Emily Reimer-Barry, 'On Naming God: Gendered God-Talk in *Laudato Si*'', Catholic Moral Theology blog, 30 June 2015, https://catholicmoraltheology.com/on-naming-god-gendered-god-talk-in-laudato-si/ (accessed 19 August 2021). *Querida Amazonia* praises Mary similarly for her 'tender strength' (101), while unfortunately also insinuating that only men can image Christ (and not bringing up Joseph).

61. *Vatican News*, 'Amazon Synod Briefing'.

62. Pope Francis, *Querida Amazonia* (Rome: Libreria editrice Vaticana, 2020), §103.

dredging parts of three rivers. Disruption endangers not only people, plants and animals but also the spirits believed to inhabit the waters. Berjón and Cadenas are scholars of the Kukama cosmovision. Their advocacy garners well-deserved media attention and praise.[63] Moreover, regional Catholic agencies have helped supply legal counsel and training of Indigenous leadership for court battles over land rights and toxicity resulting from mining and other sorts of resource exploitation.

Less publicized is the indispensable role of women activists and allies. In La Oroya, women are principal environmental leaders who brought and won a lawsuit against the owners of the smelter. In Loreto, Kukama women won a court battle over the legal requirement that the regional government invest a percentage of taxes from extractive companies in the affected communities, specifically, to finance a maternity home, a shelter for abused women, and intercultural education. Peruvian women religious of the Congregation of the Sacred Heart of Jesus have for decades formed a parish team and a faith community with the Augustinian priests of Santa Rita de Castilla parish (including Cardenas and Berjón) to minister in Cuininico and other communities in the region. The sisters' mission is in part to support women's rights, educate women and prepare women leaders. In fact, some community women look to the sisters especially as positioning them for effective leadership.[64]

In Cuininico, women formed three grassroots organizations and successfully demanded compensation from the government after the oil spill.[65] Their cause was motivated by their responsibilities as mothers to care for their children's health and education, to put food on the family table, and by their hope that their children would leave the community for an education, even if the spill were never cleaned up. Signs of changing social expectations are that the women were supported by the Vicariate of Iquitos, which provided information and legal defence, as well as by husbands who took over some family duties to contribute to the collective fight.[66] The growing conviction of both women and men that they are equal participants

---

63. See Barbara Fraser, 'Peruvian Parish Follows the Flow of the River', *National Catholic Reporter*, 28 July 2015, www.ncronline.org; Paolo Moiola, 'Peru: Interview with Augustine Missionaries Miguel Ángel Cadenas and Manolo Berjón', *Eurasia Review* (Latinamerica Press), 13 September 2011; Manolo Berjón and Miguel Ángel Cadenas, 'Seminarians, Some Challenges for the Church from Indigenous Peoples', 31 December 2017 (REPAM. redamazonica.org/).

64. Francesca García Delgado and Vanessa Romo, 'In an Oil Spill's Aftermath, New Voices Lead an Indigenous Fight for Justice', *Mongaby*, 18 December 2020, https://news.mongabay.com/2020/12/in-an-oil-spills-aftermath-in-peru-new-voices-lead-an-indigenous-fight-for-justice/ (accessed 4 March 2021).

65. On the women of Cuininico, see Delgado and Romo, 'In an Oil Spill's Aftermath'; and Deborah Delgado and Vania Martinez, *En un Ambiente Tóxico: Ser Madres Después de un Derrame de Petróleo* (Lima: OXFAM and Consejo Latinoamericano de Ciencias Sociales, 2020).

66. Delgado and Martinez, *En un Ambiente Tóxico*, pp. 50–6.

in demanding accountability for the Cuininico oil spill has been fostered by women's opportunities to speak in local meetings, trainings by the local parish, respect from Archdiocesan representatives, outside speakers and workshops, and by the attitudes of state and Petroperú representatives.[67]

Women's religious orders and the International Federation of Superiors General can bring enhanced visibility, personal, institutional and financial resources, and political clout to communities around mining sites. The Global Sisters Report[68] showcases the work of religious sisters who help local communities to fight the unjust effects of mining, especially toxicity, featuring a series on mining and murders in Honduras. 'Catholicism' and 'the Church' are of course not limited to the clergy, to parishes, episcopal initiatives, Vatican dicasteries, or men's and women's religious orders. All Catholics are the church. In Chile, for instance, a Women-Church group (Mujeres-Iglesia) formed in 2016 and joined a national women's march in 2020,[69] contributing to a Catholic advocacy culture that supports women like the community-level mining resisters.

Empowerment of women must be carried out in prophetic yet culturally appropriate ways, respecting women's own perceptions of gender identity and the gender-related values which define their goals and inspire their commitment. It must prioritize local women's leadership and ownership by the Catholic community as a whole. These women have shown that maternal identities can become politically potent forces that subvert hierarchies of gender, religion, class and economics. At the same time, as attested by the women of Cuininico, women can gain confidence in their own voices and equality with the example and support of 'outside' allies.

More attention by official Catholic Social Teaching could make equal inclusion of women normative for all Catholic activities, making inroads in resistant cultures. An outstanding advocate of Indigenous communities is the Archbishop of Huancayo and President of the Pan-Amazonian Ecclesial Network (REPAM), Cardinal Pedro Ricardo Barreto, S.J. As Archbishop, Barreto established an environmental task force, campaigned personally for the credibility of scientific evidence of lead exposure and joined forces with an interfaith regional environmental project called Mantaro Revive.[70] He testified before the US Congress against the US-based company that ran the La Oroya smelting plant.[71] As REPAM President, Barreto has

---

67. Delgado and Martinez, *En un Ambiente Tóxico* p. 56.

68. The Global Sisters Report is a project of the *National Catholic Reporter*. Available online: https://www.globalsistersreport.org/content/about-global-sisters-report.

69. Roberto Urbino Avedaño, 'Women-Church Present at the Historic Women's Demonstration in Chile', *Vida Nueva*, 10 March 2020, https://www.vidanuevadigital.com/2020/03/10/mujeres-iglesia-presentes-en-historica-manifestacion-de-mujeres-en-chile/ (accessed 30 June 2021).

70. Stefanie Graeter, 'To Revive an Abundant Life: Catholic Science and Neoextractivist Politics in Peru's Mantaro Valley', *Cultural Anthropology* 32:1 (2017), pp. 117–48.

71. Wright, 'Women Force New Path for Catholic Church in Amazon'.

integrated women into the leadership of the Panamazonian Network, appointing a Harabut woman and a religious sister to the presidency team.[72]

Conclusion

The extractive industries are a blight on local environments worldwide, and this is certainly true in the Amazon region. Women are affected in special ways by the damage, and women are among the most committed mining resisters and advocates for reform. Yet women's political change-agency is obstructed by cultural and ecclesial gender norms that aim to confine women's influence to the domestic sphere. While many Latin American women are inspired to environmental advocacy precisely by maternal and familial values, they interpret these values to demand political engagement to protect children, families, land and traditions. In practice, the 'maternalist' rhetoric of women mining activists redefines maternal space and reconfigures gendered power in the community as a whole.

Networking among women and women's groups can strengthen women's political effectiveness, as can the support of male allies, clerical and pastoral allies, and 'outsider' allies, including regional, national and international supporters. Representatives of and organizations within the Roman Catholic Church, especially at the local and regional levels, increasingly recognize the importance of empowering women to be effective environmental leaders. But the voice of Catholic Social Teaching in support of women's political agency remains muted. While official teaching documents occasionally praise women, they fail to champion women's active confrontation with and direct resistance to unjust structures, economic exploitation and political corruption.

Catholic initiatives at the practical, political level can and should do more to incorporate, promote and expand the equal agency of women against very specific threats to 'our common home', like mining toxicity. As demonstrated by initiatives of REPAM, formal ecclesial affiliation and recognition lend support to community leaders and can position individuals and organizations to take advantage of the global institutional structures and networks of Roman Catholicism to expand their advocacy work. Reinforcement in formal teaching documents would publicize that women's full participation and leadership are expected and indeed mandated for all Catholic ministries and communities. Moreover, it would name, claim and commission women as crucial agents of the Catholic environmental justice mission.

72. REPAM, 'Yésica Patiachi, from the Harakbut Indigenous People, Appointed REPAM Councilor', 6 March 2021, https://redamazonica.org/2021/03/yesica-patiachi-del-pueblo-indigena-harakbut-nombrada-consejera-de-la-repam/ (accessed 23 June 2021).

A PRACTITIONER'S RESPONSE TO DEBORAH DELGADO PUGLEY AND LISA SOWLE CAHILL

Kuzipa Nalwamba

Lisa Sowle Cahill's chapter, 'Mining and women's activism: Still under the surface of Catholic Social Teaching', observes that women's activism against mining has not found expression in Catholic Social Teaching (CST), despite its prominence in South America. She outlines this lacuna with illustrations from the 2014 Pan-Amazonian Ecclesial Network (REPAM), the 2015 Papal encyclical, *Laudato Si'*, and the 2019 Synod on the Amazon. Debora Delgado Pugley's 'Toxicity in the times of project-based development: Indigenous women facing oil and gold pollution in the Peruvian Amazon basin' offers a critical assessment of the project-based logic in developmental projects, illustrating with examples its limited impact to remedy toxic contamination. Pugley names the systemic outcomes of the project-based logic, which benefits the elite and unduly burdens Indigenous communities. Her case studies specifically depict the adverse effects of mining on Indigenous women, while also highlighting Indigenous women's resilience and resistance in face of powerful and pervasive and governmental interests.

In this response, I will apply a 'see and lament' lens to the situations described by Pugley and Cahill. Such a lens allows us to move from merely voicing grievance to expressing hope. As Emmanuel Katongole says, 'the ability to name pain and voice grief is itself a form of hope'.[1] This response chapter further draws on studies by the World Council of Churches, my current vocational location. My own native African theological context also informs this chapter, specifically my experience as a minister in the United Church of Zambia (UCZ) and as a lecturer and Dean at the UCZ Theological College.

---

1. E. Katongole, *Born from Lament: The Theology and Politics of Hope in Africa* (Grand Rapids, MI: William B. Eerdmans, 2017). Roman Catholic theologian, Emmanuel Katongole's book explores a biblically grounded theology of hope through the lens of the war-torn eastern Democratic Republic of Congo in which he highlights the particular suffering of women. Against that backdrop, he affirms hope as the essence of Christian identity and a logic located within the narrative of Christ's death and resurrection, affirming that stories that display hope provide evidence of the lived reality of hope in action.

Responding to Lisa Sowle Cahill

Cahill problematizes keeping women's agency 'under the surface' of the CST. She notes that recent CST does not go far enough in naming the structural marginalization of women and fails to acknowledge their contributions in the fight against resource extraction and deforestation. Thus, while *Querida Amazonia* (2020) acknowledges women's suffering, it does neither repudiate patriarchy nor highlight the vital work of women as agents of transformation and popular mobilization for climate justice that the Pope's landmark encyclical *Laudato Si'* calls for. The structural resistance and potential for transformation inherent in women's actions have not yet inspired theological imagery that challenges stereotypes. This is the case even though the development of *Laudato Si'* was a consultative process and women constitute the grassroot majority of the Catholic Church.

Cahill further provides research-based depictions of the effects of large-scale mining on women's lives. The accounts of toxic contamination, social dislocation and gender-based violence are all too familiar and should inform and shape the theological grammar of CST. Women's multi-layered performances of lament over environmental damage and their resistance against powerful political and economic interests provide a grammar for an Indigenous Christian narrative that arises at the intersection of despair and resilient hope.

Despite her critique, Cahill admits that the papal documents she references have moved the needle on women issues. Specifically, she refers to Vatican II's endorsement of gender equality and the call for 'social friendship' in Pope's Francis' 2020 encyclical *Fratelli Tutti: On Fraternity and Social Friendship.* These advancements, however, have taken place without structural renewal of the frame of reference.[2] It is true that paradigms are overturned only incrementally; they do not usually replace one another in a dramatic form but often overlap and exist side by side, mutually influencing and even subverting one another. Yet, for true progress on gender issue to occur, CST will need to press for a more fundamental shift in paradigm.

In her chapter, Cahill offers some 'building stones' for such a shift by way of her 'thick' description of women's 'everyday resistance'. Her section on feminist theological reflections further sketches a compelling cluster of ideas, which valourizes transformation through hopeful resistance and daily struggle (*lo cotidiano la lucha*). I agree that these ideas, nurtured by faith and lived experience, are readily available theological resources to fill the lacuna Cahill identifies in CST.

---

2. Catholic Social Teaching nurtured my own 'voice' on social justice issues through my involvement with the Jesuit Centre for Theological Reflection in Zambia during my formative years as a young woman Christian leader. Cf. Kuzipa Nalwamba, 'Cultural Values and Public Life', *JCTR Bulletin* 3 (2009), pp. 17–19.

Catholic religious sister, Bernadette Mbuy Beya, in her book chapter 'Women in the Church in Africa: Possibilities for Presence and Promises', depicts the role of women in the church in this way: '(h)er activity is seen in the liturgy; she devotes her talents to the choir; she directs and guides the young: and at the offertory, alongside a man, she offers to God "the fruit of the earth and the work of her hands"'.[3] Despite this often invisible presence, Sr Beya affirms the presence of theologies of African women through the work of the Circle of Concerned African Women Theologians (hereafter the Circle). She refers to *The Will to Arise: Women, Tradition and the Church in Africa*[4] as an example of women breaking silence through lament and hope in writing about their real lives. The Circle critically engages a patriarchal mind-frame through feminist theological reflection. As an ecumenical gathering of women's 'written voices', the Circle is a lived example of ongoing transformation that critically assesses male-dominated theological frameworks as it affirms, nourishes and nurtures women's theologies so that 'power flows from all to all among those who are in the circle of life'.[5]

Keeping these women's theologies on the periphery of churches (not only CST) and theological discourse is feeding into the continuation of structural violence against women, even as they defend life. Cahill's contribution, then, is an invitation to an unambiguous theological engagement with God in the place where the loss of life, loss of community and loss of land to mining contamination meet with resistance and resilience of Amazon women. This is the good news we witness; it is a witness to which we are *all* called because witnessing to the good news of Jesus is our *common* baptismal calling. Through the gifting of the Holy Spirit, *all* believers become co-workers with God. The Faith and Order's ecumenical convergence document, which the Catholic Church has affirmed, asserts that.[6]

For many women in the church, however, the invitation to ministry is not tantamount to an invitation to leadership. To them baptism and the gifting of the Spirit as Christians' joyful common calling to service in Christ still are not

---

3. M. B. Mbey, 'Women in the Church in Africa: Possibilities for Presence and Promises', in Nyambura J. Njoroge and Musa W. Dube (eds), *Talitha Cum! Theologies of African Women* (Pietermaritzburg: Cluster Publications, 2001).

4. Mercy Amba Oduyoye and Musimbi R. A. Kanyoro, *The Will to Arise: Women, Tradition and the Church in Africa* (Maryknoll: Orbis Books, 2005).

5. Nyambura J. Njoroge and Musa W. Dube (eds), *Talitha Cum! Theologies of African Women* (Pietermaritzburg: Cluster Publications, 2001), p. 1.

6. *Baptism, Eucharist and Ministry (BEM)*, also called the Lima Document, is an ecumenical convergence document adopted by members of the World Council of Churches in Lima in 1982. Such ecumenical agreements in sacramental theology have affected Catholic–Orthodox relations and Catholic–Protestant relations, especially the recognition of Trinitarian baptisms that signify common gifting by the Spirit and common witness to the good news of Jesus Christ.

a lived reality. Cahill demonstrates, however, that despite multiple intersecting disadvantages, it would be wrong to conclude that women do not exercise agency. Indeed, in the Amazon, women activists use their traditional gender roles to subversive ends. Moreover, without essentializing women, the fact remains that as the primary caretakers of their families, women in the Amazon do endure most of the negative effects of the toxicity of large-scale mining. Cahill's contribution thus valourizes women's experiences as a resource for theologizing. How can those experiences be systematized so that they take root in the Church and in CST?

Responding to Deborah Delgado Pugley

Using case studies, Pugley's chapter offers a critical assessment of the project-based logic applied to resource development and to solving toxic mining contamination. The case studies make the analysis specific and concrete. The references to women's activism against the toxic contamination of mining allow for deeper reflection and theological reorientation. Unlike Cahill, Pugley does not write as a theologian or an ethicist, yet she does make space for ethical reflection in pursuit of the common good and, hence, creates an opening for a cross-disciplinary conversation with theologians. Her reference to toxic environments as socio-ecologically connected landscapes evokes the theological significance of the *oikoumene*, i.e. the whole inhabited world that is our interconnected shared home, also echoing the papal encyclical *Laudato Si'*.

The 2004 Accra Confession, a document of the World Communion of Reformed Churches (formerly World Alliance of Reformed Churches), discerns and declares the global economic system as fundamentally unjust. It names the role theology must play in public spaces as a reflective building block for social transformation and the pursuit of the flourishing of life and justice for the whole inhabited world. Such theological endeavour would necessarily be collaborative and must open itself up to the lived experiences of (minoritized) women when critically assessing dominant power structures as they 'seek liberation for the entire community in an overarching oppressive social order'.[7] The latter requires a 'mediating ethics' that renounces privilege.

Pugley's case study titled 'Cuninico: Building a voice for justice out of environmental grief' is a story of resistance that grows out of vulnerability. She speaks of 'remediated suffering' that gives the community dignity and purpose. Lately, vulnerability and conviviality have made their way into academic

---

7. Emily M. Townes, 'Womanist Theology', https://ir.vanderbilt.edu/bitstream/handle/1803/8226/Townes-WomanistTheology.pdf?isAllowed=y&sequence=1#:~:text=W OMANIST%20THEOLOGY%20is%20a%20form,are%20seen%20as%20theological%20 problems (accessed 12 August 2022), p. 161.

theological discourse. Are Indigenous women, who may not insist on visibility and recognition of their activism, exemplifiers of those notions?

The 'anthropological constants'[8] of embodiment, relational dependence, ambiguity and mortality mean that we live on the verge of harm, which makes vulnerability the matrix in which we negotiate life and encounter God's redemption.[9] The human search for a life without pain, suffering and fragility reveals how dependably tethered to our vulnerability we are. Yet that inherent desire to escape vulnerability carries with it the propensity to exploit the vulnerability of others. Indeed, the Covid-19 pandemic revealed scourges of discrimination that deny our common humanity.

Pugley decries project-oriented logic and solutions because they shrink the space for moral and ethical considerations and compartmentalize otherwise structurally connected realities. She points to mujerista theology that recognizes intersections and interdisciplinarity. While I applaud this type of inter-disciplinarity, I wonder at the same time whether Christian theology is always faithful to its foundational relational truth. The anthropocentric, hierarchical and patriarchal system too often only contributes to the problem. Kwok Pui-Lan therefore proposes 'recycling Christianity',[10] alluding to a need for *metanoia* (repentance) and resurrection in order to move from an ecclesial to an ecological solidarity[11] as a radical (going back to the roots) transformation.

The World Council of Churches' Ecological Solidarity and the Ecumenical Decade of Churches in Solidarity with Women from 1988 to 1998 urged the full participation of women in church and societal life, decrying racist, classist and sexist ideas as a struggle for justice, peace and the integrity of creation.[12] Mercy Amba Oduyoye saw this decade as a time 'for women, to dream bold dreams for a new community ... and raise awareness that a society's attitude towards women directly relates to what it means to be authentically human and truly religious'.[13] Yet while the ecumenical focus on ecological solidarity with women and the earth was intended to inspire radical transformation, it has mainly led to

---

8. Edward Schillebeeckx, *Christ: The Experience of Jesus as Lord* (New York: Herder & Herder, 1980), p. 733.

9. Elizabeth O'Donnell Gandolfo, *The Power and Vulnerability of Love: A Theological Anthropology* (Minneapolis: Fortress Press, 2015), p. 34.

10. Kwok Pui-Lan, *Globalization, Gender and Peacebuilding: The Future of Interfaith Dialogue* (New York/Mawah, NJ: Paulist Press, 2011), pp. 109–10.

11. Kwok Pui-Lan, 'Ecology and the Christian Recycling of Christianity' in David Hallman (ed.), *Ecotheology: Voices from South and North* (Geneva: World Council of Churches Publications, 1994), pp. 107–11.

12. Kwok, 'Ecology and the Christian Recycling of Christianity', p. 11.

13. Mercy A. Oduyoye, *Who Will Roll the Stone Away? The Ecumenical Decade of the Churches in Solidarity with Women* (Geneva: World Council of Churches Publishing, 1991).

incremental change.[14] Nonetheless these inspirational movements and initiatives remain an important source of inspiration for re-imagining our shared life together on a fragile planet.

Conclusion

Pugley and Cahill each interweave lament and hope and thereby invite the reader to be in solidarity. They both see and name the situation of women in the Amazon in a way that moves one with rage, helplessness and hope. Their telling of the women's courageous resilience grasps the complexity of structural violence and reveals the complicity of multiple actors, including the church. Epistemologically, their ability to see and lament underlines that those who suffer discover new ways of knowing and seeing reality. The experiences of Amazonian Indigenous women chronicled by Pugley and Cahill have a *theological* shape in that they move us from seeing to lament. How may their lament shape Christian teaching and action against the existential crisis posed by the toxic contamination of large-scale mining?

14. E. Mombo, 'Reflections on Peace in the Decade to Overcome Violence', *Ecumenical Review* 61 (2021), pp. 71–6. Even though the assessment in this article is not about the decade, the author focuses on violence against women in the context of evaluating the declaration by the World Council of Churches (WCC) of the Decade to Overcome Violence 2001–2010: Churches Seeking Reconciliation and Peace (DOV). The DOV was a call to churches and all people of goodwill to commit themselves to peace and an appeal to work for the empowerment of victims of violence and to act in solidarity with those in the struggle for justice, peace and integrity of creation. The DOV urged repentance for complicity in violence and reflection in order to overcome the spirit, logic and practice of violence. For that reason and because it came later, this evaluation is apt.

Part 4

GLOBAL SOLIDARITY

Chapter 8

#FRACK OFF

TOWARDS A DECOLONIAL, ECO-FEMINIST THEOLOGICAL ENGAGEMENT WITH FRACKING AND THE MMIWG2S CRISIS ON THE BERTHOLD RESERVATION IN NORTH DAKOTA

Hilda P. Koster

Extractive industries treat Mother Earth like they treat women ... They think they can own us, buy us, sell us, trade us, rent us, poison us, rape us, destroy us, use us as entertainment and kill us. I am happy to see that we are talking about the level of violence that is occurring against Mother Earth because it equates to us [women]. What happens to her happens to us ... We are the creators of life. We carry the water that creates life just as Mother Earth carries the water that maintains our life.

Lisa Brunner, White Earth Ojibwe Nation, Executive Director
of Sacred Spirits First Nations Coalition[1]

In 2008 the United States' Geological Service estimated that the Bakken rock formation in Western North Dakota and Montana held between 3 and 4.3 billion of barrels of 'undiscovered' oil trapped in microscopic pores in shale rock. These previously inaccessible shale oil reserves became available for

---

#Frack Off started as a grassroots' campaign against unconventional gas extraction by way of hydraulic fracturing (fracking) in the UK. The motto has been adopted by Indigenous activist groups, most notably by the Indigenous anti-fracking coalition in the greater Chaco region in New Mexico. Cf. https://www.frackoffchaco.org/.

1. Cited by Mary Annette Pember, 'Brave Heart Women Fight to Ban Man-Camps, Which Bring Rape and Abuse', *Indian Country Today Media Network*, 28 August 2013. Available online https://indiancountrymedianetwork.com/news/brave-heart-women-fight-to-ban-man-camps-which-bring-rape-and-abuse/ (accessed 8 February 2022).

recovery by way of the new, and highly controversial, technology of hydraulic fracturing or fracking, which started a modern-day oil rush that lasted from 2009 through 2018.[2] One-third of the Bakken oil development is on or near the Fort Berthold Indian reservation, which is the home of the three affiliated tribal nations of the Mandan, Hidatsa and Arikara (MHA Nation). In April 2017 Fort Berthold had 1,582 active wells producing 187,519 barrels of oil per day, with 114 wells awaiting completion and 507 drilling permits. At the height of the boom, oil production on the Berthold became so large that, if the Berthold would have been a state, it would rank among the seventh largest oil-producing states in the United States.[3]

The Berthold boom has brought much-needed income, and even wealth, to the MHA nation, which had been $100 million in debt and had a 70 per cent unemployment rate prior to the boom. Yet while tribal leadership has actively promoted fracking on the Berthold, oil development is shaped by past and settler colonial violence. The Berthold was established in 1868 when the Treaty of Fort Laramie reduced the more than 12 million acres of the traditional territories of the MHA nation to a mere 1 million acres.[4] Further dispossession came in the wake of the allotment policy by the ill-fated 1887 Dawes Act, which divided tribal lands into private property; lands that were not alloted to tribal members were put up for sale. This dramatically carved up the reservation – of the 988,000 acres (4,000 km²) spanning the Berthold reservation, only 457,837 acres (1,853 km²) are currently in tribal possession. Yet perhaps most devastating for the three affiliated tribes has been the 1953 construction of the Garrison Dam, which created Lake Sakakawea – a more than 300,000 acres lake – by flooding the reservation's rich agricultural lands. As a result, 80 per cent of reservation's residents had to leave their homes

2. Despite decline in production, the Bakken still produced 900,600 barrels of oil each day in April 2022. Christa Case Bryant, 'Demand for Oil Is Spiking. So Why Are North Dakota Rigs Lying Idle?', in *The Christian Science Monitor*, 15 April 2022. Available online: https://www.csmonitor.com/Environment/2022/0415/Demand-for-oil-is-spiking.-So-why-are-North-Dakota-rigs-lying-idle (accessed 22 June 2022). Cf., https://www.usnews.com/news/best-states/north-dakota/articles/2022-06-16/nd-oil-production-drops-below-1-million-barrels-a-day (accessed 22 June 2022).

3. Cf., Sierra Crane-Murdoch, 'The Other Bakken Boom: America's Biggest Oil Rush Brings Tribal Conflict', *High Country News*, 23 April 2012. Available online: https://www.hcn.org/issues/44.6/on-the-fort-berthold-reservation-the-bakken-boom-brings-conflict (accessed 8 February 2022).

4. I am relying here on the excellent telling of the story of oil development on the Bakken by Katherine Wiltenburg Todrys, *Black Snake: Standing Rock, the Dakota Access Pipeline,*

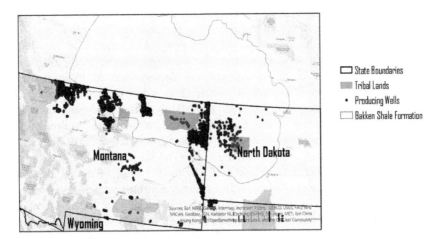

Figure 8.1 Map of active oil wells in Montana and Western North Dakota. Prepared by Hannah Gilsdorf (Concordia College, Moorhead, MN, USA, Class of '22).

Data Sources: Crude Oil Pipelines (2020) [downloaded shapefile]. United States Energy Information Administration website. URL: https://www.eia.gov/maps/layer_info-mphp; Bakken Formation (2013) [downloaded file]. United States Geological Survey ScienceBase-Catalog. URL: https://www.sciencebase.gov/catalog/item/529fbb60e4b01942f4ab9f19; TIGER/Line Shapefile, 2017, nation, Current American Indian Tribal Subdivision (AITS) National (2017) [downloaded shapefile]. United States Census Bureau on Data.gov. URL: https://catalog.data.gov/dataset/tiger-line-shapefile-2017-nation-u-s-current-american-indian-tribal-subdivision-aits-national; WellSurface (2015) [downloaded file]. Montana Board of Oil and Gas Conservation GIS Data. URL: http://www.bogc.dnrcmt.gov/gisdata/; Wells (2020) [downloaded shapefile]. North Dakota Department of Mineral Resources Oil and Gas Division on Oil and Gas: ArcIMS Viewer. URL: https://www.dmr.nd.gov/OaGIMS/viewer.htm; download database of wells, recovery units and field boundaries [downloaded geodatabase]. South Dakota Department of Environment and Natural Resources. http://www.sdgs.usd.edu/SDOIL/oilgas_databases.aspx; States (2018) [downloaded shapefile]. United States Census Bureau. URL: https://www.census.gov/geographies/mapping-files/time-series/geo/carto-boundary-file.html.

and Environmental Justice (Lincoln, NE: Bison Books, 2021), chapters 1 and 2. The 'Black Snake' refers to an ancient Indigenous prophecy about a terrible black snake that will one day devour the earth, when talking about the oil pipelines that criss-cross underneath Indigenous land, lakes and rivers. For an in-depth historical account of the history of the tribal nations on the High Plains, see David Treuer, *The Heartbeat of Wounded Knee: Native America from 1890 to the Present* (New York: Riverhead Books, 2019), Part 4.

behind and relocate to the poor soil of the higher plains; they were to be settled in newly formed communities scattered across the reservations. The loss of land not just meant a loss of livelihood and, hence, deep poverty for most of the Berthold's residents, but also very much a disconnect from identity, belonging and spirituality.[5]

Given this background of displacement and dispossession, MHA leadership's promotion of oil development on the Berthold as a way to political-economic independence is not surprising. Indeed, the MHA's former chairman Tex Hall (Mandan/Arikara) famously stated that 'our sovereignty, our independence, can be maximized by the number of barrels of oil taken from Mother Earth. We call it "sovereignty by the barrel."'[6] Yet, according to Lisa DeVille (Mandan), co-founder of Fort Berthold's Protectors of Water and Earth Rights (POWER), oil development on the Berthold happened too hastily and without proper environmental risk assessment.[7] Deville describes how due to lack of legal protection fracking has led to staggering levels of pollution that has caused spikes in cancers, cardiovascular and respiratory diseases among Berthold's residents, who already battle poverty-related diseases and generally have poor access to proper health care.[8] The fracking and pipeline industry has further brought thousands of unattached male oil workers to the Bakken region, who are typically housed in so-called man-camps, which are known breeding grounds for sex trafficking and other forms of gender-based violence. The proximity of these camps to the Berthold has created a tremendously unsafe environment for Indigenous women, girls and two-spirit persons, who have been targeted for abduction, rape and murder: in 2016 alone 125 Native women went missing in North Dakota and Montana. Tragically, then, fracking turned the Berthold into the epicenter of the Missing and Murdered Women, Girls and Two Spirit Persons (MMIWG2S) crisis.[9]

There are multiple ways environmental pollution and the explosion of gender-based violence on the Berthold are interconnected with settler colonialism. The first part of this chapter focuses on the complicated legal structures that prevents MHA leadership from adequately implementing environmental legislation and prosecute violent crimes committed by non-Natives on Native land. Drawing on the important work by Indigenous legal scholars Sarah Deer (Creek) and Elizabeth

---

5. On the use of dams as a tool of settler colonial violence see Dina Gilio-Whitaker, *As Long as Grass Grows: The Fight for Indigenous Environmental Justice from Colonization to Standing Rock* (Boston: Beacon Press, 2017), pp. 60–2. The social and cultural disintegration caused by the creation of Lake Sakakawea greatly exacerbated the intergenerational trauma caused by the shameful history of boarding schools, by which settler society forcefully removed Native children from their families with the aim to assimilate them into settler society, a practice that in the Dakotas started as early as 1876 and lasted till 1961.

6. Crane-Murdoch, 'The Other Bakken Boom.'

7. Todrys, *Black Snake*, Chapter 1.

8. Todrys, *Black Snake*, p. 22.

9. Adamson, 'Vulnerabilities of Women in Extractive Industries', p. 28. Two-spirit refers to someone who '[identifies] as having both a masculine and a feminine spirit and is used by some Indigenous people to describe their sexual, gender and/or spiritual identity'. Cf., https://lgbtqhealth.ca/community/two-spirit.php (accessed 11 February 2022).

Ann Kronk (Chippewa), I argue that it is the persistent legal infringement on tribal sovereignty by the United States' government that continues to fuel the rape of Indigenous lands and people by settler society.[10]

Building on this analysis, the second half of the chapter offers an eco-feminist and decolonial engagement with extractivism – an engagement that connects the gender ideology operative in extractive capitalism with the logic of coltoniality (the systemic codifications of knowledge and being that continue to render certain people and lands extractable). I further turn to Potawatomi environmental philosopher Kyle Whyte, who stresses the significance of attending to Indigenous accounts of environmental justice, i.e. environmental justice that promotes Indigenous eco-social resilence, or what Whyte calls 'social continuance'. The final section of the chapter confronts Amer-European Christianity's entanglement with settler colonial extractivism. Following Whyte, I read settler Christianity as a form of 'vicious sedimentation', and hence itself constitutive of the extractive colonial logic undergirding late-modern capitalism. In order to disrupt and subvert this dynamic I argue in favor of a decolonial, eco-feminist theology; a theology that grants hemeneutical privilege to the experiences of Indigenous women and SLGBTQQIA activists in extractive zones and that is fully attuned to Indigenous struggles for environmental justice.

Before moving into the body of my argument, I want to take a moment to position myself. I write from my location as a white Amer-European settler whose writing is informed by first-hand accounts of the detrimental effects of the oil development on Indigenous communities throughout North Dakota and Minnesota. While researching this chapter I had the privilege to work and live on the ancestral lands of the Red Lake Bands of Ojibwe and the Dakota Oyate (presently existing as composite parts of the Red Lake, Turtle Mountain, White Earth Bands, and the Dakota Tribes of Minnesota and North Dakota), where I learned from the Indigenous water protectors at Standing Rock (2016) and the Indigenous women and two-spirit people led coalition protesting the Enbridge's line 3 pipeline (2021).[11] I am especially grateful for the Indigenous activists, scholars, politicians and authors who gave their time and shared their work, experience and wisdom with me.[12] As a settler Christian theologian, I am part

---

10. Sarah Deer and Elizabeth Ann Kronk Warner, 'Raping Indian Country', University of Utah College of Law Research Paper No. 344 (December 2019), pp. 1–49 (5). Available online https://papers.ssrn.com/sol3/papers.cfm?abstract_id=3497007 (accessed 18 June 2022).

11. For background on the Standing Rock protests, cf. https://americanindian.si.edu/nk360/plains-treaties/dapl (accessed 8 December 2022). For the line 3 protests, cf. https://www.stopline3.org (accessed 8 December 2022). The Giniw Collective, Camp Migizi, Red Lake Treaty Camp, RISE Coalition, and Honor the Earth among others have been at the centre of the pipeline 3 resistance.

12. I am especially grateful to the following persons for sharing their knowledge and wisdom with me: Lisa Brunner (Ojibwe), Ruth Buffalo (Mandan/ Arikara), Sarah Deer (Creek), Annita Luchessi (Cheyenne) and Katherine Wiltenburg.

of ecclesial and theological traditions that have been deeply complicit with settler colonialism, white supremacy, racism and sexism. I wrestle with these historical and present-day entanglements as I seek to trace the Spirit of 'God's justice making and Earth honoring love' within movements for ecological justice and ecological flourishing.[13]

Rape of the Land: Pollution as settler colonial violence

Hydraulic fracturing is a hugely invasive technique that evokes, in a visceral manner, the image of rape. Fracking involves drilling a vertical hole followed by a horizontal branch in shale rock formations which is then forcefully punctured.[14] The perforations are subsequently used to press fracking fluids (consisting of water, chemicals and silica sands) into the shale rock under extremely high pressure, shattering (fracking) layers of rock formation forcing oil and gas to be released. This then allows the oil and gas to be pumped to the surface for gathering, processing and transportation.

Fracking thus shatters the subsurface of the earth. It also is staggeringly wasteful and poisonous. Fracking fluids consist of highly toxic chemicals (many of which oil companies do not need to disclose).[15] The regurgitated wastewater emitted from fracking wells is heavily contaminated by these chemicals and, hence, cannot be repurposed. It therefore is disposed of deep underground or, as is the case in western North Dakota, in so-called holding tanks, where it evaporates into the air. The wasteful use of water by fracking – it can take between 1.5 million and 9.7 million gallons of water to frack a single well – obviously is a matter of grave concern on the high plains of North Dakota, which receives only about fifteen inches of rain each year.[16] Equally disturbing are the

---

13. The concept of 'God's justice making and Earth honoring love' was first introduced to me by Lutheran eco-theologian Cynthia Moe-Lobeda. Cf., Cynthia Moe-Lobeda, *Resisting Structural Evil: Love as Ecological-Economic Vocation* (Minneapolis: Fortress Press, 2013), p. 163.

14. For an explanation of hydraulic fracking for oil and gas, including its environmental implications, see Melissa Denchak, 'Fracking 101', *The National Resource Defense Council*, 19 April 2019; https://www.nrdc.org/stories/fracking-101 (accessed 8 February 2022).

15. Known chemicals that are part of fracking fluids are methanol, ethylene glycol, propargyl alcohol, lead and hydrogen fluoride, all of which are considered hazardous to human health.

16. On the implications of fracking for freshwater resources, see the first edition of Christiana (Zenner) Peppard's excellent book *Just Water: Theology, Ethics, and the Global Water Crisis* (Maryknoll: Orbis, 2014). Note that in the second edition of Peppard's book (published by Orbis in 2018 under her maiden name, Zenner) this chapter is replaced by the equally fine chapter on the 2016 Standing Rock protests.

countless large and smaller wastewater spills, many on or near the Berthold. An underground pipeline owned by Crestwood Midstream/Arrow ruptured in 2014 (the largest rupture in the state to date) and spilled a million gallons of brine down a ravine into Bear Den Bay and Lake Sakakawea, critically endangering the MHA nations' drinking water. In 2016 a team of researchers of the Duke University's Nicholas School of the Environment found very high levels of lead and radium in the waters, but also detected selenium at levels as high as thirty-five times the federal thresholds set to protect fish, mussels and other wildlife, including those that people eat.[17] Unlike spilled oil, which eventually breaks down in the soil, the chemicals, metals and salts in spilled wastewater do not break down, creating a legacy of radioactivity and toxicity.

An additional problem is that there is very weak governmental oversight of the treatment of wastewater. Because drilling fluids and wastewaters are not treated as hazardous waste and, hence, do not fall under the hazardous waste regulations of the federal Environmental Protection Agency (EPA), the industry is not required by law to clean up wastewater spills.[18] Indigenous leadership, moreover, faces the difficulty that it cannot enforce environmental regulatory laws on non-Native industries operating on Native lands. While federal environmental and energy laws are considered 'laws of general application' and, hence, apply in Indigenous country, the EPA has delegated implementing these laws to the tribes. Yet because tribes do not have authority over non-members and non-Indians, tribal leadership are in fact unable to enforce environmental regulatory laws (such as the Safe Drinking Water Act) on non-Native polluting industry. Moreover, by virtue of the Doctrine of Christian Discovery – a legal principle informed by medieval papal bulls, most notably *Inter Caetera* (1493) issued by Pope Alexander IV, that insists that land not inhabited by

17. Nancy E. Lauer, Jennifer S. Harkness and Avner Vengosh, 'Brine Spills Associated with Unconventional Oil Development in North Dakota', *Environmental Science & Technology* 50:10 (2016), pp. 5389–97 (5390–1). https://doi.org/10.1021/acs.est.5b06349 (accessed 18 February 2022).

18. The loophole was closed in New York State in 2020 but is still in effect in the Dakotas. Another complicating issue is the so-called Halliburton loophole in the 2005 Energy Policy Act, which exempts the fracking industry from the Safe Drinking Water Act (SDWA) and makes that many of the chemicals used in fracking go largely unregulated. The nickname 'Halliburton' refers to the contributions to this legislation by then Vice President Dick Cheney. Cheney had personal and financial ties to the Halliburton Corporation, which performed the first commercial fracturing treatment in the United States and greatly benefits from it. See Peppard, *Just Water*, pp. 153–7.

Christians was available to be 'discovered' and taken possession of by European conquerors[19] – the supreme court determined in the *Johnson vs Macintosh* case (1823) that while the tribes have the beneficial use of the lands they traditionally occupied, the federal government owns the naked fee title to such lands. In terms of energy development this has come to mean that tribes fully depend on the Secretary of Interior to regulate pipeline construction and oil and gas leases in their territories.[20] The destructive toxicity of extractive industries and the encroachment on the sovereignty of tribal nations by the federal government are, in other words, intrinsically connected.

The latter is evident also when it comes to gas flaring, which is yet another way fracking poses a grave environmental and health concern for Berthold residents. Satellite data analysed by the Howard Center for Investigative Journalism showed that between 2012 and 2020 oil companies flared 140 billion cubic feet of gas on the Fort Behold Reservation.[21] As is the case with brine spills, the health implications of flaring are serious. Gas flaring releases carbon dioxide, methane and black carbon (a component of fine particulate matter) all potent greenhouse gases. Black matter has moreover been associated with a sharp increase in miscarriages, birth defects, asthma and cancers. Yet because tribes cannot hold non-Native oil companies accountable, they are dependent on various federal agencies for enforcing the Clean Air Act.[22] Oil companies therefore have little

19. What became known as the Doctrine of Discovery actually originated in three infamous papal bulls: *Dum Diversas* (1452), *Romanus Pontifex* (1454) and *Inter Ceatera* (1493). Under the terms of the doctrine of discovery, Indigenous people only had use or 'occupancy' of their lands, while Christian rulers claimed pre-emptive title. The American revolutionary government insisted it inherited the discovery claims of the English crown. These claims were codified in settler law and became an instrument of further Indigenous dispassion by the US Supreme Court in its *Johnson v. MacIntosh* decision, which granted the US government 'an exclusive right to extinguish the Indian title of occupancy, either by purchase or by conquest'. George E. 'Tink' Tinker, 'The Doctrine of Christian Discovery: Lutherans and the Language of Empire', *Journal of Lutheran Ethics* 17:1 (2017), p. 18. Available online: https://elca.org/JLE/Articles/1203 (accessed 8 December 2022).

20. Subsequent legal cases, most notably *Worcester vs. Georgia* determined that a wardship existed between tribes and the federal government and that the federal government has plenary power over Indian country. Cf., Deer and Kronk Warner, 'Raping Indian Country', pp. 9–10.

21. Cf., Isaac S. Simonelli, Maya Leachman and Andrew Onodera, 'How One Native American Tribe Is Battling Control over Flaring', *Inside Climate News* (26 February 2022). Available online: https://insideclimatenews.org/news/26022022/north-dakota-three-affiliated-tribes-natural-gas-flaring-venting/ (accessed 16 April 2022).

22. It is indeed telling that the EPA's regional headquarters are in Denver (CO), which is roughly 750 miles from the reservation. The headquarters are moreover tasked with enforcing the Clean Air in six states and twenty-eight tribal nations, including Fort Berthold. Cf., Simonelli et al., 'How One Native American Tribe Is Battling Control over Flaring'.

incentive to build gas-capturing pipelines on the reservation (which they are now increasingly doing in the rest of the Bakken). As a result, Berthold residents remain excessively exposed to flaring, despite ongoing efforts of current tribal leadership to gain the authority to regulate flaring on the reservation and build gas-capturing facilities.

Tribal sovereignty and the MMIWG2S crisis

Issues of sovereignty, are also fuelling the MMIWG2S crisis. Sarah Deer details how the 1978 case *Oliphant v. Suquamish Indian Tribe* stripped away the authority of tribal nations to prosecute non-Indians for any crime.[23] As a result of this ruling, tribal governments depend upon state or federal officials to prosecute crimes committed by non-Natives on Native territory. While, as we saw, this makes it difficult for MHA Nation's leadership to implement environmental regulations, it also has made Indigenous reservations into a 'free' zone for gender-based violence committed by non-Native perpetrators. Indigenous women thus are extremely vulnerable to rape, abduction and murder. A 2016 federal *American Indians and Crime* report concludes that over 80 per cent of Native women will experience some form of violent crime during their lifetime; 56 per cent of Native women will be the victim of sexual violence. The report further concluded that 90 per cent of these crimes are committed by non-Native perpetrators.[24]

In 2013 the Obama administration re-authorized the Violence against Women Act (VAWA) and included a provision—the Special Domestic Violence Criminal Jurisdiction (SDVCJ)—that enabled tribal courts to prosecute select non-Indians for a small number of crimes.[25] Most notably the SDVCJ allowed tribes to prosecute non-Native offenders that have 'ties to the Indian tribe' and commit an

---

23. *Oliphant v. Suquamish Indian Tribe*, 435 US 191 (1978) quoted in Deer and Kronk Warner, 'Raping Indian Country', p. 16. For further important scholarship on federal Indian law and the violence against Native women see Sarah Deer, *The Beginning and End of Rape: Confronting Sexual Violence in Native America* (Minneapolis: University of Minnesota Press, 2015). Deer also is the co-editor (together with Bonnie Clairmont, Carrie A. Martell and Maureen L White Eagle) of *Sharing Our Stories: Native Women Surviving Violence* (Lanham: Alta Mira Press, 2008).

24. Bureau of Justice Statistics, American Indians, and Crime (2016), quoted by Deer and Warner, 'Raping Indian Country', p. 17.

25. The SDVCJ went into effect for most of the country's 566 federally recognized Indian tribes (it does not extend to Alaskan tribes) in March 2015. See further Sari Horwitz, 'New Law Offers Protection to Abused Native American Women', *The Washington Post*, 8 February 2014. Available online: https://www.washingtonpost.com/world/national-security/new-law-offers-a-sliver-of-protection-to-abused-native-american-women/2014/02/08/0466d1ae-8f73-11e3-84e1-27626c5ef5fb_story.html?utm_term=.83102af7e4d8 (accessed 18 February 2022).

act of domestic violence, dating violence or a violation of protection orders against a Native American victim on tribal lands.[26] While this legislation is a milestone in addressing the violence against Native women, the SDVCJ amendment sadly failed to make provisions for tribal courts to prosecute *non-domestic* sexual crimes committed by non-Native perpetrators on Indigenous lands.

This blatant lack of legal protection of Indigenous women, girls and two spirit persons intersects with the lack of response by law enforcement and poor or non-existent data collection.[27] Responding to this reality, Indigenous women activists have played a major role in tracking down and reporting cases, and in collecting data. The Sovereign Bodies Institute (SBI),[28] founded by Annita Luchessi (Cheyenne) in 2018, established a MMIWG2S data base by searching through news coverage, social media posts and tribal archives, as well as connecting directly with family members of Indigenous women and girls that have gone missing or been murdered. Using such personal methods of data collection not only allows for the acquisition of statistics, typical for Western modes of 'fact' finding, but also and more importantly aims at 'generating knowledge' that restores the memory and dignity of the women who have been murdered or gone missing to their families and communities.[29]

In September 2020, after much lobbying by Indigenous activists and a handful of congress women and senators, the US Congress passed *Savanna's Act* (named after Savanna La Fontaine-Greywind, a member of the Spirit Lake Sioux Nation who was abducted and brutally murdered in Fargo, ND), which offers Indigenous nations access to federal data bases. Savanna's act was followed by *The Not Invisible*

---

26. Tribal Jurisdiction over Crimes of Domestic Violence, 25 U.S.C. §1304 (2013). '[T]ies to the Indian tribe' are defined as if the defendant '(i) resides in the Indian country of the participating tribe; (ii) is employed in the Indian country of the participating tribe; or (iii) is a spouse, intimate partner, or dating partner of – (I) a member of the participating tribe; or (II) an Indian who resides in the Indian country of the participating tribe'. The protection orders are identified as an act that '(A) occurs in the Indian country of the participating tribe; and (B) violates the portion of a protection order that – (i) prohibits or provides protection against violent or threatening acts or harassment against, sexual violence against, contact or communication with, or physical proximity to, another person; (ii) was issued against the defendant; (iii) is enforceable by the participating tribe; and (iv) is consistent with section 2265(b) of title 18'.

27. In 2016, 5,712 Native American and Alaska Native women and girls were reported missing, but only 116 missing cases were officially recorded in the US Department of Justice's federal missing-persons database.

28. The SBI's webpage states its mission as 'generating new knowledge and understandings of how Indigenous nations and communities are impacted by gender and sexual violence, and how they may continue to work towards healing and freedom from such violence'. Cf., https://www.sovereign-bodies.org/

29. Zoom interview (20 May 2020).

Figure 8.2 Missing and Murdered Women Protest in memory of Savanna LaFontaine-
Greywind (Spirit Lake Sioux), Fargo, ND (February 14, 2019), copyright Jan H. Pranger, 2019.

Act, which aims at improving the coordination between state, federal and tribal
governments and agencies.[30] Building on the new legislation, Secretary of the
Interior, Deb Haaland (Laguna Pueblo), the first Indigenous person to hold
this position, has subsequently formed a Missing and Murdered Indigenous
Women Unit within the Bureau of Indian Affairs Office of Justice Services. This
unit strengthens existing law enforcement by directing cross-departmental
and interagency work on MMIWG2S cases.[31] Yet while of great significance,

30. Heidi Heitkamp, a former Democratic senator from North Dakota, introduced
Savanna's Act in 2017. The bill passed unanimously in the Senate but stalled in the House
after outgoing US Representative Bob Goodlatte, a Republican of Virginia and chair of the
Judiciary committee, objected that the bill would provide undue benefits to law enforcement
agencies that comply with the reporting requirements in Savanna's Act. Cf., https://www.
washingtonpost.com/local/virginia-politics/before-leaving-office-rep-bob-goodlatte-
blocked-a-bill-intended-to-help-abused-native-american-women/2018/12/27/f4872d50-
09f3-11e9-85b6-41c0fe0c5b8f_story.html (accessed 22 February 2022). The bill was
reintroduced in January 2019 by US Senators Lisa Murkowski (R-AK) and Catherine
Cortez Masto (D- NV). It was then introduced in the House by US Representatives Norma
J. Torres (D-CA), Dan Newhouse (R-WA) and Deb Haaland (D-NM), alongside the *Not
Invisible Act*.

31. Cf., https://www.doi.gov/news/secretary-haaland-creates-new-missing-murdered-
unit-pursue-justice-missing-or-murdered-american (accessed 21 June 2022).

neither the new legislation nor the MMIW Unit includes provisions to assess and regulate the safety risks to Indigenous women, girls and two-spirit persons when approving resource development projects.[32] And because tribes still cannot prosecute non-Native perpetrators, oil workers can still target Native women and girls on reservations without impunity. In an interview with Al Jazeera, activist Lisa Brunner (Ojibwe) poignantly describes the situation that Native women on reservations face: 'I call it hunting – non-natives come here hunting. They know they can come onto our lands and rape us with impunity because they know that we can't touch them … The US government has created that atmosphere.'[33]

Rape and the logic of coloniality

Naming unspeakable evil is a first step in making the suffering it causes visible. As we saw, Native women use the language of 'rape' when naming the evil committed by the extraction industry in the name of fossil capitalism. The analogy of extractivism and rape has been widely documented by eco-feminist scholars, as well. For instance, in her seminal 1980 book *The Death of Nature*, Carolyn Merchant recounts how Francis Bacon (1561–1626), the founder of the modern scientific method, describes nature as 'a "disorderly woman" whose secrets wait to be penetrated'.[34] Yet while the language of rape evokes a strong connection between the suffering of women and the earth, using the term 'rape' for talking about environmental destruction and pollution has not been without controversy. Activists in the anti-rape movement have argued that the use of the language of 'rape' outside the context of criminal law only serves to relativize the experience of victims of sexual violence. This perspective is shared by third-wave eco-feminist theologians. For instance, Sigridur Gudmarsdottir observes that 'when the metaphor of rape is used loosely, the violence against women somehow becomes the "absent referent"'.[35]

Deer and Kronk Warner, however, defend using the language of rape for three main reasons: first, '[b]ecause many tribal cultures ascribe feminine qualities to the land', the use of the term rape carries salient relevance in the context of Native

32. The report *Reclaiming Power and Place: The Final Report of Canada's Inquiry into Missing and Murdered Indigenous Women and Girls*, which was released in the summer of 2019, does make such recommendations. Available online: https://www.mmiwg-ffada.ca/final-report/ (accessed 22 February 2022).

33. Kavitha Chekuru, 'Sexual Violence Scars Native American Women', *Al Jazeera*, 6 March 2013, Available online: https://www.aljazeera.com/indepth/features/2013/03/201334111633172507.html.

34. Carolyn Merchant, *The Death of Nature: Women, Ecology, and the Scientific Revolution* (New York: HarperCollins, 1980), p. 174.

35. Sigridur Gudmarsdottir, 'Rapes of Earth and Grapes of Wrath: Steinbeck, Ecofeminism and the Metaphor of Rape', *Feminist Theology* 18:2 (2010), pp. 206–22 (208).

communities who are seeking to protect their land and water from the onslaught of the extraction industry.[36] Second, as is the case with rape, there is a lack of consent: Native leaders often are not consulted when it comes to extractive projects and, when consulted, the wishes and needs of Native communities are systematically ignored. Finally, Deer and Warner insist that in the context of tribal lives the rape of mother earth and the rape of women are 'part of the same colonial power dynamics by which Indigenous people have been conquered and annihilated'.[37] As Indigenous studies' scholar Andrea Smith explains 'the project of colonial sexual violence establishes the ideology that Native bodies are inherently violable – and by extension, that Native lands are also inherently violable'.[38]

Naming the violence done to the land by fracking as 'rape' thus connects gender-based violence perpetrated against Native women, girls and two-spirit persons with (settler) colonialism. Smith's analysis is indeed instructive here. In her 2005 book *Conquest: Sexual Violence and American Indian Genocide* she demonstrates that by constructing the bodies of Indigenous people as dirty receptacles of sexual sin, colonizers justify their elimination as a means of purifying the colonized land of the 'pollution' that Indigenous people have come to represent.[39] Smith thus traces how rape connects the violability of Indigenous women to colonial devastation of the land. Significantly, her analysis resonates with the connection womanist scholar Delores Williams makes between the rape and impregnation of black slave women by their slave owners and the strip mining of the Appalachian' mountains. Williams calls the extractive logic connecting mining and the abuse of black women's bodies 'the sin of defilement': 'Stripping and strip-mining, their violence and degradation govern both.'[40] Environmental ethicist Larry Rasmussen, in an essay on climate injustice, adds that this logic is the logic of extractive capitalism: 'Bodies, together with labor and land, were possessed and commodified. Their status as sacred and their value as ends were lost. They were means and means only.'[41] Similarly, and building on Williams' important analysis, eco-womanist theologian Melanie Harris

36. Deer and Warner, 'Raping Indian Country', p. 16.

37. Deer and Warner, 'Raping Indian Country', p. 17.

38. Andrea Smith, *Conquest: Sexual Violence and American Indian Genocide* (Durham: Duke University Press, 2015, orig. publication 2005), p. 12.

39. Smith, *Conquest*, p. 15.

40. Delores Williams, 'Sin, Nature, and Black Women's Bodies', Carol J. Adams (ed.), *Ecofeminism and the Sacred* (New York: Continuum, 1993), pp. 24–9 (p. 26). On this point, see also M. Shawn Copeland, *Enfleshing Freedom: Body, Race, and Being* (Minneapolis: Fortress Press, 2009). Copeland analyses the brutalized Black female body under 'slavocracy' as constructed as object of both production and reproduction in the service of the plantation economy.

41. Larry Rasmussen, 'Climate Injustice', in Kathy Day and Sebastian Kim (eds), *Companion to Public Theology* (Leiden: Brill, 2017), pp. 349–69 (p. 55).

demonstrates that African American women parallel a female gendered concept of earth: both are subject to the racist project of colonization that commodifies and devalues the earth and poor women of color.[42]

Catholic Latinx decolonial theologian Melissa Pagán connects the commodifying logic operative in extractive capitalism with the 'coloniality of being/coloniality of gender'.[43] Drawing on the scholarship of Anibal Quijano, Nelson Maldonado-Torres, Marcelle Maese-Cohen and others, Pagán explains that the colonial project relied upon the creation and sustenance of racialized hierarchical categories of being that marked black and Indigenous bodies as subhuman and, hence, available for domination and exploitation. Christian appropriation of natural law thinking played a constitutive role in creating and justifying these hierarchal categories of identity. Thus, Pope Paul III in his 1537 bull *Sublimis Deus* conceived of 'Indigenous people's soul as an empty receptacle, an *anima nullius*, very much like the *terra nullius*'.[44] This theological informed colonial logic produced what Maldonado-Torres's identifies as the 'sub-ontological colonial difference' – a difference that grants racialized others being only insofar as 'they approximate the white European, male, normative center of humanity'.[45]

Yet while born from the fifteenth-century colonial encounter, the sub-ontological difference is still 'being normalized under neo-colonial capitalist regimes'.[46] As Pagán observes, 'those who have been marked as subhuman, perversely human, or only bearing instrumental value (the land, women, and racial minorities), the residents bodies of the colonial difference, find themselves within an *extractive zone*, a zone characterized by capitalistic violences that have been deemed justifiable, even necessary, to maintain the subjugation of the colonized'.[47] Within the extractive zone racialized female and queer bodies are especially constructed as being available for profit, pleasure or release of White rage and aggression.

---

42. Melanie Harris, *Eco-Womanism: African-American Women and Earth-Honoring Faiths* (Maryknoll: Orbis Books, 2017).

43. Melissa Pagán, 'Cultivating a Decolonial Feminist Integral Ecology: Extractive Zones and the Nexus of the Coloniality of Being/Coloniality of Gender', *Journal of Hispanic/Latino Theology* 22:1/6 (2020), pp. 72–100. Available online: https://repository.usfca.edu/jhlt/vol22/iss1/6.

44. Bonaventure de Sousa Santos, *Epistemologies of the South: Justice against Epistemicide* (New York: Routledge, 2014), p. 122. Quoted in Pagán 'Cultivating a Decolonial Feminist Integral Ecology', p. 82. *Terra Nullius* translates as 'land belonging to nobody'. This notion has fed the myth that prior to European colonization the Americas were unoccupied.

45. Nelson Maldonado-Torres, 'On the Coloniality of Being: Contributions to the Development of a Concept', *Cultural Studies* 21:2–3 (March/May 2007), pp. 240–702 (252). Quoted in Pagán, 'Cultivating a Decolonial Feminist Integral Ecology', p. 83.

46. Pagán, 'Cultivating a Decolonial Feminist Integral Ecology', p. 83.

47. Pagán, 'Cultivating a Decolonial Feminist Integral Ecology', p. 84.

Aiming to disrupt and subvert the coloniality of being/coloniality of gender Pagán therefore insists on granting *epistemological* privilege to those who have historically been constructed as not knowing and not being. Indeed, she proposes that the Catholic church commits to a preferential option for those 'at the ontological difference, for those trapped in extractive zones'.[48] This, she believes, would be a helpful reframing of the important contention by the 2019 Synod of Bishops for the Pan-Amazon region that the church has a preferential option not just for the poor but also for the Indigenous.[49]

Settler colonialism, fracking and Indigenous environmental justice

From the perspective of fracking on the Berthold reservation a preferential option for Indigenous communities living in or near extractive zones discloses the crucial importance of confronting legislative structures that undermine Native American sovereignty. As we saw, issues of Indigenous nationhood and self-determination and, hence, the unjust structures imposed by settler colonialism, are at the heart of Indigenous struggles for environmental justice. In his pivotal article 'Settler Colonialism, Ecology, and Environmental Justice' Indigenous environmental theorist Kyle Powys Whyte (Potawatomi) therefore insists that settler colonialism *itself* is a structure of environmental injustice.[50] Whyte's account of settler colonialism as environmental injustice offers an important additional way of reading the interconnecting violations of the land and women on the Berthold, as also for charting a path for solidarity with Indigenous communities. I will therefore briefly engage with Whyte's argument, which in turn informs my theological reflection.

Whyte defines settler colonialism as

> complex social processes in which at last one society seeks to move permanently onto the terrestrial, aquatic, and aerial places lived in by one or more 'other' societies who already derive economic vitality, cultural flourishing, and political self-determination from the relationships they have established with the plants, animals, physical entities, and eco-systems of those places.[51]

---

48. Pagán 'Cultivating a Decolonial Feminist Integral Ecology', p. 85.

49. Pagán 'Cultivating a Decolonial Feminist Integral Ecology', p. 85. Cf., *Final Document, The Amazon: New Paths for the Church and for an Integral Ecology* (26 October 2019). https://secretariat.synod.va/content/sinodoamazonico/en/documents/final-document-of-the-amazon-synod.html (accessed 8 December 2022). Cf, Pope Francis, Post-Synodal Exhortation *Querida Amazonia* (2020) https://secretariat.synod.va/content/ sinodoamazonico/en/documents/final-document-of-the-amazon-synod.html (accessed 8 December 2022).

50. Kyle Powys Whyte, 'Settler Colonialism, Ecology and Environmental Justice', *Environment and Society* 9 (2018), pp. 125–44; Cf. Gilio-Whitaker, *As Long as Grass Grows*, p. 12.

51. Whyte, 'Settler Colonialism, Ecology and Environmental Justice', p. 134.

Unlike other forms of historical and material colonialisms, settler colonialism is the ongoing process by which settler societies seek to erase, not just use or exploit, colonized societies. According to Whyte this process of erasure has a clear *ecological* dimension in that 'settler populations are working to create their own ecologies out of the ecologies of Indigenous peoples'.[52] Oil and gas development on or near Indigenous lands simply are one of the many ways settler societies transform Indigenous ecologies into settler ecologies.

Settler colonialism thus is a form of ecological domination: it seeks to undermine and ultimately erase Indigenous social resilience, or what Whyte calls 'collective continuance'. Collective continuance refers to 'a society's capacity to self-determine how to adapt to change in ways that avoid reasonably preventable harm'.[53] In contrast to settler cultures, Indigenous' collective continuance is deeply rooted within *reciprocal* relationships with land and non-human species. Indeed, Potawatomi botanist and writer Robin Kimmerer calls this relationship of interdependece the 'covenant of reciprocity': the notion of relationships organized among relatives who have gift-giving and gift-receiving responsibilities to each other.[54] Most importantly, the Indigenous notion of interdependence assumes that the human does not exist independently of its relationships with the more-than-human. These relationships are the source of identity for how Indigenous people understand whom and what they are in the world: responsibilities to creation are a matter of taking care of one's relatives with which one's very being is interwoven.

Whyte explains that the social resilience or adaptive capacity of a society is facilitated by ways in which responsibilities are organized into interdependent systems. In other words, the extent to which systems of responsibilities are capable of high degrees of adjustability correlates with 'ways the qualities of reciprocal responsibilities that have developed over time are organized to foster interdependence'.[55] Against this background Whyte understands collective continuance as ecology: it encompasses both ecosystems and the calculated stewardship of ecosystems. Settler colonialism, then, is environmental injustice because it consistently and systematically destroys Indigenous communities' adaptive abilities by undermining its collective continuance.

According to Whyte, two important patterns of environmental injustice arose from settler colonialism, i.e. vicious sedimentation and insidious loops. Both, I believe, are important for assessing fracking on the Berthold.[56] Vicious sedimentation refers to the process by which 'the constant ascription of settler

---

52. Whyte, 'Settler Colonialism, Ecology and Environmental Justice', p. 135.

53. Whyte, 'Settler Colonialism, Ecology and Environmental Justice', p. 127.

54. Robin W. Kimmerer, *Braiding Sweetgrass: Indigenous Wisdom, Scientific Knowledge, and the Teachings of Plants* (Minneapolis: Milkweed Editions, 2013), pp. 143–4. Quoted in Whyte, 'Settler Colonialism, Ecology and Environmental Justice', p. 127.

55. Whyte, 'Settler Colonialism, Ecology and Environmental Justice', p. 132.

56. Whyte, 'Settler Colonialism, Ecology and Environmental Justice', pp. 138–40.

ecologies onto Indigenous ecologies fortify settler ignorance against Indigenous people over time'.[57] This sedimentation is 'vicious' because it seriously impedes settlers' inclination for consensual decision-making with Indigenous nations and leads to selective and ineffective forms of solidarity. As we saw, the latter happens when settler advocacy on behalf of MMIWG2S fails to attend to issues of Indigenous sovereignty. Viewing sexual violence or pollution in isolation from past acts of colonial injustice makes it moreover impossible to see their 'insidious looping effects', i.e. the ways these present forms of colonial extractivism increase and deepen the detrimental effects of past extractive industries, such as the forceful removal and dispossession by large-scale damming projects.

Towards an eco-feminist decolonial theological engagement with fracking

Whyte's analysis of settler colonialism as environmental injustice thus helps us see that the problem with fracking on the Berthold lays with the multiple ways settler colonial society systematically undermines and destroys Indigenous nations' collective continuance and, hence, its adaptive abilities. The culminative effect of these destructive processes continues to make Indigenous communities extremely vulnerable to high levels of pollution and gender-based violence. Indigenous struggles for environmental justice therefore purposefully situate the fight against extractive industries and pipelines within the struggle for self-determination and, hence, the struggle against the injustices imposed by settler-colonial domination.

Amer-European Christianity has played a pivotal role in settler colonial extraction of Indigenous lands and the destruction of Indigenous social continuance. As Jan Pranger points out in his insightful essay 'Christianity, Settler Colonialism and Resource Extraction', Amer-European Christianity 'has mobilized Christianity for settler extractivist and accumulative purposes of lands and resources' and sought 'to substitute *itself* in the place of Indigenous relationships to the world and its Creator'.[58] In the process it has reshaped colonized Indigenous landscapes and ecosystems as 'vicious sedimentation' in its Amer-European image. African American theologian Willie Jennings explains that Christian colonial and missionary visions of the world imposed upon Native peoples a spatial-temporal Christian order that substituted place- and nature-based Indigenous spatial orientations with Christian notions of empty space (*terra nullius*), that is, 'space ready for capitalist cultivation'.[59] As Jennings demonstrates this venture was cast

---

57. Whyte, 'Settler Colonialism, Ecology and Environmental Justice', p. 138.

58. Jan H. Pranger, 'Christianity, Settler Colonialism and Resource Extraction', in *Dialog: A Journal of Theology* (Wiley Online Library, Summer 2023), italics added.

59. Willie James Jennings, *The Christian Imagination: Theology and the Origin of Race* (New Haven: Yale University Press, 2011), p. 215.

as a mission to free Indigenous lands from demonic influence by instituting the proper, i.e. utilitarian perspective on lands and animals.

Christianity, then, not only aided and abetted settler colonialism but also mimicked settler colonialism's objective of elimination and replacement of Indigenous cultures and religions. Pranger, drawing on Richard Hughes and Roxanne Dunbar-Ortiz, describes how this process of replacement has its roots in the racial ontological hierarchies underlying the Christian Doctrine of Discovery, as also in the biblical themes of covenant, divine election and promised land as they are told in the Exodus-Conquest narrative complex in Exodus and Joshua.[60] Settlers identified with God's chosen people and used the conquest story to justify taking possession of Indigenous lands. Thus, settlers constructed their identity as being the divinely chosen ones at the exclusion of Indigenous people who they identified with the biblical Canaanites and, hence, as deserving of being invaded, dispossessed and, if need be, annihilated. As Pranger observes, 'being uniquely party to a covenant with the divine provides settlers with a transcendently grounded sense of and an exclusive, even exceptional identity'.[61] The latter reassures settlers of their innocence amidst settler violence against Indigenous people.

Given the deep and enduring entanglement of Christianity with settler colonialism and its extractivist mindset, Christian eco-theology will need to engage with the multiple ways Christian theology continues to be shaped by the logic of coloniality. Melissa Pagán, therefore, takes issue with Pope Francis' notion of integral ecology as it is developed in *Laudato Si'* (*LS*) and that is central to the concluding document of the Synod for the Pan-Amazonian region. Like most eco-theological liberationists, she appreciates that *LS* centres 'the care of creation within a proper view of the human person and establishes a proper "human ecology" that will attend to both the "cries of the earth and the cries of the poor"'.[62] Pagán is troubled, however, by the way *LS* focuses integral ecology, and hence its eco-justice approach, on a critique of modernity and modern anthropology. While a decolonial analysis does not disagree that the modern anthropological subject sustains an extractive view of people and lands, it insists that such a view is 'borne from coloniality' – a hierarchized systems of knowing and being that constituted in the colonial encounter of the fifteenth century that shaped the modern subject.[63]

60. Pranger, 'Christianity, Settler Colonialism and Resource Extraction'. Cf., Richard T. Hughes, *Myths America Lives By: White Supremacy and the Stories that Give Us Meaning*, 2nd edition (Urbana: University of Illinois Press, 2018), pp. 34–45; Roxanne Dunbar-Ortiz, *An Indigenous Peoples' History of the United States* (Boston: Beacon Press, 2014), pp. 49–54. These authors point out how the utilization of biblical covenantal theology also underlies its more secular derivatives, American Exceptionalism and Manifest destiny, which, too, have been critically important to American settler colonialism.

61. Pranger, 'Christianity, Settler Colonialism and Resource Extraction'.

62. Pagán, 'Cultivating a Decolonial Feminist Integral Ecology', p. 72.

63. Pagán, 'Cultivating a Decolonial Feminist Integral Ecology', p. 73.

Continuing to solely focus the ecological critique of Christianity on its complicity in the 'vile' anthropocentricism of (late) modernity, as the Pope does in *LS*, tends to overlook Christianity's complicity in the creation and justification of the coloniality of being/coloniality of gender.

Not unlike Whyte, then, Pagán insists that if we do not adequately address the roots of the contemporary problem, our concept of environmental justice will be inadequate. She states that 'maintaining a view from modernity rather than from modernity/coloniality elides the deeper socio-cultural ecologies necessary for us to understand that our own anthropologies actually perpetuate these problematic logics, rather than subvert them; thus our efforts for environmental justice are proven lacking'.[64] A decolonial eco-feminist critique of the logic of modernity/coloniality aims at subverting the hierarchical ontological systems of knowing and being, which includes the anthropological structure of a gendered dichotomy perpetuated by Pope Francis' integral ecology. Indeed, as we saw, addressing the linkages between the coloniality of gender and our environmental crisis means that we will need to historicize and decolonize gender and sexuality as institutions intimately intertwined with the institution of race and the constitution of extractive zones of land, knowledge and being.

As other authors contributing to this present volume have also argued, such an endeavour starts by privileging the situated knowledges of brown, Black and Indigenous women most impacted by resources extraction and climate change. It also demands a confession of the sin of settler colonialism and of Amer-European Christianity's role in its extractivist logic and practices. Thus, the final report of the Truth and Reconciliation Commission of Canada (2015) on the history of Canada's residential schools calls upon all religious denominations and faith groups 'to repudiate concepts used to justify European sovereignty over Indigenous lands and peoples, such as the Doctrine of Discovery and terra nullius', as well as 'to implement the United Nations Declaration on the Rights of Indigenous Peoples'.[65] It is of crucial importance therefore that the Vatican officially repudiated the Doctrine of Discovery.[66] Yet, as many in the Catholic Church acknowledge also,

---

64. Pagán, 'Cultivating a Decolonial Feminist Integral Ecology', p. 88.

65. Calls to Action #49 and #48, respectively. *Honoring the Truth, Reconciling for the Future: Summary of the Final Report of the Truth and Reconciliation Commission of Canada* (2015). https://ehprnh2mwo3.exactdn.com/wp-content/uploads/2021/01/Executive_Summary_English_Web.pdf (accessed 23 February 2022).

66. The official repudiation was issued by the dicasteries for Culture and Education and for Promoting Integral Human Development on 30 March 2023. Cf., https://press.vatican.va/content/salastampa/en/bollettino/pubblico/2023/03/30/230330b.html (accessed 30 March 2023).

the process of reconciliation with Indigenous people demands that much more be done, in particular in terms of actual reparations. When it comes to environmental justice in solidarity with Indigenous women in extractive zones it is crucial that Christian eco-theology engages the many ways Amer-European Christianity has played, and continues to play, a constitutive role in settler colonialism's extractivist, commodifying logic. In particular, however, Christian churches will need to attend to the legislative injustices that undermine Indigenous collective continuance. A preferential option for the Indigenous therefore requires both repentance and active work on behalf of Indigenous sovereignty and land reparations.

Chapter 9

RARE EARTH AND RARE PRACTICE OF 'INTEGRAL ECOLOGY'

A FEMINIST POST-COLONIAL READING OF 'SAVE MALAYSIA, STOP LYNAS' PROTESTS

Sharon A. Bong

This chapter offers a feminist post-colonial reading of the grassroots activism against rare earth mining and processing plants in Malaysia. These plants include the Japanese-owned Asian Rare Earth plant (hereafter ARE) that operated in the 1980s but has, due to public protests resulting in legal action, shut down in 2012 and Australia-owned Lynas Advanced Materials Plant (LAMP) that has continued operating since 2014 with its license recently renewed rather than revoked, as was hoped for with the change in government. These rare earth processing plants are not fully held accountable for social and environmental costs, in part because the government of Malaysia has not ratified relevant and key conventions that set global standards for clean as well as clean-up technologies. With looser regulatory mechanisms, Malaysia is at risk of fast becoming a favoured dumping ground for toxic and carcinogenic materials in the name of profit and the push for development as rare earth elements (REE) are prized in the manufacture of hi-tech products, from smartphone screens to wind turbines that arguably facilitate green technologies.

As such, it behoves Malaysians and their allies (e.g. citizens living abroad, international news agencies and researchers) to adopt and insist on – as this is an activism spanning four decades – the rare (read as uncharacteristic in the context of Malaysia) practice of placing people and the environment before profits. At risk of imprisonment and censure, a host of ordinary citizens and committed environmental and social justice groups, for example, Save Malaysia, Stop Lynas (SMSL), Himpunan Hijau (Green Assembly), Sahabat Alam Malaysia (Friends of the Earth, Malaysian chapter), have fought the good fight. When read through a feminist post-colonial lens, the rhetoric and praxis of those who embrace the land as their 'common home', however contaminated, serve as counterpoints to masculinized meta-narratives of colonization that maintain boundaries of purity/pollution (i.e. through outsourced and off-shore processing of toxic waste) and the concomitant feminization of a post-colonial albeit less-developed nation state as a body that continues to be sullied for profit.

My chapter first provides a background and timeline of the planting of ARE in Bukit Merah, Perak (a north-western state), and LAMP in Gebeng, Pahang (the largest state in West Malaysia), and the corollary impact of grassroots activism. The second section of the chapter offers a feminist post-colonial theologizing of these people-centred narratives of dissent that are pit against profit-oriented narratives of compliance and co-optation of the post-colonial nation's resources. Realizing 'integral ecology' as enshrined in the Pope's encyclical *Laudato Si*[1] has been the hallmark of the green movement against ARE and LAMP. The fracturing of the inter-relationality of the earth and the human species, given the highly toxic (radioactive) processes of extracting REE, leaves tailing wastelands infected (contaminated) and infertile soilscape. Interrogating the trope of the womb that courses through these processes and narratives fleshes out the violence of REE extraction and colonization of the earth and its resources that, in turn, give rise to a revisiting of feminist post-colonial theorizing and theologizing around gender, race and nation that is uncommon in the treatment of rare earth elements.

(Im)planting ARE and LAMP in Malaysia

'Dumping radioactive waste in abandoned mines is akin to killing a rape victim. Instead of healing the piece of land, we are destroying it forever', says Member of Parliament, Wong Tack, as he lambasts Australian miner Lynas' proposal to use abandoned tin mines in Malaysia to store its radioactive rare earth waste.[2] MP Wong Tack is a member of the Democratic Action Party, one of the main component parties of the Pakatan Harapan (PH or Alliance of Hope) coalition that, in the last General Elections (GE14) in 2018, toppled the ruling National Front (Barisan National) coalition, which has been in charge since the nation's independence from the British Empire in 1957. As the chairperson of Himpunan Hijau, Wong Tack's anti-Lynas campaign is generally attributed to his GE14 success in defeating the incumbent for the parliamentary seat of Bentong in the state of Pahang, where LAMP is located. Wong Tack insists that Lynas' intent to 'rehabilitate' the mines would 'do irreparable damage to nearby land already made infertile by the mines'.[3] Whereas the previous government issued the operating license to Lynas Corporation to build LAMP (to process REE that is mined in Mount Weld, Western Australia), the then newly elected PH government reneged

---

1. Pope Francis, *Laudato Si': On Care for Our Common Home* (Rome: Libreria Editrice Vaticana, 2015).

2. Syed Jaymal Zahid, 'Anti-Lynas MP Likens Dumping Rare Earth Waste in Mines to Killing Rape Victim', *Malay Mail*, 4 August 2019, https://www.malaymail.com/news/malaysia/2019/08/04/anti-lynas-mp-likens-dumping-rare-earth-waste-in-mines-to-killing-rape-vict/1777525 (accessed 1 February 2021).

3. Quoted in Zahid, 'Anti-Lynas MP Likens Dumping Rare Earth Waste in Mines to Killing Rape Victim'.

on its electoral promises to review the license. The twice-elected nonagenarian prime minister's position belies a preferential treatment of foreign investors and a typically 'Asian' idiosyncrasy of not losing face. Tun (honorific) Dr Mahathir Mohamad says, 'We invite them (to invest) and then we kick them out … If we chase out the Lynas foreign investor, the others (foreign investors) will not come (to Malaysia).'[4] Dr Mahathir alludes to the RM1billion already invested in LAMP operations, fuelling 600 jobs for local engineers, who would lose them with LAMP's shutdown and its waste repatriated to Australia (which the anti-Lynas activists call for) and would have fallen 'sick' – but have not – from '"a very low-level" radioactive waste' based on studies conducted by Lynas-commissioned 'experts'.

What would the fuss be if only a '"very low-level" radioactive waste' is involved for environmental activists such as Wong Tack whose Himpunan Hijau has been campaigning since 2011? The PH government's decision to renew Lynas Corp's operating license for another six months is, according to MP Wong Tack, 'equivalent to telling the world that we are allowing this beautiful country to become a dumping ground … "How could we do this and allow our children to be burdened by toxic waste that will last for so many years? Why are we so stupid?"'[5] The double harm of not only raping but also killing the victim serves as a haunting refrain not unlike a recurring trauma for the victim when rapists are not held accountable by enforcement agencies. The issuance of a Temporary Operating Licence to Lynas Corp back on 1 February 2012 was made on condition that it would, in 10 months, submit a long-term plan and location of a permanent disposal facility (PDF) to the Atomic Energy Licensing Board of Malaysia (AELB) or have its licence suspended or revoked. Lynas Corp has not only reneged on this 'legally binding commitment to ship their waste out of Malaysia' – 450,000 tonnes of water leach purification residue – but is also getting off lightly, with no significant legal repercussions.[6] Wong Tack further cautions that Lynas Corp must be prevented from withdrawing funds from its RM205 million deposit with the AELB to pay for its PDF as that sum must be reserved 'to pay for the monitoring and maintenance of the "radioactive dump" in future' as well as further waste that would invariably be generated when the plant is decommissioned, entailing 'environmental remediation activities'.[7]

4. 'Can't Drive Out Lynas Because Foreign Investors Are Watching, Says Dr M', *The Star*, 8 August 2019, https://www.thestar.com.my/news/nation/2019/08/08/can039t-drive-out-lynas-because-foreign-investors-are-watching-says-dr-m (accessed 4 February 2021).

5. Teh Athira Yusof, Arfa Yunus and Nor Ain Mohd Radhi, 'Wong Tack Angry, Says Country Will Become Dumping Ground', *New Straits Times*, 16 August 2019, https://www.nst.com.my/news/nation/2019/08/513202/wong-tack-angry-says-country-will-become-dumping-ground (accessed 4 February 2021).

6. Zahid, 'Anti-Lynas MP Likens Dumping Rare Earth Waste in Mines to Killing Rape Victim'.

7. FMT Reporters, 'Don't Let Lynas Use AELB Deposit to Pay for RM400 Mil Waste Dump, Urges Critic', *Free Malaysia Today*, 31 January 2020, https://www.freemalaysiatoday.com/category/nation/2020/01/31/dont-let-lynas-use-aelb-deposit-to-pay-for-rm400-mil-waste-dump-urges-critic/ (accessed 4 February 2021).

The etymology of the word '*trauma*' as 'wound', originally referring to an injury inflicted on a body,[8] signifies, on one level, the wounds inflicted on the ecosystem which includes the clear and present danger that human communities face, especially those living in the vicinity of LAMP, its tailing wastelands and PDF. The townsfolk brace themselves for worsening effects that would afflict them and the next generation when waterways become contaminated as these are locations (on the east coast of West Malaysia) that are prone to flooding from seasonal monsoon rains. On another level, a 'double wound' persists that involves 'the wound of the mind',[9] which unlike the 'wound of the body, a simple and healable event', pries open the gap between knowing and not knowing as the traumatic event is 'experienced too soon, too unexpectedly, to be fully known and is therefore not available to consciousness until it exposes itself again, repeatedly in the nightmares and repetitive actions of the survivor'.[10] The spectre of terminal illness, birth defects and death caused by the toxicity of carcinogenic and radioactive waste of mining and processing REE is repetitively referenced in the collective consciousness of not only survivors but also potential victims.

The story of Lai Kwan and her severely disabled (both mentally and physically) twenty-nine-year-old son, Cheah Kok Leong (consonant with the prognosis that he was given), heartbreakingly exemplifies this trauma of remembering as narrated in a *New York Times* article that exposed the stealth clean-up operations of ARE, a subsidiary of Mitsubishi Chemical, tucked away in the remote jungles of Bukit Merah, Perak.[11] Madam Kwan recalls that while pregnant, she 'was told to take an unpaid day off only on days when the factory bosses said that a particularly dangerous consignment of ore had arrived'. She spent the 'last 29 years washing, dressing, feeding and otherwise taking care of her son from that pregnancy'. Leaving her former sawmill job for the seemingly better job, she adds that '[w]e saw it as a chance to get better pay. … We didn't know what they were producing'.[12] Kok Leong, her sixth and youngest son, lost sight in his left eye at five, has a hole in his heart, and 'has little or no capacity for speech and has never been out of diapers' nor out of their house; he was penned up for his own safety by a makeshift wire mesh door not unlike an adult crib.[13] Aside from those infected, another in the family most affected is one of Madam Kwan's daughters, who had to terminate

8. Cathy Caruth, *Unclaimed Experience: Trauma, Narrative, and History* (Baltimore: Johns Hopkins University Press, 1996), p. 3.

9. Caruth, *Unclaimed Experience*, pp. 3–4.

10. Caruth, *Unclaimed Experience*, p. 4.

11. Keith Bradsher, 'Mitsubishi Quietly Cleans Up Its Former Refinery', *New York Times*, 8 March 2011, https://www.nytimes.com/2011/03/09/business/energy-environment/09rareside. html?auth=login-facebook&ref=energy-environment (accessed 4 February 2021).

12. Bradsher, 'Mitsubishi Quietly Cleans Up Its Former Refinery'.

13. Malaysiakini, 'Bukit Merah Survivor: Our Tears Have Run Dry', *Malaysiakini*, 4 May 2011, https://www.malaysiakini.com/news/163166 (accessed 4 February 2021).

her basic education to help support the family as her father had abandoned them and her mother has to perpetually stay by Kok Leong's side. Her daughter adds that 'I had a hard time in school before I stopped, because my classmates would make fun of my brother … We have cried so much that our tears have run dry'.[14] Despite smelling 'something really awful' at the workplace, Madam Kwan only found out later why she along with all staff members at the plant was required to wear 'a thermometer-like pin over their chests' and only realized – too little and too late – the gravity of the exposure to radioactivity when residents started protesting against the plant (as detailed below).[15]

Trauma, as such, 'is not locatable in the simple violent or original event in an individual's [or nation's] past, but rather in the way that its very unassimilated nature – the way it was precisely *not known* in the first instance – returns to haunt the survivor later on'.[16] Remembering the trauma of the ARE plant and its human and ecological impact is what drives the anti-Lynas protests: 'To understand why there is so much opposition to the Lynas rare earth plant, we have to look at the sad history of Bukit Merah New Village' that is located just a few kilometres from Ipoh, the capital city of Perak. 'Life changed forever' for the mainly Hakka (Chinese) community when ARE first began operations in July 1982 to extract yttrium (a REE), from monazite.[17] Their 'sad history' is firstly attributed to health costs borne: physical defects in newborns similar to Madam Kwan's son, rising cases of leukaemia with medical examinations on children in the area confirming that 'nearly 40% of them suffered from lymph node diseases, turbinate congestion and recurrent rhinitis. Seven of the (eight) leukemia victims have since died (at the time of reporting)'.[18] A less-known case study is that of fifty-five-year-old Pancharvarnam Shanmugam's youngest daughter Kasturi who suffered from health complications since birth (e.g. bodily inflammation, splitting headaches, heavy nose bleeds, faint spells) and was eventually diagnosed with leukaemia at ten to eleven years of age. Shanmugam worked as a labourer clearing land next to ARE and noticed 'a lot of water being flushed out of the factory' that 'would rise to almost as high as our knees … and was very smelly'.[19]

The 'sad history' of the Bukit Merah New Villagers also lies in their exhausting anti-ARE campaign which pit them against conglomerates and both state and federal governments, then helmed by Dr Mahathir Mohamad (hereafter Dr M, his moniker). Their 'sad history' exposes 'a tragedy of betrayal of leadership … about

---

14. Malaysiakini, 'Bukit Merah Survivor: Our Tears Have Run Dry'.

15. Malaysiakini, 'Bukit Merah Survivor: Our Tears Have Run Dry'.

16. Caruth, *Unclaimed Experience*, p. 4.

17. Stanley Koh, 'Lessons from Bukit Merah', *Malaysia Today*, 21 March 2012, https://www.malaysia-today.net/2012/03/21/lessons-from-bukit-merah/ (accessed 4 February 2021).

18. Stanley Koh, 'Lessons from Bukit Merah'.

19. Malaysiakini, 'Bukit Merah Survivor: Our Tears Have Run Dry'.

people in power losing their moral compass to the pull of profit'.[20] Highlights of this two-decade saga, faithfully documented by the Consumers' Association of Penang, include first protests (June 1982) by the community on experiencing 'tinging smoke and bad smell which made them choke and cry' which led to the relocation of the first dumping site from Parit to Bukit Merah/Papan; second protests include a signed letter by 6,700 residents (to the relevant authorities) and road block by 200 residents to the ARE site (May 1984) that prompted Dr M's damage-control assurance that 'every precaution to ensure safety' has been taken but the construction of the 'radioactive dump' in Papan 'will go ahead', inciting a third demonstration (June 1984);[21] a fourth protest (July 1984) involving 3,000 including women and children ensued in response to the Minister of Science, Technology and Environment's assurance that the dumpsite is 'safe' as it is built 'according to stringent standards';[22] and a fifth protest (three days later) persisted despite the Perak Chief Police Officer's order to call it off. The Bukit Merah Action Committee is formed (July 1984) and over the next four months, on-site research is commissioned not only by the action committee but also the government. Sahabat Alam Malaysia, an ally of the Bukit Merah Action Committee, in a memorandum to the PM, states that the level of radiation at the tailing pond was '43 800 millirems/year' which is '88 times higher than the maximum level permitted by the International Commission on Radiological Protection' for the public, and international scientists (e.g. physicist and safety analyst, industrial waste expert and radiation specialist) find the site's construction 'extremely shoddy' and generally 'unsuitable for storing hazardous waste'.[23] The United Nations' International Atomic Energy Agency (IAEA), at the invitation of the Malaysian government, declares the site, on its first inspection, as 'unsafe' and in its second report states that the trenches 'did not meet required specifications'. More than 1,500 residents staged a hunger strike in response to the government's inaction and by the time Japanese radiation and genetics expert, Professor Sadao Ichikawa, is brought in by the Papan residents (December 1984), he finds that the radiation levels are 'dangerously high, the highest at 800 times above the permissible level'.[24]

20. Koh, 'Lessons from Bukit Merah'.

21. Consumers' Association of Penang, 'Chronology of Events in the Bukit Merah Asian Rare Earth Development', *CAP*, https://consumer.org.my/chronology-of-events-in-the-bukit-merah-asian-rare-earth-development/ (accessed 4 February 2021).

22. Consumers' Association of Penang, 'Chronology of Events in the Bukit Merah Asian Rare Earth Development'.

23. Consumers' Association of Penang, 'Chronology of Events in the Bukit Merah Asian Rare Earth Development'.

24. Consumers' Association of Penang, 'Chronology of Events in the Bukit Merah Asian Rare Earth Development'.

And the government's response? To relocate the dump site yet again (January 1985) to Mukim Belanja in the Kledang Range, about 5 kilometres from Papan. Retrospectively, this served as the turning point for the Bukit Merah community. They filed an application in the Ipoh High Court (February 1985) essentially to shut down the entire ARE operations. This triggers the enforcement of the Atomic Energy Licensing Act of 1984 to ensure that operators of nuclear installations which the government is not exempted from are 'held liable for nuclear damage'.[25] An Atomic Energy Licensing Board (AELB) is formed to investigate. The Ipoh High Court grant an injunction to the Bukit Merah residents (October 1985) to 'stop ARE from producing and storing radioactive waste until adequate safety measures are taken'.[26] A sixth protest, a 3,000-strong demonstration, is held against ARE's plan to keep radioactive waste in its 'permanent dump' in the Kledang Range (October 1986). An AELB team further discovers a few illegal thorium waste dump sites (November 1986) with radiation levels 'between 0.05–0.10 millirems/hour (that is, 438–876 millirems/year) above the maximum safety level of 0.057 millirems/hour set by the ICRP' (International Commission on Radiological Protection). A minister in the PM's department rather ignorantly adds that these two illegal dumps do not pose a danger as such dumps are few in number! The Malaysian AELB grants a license to ARE to resume operations despite the court injunction (February 1987), triggering a 10,000-people protest march through Bukit Merah (April 1987). Clashes with the Federal Reserve Unit personnel result in some getting hurt, including women. During the court hearing (from September 1987 to February 1990), there are more protests against ARE for breaking the court's injunction, resulting in the two-month detention (without trial) of key activists, under the draconian Internal Security Act (that curtails the rights to expression, free press and assembly in the name of national security).[27] This in turn ignites a campaign by the global network Friends of the Earth to release Malaysian environmentalists jailed on the pretext of inciting 'racial tension' (e.g. Meenakshi Raman, a lawyer representing the Bukit Merah residents).[28]

After sixty-five days of hearing stretched over thirty-two months (July 1992), the people of Bukit Merah win their suit against ARE with the latter ordered to shut down 'within 14 days'.[29] In the same month, ARE, without the consent of

---

25. Consumers' Association of Penang, 'Chronology of Events in the Bukit Merah Asian Rare Earth Development'.

26. Consumers' Association of Penang, 'Chronology of Events in the Bukit Merah Asian Rare Earth Development'.

27. Consumers' Association of Penang, 'Chronology of Events in the Bukit Merah Asian Rare Earth Development'.

28. Dianne Dumanoski, 'Groups to Campaign for Release of Malaysian Environmentalists', *Boston Globe*, 15 November 1987, p. 20.

29. Consumers' Association of Penang, 'Chronology of Events in the Bukit Merah Asian Rare Earth Development'.

Mitsubishi Chemical in Japan, files an ex-parte application to the Supreme Court which suspends (until further order), the High Court order to ARE to stop operations, on grounds that closure of ARE would 'bring hardship to the company and its 183 workers'. And in December 1993, the supreme court overturns the high court decision on two grounds: firstly, it is of the opinion that 'ARE's experts were more believable', and secondly that the residents should have turned to the AELB 'to ask that it revoke ARE's licence', on grounds that the factory's operation 'is not in the public interest'. Yet the local Atomic Energy Licensing Act does not even have any such provisions that would enable 'affected communities or the public' to appeal for the revocation of a licence granted to a company by the AELB. In a twist of events, at the ten-year mark of this drawn-out saga, ARE, despite its win, announces the closure of the plant (January 1994) with decommissioning and decontamination exercises (2003 and ongoing), due to 'public pressure both nationally and internationally', including opposition in Japan.[30] The 'image-conscious' Mitsubishi Chemical reaches an out-of-court settlement, making monthly payments to the affected community through its Development Fund which includes donating $164,000 to the community's schools while 'denying any responsibility' for the diseases striking the villages.[31]

And what of the environmental trauma – costs and impact – that is tantamount to doubly wounding the earth? Earlier phases of the Bukit Merah clean-up overseen by GeoSyntec, an Atlanta-based firm (one of Mitsubishi's contractors), involved removing '11,000 truckloads of radioactively contaminated material' and hauling away 'every trace of the old refinery and even tainted soil from beneath it, down to the bedrock as much as 25 feet below'.[32] Disposing the radioactive material – 'more than 80 000 steel barrels of radioactive waste' – then necessitated cutting the top of a hill 'three miles away in a forest reserve', with robots and workers in protective gear burying the hazardous material 'inside the hill's core' and then entombing it with cement and gypsum 'under more than 20 feet of clay and granite'.[33] The pristine Kledang range has become a permanent dump, indeed tomb. Twenty-eight years since the construction of ARE, Dr M concedes (in June 2010) that this '"small amount" of nuclear waste' renders the place 'not safe' as almost 'one square mile of that area is dangerous'.[34] This site is located only 3 kilometres away from Bukit Merah which is a tourist resort (about 15 kilometres from Ipoh, Perak's capital city). The ongoing clean-up, reputed to be 'one of Asia's largest

30. Consumers' Association of Penang, 'Chronology of Events in the Bukit Merah Asian Rare Earth Development'.

31. Bradsher, 'Mitsubishi Quietly Cleans Up Its Former Refinery'.

32. Bradsher, 'Mitsubishi Quietly Cleans Up Its Former Refinery'.

33. Bradsher, 'Mitsubishi Quietly Cleans Up Its Former Refinery'.

34. Consumers' Association of Penang, 'Chronology of Events in the Bukit Merah Asian Rare Earth Development'.

contaminated site clean-up operations',[35] is estimated to cost a 'massive RM300 million' (approximately USD120 million).[36]

'Ghosts of the health hazards leaking out of the ARE episode'[37] nightmarishly resurfaced when LAMP was made public in 2011. Haunting is, in the Malaysian imaginary, located not only in an original traumatic event – in this instance, ARE – but also made known (assimilated) through repetitive people's protests for the planet that are punctuated with celebratory and defeating outcomes (e.g. the routine lack of political will) and (irreversible social-environmental costs) magnified with LAMP, a facility that is ten times the size of ARE (with proportional damage to the health of the people and planet). Haunting returns to wound the survivor on and on and on.

Gestating hope from the womb of the earth

How does one, from a feminist post-colonial lens, theologize this trauma of the womb? The exhortation of 'integral ecology' – to 'feel intimately united with all that exists' – in *Laudato Si'*[38] is a haunting refrain as the mining and extraction of REE fractures the inter-relationality of people and planet. The gendered impact of this facture or wound, the root word for trauma, lies firstly, in the violent extraction of REE from ores that are naturally and readily yielded from the womb of the earth but deemed far less valuable. 'Rare' in REE may signify its value but not its scarcity, as they 'are not particularly rare'.[39] There are many identified sources of REE globally, notably China, the United States and Russia. In Australia, with REE projects such as Mount Weld (where its REE are shipped to LAMP in Gebeng, Malaysia, to process), there are '59 million tonnes in sub-economic rare earth element resources in addition to its 1.83 million tonnes of economic rare earth elements'.[40] Evidently, there are sufficient REE to meet global demands for 'fancy gadgets and green technology' for decades to come, with an approximate 'world annual production of the order of 130 000 tonnes'.[41] The 'problem' with REE is not with its supply but rather with the 'radioactivity associated with them': the 'impacts (of social-environmental costs) are real and

---

35. Gavin M. Mudd, 'Impacts of the Not-So-Rare Earths', *Issues* 99 (June 2012), http://www.issuesmagazine.com.au/article/issue-june-2012/impacts-not-so-rare-earths.html (accessed 4 February 2021).

36. Consumers' Association of Penang, 'Chronology of Events in the Bukit Merah Asian Rare Earth Development'.

37. Malaysiakini, Bukit Merah, 'Survivor: Our Tears Have Run Dry'.

38. Pope Francis, *Laudato Si'*, §11.

39. Mudd, 'Impacts of the Not-So-Rare Earths'.

40. Mudd, 'Impacts of the Not-So-Rare Earths'.

41. Mudd, 'Impacts of the Not-So-Rare Earths'.

not rare at all.[42] Processing REE involves the use of strong chemicals (non-natural elements) to extract rare earth elements, generating hazardous waste (defined as ignitable, corrosive, reactive or toxic)[43] such as 'radioactive thorium and uranium and their radioactive decay products such as radium and radon'.[44] An estimated '22 500 tonnes of radioactive waste (containing water) will be produced per annum' as well as 'non-radioactive waste' that includes fluoride compounds, dust particles, waste gas and acidic wastewater (mine tailings).[45] LAMP's 'liquid discharge of 500 tonnes per hour' into the nearby Balok River that flows into the South China Sea would not only damage the ecosystem – where waterway pollution is aggravated as LAMP is located in a reclaimed swampy peat land with a high water table that is further prone to flooding – but also adversely impact the fishing and beach tourist industries of the local communities already burdened with REE industry fallout (e.g. health risks and illnesses).[46]

The gendered impact of this facture or wound lies secondly in the parallelism between the womb of the earth and women's wombs. To imagine the extent of environmental damage of LAMP which at 'full capacity ... will be world's largest rare earth extraction plant',[47] is to recall Shanmugam, wading in almost knee-high 'smelly' water as she laboured to clear the land next to ARE, 'one of Asia's largest contaminated site clean-up operations'.[48] The accolade of 'largest' in both these instances – often hailed as an index of development – tragically belies the extent of wounding experienced, resulting in not only environmental injustice but also gender injustice. The hazardous material of ARE's permanent disposable facility, buried and entombed 'inside the hill's core' of the Kledang range 'under more than 20 feet of clay and granite',[49] is not unlike a cancerous tumour infecting the womb of the earth, especially if the integrity of the structure (container cells) is compromised (e.g. cracked). The spectre of decay and death is affected by the parallelism of the wombs of women like Madam Kwan and Shanmugam, among others, that are similarly 'infected', resulting in birth defects of their offspring, Kok Leong and Kasturi, suffering life-long severe disability and

42. Mudd, 'Impacts of the Not-So-Rare Earths'.

43. Kai-Lit Phua and Saraswati S. Velu, 'Lynas Corporation's Rare Earth Extraction Plant in Gebeng, Malaysia: A Case Report on the Ongoing Saga of People Power Versus State-Backed Corporate Power', *Journal of Environmental Engineering & Ecological Science* 1:1 (2012), pp. 1–5 (1). http://dx.doi.org/10.7243/2050-1323-1-2.

44. Kai-Lit Phua, 'Should Malaysia Bear the Burden of Australian Radioactive Waste?', *The Conversation,* 24 September 2012, https://theconversation.com/should-malaysia-bear-the-burden-of-australian-radioactive-waste-9566 (accessed 4 February 2021).

45. Phua, 'Should Malaysia Bear the Burden of Australian Radioactive Waste?'.

46. Phua, 'Should Malaysia Bear the Burden of Australian Radioactive Waste?'.

47. Phua, 'Should Malaysia Bear the Burden of Australian Radioactive Waste?'.

48. Mudd, 'Impacts of the Not-So-Rare Earths'.

49. Bradsher, 'Mitsubishi Quietly Cleans Up Its Former Refinery'.

leukaemia, respectively. The stark contrast between a 'thermometer-like pin' on Madam Kwan's chest to gauge her exposure to radioactive particles (and when pregnant with Kok Leong, given instructions to take unpaid leave on days when a 'dangerous consignment of ore had arrived')[50] and men in full personal protective equipment aided by robots, moving and burying ARE's hazardous material into the womb of the earth, exposes the differentiated gendered treatment of those who labour at ARE. The disproportionate burden of care endured by Madam Kwan in relation to her utterly dependent son – that is extended to her daughter who is deprived of basic education – reflects the hardships of women who are doubly marginalized on account of their sex and class. Gendered inequalities and inequities are further compounded by their having to manage the environmental fallout (e.g. contamination to water systems affecting food security, health hazards affecting job security and overall reproductive health and rights).[51] A jarring contrast is also afforded between the media attention (as cited) highlighting the plight of these women, along with their offspring and the glamorous profiling of women, including women of colour, in mostly senior managerial positions in male-dominated mining and mining-related industries, which includes Amanda Lacaze, the CEO and Managing Director of Lynas Corporation in Malaysia.[52]

Recognizing the critical intersection of environmental justice and gender justice in terms of differentiated needs, vulnerabilities and capacities among women, and between women and men, where these differences are further inflected by class, caste and ethnicity, nationalism (including stateless persons) and creed, is disappointingly absent from *Laudato Si'*. Yet while largely blind to issues of gender, *Laudato Si'*, in the spirit of liberation theologies, does spotlight the class distinction and concomitant lopsided power dynamics between developed nation states of the North and developing nation states of the South. The Pope's critique resonates with a post-colonial theorizing and theologizing of the binary of North/South that questions such systemic colonization of the Global South by the Global North, a binary reflected especially in the intergenerational 'ecological debt' that is borne (potentially in perpetuity) by the South. Pope Francis fittingly derides this as 'structurally perverse', as he opines:

> There is also the damage caused by the export of solid waste and toxic liquids to developing countries, and by the pollution produced by companies which operate in less developed countries in ways they could never do at home, in the countries in which they raise their capital: 'We note that often the businesses

---

50. Malaysiakini, 'Bukit Merah Survivor: Our Tears Have Run Dry'.

51. ARROW, 'Definitions', *ARROW for Change* 15 (2009), p. 11, http://arrow.org.my/wp-content/uploads/2015/04/AFC-Vol.15-No.1-2009_Climate-Change.pdf (accessed 4 February 2021).

52. Women in Mining, *100 Inspirational Women in Mining 2020* (2020), pp. 1–148 (80), https://www.womeninmining.org.uk/wp-content/uploads/2020/12/2020-Edition_WIM100_vf_1.pdf

which operate this way are multinationals [MNCs]. They do here what they would never do in developed countries or the so-called first world'.[53]

This structural violence that has sustained such 'ethics of international relations'[54] resonates with binaries of colonizer ('first world')/colonized (third world), master/native other and 'home'/out-of-home dumpsites that are firstly evidenced by the complicity of, in this context, the Malaysian government and secondly, global society at large through their insatiable demand for 'fancy gadgets and green technology'.[55] On the one hand, the Malaysian government is justifiably held accountable by its citizenry and their international allies. It has sold out the nation's soul to foreign investors by prioritizing (short-term) profits before people, wittingly loosening regulatory controls with less regard for international standards of health and safety of its people and the environment. Renewing LAMP's Temporary Operating Licence, giving it a twelve-year tax exemption, eschewing penalty for its contractual non-compliance and enabling it to defer the construction of a PDF, is done in the name of 'leading an international race to break China's global stranglehold on rare earths'.[56]

Yet the open wounds of China, the global leader in REE mining for over two decades, are laid bare through its wastelands and walking dead: the 'toxic lake [in Baotou that] poisons Chinese farmers, their children and their land ... is what's left behind after making the magnets [from the REE, neodymium] for Britain's latest wind turbines [perched on the Monadhliath mountains in Scotland] ... and ... is merely one of a multitude of environmental sins committed in the name of our *new green Jerusalem*' (italics mine).[57] 'In China, the true cost of Britain's clean, green wind power experiment',[58] and other news headlines succinctly capture the complex web of toxic relationships between and among the North and South with MNCs serving as catalysts and deal brokers: 'Mitsubishi quietly cleans up its former refinery'.[59] 'Should Malaysia bear the burden of Australian

53. Pope Francis, *Laudato Si'*, §51.

54. Pope Francis, *Laudato Si'*, §51.

55. Mudd, 'Impacts of the Not-So-Rare Earths'.

56. Philip Wen, 'Lynas Plant under Fire', *The Sydney Morning Herald*, 6 July 2011, https://www.smh.com.au/business/lynas-plant-under-fire-20110705-1h0pk.html (accessed 4 February 2021).

57. Simon Parry and Ed Douglas, 'In China, the True Cost of Britain's Clean, Green Wind Power Experiment: Pollution on a Disastrous Scale', *Mail Online*, 26 January 2011, https://www.dailymail.co.uk/home/moslive/article-1350811/In-China-true-cost-Britains-clean-green-wind-power-experiment-Pollution-disastrous-scale.html (accessed 4 February 2021).

58. Simon Parry and Ed Douglas, 'In China, the True Cost of Britain's Clean, Green Wind Power Experiment: Pollution on a Disastrous Scale'.

59. Bradsher, 'Mitsubishi Quietly Cleans Up Its Former Refinery'.

radioactive waste?',[60] and 'Has the western world exported cancer to China?'.[61] To alleviate such wanton wounding of poorer thus more vulnerable communities and countries, the practice of '*differentiated responsibilities*' serves only as a Band-Aid.[62] The Pope's exhortation that developed countries 'ought to help pay this [ecological] debt by significantly limiting their consumption of non-renewable energy and by assisting poorer countries to support policies and programmes of sustainable development'[63] is out of touch with the questionable ethics and hidden environmental costs of 'green' technology. That the 'poorest areas and countries are less capable of adopting new models for reducing environmental impact because they lack the wherewithal to develop the necessary processes and to cover their costs'[64] is precisely what richer countries are exploiting, which adds to the reduced costs of 'fancy gadgets' and the off-shore (at someone else's backyard and expense) processing of REE that adds to the illusory greenness of green technology at 'home'.[65] The 'globalization of indifference'[66] is the element that fuels the wounding of the South by the North with regard to REE mining and extraction.

An open wound is further lacerated with the global shift towards '"green" investment in clean-up, rather than clean technologies'[67] by 'dirty industry migration',[68] principally REE industries. This shift defeats the 'common wisdom'[69] that is consonant with the Pope's exhortation above – of richer countries aiding poorer countries in the transfer of green technology and sustainable practices – as clean-up industries are simply 'more profitable'[70] even in the short run. This is because 'large capital outlays'[71] that ensure compliance with

60. Phua, 'Should Malaysia Bear the Burden of Australian Radioactive Waste?'.

61. Matthew Currell, 'Has the Western World Exported Cancer to China?', *The Conversation*, 23 April 2013, https://theconversation.com/has-the-western-world-exported-cancer-to-china-13349 (accessed 4 February 2021).

62. Pope Francis, *Laudato Si'*, §52.

63. Pope Francis, *Laudato Si'*, §52.

64. Pope Francis, *Laudato Si'*, §52.

65. Mudd, 'Impacts of the Not-So-Rare Earths'.

66. Pope Francis, *Laudato Si'*, §52.

67. Jennifer Clapp, 'Foreign Direct Investment in Hazardous Industries in Developing Countries: Rethinking the Debate', *Environmental Politics* 7:4 (1998), pp. 92–113 (92).

68. Clapp, 'Foreign Direct Investment in Hazardous Industries in Developing Countries: Rethinking the Debate', p. 96.

69. Clapp, 'Foreign Direct Investment in Hazardous Industries in Developing Countries: Rethinking the Debate', p. 93.

70. Clapp, 'Foreign Direct Investment in Hazardous Industries in Developing Countries: Rethinking the Debate', p. 105.

71. Clapp, 'Foreign Direct Investment in Hazardous Industries in Developing Countries: Rethinking the Debate', p. 106.

international standards of hazardous waste disposal can be avoided at 'home'. It then becomes economically unsound for local governments – that house these off-shore dump sites of hazardous materials – to level the 'cost differentials between rich and poor countries'[72] by tightening regulatory mechanisms, thus increasing production costs that would inevitably serve to deter foreign investment. 'Dirty' industries could recycle REE that 'could reduce the ecological footprint of mining' but the cost of extraction 'makes recovery less competitive'.[73] And in so doing, the web of entanglement between richer and poorer countries burdened with the impossible choice between profits or people and the environment inadvertently destroys our earthly 'common home' and distances us even further away from the '*new Jerusalem* ... our common home in heaven' (italics mine).[74] The idea and experience of 'home' become a site of contestation between integrity and corruptibility, the promise of the good life and its desecration, and the fecundity of a womb to its deterioration as a tomb.

Would realizing a 'new Jerusalem' entail a meaningful commitment to green technology that begins with global society's preparedness to pay more for our 'fancy gadgets' in cognizance of these hidden and inestimable environmental costs in the mining, processing of REE and especially the disposal of its hazardous waste? Or perhaps and quite impractically, eschewing these altogether? Realizing a 'new Jerusalem' on Malaysian soil has led the Malaysian citizenry, buoyed by their international allies, to fight the good fight, finish the race and keep the faith (2 Tim. 4.7). One of the highlights of the anti-Lynas activism across numerous public demonstrations includes a 20,000-strong 300 kilometre green march on foot from Kuantan (the city next to where LAMP is located) to Kuala Lumpur, spearheaded by Himpunan Hijau.[75] The protesters were in a 'standoff with police'[76] at Dataran Merdeka (Independence Square), a site favoured for its historical significance as this is where the first PM of Malaysia had declared independence from its fourth and final colonizer, the British Empire in 1957. One demonstrator says, 'We hope the government can hear his people's voices. I believe they can't handle any untoward consequences. Advanced countries like Japan couldn't handle (radiation-related disasters) [referring to ARE that was eventually shut down], let alone Malaysia.'[77] One of the principle movers and shakers of the

---

72. Clapp, 'Foreign Direct Investment in Hazardous Industries in Developing Countries: Rethinking the Debate', p. 109.

73. Saleem H. Ali, 'Social and Environmental Impact of the Rare Earth Industries', *Resources* 3:1 (2014), pp. 123–34 (128). https://doi.org/10.3390/resources3010123.

74. Pope Francis, *Laudato Si'*, §243.

75. Malaysiakini Team, '20 000 Join Green March against Lynas', *Malaysiakini*, 25 November 2012, https://www.malaysiakini.com/news/215072 (accessed 4 February 2021).

76. Talia Ralph, 'Kuala Lumpur: 10,000 Protest Rare Earth Plant over Health Concerns', *Global Post*, 25 November 2012, https://www.pri.org/stories/2012-11-25/kuala-lumpur-10000-protest-rare-earth-plant-over-health-concerns (accessed 4 February 2021).

77. Ralph, 'Kuala Lumpur: 10,000 Protest Rare Earth Plant over Health Concerns'.

anti-Lynas protests, Save Malaysia, Save Lynas's (SMSL), Tan Bun Teet explains: 'We cannot simply stay silent just because we have been betrayed by self-interested politicians who have made decision against Rakyat's [citizenry] wishes.'[78] Tan refers to Lynas leaving 'close to 600 000 tonnes' of radioactive waste from its water leach purification stream and 'over 1.5 million tonnes of scheduled waste (less contaminated but hazardous) in open dams [that are] exposed to flooding and gale-force wind'.[79] The SMSL press statement adds that 'Malaysia's reputation is once again put on the line by allowing a foreign company to continue to generate toxic radioactive waste which nobody wants in their backyard'.[80] The 'NIMBY Syndrome – Not In My Back Yard'[81] used by environmental scholars refers to how the lack of public engagement with local communities typically leads to a public distrust of foreign-owned industries operating, in the case of LAMP, over 4,000 kilometres away from 'home' (Mount Weld, Australia). Lynas and, by extension, the government of Malaysia had also underestimated the 'awakening of fervent environmentalism' among resistant residents,[82] in memory of the trauma of ARE and resilience of its protestors.

Malaysians and their allies living abroad staged an 'occupy' event (November 2013) at Lynas Corporation's headquarters in Sydney, Australia. They camped out on-site for three days to confront shareholders to protest Lynas' 'incompetent, irresponsible and immoral acts' and seek the shutdown of LAMP.[83] This Occupy Lynas act of resistance is reminiscent of the global Occupy movements in 2011 (e.g. Occupy Wall Street, Arab Spring, etc.). The ground-up or grassroots movement of anti-ARE and anti-Lynas protests, as elucidated, that begin with local communities directly affected by improper and illegal hazardous waste disposals of these 'dirty' RE industries, swell up as Malaysians, men and women, young and old, from diverse ethnic and religious groups from metropolitan cities, stand in solidarity with them. The support that ripples outwards includes international researchers and both Malaysians and allies living abroad. Consonant with the Occupy movements is the foregrounding of the '99 percent' or 'the multitude'[84] who, in this context, range from the afflicted, such as Madam Kwan, Shanmugam and their offspring who courageously spoke out, activists who were pelted with

---

78. Save Malaysia, Stop Lynas, 'Press Statement: SMSL to Pursue Legal Actions after the Protest Action', *SMSL*, 18 August 2019, http://savemalaysia-stoplynas.blogspot.com/2019/08/press-statement-18th-august-2019-smsl.html (accessed 4 February 2021).

79. Save Malaysia, Stop Lynas.

80. Save Malaysia, Stop Lynas.

81. Ali, 'Social and Environmental Impact of the Rare Earth Industries', p. 130.

82. Ali, 'Social and Environmental Impact of the Rare Earth Industries', p. 130.

83. Aliran Admin, 'Malaysian Activists "Occupy" Lynas' Headquarters in Sydney', *Aliran*, 28 November 2013, https://aliran.com/civil-society-voices/2013-civil-society-voices/malaysian-activists-occupy-lynas-corps-headquarters-in-sydney/ (accessed 4 February 2021).

84. Joerg Rieger and Kwok Pui-Lan, *Occupy Religion: Theology of the Multitude* (Plymouth, UK: Rowman and Littlefield, 2012), p. 5.

tear gas, faced off with the police and were detained under the Internal Security Act, and the countless acts of civil disobedience (e.g. petitions, hunger strikes, demonstrations, marches) that manifest a 'rare mobilization of "people power" in politically authoritarian Malaysia' to defeat 'state-backed transnational corporate power'.[85] A 'theology of the multitude', according to Kwok Pui-Lan, a pioneer in post-colonial theology, in particular, Asian feminist post-colonial theology, along with her collaborator, Joerg Rieger in *Occupy Religion*, speaks of continuing reflection and praxis where hope is embodied in such anti-ARE and anti-Lynas protests that seek to transform the hearts and minds of not only the Malaysian citizenry but also the world in upholding the 'humanity of the 99 percent', the differently abled, downtrodden and disenfranchised.[86]

Conclusion

This chapter offers a feminist post-colonial reading of anti-ARE and anti-Lynas protests that are emblematic of the praxis of the multitude. The trope of the womb is revelatory in showing how dumping hazardous waste (that is chiefly radioactive) from REE mining and processing and entombing it in a pristine mountain range is tantamount to committing the double crime of not only raping the earth but also killing it. Repetitive acts of violence are entailed in the extraction of REE through use of harmful chemicals in the environment where they are naturally deposited in abundance albeit scattered (hence their rarity). A gendered reading also foregrounds the differentiated treatment of women at these REE plants whose lived realities of begetting offspring with birth defects and leukaemia are traumatic (the wounding of these bodies parallels the wounding of the earth). They embody the inestimable environmental costs that are purposefully suppressed to lure foreign conglomerates.

A post-colonial reading of anti-ARE and anti-Lynas protests exposes the inferiorized positionality of developing countries like Malaysia (as dumpsites) in relation to the imagined superiority of countries like Japan (ARE) and Australia (LAMP) who can afford to outsource and get away with improper and illegal waste management methods. The unceasing global demand not only for hi-tech gadgets at competitive prices but also 'green' technology which belies a preference for clean-up rather clean industries hardens the stranglehold of the first world on the Third World economies and the irreversible sullying of the environment. A feminist post-colonial reading insists on the prioritization of the intersectionality between environmental justice and reproductive justice that continues to be elusive for the Malaysian people in their inexhaustible fight against 'dirty' industries.

85. Phua and Velu, 'Lynas Corporation's Rare Earth Extraction Plant in Gebeng, Malaysia', p. 1.
86. Rieger and Kwok, *Occupy Religion*, pp. 117–18.

Hope that is embedded in a post-colonial 'theology of the multitude'[87] coheres with the practice of 'integral ecology' that has sustained anti-ARE and anti-Lynas protests through the decades. Theirs is a praxis 'made up of simple daily gestures [saying no, standing up and crying out] which break with the logic of violence, exploitation and selfishness. In the end, a world of exacerbated consumption is at the same time a world which mistreats life in all its forms.'[88]

---

87. Rieger and Kwok, *Occupy Religion*, p. 6.
88. Pope Francis, *Laudato Si'*, §230.

A PRACTITIONER'S RESPONSE TO HILDA P. KOSTER AND SHARON BONG

Josianne Gauthier

I am deeply grateful to have the opportunity to comment on these two specific chapters that touch so directly on my own story as a Canadian and as a Catholic feminist dedicated to human rights and to integral ecology, yet struggling with my own true integral conversion and identity as a settler – a colonizer. I was particularly inhabited and haunted by the accounts of resistance and resilience of the Indigenous women and the common thread of colonialism that tie the two chapters together and which I consider to be the backdrop of the systemic injustice and violence holding up our extractivist and fossil fuel economy.

This response and experience with essay is based on practical experience, as well as knowledge of international law, climate justice and human rights work with partner organizations close to local communities around the world. Experiences lived through active participation in some important events related to the rights of Indigenous peoples both in Canada and in a more global context will also inform this commentary, as well as my reading of Catholic Social Teachings and Thought around integral ecology and ecological conversion.

This response is further informed by the other chapters included in this collective work. The topics discussed by Koster and Bong should not be seen as isolated, not from each other or from the rest of the reflections on the impacts of mining, extractivism and toxicity on the lives of women.

We cannot dissociate the current conversation from the revelations of past acts of violence and racism towards Indigenous cultures and people in North America, especially children who were wilfully torn from their land and families in a colonial project with which the Catholic and Protestant churches were involved. These acts of settler colonial violence remind us of the intimate and toxic relationship between the extractivist economic models and the destruction of social and ecological lived realities.

This book demonstrates that the response to the identified pain and destruction should be one of global solidarity. Indeed, the crimes committed against women and the land in one place, and in one given time, have an impact on all of us and deserve our collective response. So it is useful to consider how this solidarity is formed, how we feed and harness this solidarity and how we can come to practise it fully.

In the previous two chapters, both authors detail the devastating impact of the extractive industry on women's lives in connection to the land but also brought forward the strength and power of mobilization and solidarity within the community to stand up to the abuse and greed of the corporations occupying their territories and homes. Koster and Bong both make the point of connecting the issue of extractive industry to the violence against women. They both touch on the gendered impact of the ecological crisis and the critical intersection of environmental justice and gender justice, connecting the rape of women to the rape of the land. In this, we recognize the truth of what Pope Francis said in *Laudato Si'*,[1] reminding us of the words of Brazilian theologian Leonardo Boff, in that there is only one cry: the cry of the earth and the cry of the poor.[2] It is significant that this reference is rooted in the plight of the Amazon, a region full of significance for human rights, natural resources and the rights of Indigenous cultures.

We could extrapolate to say that the cry of the earth and the cry of the poor (or oppressed) are also the cry of women or of the feminized nature of life, embodied in the exploited earth and communities. By way of our own colonial, patriarchal constructs, the feminine is portrayed as weakness, and vulnerability is seen as feminine and therefore considered with disdain. In turn, these constructs legitimize the abuse and exploitation that women, especially Indigenous women, are subjected to. As we will see, however, this entire framing is what needs to be questioned and challenged. For women and communities that are already resisting this colonial worldview have power and knowledge. If we are prepared to listen and learn, they can teach us how to heal and find the courage to act.

Calling for intergenerational justice

In her chapter, Sharon Bong relates the grassroots activism against rare earth mining and processing plants in two regions of Malaysia: a story of forty years of resistance by the communities who overcame their pain in order to fight for the land. Bong examines the struggle through a post-colonial feminist lens as a counterpoint to the masculinized meta-narratives of colonization. She draws a relationship between the masculinity of colonization and the femininity of being colonized, raped, possessed and dominated. This is particularly interesting because it takes us into a reflection on the rape of the land, and on the wounds

---

1. Pope Francis, *Laudato Si': On Care for Our Common Home* (Rome: Libreria Editrice Vaticana, 2015), p. §49.
2. Leonardo Boff, *Cry of the Earth, Cry of the Poor* (Maryknoll: Orbis Books, 1997).

that dumping carcinogenic toxic waste in and on the land creates. The violence of the extraction of rare earth and the violence with which the waste is left behind reminds us of the killing or silencing of a rape victim (as noted by Bong quoting a member of parliament). Not only do we harm and violate, but we also try to hide the evidence that a heinous act was ever committed, by making the victim's voice disappear forever. Bong further provides us with powerful language to express the lasting hurt and the depth of the harm. She speaks of 'wound' and 'trauma', which truly express the intergenerational nature of the violence. Indeed, we are seeing intergenerational trauma emerge as an idea worth exploring even further.

In my own encounter with the Truth and Reconciliation process in Canada, I learned that the Indigenous peoples of the region where my ancestors settled, the Iroquois Nation, speak of the principle of seven generations. Decisions made today will have an impact for seven generations to come. (This is now often being referenced in discussions on ecology and green renewal.) But the other side of this idea is that an injustice committed today also has impacts for the seven generations that follow. If we apply this principle to trauma and reparation, we recognize that the trauma lasts, and therefore the reparation, and eventually the healing and reconciliation, will take time as well. Thus, Pope Francis reminds us of the importance of intergenerational justice and solidarity by way of the important concept of 'integral ecology'.[3]

The healing power of resistance

Koster's chapter invites us to explore the relation between the ecological crime and sin of fracking and the epidemic of Missing and Murdered Indigenous Women (MMIW) on the Great Plains (North Dakota). Her chapter is passionate and emotionally engaging as it draws the relationship between acknowledging sin, through confession and repentance as a precondition to solidarity. This is another way of stating that there can be no reconciliation without truth, as the mediators of delicate peace processes will remind us, and that there can be no justice without remediation of some sort.

There is great power in this proposal, that through our action, through our refusal of what is wrong we can save not only the planet and others, but ourselves. This implies that we recognize the evil of what we are taking part in or witnessing. It also implies that our own solidarity can redeem us and others. In reading Koster's chapter, I felt physical and emotional pain with regard to the stories of the Missing and Murdered Indigenous Women. The laws and systems of the settlers are inadequate and perhaps often disinterested in protecting the Indigenous women, who suffer from deep-rooted racism and neglect. One must question the inefficiencies and inherent flaws of the legislative and

3. *Laudato Si'*, pp. §159–62.

judicial systems in the United States but also in Canada. In Canada there is systematic violence targeted against Indigenous women due to erroneous or non-application of existing laws and lack of protection by law enforcement. In my home province of Québec,[4] recent enquiries proved that police not only were not investigating the disappearances and abuse cases but were themselves assaulting Indigenous women and extorting them for sexual favours. This is only possible in a society that has an established colonial rule; a society where some communities are not entitled to the same rights, nor the same respect and dignity.

Koster correlates between the violation of the earth by extractive industries and the violence against Indigenous women. Violence against women has indeed often been tied to the presence of extractive industry in marginalized communities, both in the Global North and South. This phenomenon is well documented by the various contributions to this volume and results especially from transnational corporations, most particularly Canadian mining corporations.[5] This is an indication of neocolonial economic patterns. Indeed, the question to ask is whether this type of systemic gender-based violence is present because of the various ways this type of extractivism is entangled with a colonial model of so-called development.

We know that there is an impressive body of national and international laws and legal instruments that are supposed to defend and protect the rights of women and Indigenous peoples, and even treaties that are meant to safeguard our environment, our fundamental rights to food, to clean water, to live in dignity in our own countries, and to work towards more sustainable futures for our planet.

---

4. Report from the National Inquiry into Missing and Murdered Indigenous Women and Girls (MMIWG), *Reclaiming Power and Place,* with twenty-one calls to justice aimed specifically at Québec, 2019, https://www.mmiwg-ffada.ca/final-report/ (accessed 26 July 2022). Canada had previously held a Truth and Reconciliation Commission inquiry into the crimes committed against Indigenous children in the Residential Schools. Published in 2015, the Commission's final report and 94 Calls to Action are directed at both the State and the Churches. Cf., *Honouring the Truth, Reconciling for the Future: Summary of the Final Report of the Truth and Reconciliation Commission of Canada* (2015), available online: https://irsi.ubc.ca/sites/default/files/inline-files/Executive_Summary_English_Web.pdf (accessed 26 July 2022).

5. The involvement of Canadian mining corporations in the Philippines is especially infamous. Cf., https://www.regionalstudies.org/news/poorly-understood-underground-politics-of-canadian-transnational-mining-in-the-philippines/ (accessed 26 July 2022). Canadian mining companies are also said to make up around 75 per cent of the mining activities in Africa. Cf., https://miningwatch.ca/open4justice (accessed 26 July 2022).

Several international civil society organizations, such as CIDSE[6] – a network of Catholic Social Justice organizations – have successfully fought for European Union (EU) legislation on conflict minerals[7] and are continuing to fight for European due diligence legislation on protecting environmental and human rights in supply chains[8] as well as for a United Nations Binding Treaty on Business and Human Rights.[9] Of course, much more needs to be done to extend the protection of human rights and ensure ecological safeguards. Yet, in spite of international legislation and treaties, some countries refuse to support them. Why do national interests, economic interests and commercial interests always seem to trump all obvious principles to protect and defend what is sacred or what should be sacred?

We would suggest that it is not just a matter of laws being inadequate or poorly applied, nor is it due to confusion or intentional avoidance between jurisdictions (between tribal and state or federal laws); it is yet another sign of pervasive and continuing colonialism. We are addicted to growth. We are addicted to our power and privilege and comforts. We lack the courage to truly transform our economies

---

6. Cf., CIDSE, https://www.cidse.org/areas-of-work/corporate-regulation/?_sft_topic=mining (accessed 26 July 2022). CIDSE is a family of eighteen Catholic Social Justice organizations across Europe and North America, working for transformational change to end poverty and inequalities, challenging systemic injustice, inequity, destruction of nature and promoting just and environmentally sustainable alternatives. CIDSE Secretariat is based in Brussels and carries out its advocacy work towards International and EU bodies by contributing to and partnering with global movements and alliances. Cf., https://www.cidse.org/.

7. EU Conflict Minerals Regulation, adopted in 2017, applicable as of 1 January 2021. This regulation seeks to implement 'supply chain due diligence obligations' for EU countries importing tin, tantalum and tungsten, ores, and gold originating from conflict-affected and high-risk areas. Available online: https://eur-lex.europa.eu/legal-content/EN/TXT/?uri=OJ:L:2017:130:TOC (accessed 26 July 2022).

8. European Commission Directive on corporate sustainability and due diligence (EU 2019/1937. At this point it is still a proposal under debate but if adopted it would allow extraterritorial application of the EU law to European-based corporations: https://eur-lex.europa.eu/legal-content/EN/TXT/?uri=CELEX%3A52022PC0071.

9. Since 2014, the UN Human Rights Commission has been working on a draft of a Binding Treaty that would regulate human rights abuses committed by corporations registered in signatory countries. UN Human Rights Council, Office of the High Commissioner for Human Rights. HRC, Resolution 26/9 (14 July 2014) https://documents-dds-ny.un.org/doc/UNDOC/GEN/G14/082/55/PDF/G1408255.pdf?OpenElement. The third draft was revised in 2021 at the seventh session of the Working Group. This long process has been supported and pushed for by a broad coalition of human rights, Indigenous rights and now environmental rights activists from around the world. The eighth session will be in October 2022. Third Draft available here: United Nations Binding Treaty on Human Rights, currently working with the third draft (2021), https://www.ohchr.org/sites/default/files/Documents/HRBodies/HRCouncil/WGTransCorp/Session6/LBI3rdDRAFT.pdf.

away from the growth paradigm, to protect the common good, and to truly imagine a new way of sharing this planet together. Sadly, laws are written by those with the most power, the colonizer, the foreign state, the investor, the consumer, as we have seen in numerous examples of communities trying to seek justice for corporate abuse, particularly in the extractive industry.

Rethinking, reimagining 'development' and the cultural dream

The two chapters could perhaps have further reflected on the *cultural impacts* of colonial extractivist practices. Many have called for the recognition of the systematic violations of Indigenous rights and the wanton destruction of Indigenous cultures and practices as cultural genocide. Certain countries, such as Canada through its Truth and Reconciliation Commission, are looking at the impacts of their colonial past on other cultures and on culture in general. In the Synod on the Amazon,[10] the discussion about the sacredness of culture for the survival and flourishing of any community was discussed at length, and we know that full and integral development includes our cultural needs being met as well.

It is a throwaway culture that has brought us to this point of destruction of others and of the environment, and it is a deep transformation that is required to embrace a culture of care. Culture is defined in Merriam-Webster as 'the customary beliefs, social forms, and material traits of a racial, religious or social group' and also 'the characteristic features of everyday existence (such as diversions or a way of life) shared by people in a place or time'.[11] Culture is used and referenced often by Pope Francis in many different ways, as something that we can both change when it is harmful and celebrate in its diversity and beauty. In *Laudato Si'* and *Fratelli Tutti*, Francis speaks of a 'culture of encounter' as opposed to a 'throwaway culture'.[12] In *Querida Amazonia*, his exhortation following the Synod on the Amazon, he proposes that we engage in a 'cultural dream', speaking of intercultural dialogue and the wealth of cultures in the Amazon, urging the Christians to listen and learn from Indigenous cultures and challenge our colonial pasts and patterns.

In Pope Francis' latest encyclical on fraternity and solidarity, *Fratelli Tutti*,[13] we are reminded that all sources of knowledge and wisdom, all traditions must

---

10. Synod on the Amazon: Special Assembly of the Synod of Bishops for the Pan-Amazon Region, 6–27 October 2019. Final Document: *Amazonia: New Paths for the Church and for an Integral Ecology* (2019). Available online: http://secretariat.synod.va/content/sinodoamazonico/en/documents/final-document-of-the-amazon-synod.html (accessed 25 July 2022).

11. 'Culture', Merriam-Webster, https://www.merriam-webster.com/dictionary/culture (accessed 27 July 2022).

12. *Laudato Si'*, p. §22. Pope Francis, *Fratelli Tutti: On Fraternity and Social Friendship* (Rome: Libreria Editrice Vaticana, 2020), p. §216.

13. *Fratelli Tutti*, p. §50.

be valued the same way we value our own traditions. We can only care for our Common Home if we see others as our sisters and our brothers. We can only live in solidarity as it were if we see each one of us as sacred, in our common dignity, and deserving of our care. In *Querida Amazonia*,[14] the exhortation published after the Synod, we are reminded that we must share a cultural dream and enter onto a path of cultural conversion which sees the beauty and value in all cultures and traditions.

Perhaps we need to think of redemption both through solidarity earth-honoring and culture and derive a new form of hope and strength from the power of traditions which have for so long been treated as inferior. If this knowledge were recognized, if these experiences of living in a sacred relationship with nature and the land were shared and we allowed ourselves to learn from them, perhaps we might find new paths for our own flourishing and healing. Beyond the collective, intergenerational trauma of women in their struggles against the extractive industry and the systems that enable it, there is also great power, harnessed in their resistance and courage and vision. As these women faced every kind of danger and threat because they believed in their culture, they felt tied to what happened to the land; they understood it to be part of them.

We can learn so much from their courage and actions. These women adding our voice to the courageous action of these women is our hope and strength. This too is solidarity.

---

14. Pope Francis, *Querida Amazonia* (Rome: Libreria Editrice Vaticana, 2020), pp. §§28–40.

Chapter 10

SOLIDARITIES OF DIFFICULT DIFFERENCE

TOWARDS A CONVIVIALITY OF THE EARTH

Catherine Keller

So much eco-theology has already been communicated, and persuasively, that many feel what we need at this point is not more words but action. Nonetheless, and in solidarity with that impatience, I will offer some closing words on that most eco-famous of subtitles: *on care for our common home*.[1] For the sake of the action we need on behalf of that earth home, of practices that must arise across difficult differences, we cannot cease to clarify the meaning of care for that home. After all, those metaphors trigger the question of woman, as traditional keeper of the home. And that question marks women's long-time struggle for liberation from androcentric assignations and toxifications. This conversation has gathered us under that mark because the language of the 'common home' invites an immense alternative to the patriarchal home-owning and planet-possessing commodification of our place of dwelling, of domicile.

Indeed, *Laudate Si's* 'care for our common home' humbly but radically signals the chance of solidarity.[2] No mere fist in the air, solidarity signals a commitment to a shared, a common, reality. And in naming that collective in this case as the common home, the signifiers do not communicate their meaning automatically. For feminist theology has long laboured – in different contexts and ways – to dispel any presumption of a commonality won by repressing difference: sex/gender or class or race or religious or species difference. Common home, however, need signal no dull domestic unity. In Francis' usage, home, *oikos*, names our collective habitat, our ecology – the logos of our *oikos*, our dwelling place. So now we face

1. Pope Francis, *Laudato Si': On Care for Our Common Home* (Rome: Libreria Editrice Vaticana, 2015).
2. The problematic concept of 'global solidarity' with its issues of international cooperation was, for example, the subject of a recent exchange on the *Great Transition* platform in response to Richard Falk, 'Can Human Solidarity Globalize?' See also my response: https://greattransition.org/forumsearch?childforums=1&query=Catherine%20Keller&searchdate=all.

ecocide or what an important partner in the Pope's project calls '*oikos*-cide': home-killing.[3] The opposite of home-keeping. Of 'tilling the earth and keeping it' (in the encyclical's key exegesis). *Oikocide* marks not anyone's intention but a mounting side effect of business as usual: the business of global economics, *oikonomia*, the ultimate in carelessness. And so, with such smooth transnational power, the nomos, the 'law', of the global economics of neoliberal capitalism justifies the devastation of its own planetary *oikos*.

It is however another encyclical locution that has haunted me, a proposition printed in bold as the first section title: 'Nothing in this world is indifferent to us.' In context the 'thing' of nothing signifies *everything* – with emphasis upon the non-human, on the animal, the vegetal, the mineral. Does this mean then that everything *cares* about us? But that might seem to anthropomorphize, even sentimentalize, the sort of relation that all creatures have to each other. Caring for a pet may involve an affectively rich, almost interpersonal, reciprocity. Not so, my relation to the tick that delivered me a disease this summer. Strictly speaking, however, indifference is the precise opposite not of care but of *difference*. So the claim is that everything *makes* a difference – everything affects us. Each thing matters. (I no doubt made a nutritious difference to that tick.) Nothing as it materializes fails to make a difference, even as *we* make a difference to all that makes up our world. And yet despite this fundamental interdependence, civilization as we know it systemically numbs its units. Accordingly, the global *oikonomia* is free to pit itself *oikocidally* against not just 'nature' out there but our own 'nature' as creatures – and so against a cosmos of interrelation.

In other words, integral ecology presumes an ontological relationalism. Its cosmology has deep resonance with the ecumenical movement of process theology. The latter unfolds the century-old thought of the British mathematical cosmologist Alfred N. Whitehead – that 'everything is in a certain sense everywhere at all times'.[4] Every thing – in its *difference*. This universe of endlessly creative difference is far from indifferent. Indeed, it is a universe in which everything 'feels' its world – not in the case of non-humans in conscious, human-like emotion, but in varied layers of material sentience. So it was the leading process theologian John B. Cobb, Jr, who within three months of the encyclical's release, called forth a collection of sixty essays – multidisciplinary, multi-religious, multi-secular. The anthology is called *For Our Common Home: Process-Relational Responses to 'Laudato Si'*.[5] Not accidentally, the process-relational cosmology has long been a

3. Joshtrom Kureethadam, *Creation in Crisis: Science, Ethics, Theology* (Maryknoll: Orbis, 2014), p. 73.

4. Alfred N. Whitehead, *Science and the Modern World* (New York: Free Press, 1953), p. 114.

5. John B. Cobb, Jr. and Ignacio Castuera (eds), *For Our Common Home: Process-Relational Responses to 'Laudato Si'* (Anoka, MN: Process Century Press, 2015).

crucial resource for much ecological, feminist and ecofeminist theology – indeed, for its own broadly integral vision.

In this chapter, and for the sake of the integral work of this anthology, I want to offer two lines of enquiry into gender difference and the common home. First, the matter of gender in relation to the materiality of the earth: how does *gender* difference make a difference in relation to all of the differences that materialize as our terrestrial ecology? For example, how important is the masculinity of mining? Those questions will hook us into the second line of enquiry: how does gender difference pertain to *religious* difference in the common home? Even to the ecumenical difference marked by my role in this conversation as a Protestant feminist theologian? Finally, the most poetic of Puritans, John Milton, unexpectedly pops in to offer an early, gender-inflected critique of mining. In the end I hope we agree that the common, the commons, the commonality of the world means that no creature – however well oiled – can be extracted from the entangled differences that make a world. Like it or not, and with unthinkable differences of power, all unexceptionally exemplify that material entanglement.

The matter/materiality of gender and earth

How then does the non-indifference of the earth relate to gender? Specifically, how does gender play out as extractivism? It is surely not that males are inherently *oikocidal*. But we might agree that a toxic version of masculinity has penetrated the depths of the earth and the breadth of its climate. There are endless factual connections of gender and global warming. Here are four US examples: men make up 72 per cent of workers producing energy and fuels; women suffer more from respiratory conditions during the lengthening wildfire seasons; and extreme weather events figure in low birthweight and preterm births. The fourth: studies repeatedly show that among Americans more women than men (and disproportionately women of colour) believe that the climate crisis is harmful to the United States, the world and the future.[6]

Again, the issue is not gender difference as such, not some essential supremacism of Man over and against Woman and Mother Nature, but the tragic world history in which oppressive schemes of gender, race and economics have congealed into potent systems of exploitation. As the late modern economics of fossil fuel extraction continues warming the globe, the dominant form of White Man can do us all in – in a quite egalitarian mass extinction. Northern estates or extraterrestrial escapes for the exceptional few of 'us' notwithstanding. But long before modernity, that penetrating masculinity had already projected its colourless indifference

---

6. https://oxfordre.com/climatescience/view/10.1093/acrefore/9780190228620.001.0001/ acrefore-9780190228620-e-412; https://climatecommunication.yale.edu/publications/gender-differences-in-public-understanding-of-climate-change/ (accessed 14 September 2022).

beyond the world, in the form of the omnipotent Lord: the Unmoved Mover, untouched, unaffected in his high He-ness, his heinous Highness. Enthroned in His transcendent indifference, His old pedigree of love can then sub-serve, rather than subvert, the love of power.

Feminist, and very quickly ecofeminist, theology has answered with a half-century-long choir of protest. With a distinctive focus on matters of extraction and energy, one group of scholars of religion and theologians, in a fresh form of interdisciplinarity, is tracking the sacralized patriarchy of Christian history as it then fuels masculinization as modernization.[7] In this vein, Hilda Koster has succinctly captured the relations between the violence of sex trafficking, oil and structural evil as enacted close to her own neighborhood.[8] Terra Schwerin Rowe, as a Lutheran feminist theologian, has written *Of Modern Extraction: Experiments in Critical Petro-Theology*.[9] It demonstrates how the knowledge-as-power driving early modernity was always already an extractivism. It worked to surface and expose the deep dark secrets of Christian dogmas as well as of magicians, witches, midwives, but especially nature. This extractive epistemology did sometimes serve to democratize knowledge. But, as Rowe shows, it served something more and other than an epistemology of equality. 'A masculinist desire to penetrate, dominate and control nature, corresponding to the wild, unruly female and "uncivilized" peoples encountered in the colonial project, is also at play.' The petrol industry's plumbing of the dark fluid depths reads, in other words, as a late phase of the hypermasculine penetration of the feminized earth. In the colonizing projects of extraction, Rowe writes, '[W]hiteness emerges as the active exception to inhumanity while blackness emerges as a feminized passivity, identified with the passive matter from which white masculinity has triumphantly disentangled itself.' As background for this modernity, Rowe dives into the medieval argument between Thomists, for whom God's will remains at one with the good, and thereby limited by God's own law, and the nominalists, for whom God's power could not be limited. So then as Jean Bethke Elshtain tracks it, the question arose: 'If God acts outside the laws, can an earthly sovereign act outside the established laws

7. A community of thinkers in and beyond theology and religion, including a high proportion of feminist theologians, have been addressing the Christian patriarchies of petroleum, forming an Exploratory Seminar working group for the American Academy of Religion, called 'Energy, Extraction, and Religion'. Among the scholars involved are Marion Grau, Jan Pranger, Terra Schwerin Rowe, Evan Berry, J. Kameron Carter, Jacob Erickson, Clayton Crockett, Kate Rigby, Desmond Coleman and Lisa Sideris.

8. Hilda P. Koster, 'Trafficked Lands: Sexual Violence, Oil, and Structural Evil in the Dakotas', in Grace Ji-Sun Kim and Hilda P. Koster (eds), *Planetary Solidarity: Global Women's Voices on Christian Doctrine and Climate Justice* (Minneapolis: Fortress Press, 2017), pp. 155–78.

9. Terra Schwerin Rowe, *Of Modern Extraction: Experiments in Critical Petro-Theology* (London and New York: T&T Clark, 2022).

of a polity? Yes, it follows that rulers may suspend the laws if the need arises.'[10] In this version of political theology, *potestas* becomes unlimited and exceptional *potentia*. Extracted from other constitutive ties, such sovereign power makes way for multiple forms of exceptionalism: resource extraction, political sovereignty, colonization, slavery and race merge to energize the modern conquistador masculinity. With that trans-Atlantic conquistador, one pictures perhaps a Spanish Roman Catholic extractivism – vis-à-vis the mining of gold and silver. But it was in Protestant North America that a voracity for 'liquid gold' morphed into what can now be called 'petromasculinity'.[11]

In *Political Theology of the Earth* (2018) I had linked US exceptionalism to that of Man – both anthropo- and androcentric.[12] To except, from *excipere*, to take out, signifies quite literally to extract. Exceptionalism, with its aggressive political, social and economic manifestations, is bred of an onto-relational indifference to our constitutive relations. We might in the present context name the alternative 'intersectionalism' in which attention to our bottomlessly common interdependence sustains an ontology of entangled difference. Intersectionality as a social justice discourse arises in the work of Black feminists, first of all Beverly Crenshaw, insistent on the inseparability of gender from race, LGBTQI and class dynamics.[13] If we map the human social intersections onto their earth ground, we find ourselves in a dense field of relations human and otherwise, an entire planet of relations dangerously out of balance. Of course, those least responsible for the climate crisis, the toxifications, the extinctions, will suffer the materially worst consequences. Among humans that means non-white and, yes, also disproportionately female populations.

Nonetheless – before sliding into the paralyzing indifference of resignation and despair – we must bear this irony in mind: the disease may be its own cure. The vulnerability of the human species, including much of its privileged population, to the effects of climate change – a precarity that is almost everywhere, with each flood, hurricane and forest fire – is getting ever harder to miss. Isn't that awareness, that dawning recognition, a source not just of threat to our world but of hope for mass global action? The timing is unthinkably tight. Nonetheless, such dawning awareness would mean true apocalypse in the ancient sense. After all, *apokalypsis*, means 'unveiling', revelation' not The End of the world. Despite Protestant fundamentalism, The End is *not* a biblical concept. Revealing across the

10. Jean Bethke Elsthain, *Sovereignty: God, State, and Self* (New York: Basic Books, 2008), p. 38.

11. See Cara Daggett, 'Petro-Masculinity: Fossil Fuels and Authoritarian Desire', *Millennium* 47:1 (2018), pp. 25–44 (p. 29). https://doi.org/10.1177/0305829818775817.

12. Catherine Keller, *Political Theology of the Earth: Our Planetary Emergency and the Struggle for a New Public* (New York: Columbia University Press, 2018).

13. For an exposition of the conceptualization and praxis of intersectionality as such, see Patricia Hill Collins and Sirma Bilge, *Intersectionality* (Cambridge: Polity Press, 2016).

warming world is certainly happening: an unveiling that no amount of capitalist propaganda can quite re-veil. And with it stirs perhaps a hope not to be reviled? The biblical Apocalypse plays out ugly imperialism, political and economic, catastrophic human and non-human losses, and it lands in the ecologically and multinationally viable new Jerusalem. Even its ancient signs of environmental destruction (vast losses of forests to fire, of sea life to toxicity, are for instance 'prophesied') disclose a world of human and non-human interdependence. And the visions do in their archaic medium reveal this entangled difference as the fibre and the vulnerability of our common life.[14]

The masculinity of indifference of course scorns vulnerability as weakness, vulnus, wound. Yet without acceptance of our vulnerability – and so attention to the deadly growing wounds of our world – how is responsibility possible? And without the ability to respond, how is hope anything but hype? We are not only vulnerable under threat, though threat may reveal that vulnerability. Theological ethicist and ecumenist Linda Hogan has solicited the ontology of vulnerability with precision: 'The modes of relationality constituted through a sense of shared vulnerability are of an altogether different kind than those based on an ontology which seeks to foreclose this aspect of the human condition.' She asks if this existential experience of vulnerability can generate a fresh sort of conversation about our obligations towards each other. How then do we oppose the conditions under which some are more vulnerable than others, and how do we generate new alliances lived within 'the horizon of a counter-imperialist egalitarianism'?[15] That horizon, we might add, remains concealed by an atmosphere – not only metaphoric – polluted by entitlement and privilege. The possibility of a worldwide egalitarianism only comes into its visibility when the well-oiled penetration of the planet by the neo-imperialism of extraction is exposed.

The difference gender makes to religious difference

This conference, and all the conversations that the Laudato Si' Research Institute will host, surely signals the advance of such new alliance. Hence my second line of enquiry: how does gender difference translate across religious difference? Specifically, as the difference staged here by my role as a Protestant ecofeminist theologian? It is all too easy to grimace at the irony of any feminist egalitarianism 'making nice' with an institute based on a papal encyclical, carrying the seal of one of the most persistent patriarchal – and indeed global – hierarchies in human history. But irony sometimes facilitates alliance. Especially where the stakes are high, and the terms of cooperation are on the table, not mistaken for a hoped-for but elusive equality.

14. Cf., Catherine Keller, *Facing Apocalypse: Climate, Democracy and Other Last Chances* (Maryknoll: Orbis Press 2021).

15. Linda Hogan, 'Human Rights and the Vulnerabilities of Gender in a Climate Emergency', Chapter 1 of this volume.

Solidarity, we recall, is not a matter of sameness but of difficult difference. The greater the stakes, the broader is that needed solidarity. And the more difficult the difference. So, for a 'planetary solidarity' – a symbol already supercharged with ecofeminist and ecumenical articulation – the challenge of difference could hardly be greater in difficulty and at the same time in importance.[16]

Francis wasn't arguing for egalitarian but for 'integral' ecology. The cry of the poor may be for equality, but the cry of the earth is for a far broader relationality. To cite *Laudato Si'*: 'Just as the different aspects of the planet – physical, chemical, and biological – are interrelated, so too living species are part of a network, which we will never fully explore and understand. A good part of our genetic code is shared by many living beings.' This terrestrial network, this earth of intersecting intersections, does not reveal all creatures as equal. But it may well discern with Whitehead a 'democracy of fellow creatures'.

In fact, it was the study of Whitehead by way of a radically ecumenical form of Protestantism that sucked me irreversibly into theology. Process theology converged with early feminist intuitions as to the web of life – and its brokenness.[17] A few years later, my first teaching position was in a Jesuit university, in a department headed non-accidentally by a leading process theologian, Joseph Bracken, a Jesuit. But the story would not be honest if it did not acknowledge that my sense of ontological relationality as a woman's issue depended from the get-go on Roman Catholic feminists – first on *Gyn/Ecology* (1979),[18] written by that feminist with two doctorates in medieval theology and Aquinas who taught for three decades at (Jesuit) Boston College – I count Mary Daly to the venerable old tradition of brilliant Roman Catholic dissidents. But remaining Roman Catholic while inaugurating ecofeminist theology as such was Rosemary Radford Ruether, who would forge the alliance between *Gaia and God* (1992).[19] And soon came forth the ecofeminist theologies of (Sisters) Elisabeth Johnson and Ivone Gebara.

Why was there nothing comparable in Protestant theology? Could it be because half a millennium ago the Protestant Reformation had eviscerated theological cosmology? Any serious interest in the creation and in non-human creatures could be judged a Papist distraction from what we deemed the heart of faith: the personal relation of 'me and my God'.[20] This fixation on the one on one

16. Kim and Koster (eds), *Planetary Solidarity*. See also Krista E. Hughes, Dhawn B. Martin and Elaine Pedilla (eds), *Ecological Solidarities: Mobilizing Faith and Justice for an Entangled World* (Philadelphia: Penn State University Press, 2019).

17. Catherine Keller, *From a Broken Web: Separation, Sexism and Self* (Boston: Beacon Press, 1986).

18. Mary Daly, *Gyn/Ecology: The Metaethics of Radical Feminism* (Boston: Beacon Press, 1979).

19. Rosemary Radford Ruether, *Gaia and God: An Ecofeminist Theology of Earth Healing* (San Francisco: Harper One, 1992).

20. I thank the theologian Michael Welker for conversations in which he mockingly characterizes (his own) Protestant tradition with that phrase.

between the human and divine persons gradually brewed up the white Protestant individualism. It leant a Puritan potency to the extraction – the exception – of Man Himself not just from inter-human but from creaturely interdependence. The force of Western modernization can then be read as the secularization and its economization of this religious individualism. It is not until process theology, with its ecological concern going back over half a century to John Cobb's *Is It Too Late?* (1971), that a significant network of theologians, among them many Protestants, reclaimed the cosmology of the creation. Not that Roman Catholics ever lost it. So the ecofeminist ecumenism significantly criss-crosses the process network.

Am I implying that ecofeminist Protestants have no problem with the theology behind the encyclical? That would be misleading. We share the Catholic feminist assessment of magisterial gender dogma. But I doubt that we would help by banging on about women's ordination or reproductive rights from our own theological contexts, in the liberal versions of which both have been for so long presumed (if often incompletely). What I do not doubt is this: we must continue to avow and advance women's rights, needs and aspirations, and at the same time, we must not hold the ecological alliance hostage to the struggle for gender equality. No single human rights issue can be allowed to trump the urgency of environmental justice. The intersectionality of gender, sex, race, class is woven of the life of non-human bodies. Human justice itself does not materialize in abstraction from our common material life. So integral ecology cannot be dissociated from the ecumenism of feminist struggles. The *ecu* of religious diversity – the *oikumene* – stems etymologically and materially from the same *oikos* that is threatened with *oikocide*.

When ancient Hellenic geographers used the term 'ecumene' they meant the (humanly) inhabited world. I will say this much: the ecological pressure of an *over*-inhabited (i.e. overpopulated), human world has been a sticking point for Protestant/Catholic ecumenism. But that pressure may be alleviated differently than expected; I learned rather recently and to my surprise that the rate of human population growth is already dropping significantly. Recent studies indicate that women's education and reproductive choices, possibly in combination with routine chemical pollutants and climate change, are bringing down population across most of the planet.[21] This is complex data that can of course be misused in anti-feminist ways. And given, as I write, renewed pressure against women's reproductive freedom – driven by right-wing *evangelical* politics as re-inaugurated in Texas in 2021 – the struggle to keep abortion legal may provoke new ecumenical hurdles. But the downward trend of population is surely good news for the habitable

21. https://www.thelancet.com/journals/lancet/article/PIIS0140-6736(20)30677-2/fulltext
https://www.bbc.com/news/health-53409521

https://www.theguardian.com/world/2021/jan/24/as-birth-rates-fall-animals-prowl-in-our-abandoned-ghost-villages

https://www.nytimes.com/2021/05/22/world/global-population-shrinking.html?action=click&module=Spotlight&pgtype=Homepage (accessed 13 September 2021).

ecumene. It portends not some movement towards zero humanity but hopefully towards zero growth. Integral ecology offers wisdom less for growing the same old, all too common, nuclear families than for embracing social and cross-species life together in our common home – a life together, a convivium, that must relativize the 'nuclear' units, inviting them into the greater relativity.

The complicated alliance that *oikos* needs can only grow if we can raise difficult questions without shutting down conversation. The work of solidarity must keep our varying theologies intersecting within the vulnerabilities of ecumenical encounter. These have not only to do with long-entrenched moral practices but with doctrinal habits. For instance, one might contest the encyclical's strategy of questioning human ownership by asserting God's possession of the earth. Doesn't that metaphor sacralize ownership itself, recharging capitalist ideals more than it relativizes them? Or for another example, I have elsewhere pushed respectfully back against a certain edge of the encyclical that presumes divine omnipotence and its *ex nihilo* power. This difference will persist even though, as the ecotheological Father Kureethadam emphasizes, Francis means a non-arbitrary power.[22] Yet the shadow of the controlling God will always tend to undermine any rigorous sense of collective responsibility. That is an argument that exceeds feminist or ecological sensibilities but belongs to the core of process theology.

Those residual patriarchalisms, however, are no less true of Protestant theology. And they play a minor role in the encyclical in comparison to the energy of its wake-up call. Perhaps indeed they are concessions pragmatically crucial to awakening the more conservative public that an integral ecology most needs to reach. The encyclical's reading of the world as 'web of relationships' draws an orthodox Trinitarianism into a radically ecological vision: 'Everything is interconnected, and this invites us to develop a spirituality of that global solidarity which flows from the mystery of the Trinity.'[23] Such a spirituality of interconnection does not exclude non-Christian or non-Trinitarian perspectives from its invitation. Any effectually global solidarity can only arise across difficult differences requiring multiple strategies. Our constructive theological differences at any rate will remain resilient and self-critical or else drift towards dogmatic certitudes. There is no time (and I must repeat this to myself) to waste in theological bickering. It is our earth home that is getting wasted.

A spacious wound

And now suddenly an unexpected Puritan voice insists itself upon this discussion of gender and mining. Its poetry rises up out of the seventeenth-century British world of rapid modernization and urbanization. John Milton here describes the

---

22. Catherine Keller, 'Climate Change Brings Moral Change', in Cobb and Castuera (eds), *For Our Common Home*.

23. Pope Francis, *Laudato Si'*, §154f.

construction of the city of Pandemonium. It is the urban centre of Hell in his epic poem, *Paradise Lost* – 'the high Capital of Satan and his Peers'.[24] All those demons form the 'pan' of Pandemonium. But it is not Satan himself who envisioned this elegant new city. It is none other than *Mammon*, the biblical demon of economic avarice, who directs its construction. In order to build the golden splendour of Pandemonium Mammon organizes demons and humans together to mine the Earth for its 'treasures':

> Men also, and by [Mammon's] suggestion taught,
> Ransack'd the Center, and with impious hands
> Rifl'd the bowels of their mother Earth
> For Treasures better hid. Soon had his crew
> Op'nd into the Hill a spacious wound
> And dig'd out ribs of Gold.[25]

There can hardly be more violently rapacious an image than this 'rifling' of the earth, the mother's bowels. In view of this violent plunder of the planet, Milton goes on to warn, 'let none admire / That riches grow in Hell'.[26] By a noteworthy synchronicity, Milton was not writing *Paradise Lost* at home in the capital city of London, which he had fled with his family in 1664 to escape the last outbreak of bubonic plague. On the wake of increased global travel and trade, thought to have come from a region in China by way of the Silk Road or the new schooner ships, that plague remains the second worst pandemic in history, at least for now. It killed a quarter of the city's population in eighteen months: an estimated 100,000. But I hope as you read this the eerie reverb with the Covid-19 pandemic is fading into history.

Milton, meditating on the open wounds of mining, reminds us that the prefix of ecumene, like that of ecology, comes inseparably linked to that of economy: here at his early capitalist moment exposed as the demonic *oikos* of wealth. Gold mining might be particularly associated in the new world with Spanish, hence Catholic conquistadors, but he is not singling out any denomination for blame. As 'riches grow in Hell' the extraction of gold was gradually outdone by the mining (more associated with the Protestant United States) of liquid gold. As the 'ribs of gold' were extracted, so now are the veins of oil. The 'spacious wound' of the earth by the fossil fuel industry is now steadily bringing human civilization truly into pandemonium.[27] Not just paradise, but planet lost? Specifically, the humanly habitable planet.

24. John Milton, *Paradise Lost* (Chicago: Thompson and Thomas, 1901, Originally Published 1667), p. 30.

25. Milton, *Paradise Lost*, p. 28.

26. Milton, *Paradise Lost*, p. 28.

27. Catherine Keller, 'The Gallop of the Pale Green Horse: Pandemic, Pandaemonium and Panentheism', in Alexander J. B. Hampton, *Pandemic, Ecology and Theology: Perspectives on COVID-19* (London: Routledge, 2021), pp. 41–54.

Pandemonium suggests a hellishly structured disorder of dissociated differences – the opposite not of mere order but of the creative chaos of mindfully interdependent differences. An alternative order for the human habitation of the planet will demand challenging alliances. And it will never evade what complexity theory calls the 'edge of chaos'. If what matters is the genesis – across genders and sexes, across traditions and species – of a vigorous new solidarity of difference, it will span the earth. For such a planetary solidarity – a symbol already layered with ecofeminist and ecumenical motives – the challenge of difference could hardly be greater in difficulty and at the same time in importance.

We can work those differences not through heightened opposition but through what Celia Deane-Drummond calls 'the wisdom of the liminal'.[28] Such wisdom, theological and practical, invokes the liminality that shadows the edge of every difference. Attending to the folds of liminality, we find that limit itself exposes our creaturely finitude without reducing our complexity, our plex-together, our mutual enfoldedness. Then, rather than succumbing to old careless antagonisms, we might grow into the agonisms of shared struggle.[29] Attending to the limits rather than ransacking 'The Center', an alternative to the extractive economy and its abstractive justifications might be discerned emerging. Already and still possible, if hardly probable.

Beyond all the home-killing, a planetary home-keeping. It would not be about a happy ending but about a creaturely conviviality, an eco-convivium. This cosmos cannot be abstracted from its creator, who cannot be subtracted from any creature – and who does not, will not, do our work of world-healing for us. In the liminally possible commons of planetary care, amidst all of us animals, plants, rocks, molecules, amidst all our difficult differences, none of the lives are indifferent to each other. At our limits, enough of the human animals realize that truth – to make the difference.

28. Cf., Celia Deane-Drummond, *The Wisdom of the Liminal: Evolution and Other Animals in Becoming* (Grand Rapids: Eerdmans, 2014).

29. Cf., my discussion of William Connolly's distinction (also developed by Chantal Mouffe) of agonism and antagonism, in Keller, *Political Theology of the Earth*, especially chapter 1.

Epilogue

ARE WE READY TO LISTEN?

CONSIDERATIONS ON THE ROLE OF WOMEN IN DEVELOPMENT PROCESSES WITH PARTICULAR REFERENCES TO POLLUTION AND MINING

Tebaldo Vinciguerra

When I started writing this text, the front page of the *Osservatore Romano* denounced the murder of two Indigenous women activists. Clearly these women were disturbing some big particular interest. The furrow of blood connects those Indigenous women to Sr. Dorothy Stang and Berta Caceres, and to many other, less-known women in their fight for human rights, human dignity, environmental stewardship and peace. The United Nations has underscored that human rights defenders and conservationists with their families frequently face violence 'including killings and sexual violence, smear campaigns, and other forms of intimidation'.[1] Even the judicial system seems unfair, and the burden of proof appears especially heavy if the plaintiff is a woman. This is obvious already in the parable of the persistent widow (cumulative weakness: woman and widow!): 'In a certain town there was a judge who neither feared God nor cared what people thought. And there was a widow in that town who kept coming to him with the plea, "Grant me justice against my adversary". For some time he refused' (Lk. 18. 2-4 [NIV]).

The former Pontifical Council for Justice and Peace received similar testimonies when meeting with representatives of communities affected by mining in July 2015. Let us recall the role of Native American women activists in the 2016 Dakota Access pipeline protests near the Standing Rock reservation in North Dakota (US) described in this volume by Marion Grau, or the nun recently kneeling in front of the police in Myanmar, or the half-naked women demonstrating in the Niger Delta against an oil company in 2014. When everything seems to collapse

---

1. United Nations Environmental Programme (UNEP), Press release, 16 August 2019. 'UNEP, UN Human Rights Office sign new agreement, stepping up commitment to protect the human right to a healthy environment' (accessed 7 September 2021).

because of cynicism, ruthless violence and irresponsible pollution, it seems that women frequently represent a strong voice of reason and wisdom. They often offer a courageous stance in face of madness and annihilation, safeguarding invisible goods such as peace, social cohesion, hope and the very conditions for life. Recognizing that not all women are mothers, motherhood nonetheless is often referred to as a special source of strength and insight. Indeed, Pope Francis insists: 'The consecrated woman … must be a mother, not a "spinster"! … motherhood in the consecrated life is important, this fruitfulness! May this joy of spiritual fecundity motivate your life; be mothers, as a figure of Mary'.[2]

Women's leadership on environmental issues is motivated by the fact that they and their children often are heavily impacted by pollution. In the majority world the negative health effects of indoor pollution caused by poor cooking conditions are now well understood. Another grave concern is inadequate access to drinking water. Because of climate change induced droughts women and girls need to walk longer distances to fetch water (which is not without risks). And while the poor typically are excessively exposed to various forms of pollution due to mining, poor women are carrying the brunt of the toxicity of resource extraction in their bodies. As Denise Humphreys Bebbington narrated in her chapter about mining in Bolivia and Peru, 'mothers talked about the experience of giving birth to contaminated children whose bodies grew discoloured and weak, and who ultimately buried their children without answers to what made them sick because they were too afraid to speak out'. Similarly, Felicia Jefferson's contribution describes the worrying impacts of endocrine disruptors on woman's bodies, affecting their health and fertility. Really, 'never has humanity had such power over itself, yet nothing ensures that it will be used wisely, particularly when we consider how it is currently being used'.[3] It is important to be reminded therefore that 'the Church has a responsibility towards creation, and she must assert this responsibility in the public sphere. In so doing, she must defend not only earth, water and air as gifts of creation that belong to everyone. She must above all protect mankind from self-destruction'.[4]

This said, we need to go deeper (without neglecting the fact that women are heavily impacted by pollution and its consequences) and tackle more structural issues. Beside the aforementioned list of assaults on human bodies – and particularly the bodies of women – we shall be aware that women and their point of view are not duly considered in economic theory. According to 'mainstream economic theory' the *homo economicus* is the 'solitary, calculating, competing and

2. Pope Francis, *Address to the Plenary Assembly of the International Union of Superiors General*, 8 May 2013, https://www.vatican.va/content/francesco/en/speeches/2013/may/documents/papa-francesco_20130508_uisg.html (accessed 7 September 2021).

3. Pope Francis, *Laudato Si': On Care for Our Common Home* (Rome: Libreria Editrice Vaticana, 2015), p. §104.

4. Benedict XVI, *Caritas in Veritate* (Rome: Libreria Editrice Vaticana, 2009), p. §51.

insatiable' man. This model turns a caricatural 'model of man ... into a model' for the whole society.[5] A model blatantly unable to consider and take care of the commons, unable to respect women's wisdom, unable to operate according to what economist Alessandra Smerilli has called 'We-rationality',[6] let alone consider its relevance for solidarity and collaboration. Pollution of local water sources is a grave example of disrespect for the commons. In her chapter, Deborah Delgado Pugley describes the devastating effects of an oil spill on the local water supply of the community of Cuninico (Peru): 'before the oil spill it was common to drink and cook with stream water in Cuninico. Water remains contaminated to this day, so the residents mainly rely on rainwater'. A common was ruined. Frequently in this kind of situation local governance structures are not involved in the decisions leading to drilling, and local communities do not benefit from the project. This despite the warning issued by the Pastoral Constitution *Gaudium et Spes*: 'imprudent action should not be taken against respectable customs' since 'in economically less advanced societies the common destination of earthly goods is partly satisfied by means of the customs and traditions proper to the community, by which the absolutely necessary things are furnished to each member'.[7] In the example we are discussing – the pollution of a river no longer suitable for drinking or cooking – the whole community is penalized. It now relies chiefly on unsafe and unpredictable rainwater.

It is worthwhile noting that in 1911 Katharine Coman (1857–1915), a Professor of Economics and Dean of Wellesley College (Wellesley, MA), studied water management in the western part of the United States, where water rights were 'a matter of serious concern'. Yet, progressively, a desire emerged to encourage 'a more democratic form of irrigation by cooperating communities' because 'what might be accomplished by cooperative effort had already been demonstrated in ... Colorado'. The Wright Act, the California law of 1887, stipulated that an irrigation district could be 'organized under state supervision wherever a majority of the resident freeholders should petition for the privilege'.[8] A district, once established according to this framework, 'had authority to issue bonds, secured by a mortgage on the lands in question, for the purchase or construction of waterworks' and could also 'levy taxes assessed on the real estate represented sufficient to

5. Kate Raworth, *Doughnut Economics: Seven Ways to Think Like a 21st Century Economist* (London: Penguin Random House, 2018), pp. 95–127.

6. Cf., Alessandra Smerilli, '"We-rationality", per una teoria non individualistica della cooperazione', *Economia politica* XXIV:3 (December 2007), pp. 407–25 (409).

7. Paul VI, *Gaudium et Spes: Pastoral Constitution on the Church and the Modern World* (Rome: Libreria Editrice Vaticana, 1965), p. §69. Available online: https://www.vatican.va/archive/hist_councils/ii_vatican_council/documents/vat-ii_const_19651207_gaudium-et-spes_en.html (accessed 7 September 2021).

8. Katharine Coman, 'Some Unsettled Problems of Irrigation', reprinted after a century in *American Economic Review* 101:1 (February 2011), pp. 36–48 (37).

meet interest on the bonds and the annual costs of maintenance'.[9] Similarly, in 2009 Elinor Ostrom (1939–2012) received a Nobel Prize in Economics because she 'challenged the conventional wisdom by demonstrating how local property can be successfully managed by local commons without any regulation by central authorities or privatization'.[10] The Nobel webpage states that

> it was long unanimously held among economists that natural resources that were collectively used by their users would be overexploited and destroyed in the long-term. Elinor Ostrom … showed that when natural resources are jointly used by their users, in time, rules are established for how these are to be cared for and used in a way that is both economically and ecologically sustainable.[11]

Evoking these two women economists, Luigino Bruni – a historian of economic thought and one of the driving forces behind the *Economia di Francesco* initiative[12] – observed that it should not surprise us that 'at the beginning and at the end (for now) of the theory of commons, there are two women' since commons are 'relationships between people mediated by goods'.[13] Without attention to the relational dimension of life and the economy, without a relationship that transcends time and generations, commons first cannot be seen, then they cannot be understood, and finally they perish. Moreover, if we 'look at relationships intrinsically, women have a vocation to take a leading role, and so to pass on life, their look and their flesh connect generations and create brothers and sisters out of their members'.[14] Mainstream capitalist economy often has failed 'to understand commons because in general it does not address problems in a historical (or geographical) perspective. In fact, it does not see relations but separate individuals, and it is defined entirely within the registry of male rationality'.[15] It is worthwhile noting that a few years before Ostrom was awarded the Nobel Prize in Economics, Wangaari Muta Maathai received the Nobel Prize for Peace – the first African woman to receive the Prize – for her environmental activism and her work empowering rural women through tree planting in her native Kenya. Married and

---

9. Coman, 'Some Unsettled Problems of Irrigation', pp. 39–40.

10. 'Elinor Olstrom Facts', https://www.nobelprize.org/prizes/economic-sciences/2009/ostrom/facts/ (accessed 7 September 2021).

11. 'Elinor Olstrom Facts', https://www.nobelprize.org/prizes/economic-sciences/2009/ostrom/facts/ (accessed 7 September 2021).

12. Cf., https://francescoeconomy.org/.

13. Luigino Bruni, 'The Future Is Not a Club', English translation of an article originally published in *Avvenire*, 1 December 2013. Available online: https://www.edc-online.org/en/publications/articles-by/luigino-bruni-s-articles/avvenire-editorial/other-series/the-vocabulary-of-good-social-life/8260-the-future-is-not-a-club.html (accessed 7 September 2021).

14. Bruni, 'The Future Is Not a Club'.

15. Bruni, 'The Future Is Not a Club'.

a mother, she was also the first female scholar from East and Central Africa to earn a doctorate. Maathai played an active part in the struggle for democracy in Kenya.

In her chapter, Bebbington asks, 'Do women have a better ethics of care towards the environment than men?' and I am tempted to answer, 'In many cases, yes'. Nonetheless, the struggle to respect women's role as leaders and activists is not easy.

The fight for and with women fighting for human rights and for the care of our common home is a major challenge for integral human development and for the Church. I will conclude invoking Our Lady who was called 'Woman' by her son, Christ the Son, precisely at the beginning and at the end of his public life: 'Woman, why do you involve me?' and 'Woman, here is your son' (Jn 2.4; 19.26). In a mysterious way, she has already experienced many of the difficulties which poor women often experience today: the mockery of an unusual (out of wed-lock) pregnancy (Nazareth), the lack of housing (Bethlehem), the threat and forced migration (Egypt), the awareness of daily logistical needs (Cana), the criminalization of her Son (Jerusalem) and the heartbreak of his death (Golgotha). Perhaps Mary – represented also as *Pietà* or as a woman crowned with stars crushing the head of a serpent – is waiting and ready to welcome and comfort the women in each of these places. It seems particularly important, especially for countries with a strong Marian tradition, to be concerned and proactive about the themes discussed in this book. As *Laudato Si'* insists, genuine religious values can offer a strong motivation for conversion, commitment and preservation.

SELECTED BIBLIOGRAPHY

Ali, Saleem H., 'Social and Environmental Impact of the Rare Earth Industries', *Resources* 3:1 (2014), pp. 123–34.

Arbuckle, T., 'Are There Sex and Gender Differences in Acute Exposure to Chemicals in the Same Setting?', *Environmental Research* 101:2 (2006), pp. 195–204.

Auyero, J. and D. Swistun, *Flammable: Environmental Suffering in Argentine Shantytown* (Oxford: Oxford University Press, 2009).

Barclay, J. M. G., *Paul and the Gift* (Grand Rapids: Eerdmans, 2015).

Bartlett, R., *Why Can the Dead Do Such Great Things? Saints and Worshippers from the Martyrs to the Reformation* (Princeton: Princeton University Press, 2013).

Bebbington, A. (ed.), *Social Conflict, Economic Development and the Extractive Industry: Evidence from South America* (London: Routledge, 2011).

Bebbington, A., 'The New Extraction: Rewriting the Political Ecology of the Andes?', *NACLA Report on the Americas* 42:5 (2009), pp. 12–20.

Bebbington, A. and J. Bury (eds), *Subterranean Struggles New Dynamics of Mining, Oil, and Gas in Latin America* (Austin: University of Texas Press, 2013).

Bebbington, A. and M. Williams, 'Water and Mining Conflicts in Peru', *Mountain Research and Development* 28:3–4 (2008), pp. 190–5.

Benotti, M. J., R. A. Trenholm, B. J. Vanderford, J. C. Holady, B. D. Stanford and S. A. Snyder, 'Pharmaceuticals and Endocrine Disrupting Compounds in U.S. Drinking Water', *Environmental Science & Technology* 43:3 (2009), pp. 597–603.

Berger, R. G., T. Hancock and D. DeCatanzaro, 'Influence of Oral and Subcutaneous Bisphenol-A on Intrauterine Implantation of Fertilized Ova in Inseminated Female Mice', *Reproductive Toxicology* 23:2 (2007), pp. 138–44.

Bergmann, S., *Religion, Space and the Environment* (New Brunswick: Transaction, 2014).

Birnbaum, L. S. and S. E. Fenton, 'Cancer and Developmental Exposure to Endocrine Disruptors', *Environmental Health Perspectives* 111:4 (2003), pp. 389–94.

Björvang, R. D. and P. Damdimopoulou, 'Persistent Environmental Endocrine – Disrupting Chemicals in Ovarian Follicular Fluid and In Vitro Fertilization Treatment Outcome in Women', *Upsala Journal of Medical Sciences* 125:2 (2020), pp. 85–94.

Blacksmith Institute, *The World's Worst Polluted Places: The Top Ten of the Dirty Thirty* (New York: Blacksmith Institute, 2007).

Bolz-Weber, N., *Accidental Saints: Finding God in All the Wrong People* (New York: Convergent Books, 2015).

Brody, J. G. and R. A. Rudel, 'Environmental Pollutants and Breast Cancer', *Environmental Health Perspectives* 111:8 (2003), pp. 1007–19.

Buller, M., M. Audette, B. Eyolfson and Q. Robinson, *Reclaiming Power and Place: The Final Report of the National Inquiry into Missing and Murdered Indigenous Women and Girls*, June 13, 2019, Volume 1a, available at https://www.mmiwg-ffada.ca/wp-content/uploads/2019/06/Final_Report_Vol_1a-1.pdf.

Bury, J., 'Livelihoods in Transition: Transnational Gold Mining Operations and Local Change in Cajamarca, Peru', *The Geographical Journal* 170:1 (2004), pp. 78–91.

Caruth, C., *Unclaimed Experience: Trauma, Narrative, and History* (Baltimore: Johns Hopkins University Press, 1996).

Castillo Guzmán, G. and L. Soria, *Gender Justice in Consultation Processes for Extractives Industries in Bolivia, Ecuador, and Peru* (Lima, Peru: Oxfam, 2011).

Chan, M., C. Mita, A. Bellavia, M. Parker and T. James-Todd, 'Racial/Ethnic Disparities in Pregnancy and Prenatal Exposure to Endocrine-Disrupting Chemicals Commonly Used in Personal Care Products', *Current Environmental Health Reports* 8:2 (2021), pp. 98–112.

Charles L., S. Cissoko and Osprey Orielle Lake, 'Gendered and Racial Impacts of the Fossil Fuel Industry in North America and Complicit Financial Institutions' (Women and Earth, Climate Activist Network, 2021), available at https://www.wecaninternational. org/_files/ugd/d99d2e_918b1e133b2548549b686e4b6eac4cc3.pdf.

Christian Aid, *Engendering Business and Human Rights: Applying a Gender Lens to the UN Guiding Principles on Business and Human Rights and Binding Treaty Negotiations* (2019), available at https://www.christianaid.org.uk/sites/default/files/2019-05/ Engendering%20Business%20and%20Human%20Rights_1.pdf.

Christian Aid, *Song of the Prophets: A Global Theology of Climate Change* (2020), available at https://www.christianaid.org.uk/sites/default/files/2020-05/song-of-the-prophets-theology-climate-change-report-May2020.pdf.

Chung, H. K., 'Ecology, Feminism and African and Asian Spirituality: Towards a Spirituality of Eco-Feminism', in D. Hallman (ed.), *Ecotheology: Voices from the South* (Geneva: WCC Publications, 1994), pp. 175–8.

Clapp, J., 'Foreign Direct Investment in Hazardous Industries in Developing Countries: Rethinking the Debate', *Environmental Politics* 7:4 (1998), pp. 92–113.

Colborn, T., D. Dumanoski and J. P. Myers, *Our Stolen Future: Are We Threatening Our Fertility, Intelligence, and Survival? A Scientific Detective Story* (New York: Plume Publishing, 1996).

Cowie, R. H., P. Bouchet and B. Fontaine, 'The Sixth Mass Extinction: Fact, Fiction or Speculation?' *Biological Reviews* 97 (2022), pp. 640–63.

Daggett, C., 'Petro-Masculinity: Fossil Fuels and Authoritarian Desires', *Millennium: Journal of International Studies* 47:1 (2018), pp. 25–44.

Daggett, C., 'Energy and Domination: Contesting the Fossil Myth of Fuel Expansion', *Environmental Politics* 30:4 (2021), pp. 644–62.

Damonte, G., *The Constitution of Political Actors: Peasant Communities, Mining and Mobilization in Bolivian and Peruvian Andes* (Saarbrucken-Berlin: VDM Verlag, 2008).

De Echave, J., R. Hoetmer and M. Palacios (eds), *Mineria y Territorio en el Peru, Dialogos y Movimientos* (Lima, Peru: CooperAcción, Confederacion Nacional de Comunidades del Peru Afectadas por la Mineria, Universidad Nacional Mayor de San Marcos, 2009).

Deer, S. and E. A. Kronk Warner, 'Raping Indian Country', University of Utah College of Law Research Paper No. 344 (December 2019). Available online https://papers.ssrn. com/sol3/papers.cfm?abstract_id=3497007.

Deonandan, K. and R. Tatham, 'The Unexplored Dimensions of Resistance to Extractivism in Latin America: The Role of Women and NGOs', in Kalowatie Deonandan and Michael L. Dougherty (eds), *Mining in Latin America: Critical Approaches to the New Extractivism* (London and New York: Routledge, 2016), pp. 273–83.

Deonandan, K., R. Tatham and B. Field, 'Indigenous Women's Anti-Mining Activism: A Gendered Analysis of the El Estor Struggle in Guatemala', *Gender and Development* 25 (2017), pp. 405–19.

Dochuk, D., *Anointed with Oil: How Christianity and Crude Made Modern America* (New York: Basic Books, 2019).

Dube, M. W., 'Introduction: "Little Girl, Get Up"', in Nyambura J. Njoroge and Musa W. Dube (eds), *Talitha Cum! Theologies of African Women* (Pietermaritzburg: Cluster Publications, 2001), pp. 3–24.

Eftimie, A., K. Heller and J. Strongman, *Mainstreaming Gender into Extractive Industries Projects* (Extractive Industries and Development Series; Washington, DC: The World Bank, 2009).

Estes, N. and J. Dhillon, *Standing with Standing Rock: Voices from the #NODAPL Movement* (Minneapolis: University of Minnesota Press, 2019).

Francis, Pope, *Laudato Si': On Care for Our Common Home* (Rome: Libreria Editrice Vaticana, 2015).

Gebara, I., 'Women, Climate, God, and Pope Francis', in Grace Ji-Sun Kim and Hilda P. Koster (eds), *Planetary Solidarity: Global Women's Voices on Christian Doctrine and Climate Justice* (Minneapolis: Fortress, 2017), pp. 67–79.

Geyer, R., J. R. Jambeck and K. L. Law, 'Production, Use, and Fate of All Plastics Ever Made', *Science Advances* 3 (2017), e1700782. DOI: 10.1126/sciadv.1700782.

Gibson, G. and D. Kemp, 'Corporate Engagement with Indigenous Women in the Minerals Industry: Making Space for Theory', in Ciaran O'Faircheallaigh and Saleem Ali (eds), *Earth Matters: Indigenous Peoples, the Extractive Industries and Corporate Social Responsibility* (Sheffield, UK: Greenleaf, 2008), pp. 104–22.

Gideon, J. and A. Ramm (eds), *Motherhood, Social Policies, and Women's Activism in Latin America* (Cham, Switzerland: Palgrave Macmillan, 2020).

Gil, V., *Aterrizaje Minero: Cultura, conflicto, negociaciones y lecciones desde la minería en Ancash, Perú* (Lima, Peru: Instituto de Estudios Peruanos, 2009).

Gilio-Whitaker, D., *As Long as Grass Grows: The Fight for Indigenous Environmental Justice from Colonization to Standing Rock* (Boston: Beacon Press, 2017).

Grieco, K., 'Motherhood, Mining and Modernity in the Peruvian Highlands from Corporate Development to Social Mobilization', in *Negotiating Normativity* (Cham: Springer, 2016), pp. 131–46.

Harris, M., *Eco-Womanism: African-American Women and Earth-Honoring Faiths* (Maryknoll: Orbis Books, 2017).

Helm, J. S., M. Nishioka, J. G. Brody, R. A. Rudel and R. E. Dodson, 'Measurement of Endocrine Disrupting and Asthma-Associated Chemicals in Hair Products Used by Black Women', *Environmental Research* 165:208 (2018), pp. 448–58.

Hogan, L., *Keeping Faith with Human Rights* (Washington, DC: Georgetown University Press, 2015).

Hollenbach, D. S.J., *Humanity in Crisis Ethical and Religious Responses to Refugees* (Washington, DC: Georgetown University Press, 2019).

Howles, T., J. Reader and M. Hodson, '"Creating an Ecological Citizenship": Philosophical and Theological Perspectives on the Role of Contemporary Environmental Education', *Heythrop Journal* 59:6 (2018), pp. 997–1008.

Humphreys Bebbington, D. and A. Bebbington, 'Extraction, Territory, and Inequalities: Gas in the Bolivian Chaco', *Canadian Journal of Development Studies/Revue canadienne d'études du développement*, 30:1–2 (2010), pp. 259–80.

Isasi-Díaz, A. M., *La Lucha Continues: Mujerista Theology* (Maryknoll: Orbis, 2004).

Jenkins, K., 'Unearthing Women's Anti-Mining Activism in the Andes: Pachamama and the "Mad Old Women"', *Antipode* 47:2 (2015), pp. 442–60.

Jenkins, K., 'Women Anti-mining Activists' Narratives of Everyday Resistance in the Andes: Staying Put and Carrying on in Peru and Ecuador', *Gender, Place & Culture*, 24:10 (2017), pp. 1441–59.

John, Paul II, Pope, *Letter to Women* (Rome: Editrice Libreria Vaticana, 1995).

Johnson, D. M., 'Reflections on Historical and Contemporary Indigenist Approaches to Environmental Ethics in a Comparative Context', *Wicazo Sa Review* 22:2 (Fall 2007), pp. 23–55.

Johnson, E. A., *Friends of God, and Prophets: A Feminist Theological Reading of the Communion of Saints* (Ottawa: Novalis, 1998).

Kahn, L. G., C. Philippat, S. F. Nakayama, R. Slama and L. Trasande, 'Endocrine-Disrupting Chemicals: Implications for Human Health', *Lancet Diabetes & Endocrinology* 8:8 (2020), pp. 703–18.

Kanyoro, M., *Introducing Feminist Cultural Hermeneutics: African Perspective* (Cleveland: Pilgrim Press, 2002).

Katongole, E., *Born from Lament: The Theology and Politics of Hope in Africa* (Grand Rapids, MI: William B. Eerdmans, 2017).

Keenan, J., D. Kemp and R. Ramsay, 'Company–Community Agreements, Gender and Development', *Journal of Business Ethics* 135:4 (2016), pp. 607–15.

Kidwell, C., N. Homer, G. E. Tinker and J. Weaver, *A Native American Theology* (Maryknoll: Orbis Books, 2001).

Kim, G. Ji-Sun and H. P. Koster (eds), *Planetary Solidarity: Global Women's Voices on Christian Doctrine and Climate Justice* (Minneapolis: Fortress, 2017).

Kimmerer, R. W., *Braiding Sweetgrass: Indigenous Wisdom, Scientific Knowledge, and the Teachings of Plants* (Minneapolis: Milkweed Editions, 2013).

Kwok, P. L., 'Ecology and the Christian Recycling of Christianity', in D. Hallman (ed.), *Ecotheology: Voices from South and North* (Geneva: WCC Publications, 1994), pp. 107–11.

Kwok, P. L., *Globalisation, Gender and Peacebuilding: The Future of Interfaith Dialogue* (Mahwah, NJ: Paulist Press, 2012).

Lahiri-Dutt, K., 'The Megaproject of Mining: A Feminist Critique', in Stanley D. Brunn (ed.), *Engineering Earth* (New York: Springer, 2011), pp. 329–51.

Langston, N., *Toxic Bodies* (New Haven: Yale University Press, 2010).

Laplonge, D., 'The "Un-Womanly" Attitudes of Women in Mining towards the Environment', *The Extractive Industries and Society* 4:2 (2017), pp. 304–9.

Leduc, T. B., *A Canadian Climate of Mind: Passages from Fur to Energy and Beyond* (Montreal: McGill-Queen's University, 2016).

Li, F., 'Negotiating Livelihoods: Women, Mining and Water Resources in Peru', *Canadian Woman Studies* 27:1 (2008), pp. 97–102.

Li, F., *Unearthing Conflict* (Durham, NC: Duke University Press, 2015).

Macdonald, I. and C. Rowland, *Tunnel Vision: Women, Mining and Communities* (Victoria, Australia: Oxfam Community Aid Abroad, 2002).

Maddow, Rachel, *Blowout: Corrupted Democracy, Rogue State Russia, and the Richest, Most Destructive Industry on Earth* (New York: Crown, 2019).

Madrid L., E., Sempértegui, A., Tito, S., Canelas, E. and J. L. Alanez, 'Coro Coro and Challapata: Defending Collective Rights and Mother Earth against Development Mining Fetishism', *Environmental Justice* 5:2 (2012), pp. 65–9.

Mann, M., *The New Climate War: The Fight to Take Back Our Planet* (New York: Public Affairs, 2021).

Mbey, M. B., 'Women in the Church in Africa: Possibilities for Presence and Promises', in Nyambura J. Njoroge and Musa W. Dube (eds), *Talitha Cum! Theologies of African Women* (Pietermaritzburg: Cluster Publications, 2001).

Merchant, C., *The Death of Nature: Women, Ecology, and the Scientific Revolution* (New York: HarperCollins, 1980).

Mikołajewska, K., J. Stragierowicz and J. Gromadzińska, 'Bisphenol A – Application, Sources of Exposure and Potential Risks in Infants, Children, and Pregnant Women', *International Journal of Occupational Medicine and Environmental Health* 28:2 (2015), pp. 209–41.

Mikołajewska, K., J. Stragierowicz and J. Gromadzińska, 'Mining, Meaning and Memory in the Andes', *The Geographical Journal* 184:3 (2018), pp. 229–41.

Molyneux, Maxine, 'Mothers at the Service of the New Poverty Agenda: Progresa/ Oportunidades, Mexico's Conditional Transfer Programme', *Social Policy & Administration* 40 (2006), pp. 425–49.

Mombo, E., 'Reflections on Peace in the Decade to Overcome Violence', *Ecumenical Review* 61 (2021), pp. 71–6.

Moyn, S., *Not Enough Human Rights in an Unequal World* (Cambridge, MA: Belknap Press, Harvard University Press, 2018).

Mudd, Gavin M., 'Impacts of the Not-So-Rare Earths', *Issues* 99 (June 2012), available at http://www.issuesmagazine.com.au/article/issue-june-2012/impacts-not-so-rare-earths.html.

Muigua, K., 'Gender Perspectives in Biodiversity Conservation', *Journal of Conflict Management & Sustainable Development* 7:4 (2021), pp. 77–93.

Nalwamba, K., 'Cultural Values and Public Life', *JCTR Bulletin* 3 (2009), pp. 17–19.

Nikiforuk, A., *The Energy of Slaves: Oil and the New Servitude* (Vancouver: Greystone Books /D&M Publishers, Inc., 2012).

O'Donnell Gandolfo, E., *The Power and Vulnerability of Love: A Theological Anthropology* (Minneapolis: Fortress Press, 2015).

O' Neill, W., *Reimagining Human Rights Religion and the Common Good* (Washington, DC: Georgetown University Press, 2021).

Oduyoye, M. A., *Who Will Roll the Stone Away? The Ecumenical Decade of the Churches in Solidarity with Women* (Geneva: World Council of Churches, 1991).

Pacyga, D. C., S. Sathyanarayana and R. S. Strakovsky, 'Dietary Predictors of Phthalate and Bisphenol Exposures in Pregnant Women', *Advances in Nutrition (Bethesda, Md.)* 10:5 (2019), pp. 803–15.

Pagán, M., 'Cultivating a Decolonial Feminist Integral Ecology: Extractive Zones and the Nexus of the Coloniality of Being/Coloniality of Gender', *Journal of Hispanic/ Latino Theology* 22:1/6 (2020), pp. 72–100. Available online: https://repository.usfca.edu/ jhlt/ vol22/iss1/6.

Pérez, L., L. De la Puente and D. Ugarte, *Las cuidadoras de los mineros: género y gran minería en Cotabambas* (Lima, Perú: Fondo Editorial Universidad del Pacífico, 2019).

Perreault, T., 'Climate Change and Climate Politics: Parsing the Causes and Effects of the Drying of Lake Poopó, Boliva', *Journal of Latin American Geography* 193 (2020), pp. 26–46.

Persson, L., B. M. Carney Almroth, C. D. Collins, S. Cornell, C. A. de Wit, M. L. Diamond, P. Fantke, M. Hassellöv, M. MacLeod, M. W. Ryberg, P. Søgaard Jørgensen, P. Villarrubia-Gómez, Z. Wang and M. Z. Hauschild, 'Outside the Safe Operating Space of the Planetary Boundary for Novel Entities', *Environmental Science & Technology* 56:3 (2022), pp. 1510–21.

Phua, Kai-Lit, 'Should Malaysia Bear the Burden of Australian Radioactive Waste?', *The Conversation*, 24 September 2012, available at https://theconversation.com/should-malaysia-bear-the-burden-of-australian-radioactive-waste-9566.

Pranger, J. H., 'Christianity, Settler Colonialism, and Resource Extraction', in *Dialog: A Journal of Theology* (Wiley Online, 2023). https://doi.org/10.1111/dial.12799.

Ranjit, N., K. Siefert and V. Padmanabhan, 'Bisphenol-A and Disparities in Birth Outcomes: A Review and Directions for Future Research', *Journal of Perinatology: Official Journal of the California Perinatal Association* 30:1 (2010), 2–9.

Reclaiming Power and Place: The Final Report of Canada's National Inquiry into Missing and Murdered Indigenous Women and Girls (2019). Available online hhttps://www.mmiwg-ffada.ca/final-report/.

Rieger, J. and Kwok Pui-Lan, *Occupy Religion: Theology of the Multitude* (Plymouth, UK: Rowman and Littlefield, 2012).

Robinson, M., *Climate Justice Hope, Resilience, and the Fight for a Sustainable Future* (London: Bloomsbury, 2018).

Ruiz, D., M. Becerra, J. S. Jagai, K. Ard and R. M. Sargis, 'Disparities in Environmental Exposures to Endocrine-Disrupting Chemicals and Diabetes Risk in Vulnerable Populations', *Diabetes Care* 41:1 (2018), pp. 193–205.

Schlabbach, T. and V. Wesselak, *Energie: Den Erneuerbaren Gehört die Zukunft* (Berlin: Springer, 2020).

Schmidt, A., *Conquest: Sexual Violence and American Indian Genocide* (Durham: Duke University Press, 2015).

Silva Ontiveros, L., P. Munro and M. Melo Zurita, 'Proyectos de Muerte: Energy Justice Conflicts on Mexico's Unconventional Gas Frontier', *The Extractive Industries and Society* 5:4 (2018), pp. 481–9.

Steffen, W., K. Richardson, J. Rockström, S. E. Cornell, I. Fetzer, E. M. Bennett, R. Biggs S. R. Carpenter, W. de Vries, C. A. de Wit, C. Folke, D. Gerten, J. Heinke, G. M. Mace, L. M. Persson, V. Ramanathan, B. Reyers and S. Sörlin, 'Planetary Boundaries: Guiding Human Development on a Changing Planet', *Science* 347:6223 (2015), pp. 1259855-1–10.

Stoekl, A., *Bataille's Peak: Energy, Religion, and Postsustainability* (Minneapolis: University of Minnesota Press, 2007).

Sze, J., *Environmental Justice in a Moment of Danger* (Berkeley: University of California Press, 2020).

Teteh, D., M. Ericson, S. Monice, L. Dawkins-Moultin, N. Bahadorani, P. Clark, E. Mitchell, L. S. Treviño, A. Llanos, R. Kittles and S. Montgomery, 'The Black Identity, Hair Product Use, and Breast Cancer Scale', *PloS one* 14:12 (2018), p. e0225305.

Tinker, 'Tink', G. E., 'The Doctrine of Christian Discovery and the Language of Empire', *Journal of Lutheran Ethics* 171: 1 (2017). Available online https://elca.org/JLE/Articles/1203.

Todrys, Wiltenburg K., *Black Snake: Standing Rock, the Dakota Access Pipeline Pipeline, and Environmental Justice* (Lincln NE: Bison Books, 2012).

United Nations Office of the High Commissioner for Human Rights, *Analytical Study on Gender-Responsive Climate Action for the Full and Effective Enjoyment of the Rights of Women* (United Nations: Geneva, 2019).

Watt-Cloutier, S., *The Right to Be Cold: One Woman's Story of Protecting Her Culture, the Artic and the Whole Planet* (Toronto: Penguin, 2015).

Willie James Jennings, *The Christian Imagination: Theology and the Origin of Race* (New Haven: Yale University Press, 2011).

Whyte Powys, K., 'Settler Colonialism, Ecology and Environmental Justice', *Environment and Society* 9 (2018), pp. 125–44.

Willow, A. J., *Understanding ExtrACTIVISM: Culture and Power in Natural Resource Disputes* (New York: Routledge, 2019).

Wilson, S., A. Carlson and I. Szeman (eds), *Petrocultures: Oil, Politics, Culture* (Montreal: McGill-Queen's University Press, 2017).

World Wildlife Fund for Nature, 'Living Planet Report 2020. Bending the Curve of Biodiversity Loss', available at https://livingplanet.panda.org/en-us/.

Zahid, Syed Jaymal, 'Anti-Lynas MP Likens Dumping Rare Earth Waste in Mines to Killing Rape Victim', *Malay Mail*, 4 August 2019, available at https://www.malaymail.com/news/malaysia/2019/08/04/anti-lynas-mp-likens-dumping-rare-earth-waste-in-mines-to-killing-rape-vict/1777525.

Zalasiewicz, J., C. N. Waters, J. A. Ivar Do Sul, P. L. Corcoran, A. D. Barnosky, A. Cearreta, M. Edgeworth, A. Gałuszka,C. Jeandel, R. Leinfelder, J. R. McNeill, W. Steffen, C. Summerhayes, M. Wagrech, M. Williams, A. P. Wolfe and Y. Yonan, 'The Geological Cycle of Plastics and Their Use as a Stratigraphic Indicator of the Anthropocene', *Anthropocene* 13 (2016), pp. 4–17.

Zenner, C. *Just Water: Theology, Ethics, and the Global Water-Crisis* (Maryknoll, NY: Orbis, 2014).

Zlatnik M. G., 'Endocrine-Disrupting Chemicals and Reproductive Health', *Journal of Midwifery & Women's Health* 62:4 (2016), pp. 442–55.

INDEX

Q'eqchi 146
Querida Amazonia, Post-Synodal
    Exhortation (2 February 2020)
    11, 152–3, 158, 179, 207–8

rare earth 6, 11, 185–6, 189, 203–4
    minerals/elements (REE) 6, 185–6
    mining 185, 203
    processing plants 185, 189
REPAM (*see* Panamazonian Ecclesial
    Network)
reproductive health 73, 88, 195
resource extraction 7, 8, 25, 31, 35, 40, 125,
    139–40, 158, 181–2, 213, 221
    see also extraction; extractivism;
        ExtrACTIVISM
Rieger, Joerg and Kwok Pui-Lan, *Occupy
    Religion* 200
rights (*see* human rights; Indigenous
    rights)
Robinson, Mary, *Climate Justice* 14

San Martin mine, Honduras 141
SBI (*see* Sovereign Body Institute)
settler colonial
    ecologies 180–1
    extraction 182
    violence 11, 166, 168, 170, 202
settler colonialism 4, 11, 64, 168, 170,
    179–83
    and Christianity 181–3
sex trafficking 133, 168
'Skywoman Falling' 59
slow violence 35
Smith, Andrea, *Conquest: Sexual Violence
    and American Indian Suicide* 177
social justice 11, 13, 213, 216
social toxicity 42, 65, 67
    see also toxicity; toxic masculinity
socio-ecological crisis 106–8, 112
sovereignty (*see* Indigenous sovereignty)
Sovereign Body Institute (SBI) 174
spirituality (*see* eco-spirituality)
Standing Rock, North Dakota 18, 44,
    47–52, 55, 66, 166, 168–70, 220
    see also #NODAPL; Mni Wiconi
state
    actors 19, 21–4
    of exception 18

Nation 11, 23, 24, 40, 136, 140
    a rogue 50
    sponsored violence 53
    see also Agambden
Stoekl, Allan, *Bataille's Peak* 46
    see also post-sustainability
Stop Lynas 11, 185, 199
subsidiarity, principle of 26
    see also Catholic Social Thought
survival 1, 20, 46, 58, 72, 99, 102, 115,
    207
    and biological success 99
    human 72, 107
    mechanisms 20
    of the planet 107
sustainable development 17–19, 112, 197
sustainability 42, 206
    see also Stoekl
Synod on the Amazon (Synod of Bishops
    for the Pan-Amazonian Region,
    October 6–26 2019) 18, 138,
    153, 157, 166, 207
Sze, Julie, *Environmental Justice in a
    Moment of Danger* 45–9, 51

'tactics of dispossession' division 42
technocracy
    Pope Francis' critique of 108
Tegucigalpa, Honduras 141
toxicity
    environmental 8, 9, 10, 37, 42, 64–6,
        125, 128, 135, 137, 140–2, 155–6,
        171–2, 188, 202, 214, 221
    social 37, 142, 65–7
truth and reconciliation 55, 85, 183,
    204–7
    see also Canada's Truth and
        Reconciliation Commission
Turkson, Peter (Cardinal) 148

Union Latino America de Mujeres –
    Union of Latin American
    Women (ULAM) 148

Vicariate of Iquitos 154
Vienna Declaration and Programme of
    Action (1993), United Nations'
    World Conference on
    Human Rights 42

Printed in the USA
CPSIA information can be obtained
at www.ICGtesting.com
LVHW010144250124
R18036300001B/R180363PG769412LVX00004B/7